International Capital Markets

Developments, Prospects, and Policy Issues

David Folkerts-Landau and Takatoshi Ito

with

Marcel Cassard, Steven Dunaway, Robert Flood, Shogo Ishii,
Laura Kodres, Charles Kramer, John Montgomery, Victor Ng,
Carmen Reinhart, Garry Schinasi, Todd Smith, Michael Spencer,
and Subramanian Sriram

INTERNATIONAL MONETARY FUND
Washington, DC
August 1995

ISBN 1-55775-516-9
ISSN 0258-7440

Price: US$20.00
(US$12.00 to full-time faculty members and
students at universities and colleges)

Please send orders to:
International Monetary Fund, Publication Services
700 19th Street, N.W., Washington, D.C. 20431, U.S.A.
Tel.: (202) 623-7430   Telefax: (202) 623-7201
Internet: publications@imf.org

recycled paper

Contents

II. Background Papers on Financial Supervisory and Regulatory Issues

Charts

Figure

The following symbols have been used in this paper:

... to indicate that data are not available;

— to indicate that the figure is zero or less than half the final digit shown, or that the item does not exist;

– between years or months (e.g., 1991–92 or January–June) to indicate the years or months covered, including the beginning and ending years or months;

/ between years (e.g., 1991/92) to indicate a crop or fiscal (financial) year.

"Billion" means a thousand million.

Minor discrepancies between constituent figures and totals are due to rounding.

The term "country," as used in this paper, does not in all cases refer to a territorial entity that is a state as understood by international law and practice; the term also covers some territorial entities that are not states but for which statistical data are maintained and provided internationally on a separate and independent basis.

Preface

The *International Capital Markets* report is an integral element of the IMF's surveillance of developments in international financial markets. The IMF has published the *International Capital Markets* report annually since 1980. The report draws, in part, on a series of informal discussions with commercial and investment banks, securities firms, stock and futures exchanges, regulatory and monetary authorities, and the staffs of the Bank for International Settlements, the Commission of the European Union, the International Swaps and Derivatives Association, the Japan Center for International Finance, and the Organization for Economic Cooperation and Development. The discussions leading up to the present report took place in Belgium, Denmark, France, Germany, Hong Kong, Indonesia, Japan, Malaysia, the Netherlands, Singapore, Spain, Switzerland, the United Kingdom, and the United States, between November 1994 and March 1995. The report reflects information available up to the end of April 1995.

The *International Capital Markets* report is prepared in the Research Department, in collaboration with the Policy Development and Review Department, under the general direction of Takatoshi Ito, Senior Advisor in the Research Department, and David Folkerts-Landau, Chief of the Capital Markets and Financial Studies Division, Research Department. Co-authors of the report from the Research Department, Capital Markets and Financial Studies Division, are Garry Schinasi, Deputy Chief; Robert Flood, Senior Economist; Marcel Cassard, Laura Kodres, John Montgomery, Victor Ng, Todd Smith, Michael Spencer, all Economists; and Subramanian Sriram, Research Officer. Co-authors of the report from the Policy Development and Review Department are Steven Dunaway, Chief, and Shogo Ishii, Deputy Chief, of the Debt and Program Financing Issues Division. Co-authors of the report from the Western Hemisphere Department are Charles Kramer and Carmen Reinhart, both Economists. Parthasarathi Shome and Janet Stotsky from the Fiscal Affairs Department provided the box on transactions taxes. Anne Jansen and Jared Romey provided research assistance, and Tammi Shear and Adriana Vohden provided expert word-processing assistance. Juanita Roushdy of the External Relations Department edited the manuscript and coordinated production of the publication.

This study has benefited from comments and suggestions from staff in other IMF departments, as well as from Executive Directors following their discussions of the *International Capital Markets* report on May 24, 1995. The analysis and policy considerations, however, are those of the contributing staff and should not be attributed to Executive Directors, their national authorities, or the IMF.

List of Abbreviations

ADRs	American Depository Receipts
Banamex	Banco Nacional de México
BIS	Bank for International Settlements
CAD	Capital Adequacy Directive
CBOT	Chicago Board of Trade
CCPC	Cooperative Credit Purchasing Company (Japan)
Cetes	short-term, peso-denominated government obligations (Mexico)
CME	Chicago Mercantile Exchange
CNB	National Banking Commission (Mexico)
DJIA	Dow Jones Industrial Average
DTB	Deutsche Terminbörse (Germany)
EMU	European Economic and Monetary Union
ERM	(European) exchange rate mechanism
EU	European Union
FAS	Financial Accounting Standard
FASB	Financial Accounting Standards Board (United States)
FISMOU	Financial Information Sharing Agreement
FOBAPROA	Fondo Bancario de Protección al Ahorro (Mexican deposit-guarantee fund)
GDP	gross domestic product
GDRs	Global Depository Receipts
HKMA	Hong Kong Monetary Authority
IASC	International Accounting Standards Committee
IFC	International Finance Corporation
IIF	Institute of International Finance
IOSCO	International Organization of Securities Commissions
ISDA	International Swaps and Derivatives Association, Inc.
LIBOR	London interbank offered rate
LIFFE	London International Financial Futures Exchange
MATIF	Marché à Terme International de France
MOU	Memorandum of Understanding
Nafinsa	government development bank (Mexico)
NAFTA	North American Free Trade Agreement
OECD	Organization for Economic Cooperation and Development
OSE	Osaka Securities Exchange
OTC	over the counter
PROCAPTE	programa de capitalización temporal (temporary capitalization program (Mexico))
REER	real effective exchange rate
S&P	Standard and Poor's
SEC	Securities and Exchange Commission (United States)
SIMEX	Singapore International Monetary Exchange
Tesobono	dollar-indexed, short security (Mexico)
TIIP	tasa interbancaria promedia (Mexico)
UDI	unit of investment

I

Introduction

International capital markets have once again passed through an eventful period since the last report on capital markets surveillance in September 1994. The re-evaluation of prospects for emerging markets by foreign investors, which accompanied the cyclical upswing in industrial countries in 1994—gathering momentum in the aftermath of the Mexican crisis at the end of December—left few developing country markets untested. Barely a little more than a decade after the Mexican debt-service moratorium opened the first chapter in the previous developing-country debt crisis, key emerging markets were again being supported by international loan packages intended to reduce the risk of a regional or global economic disruption. Meanwhile, the possibility that derivatives-related losses by firms such as Barings and Metallgesellschaft, as well as by Orange County, could have had serious spillovers suggests that there is room for further improvement in the international regulatory and supervisory infrastructure.

These events underscore the challenges that financial authorities around the world will have to meet in this new period of rapidly evolving global capital markets. They also motivate the choice of topics for this year's international capital markets surveillance report. Chapter II of the report addresses the international financial markets aspects of the current turbulence in emerging markets. After briefly reviewing the sources of capital flows to emerging markets and the developments that led to the Mexican crisis at the end of 1994 and the beginning of 1995, the report discusses five issues related to recent developments in emerging markets. These are the contagion from the Mexican crisis; the influence of resident investors in emerging market countries on cross-border flows; the extent to which the fragility of banking systems in emerging market countries limits the increases in interest rates that can be implemented to defend exchange rates; the stability of global banking and payment systems; and the impact of the changing global capital markets environment on the modalities of resolving external debt-servicing difficulties. The report then considers the challenges faced by emerging mar-

ket countries in managing the risks that are part and parcel of capital inflows. These are the risk to macroeconomic stability; risks to the financial sector; and debt-management and liquidity risks. It should be noted explicitly that this report does not take up questions about the potential role of international financial institutions in dealing with the consequences of the growing scale and speed of international capital flows to and from emerging markets.

Chapter III contains a discussion of international financial supervisory and regulatory issues. It considers the challenges for international regulators and supervisors posed by the continuing growth of international derivative markets and their impact on the activities of the major money-center banks. The chapter reviews how the successful strengthening of the supervisory and regulatory infrastructure for managing risk in these markets in recent years is continuing with a major initiative by the Basle Committee to reformulate capital requirements for international banking firms. It also briefly touches on some aspects of the resolution of banking difficulties in some major industrial countries. Chapter IV concludes by discussing various policy implications.

The report is followed by two groups of self-contained background papers. The first provides background material and analyses pertaining to the crisis in emerging markets and includes papers on recent trends in capital flows to developing countries, the evolution of the Mexican crisis, the Mexican peso crisis from the perspective of the speculative attacks literature, the macroeconomic policy responses to previous surges of capital flows, the experience with capital controls, and two sections on domestic financial sector issues in developing countries. The second group pertains to the supervisory and regulatory issues in the industrial countries, including capital adequacy and internal risk managment, initiatives relating to derivative markets, mechanisms for international cooperation in financial regulation, the regulatory implications of the Barings failure, the increasing importance of institutional investors, and a paper on bubbles and noise in speculative markets.

II

Turbulence in Emerging Capital Markets

Although sufficient historical distance has not yet been gained to present the definitive rendition of current events in key emerging markets, the broad outlines of the story are now coming into focus. Significant flows of capital, at relatively narrow spreads, surged into many of the emerging markets starting around 1990. These flows were largely due to improved economic performance and structural reforms in many recipient countries and a cyclical downturn in the early 1990s and structural changes in institutional portfolios in industrial countries. Most countries managed well the macroeconomic and prudential challenges posed by large-scale capital inflows. In others, however, these inflows may have masked weak economic fundamentals. The decline in inflows exposed these weaknesses, and, in Mexico, contributed to a serious exchange rate crisis.

The events in key emerging markets in late December 1994 and early 1995 initiated a re-evaluation of prospects for emerging markets and a rebalancing of international portfolios that are likely to continue throughout 1995. As this process evolves, several emerging market economies may continue to experience intermittent periods of turbulence. With this perspective in mind, this section examines the events in emerging markets in 1994 and early 1995, considers briefly a number of broader aspects of these events, and concludes with a discussion of the management of the risks to macroeconomic and financial stability that can be generated by substantial capital flows.

Capital Inflows to Emerging Markets

Flows During 1990–94

After four years of sharp acceleration, flows to developing countries decreased modestly in 1994. Total net capital flows to all developing countries receded to $125 billion in 1994 after having increased markedly from $40 billion in 1990 to $155 billion in 1993 (Table 1). With the benefit of hindsight, it now appears that it would have been difficult to sustain the rate of growth of inflows—almost a quadrupling in three years.[1] Some recipient countries should have expected a leveling off with the inevitable change in the cyclical position of the industrial countries.[2] Furthermore, for some regions and countries, the turnaround in the availability of external financing was even more pronounced than is suggested by the aggregate numbers for all developing countries. Countries in the Western Hemisphere, which as a group had experienced a cumulative net capital *outflow* of $116 billion during 1983–89, received a cumulative net inflow of $200 billion during 1990–94. Perhaps, the most surprising turnaround was in Mexico, where capital flows changed from a cumulative net outflow of about $15 billion during 1983–89 to a cumulative net inflow of $102 billion during 1990–94. In 1993, Mexico received $31 billion of capital inflows, which amounted to 8 percent of Mexican GDP. It also implied that Mexico was receiving fully 20 percent of total net capital flows to all developing countries, although its share of GDP in total GDP of emerging markets was only 8 percent. In contrast, the change in flows was less pronounced for Asian countries, where flows increased from a cumulative net inflow of $117 billion during 1983–89 to cumulative inflows of $261 billion during 1990–94.

There was a marked regional difference also in the composition of flows to developing countries. On average, since 1990, 41 percent of capital flows to developing countries has been in the form of portfolio investment in tradable bonds and equity shares and 37 percent has been foreign direct investment. In Asia, however, portfolio investment represented only 24 percent of inflows, while 45 percent was foreign direct investment. In the Western Hemisphere, capital flows were significantly more concentrated in yield-sensitive, and liquid, portfolio flows, which accounted for 66 percent of gross inflows in 1990–94, while foreign direct investment inflows represented 30 percent.

The inflows were accompanied by a decline in interest rate spreads over comparable U.S. Treasury securities to historically low levels. Average spreads for developing country borrowers declined from 346 basis points in 1991 to 243 basis points in the fourth

---

[1] The growing access of developing countries to international capital markets has been chronicled in past capital markets reports. Further details of capital flows to developing countries are provided in the background paper "Capital Flows to Developing Countries," pp. 33–52.

[2] See Dooley, Fernández-Arias, and Kletzer (1994).

Table 1. Capital Flows to Developing Countries[1]

(In billions of U.S. dollars)

	1977–82	1983–89	1990	1991	1992	1993	1994
	Annual average						
All developing countries[2]							
Total net capital inflows	30.5	8.8	39.8	92.9	111.6	154.7	125.2
Foreign direct investment							
plus portfolio investment (net)	0.7	19.8	25.7	51.3	77.2	141.1	118.0
Net foreign direct investment	11.2	13.3	19.5	28.8	38.0	52.8	56.3
Net portfolio investment	−10.5	6.5	6.2	22.5	39.1	88.3	61.7
Other	29.8	−11.0	14.2	41.7	34.5	13.6	7.2
Asia							
Total net capital inflows	15.8	16.7	25.6	50.7	39.2	72.0	73.4
Foreign direct investment							
plus portfolio investment (net)	3.3	6.6	9.4	18.0	27.3	59.5	65.0
Net foreign direct investment	2.7	5.2	9.8	14.9	19.9	35.6	36.9
Net portfolio investment	0.6	1.4	−0.4	3.1	7.4	23.9	28.1
Other	12.5	10.1	16.2	32.7	11.9	12.5	8.4
Western Hemisphere							
Total net capital inflows	26.3	−16.6	17.9	28.6	52.6	62.3	38.6
Foreign direct investment							
plus portfolio investment (net)	6.9	3.2	12.4	27.9	40.2	67.6	44.2
Net foreign direct investment	5.3	4.4	6.8	11.2	12.9	13.8	14.8
Net portfolio investment	1.6	−1.2	5.6	16.7	27.3	53.8	29.4
Other	19.4	−19.8	5.5	0.7	12.4	−5.3	−5.6
Other[2]							
Total net capital inflows	−11.6	8.7	−3.7	13.6	19.9	20.3	13.2
Foreign direct investment							
plus portfolio investment (net)	−9.5	10.0	3.9	5.4	9.7	13.9	8.8
Net foreign direct investment	3.2	3.7	2.9	2.7	5.3	3.3	4.6
Net portfolio investment	−12.7	6.3	1.0	2.7	4.4	10.6	4.2
Other	−2.1	−1.3	−7.6	8.3	10.2	6.4	4.4

Source: International Monetary Fund, World Economic Outlook data base.

[1]Flows exclude exceptional financing. A number of countries do not report assets and liabilities separately. For these countries, it is assumed that there are no outflows, so that liabilities are set equal to the net value. To the extent that this assumption is not valid, the data underestimate the gross value. Adjustments are also made to the World Economic Outlook data to net out the effects of bonds exchanged for commercial bank loans in debt and debt service reduction operations and to provide additional detail on selected private capital flows.

[2]Excludes capital exporting countries such as Kuwait and Saudi Arabia.

quarter of 1993. The decline was most pronounced for private sector borrowers: average spreads fell from 650 basis points in 1990 to 315 basis points in late 1993. Yields on five-year Mexican government bonds came down from 800 basis points over the comparable yield on U.S. Treasury bonds in late 1989 to less than 150 basis points in late 1993.

Reasons Behind the Surge in Inflows

The supply of capital to developing countries appears to have been driven largely by three factors. First, the success of some Western Hemisphere countries and the Philippines in restructuring their commercial bank debt, combined with the implementation of sound macroeconomic policies and wide-ranging structural reforms, including financial sector reforms, facilitated their re-entry into international capital markets. Second, the cyclical position of industrial country economies stimulated the flow of capital into emerging markets. Specifically, the

sluggishness in economic activity, the weak demand for funds, and the decline in interest rates in the industrial countries in the early 1990s contributed to investors having a greater interest in developing countries.[3]

Finally, the ongoing international diversification of rapidly expanding institutional portfolios (mutual funds, insurance companies, pension funds, proprietary trading of banks and securities houses) has contributed greatly to the flows into emerging markets. Institutional portfolios are absorbing a growing share of world saving, and hence investment decisions are becoming increasingly concentrated in the hands of professional fund managers who generally are more willing to diversify their investments to the

---

[3]In the United States, for example, the Federal Funds rate declined from 9.8 percent in April 1989 to 2.9 percent in November 1992, as the U.S. economy entered a period of sluggish growth and then recession.

international arena.[4] As a result, there has been a gradual but persistent trend toward greater international diversification of institutional portfolios. At the same time, the share of international flows going to developing countries is also increasing. For example, institutional investors in the United States, Japan, Germany, France, and the United Kingdom together increased their international investments from around $100 billion (or 4.8 percent of assets) in 1980 to roughly $900 billion (7.2 percent of assets) in 1993, significantly outpacing the growth in total assets under management over the same period.[5] In 1987, about $0.50 out of each $100 of foreign portfolio investment from industrial countries was invested in emerging markets, but by 1993 more than $16 out of each incremental $100 of foreign investment was invested in emerging markets. The $155 billion of net capital inflow to developing countries represented approximately 2 percent of world saving, compared with 0.8 percent in 1990. Developing countries are forecast to grow at approximately twice the growth rate of industrial countries over the 1995–2000 period. These growth prospects should continue to provide an impetus for growth in the share of institutional portfolios flowing into emerging markets.

Recent surveys of institutional fund managers in the United States indicate that the share of foreign investment going to emerging markets increased from 2.5 percent in 1989 to 10 percent in 1992 and to about 12 percent in 1993. Although this share is subject to cyclical developments, industry surveys suggested that it is unlikely to change radically in the coming years. The "Emerging Markets" have become a respectable asset class, together with real estate and high-yield bonds, among the dozen or so asset classes that make up the institutional investment universe. Institutional investment managers have been very clear that they intend to press steadily and purposefully ahead with the international diversification of their portfolios, although the regional allocation may change somewhat. And, indeed, there appears to be scope for further diversification in the institutional portfolios in industrial countries—not only into foreign securities, but also further diversification among the foreign holdings into emerging market assets over the next decade. For example, a frequently

cited rule of thumb employed by fund managers is that an optimally diversified portfolio can be approximated by using country weights that correspond to the share of a country's market capitalization in total world market capitalization. In 1993, institutional investors in the United States, Japan, Germany, France, and the United Kingdom invested, on average, less than 1 percent of their assets in emerging markets, significantly below the 12 percent share of emerging markets in total world equity market capitalization. Every additional 1 percentage point move in the direction of this rule of thumb would represent a net flow to emerging markets of about $130 billion.

Rebalancing Global Portfolios

The Correction in Emerging Markets

The reversal of the cyclical factors in industrial countries in 1994—strong growth momentum in the United States, accompanied by a tightening of financial conditions in several major countries—that had made emerging debt markets relatively attractive earlier, led to a general reassessment of investors' global portfolios. The volume of international bond issues by emerging market countries fell from $18 billion in the first quarter of 1994 to $8 billion in the second quarter.[6] Over February and March alone, spreads on Brady bonds issued by Argentina, Brazil, Mexico, and the Philippines widened by between 132 and 575 basis points. Emerging equity markets were also hard hit: share prices declined by more than 10 percent in Argentina, Venezuela, China, Hong Kong, Indonesia, Malaysia, the Philippines, and Thailand during the period from January to November 1994. Net portfolio investment in developing countries fell from $88 billion in 1993 to $62 billion, mostly due to a decline in investment in the Western Hemisphere from $54 billion in 1993 to $29 billion in 1994 (see Table 1).

Mexican Exchange Rate Crisis

The less favorable international capital markets environment in 1994 coincided with domestic political shocks in Mexico: the large net inflows that followed Mexico's accession to the North American Free Trade Agreement (NAFTA) declined abruptly with the assassination of presidential candidate Colosio in March 1994. The spread of Mexican Brady bond yields over comparable U.S. Treasury securities widened to more than 400 basis points in April 1994. The Mexican Bolsa fell 9 percent in February, and by a further 14 percent in March. By April 1994, the inflow of capital was no longer sufficient to finance

---

[4]The assets under management by the most important institutional investors (pension funds, insurance companies, mutual funds) in the major industrial countries stood at about $13 trillion in 1993, with U.S. institutional investors accounting for more than two-thirds of this total. The fastest growing segment has been the mutual fund industry (including hedge funds), which managed about $3 trillion of private wealth in the five largest industrial countries in 1993.

[5]The growth of institutional investors is discussed more fully in the background paper "Increasing Importance of Institutional Investors," pp. 165–74.

---

[6]Total international bond issues declined from $128 billion in the first quarter of 1994 to $87 billion in the second quarter, so the developing countries' share in total new issues declined from 12 percent to 8 percent during this period.

the outflow of funds and the current account deficit, which exceeded 8 percent of GDP, and the Mexican authorities had to intervene to prevent the peso from breaking through its lower intervention limit.[7]

The authorities sought to slow the sale of peso-denominated debt through an increased issue of a dollar-indexed, short-term security (the Tesobono). In this way, the foreign exchange risk associated with holding peso-denominated instruments was effectively transferred to the Mexican government. Domestic and foreign investors took the opportunity to exchange large amounts of their Cetes holdings—short-term, peso-denominated government obligations—for Tesobonos. From February to November 1994, Tesobonos outstanding expanded nearly tenfold to MexN$82 billion, while Cetes fell by 53 percent to MexN$42 billion. The Tesobonos, which sold at an average spread of 237 basis points above U.S. Treasury bills between January 29 and December 2, 1994, were popular with foreign bond funds, which looked upon them as dollar securities that could be used to enhance the yield on their U.S. fixed income portfolio.

Although reserves stood at $28 billion before the assassination of presidential candidate Colosio on March 23, they fell by more than $8 billion in April. Reserve levels improved slightly during the summer, but then an expansionary monetary policy contributed to further declines of $4.8 billion and $6.6 billion in November and December, respectively. By December 20, international reserves had fallen to $10.5 billion, and the Mexican authorities devalued the peso by 15 percent, but were forced to let the peso float on December 22, after losing another $4 billion of reserves in two days. The peso fell from its postdevaluation level of 4.0 pesos per dollar to a 1994 low of 5.7 on December 27, when a Tesobono refinancing auction had to be canceled because investors were no longer willing to carry the sovereign risk of these obligations at rates acceptable to the Mexican authorities.

The devaluation and the decision to allow the peso to float—after repeated pronouncements to the contrary—took international investors by surprise, despite warnings from several noted economists and market commentators. Mexico had made available only limited economic data during 1994 and now had difficulties preventing market participants from expecting the worst. This translated in early January into doubts about Mexico's economic reform package and ultimately led to questions about Mexico's ability to continue servicing its short-term debt. As a result, the quantities of bids at the Tesobono refinancing auctions in early January fell far short of the amounts offered.

The positive impact of the announcement of the U.S. support package on January 12 quickly dissipated with growing uncertainty about its approval in the U.S. Congress. Between January 13 and 30, the Bolsa fell 29 percent in dollar terms and the peso lost 17 percent of its value against the dollar. The international support package announced on January 31 temporarily calmed the waters, but uncertainty soon again continued to roil markets until the announcement of the new Mexican economic plan on March 9, when the peso hit a low of 7.45. The peso has since settled back to just below 6 pesos to the dollar as of the end of April.

Doubts about Mexico's ability to service its international debt obligations forced domestic interest rates beyond what was justified by expectations of a further depreciation of the peso. A contractionary monetary policy added to the upward pressure. Short-term interest rates soared from below 40 percent in early February to a high of 80 percent in mid-March and have remained above 70 percent since then.[8] The combined impact of the devaluation and the high interest rates produced a trade surplus of $240 million in February 1995 after a deficit of $530 million in January.

Aspects of Current Crisis and Its Management

The evolution and the resolution of the current crisis are being shaped by changes in global financial markets that have occurred since the 1982 debt crisis. First, the liberalization of capital flows to the major developing countries has meant that emerging markets have become, in essential ways, integrated into global capital markets. As a consequence, cross-border securities and banking transactions have become less costly and more accessible, not only at the wholesale, but also at the retail level. Second, securitization of international finance has meant that international syndicated bank lending is giving way to direct debt and equity as the preferred instrument of capital transfer to emerging markets. Third, the growth of global institutional investors has meant that capital flows to emerging markets are now predominantly driven by liquidity and performance considerations, rather than by longer-term banking relationships. This section discusses a number of consequences of this development.

---

[7]For further details on the evolution of the financial situation in Mexico, see the background paper "Evolution of the Mexican Peso Crisis," pp. 53–69. See also the background paper "Mexican Foreign Exchange Market Crises from the Perspective of the Speculative Attack Literature," pp. 70–79.

[8]By comparison, money market rates in the United Kingdom fell after the devaluation of sterling during the European Exchange Rate Mechanism (ERM) crisis in 1992.

Contagion from the Mexican Crisis

The substantial, albeit gradual, decline in equity prices and bond prices in the emerging markets in 1994 had been accepted by investors as a market correction that was not out of the ordinary. The Mexican crisis, however, produced a more fundamental re-evaluation of risk in emerging markets. This re-evaluation of risk led to a rebalancing of institutional portfolios that was the mechanism for transmitting the disturbance from Mexico to other emerging markets. Mexico had been the first country to regain substantial market access after restructuring its commercial bank debt in the 1980s. It had received the largest share of capital flows in the 1990s, and in addition, it had recently signed the NAFTA and joined the Organization for Economic Cooperation and Development (OECD). It was not surprising, therefore, that after the peso devaluation, market participants would ask, If it can happen to Mexico, then why wouldn't it happen elsewhere? Such doubts led to an intensive re-examination of financial exposures in other emerging markets.

Immediately after the devaluation, most of the larger Western Hemisphere developing countries experienced varying degrees of turbulence in their foreign exchange markets and registered marked declines in their equity markets. In the financial centers in Asia, however, there was no significant reaction to the events in Mexico in December. The announcement of the U.S. support package on January 11, and the beginning of negotiations between the International Monetary Fund and Mexican authorities, calmed markets and forestalled greater spillovers; however, as the Mexican crisis deepened in early January and as growing doubts about the successful completion of the support package for Mexico once again raised the possibility that Mexico might not be able to service its short-term debt spillovers extended to Asia as well. Most Asian developing country currencies came under attack in mid-January, requiring intervention and defensive interest rate increases. Securities markets in some Asian countries also dropped sharply in mid-January 1995. For instance, stock markets in Hong Kong and Singapore fell by about 9 percent between January 18 and 24, and equity prices in Indonesia, Malaysia, and the Philippines fell by roughly 10 percent in January.[9] Hong Kong's currency board exchange rate arrangement also experienced strong speculative pressure, forcing the Hong Kong Monetary Authority (HKMA) to tighten liquidity to force overnight interest rates to rise by 5 percentage points on January 13. However, exchange rates, interest rates, and stock prices quickly stabilized in most Asian countries, but at

discounted values from their earlier levels. The successful conclusion of negotiations with the IMF and the announcement of an international support package of nearly $50 billion (including $17.8 billion from the IMF) was instrumental in containing further spillovers into emerging markets in the Western Hemisphere and Asia.

Once the initial reaction subsided, the attitude of investors toward emerging markets became more discriminating. Broadly speaking, countries with low savings rates, large current account deficits, weak banking systems, and significant volumes of short-term debt experienced greater external pressure than countries that had sound fundamentals. This meant that within Asia, pressures centered on the Philippines, and to a lesser extent on Indonesia, and within the Western Hemisphere, pressures became focused on Argentina, and to some extent on Brazil.

Argentina, in particular, was seen as having some of the macroeconomic features that characterized Mexico in the run-up to the devaluation of the peso in December: a fixed exchange rate regime, a low domestic savings rate, a banking system with a large and growing volume of nonperforming loans, and a high current account deficit. Stock and bond prices in Argentina fell by as much as 50 percent from December 20, 1994 until they reached bottom in early March 1995. Yield spreads on Brady bonds (over U.S. Treasury bonds) for Argentina widened along with those of Mexico from December 1994 through the end of February 1995 (Table 2). Commercial bank deposits in Argentina fell by 16 percent (more than $7.5 billion) from mid-December 1994 to the end of March 1995. Because of the currency board system in Argentina, foreign currency withdrawals translated into contractions of the monetary base and, via the money multiplier, into a contraction of domestic credit and a rise in interest rates. Argentina's foreign reserves declined by almost $5 billion over the same period and prime interest rates rose by 33 percentage points to nearly 50 percent in mid-March. The pressures subsided after a number of financial measures were implemented, including the relaxation of reserve requirements and the announcement of the creation of a bank support fund, and, most significantly, a revised economic program with support from the IMF was announced in March.[10] Unlike Mexico, Argentina had not sterilized the capital inflows, and this precluded the buildup of a large stock of short-term foreign debt.

---

[9] In December 1994, nonresident investors in Indonesia made net sales of equity for the first time in three years.

[10] A change in market expectations, for example, regarding the credibility of future fiscal programs, may force the authorities to adopt a different set of policies. Depending on the nature of market expectations, several macroeconomic outcomes may be possible—a phenomenon of multiple equilibriums. In such a case, policy designed to influence expectations can be used to guide the economy to a particular (favorable) equilibrium.

Table 2. Brady Bond Spreads[1]
(Changes in basis points)

	Dec. 19–Dec. 30, 1994	Dec. 30, 1994–Jan. 30, 1995	Jan. 30–Jan. 31, 1995[2]	Jan. 31–Feb. 28, 1995
Argentina	218	183	−266	462
Brazil	116	281	−283	217
Mexico	384	190	−212	366
Philippines	27	43	10	109
Venezuela	374	719	−383	45

Sources: Reuters and Salomon Brothers.
[1]Stripped basis, spread over U.S. Treasury bonds.
[2]January 31, 1995 was the day on which the $50 billion loan package for Mexico was announced.

This, the existence of the currency board, and the fact that structural policies had gone further in Argentina than Mexico may explain in part its ability to maintain the exchange rate parity.

Growing Importance of Domestic Investors

The liberalization of cross-border financial transactions and the progressive integration of global capital markets have meant that domestic firms and individuals in the major developing countries are gaining access to low-cost transactions in international capital and banking markets. The more liberalized and internationalized is the domestic banking system, the greater is the ease and the lower is the cost of international financial transactions. If residents doubt the sustainability of the exchange rate regime, they can quickly, and at relatively low cost, adjust the currency denomination of their financial assets. The collective expectations of domestic and foreign holders of a country's tradable financial wealth are now reflected more quickly, and possibly more accurately, in asset prices and currency values, than had been the case during earlier crises.

In addition, there exists a type of information asymmetry in developing countries that is not as pronounced in the major industrial country markets. Domestic residents in developing country emerging markets tend to be closer to sources of information about domestic economic events and prospects than foreign investors. They generally tend to be first in redenominating their domestic financial assets into foreign currency. They also often are the first class of investors back into the market: flight capital, for example, returned to many emerging markets long before foreign investors saw the investment opportunities.

Another reason why resident investors in emerging market countries tend to be the front-runners in a currency crisis is that the class of international investors that in the past five years has assumed this role in major markets—the hedge funds and the proprietary traders for international financial institutions—tend not to be able to participate, on a large scale, in developing country currency crises. The primary mechanism of leveraged speculative position-taking (borrowing the currency from domestic banks, against a small margin, and selling the proceeds forward) is not generally available to them. First, central banks in developing countries typically impose constraints on the ability of banks to make a large liquid forward market, or they use moral suasion to inhibit the banking sector from lending for speculative position-taking against the currency. Second, even when such forward markets exist, speculative position-taking by institutions such as hedge funds is frequently curtailed by concerns about the ability of the banking system to deliver on the forward contract after the devaluation. In contrast, during the ERM crisis in 1992, most of the initial speculative position-taking against currencies perceived to be weak came from hedge funds and other international institutional investors.[11]

The available data show that the pressure on Mexico's foreign exchange reserves during 1994, and in particular just prior to the devaluation, came not from the flight of foreign investors or from speculative position-taking by these investors, but from Mexican residents. Foreign investors' net purchases of peso-denominated debt and equity instruments and net foreign direct investment during 1994 came to just over $9 billion, and official capital inflows were $2.5 billion. Together with a decline in reserves of $19 billion, these inflows financed a current account deficit of $29.5 billion. In the run-up to the devaluation, that is, from November 30 to December 19, foreign investors had net sales of about $326 million in Mexican government debt securities, and there were net purchases of equity, while reserves fell by $2.8 billion. For the entire month of December 1994, foreign investors were net sellers of about $370 million of debt and equity, while Mexican foreign exchange reserves fell by $6.7 billion, only $1.7 billion of which was accounted for by the trade deficit. Indeed, foreign investors did not start to sell their Mexican

---

[11]For details see International Monetary Fund (1993a).

equity holdings in any sizable quantity until February 1995.[12]

Furthermore, during the two weeks preceding the Mexican devaluation in December 1994, there was little or no traditional speculative position-taking in the peso forward market. Mexican banks could not make credit available to speculators to sell pesos forward, as the Mexican central bank prohibits banks from selling long-term contracts for forward delivery of pesos.[13]

One of the implications of this change in the financial environment is that the adequacy of a given stock of foreign exchange reserves under a regime of pegged rates cannot be gauged simply by tallying up external exposure: the authorities also need to consider the possibility that domestic investors can now readily redenominate their holdings of domestic financial assets into foreign currency. In addition, the general message emerging from these developments is that the room for policy slippage has been significantly reduced, because the disciplining mechanism of capital flight can be expected to be applied sooner and to be more potent in the future.

The Banking System as a Constraint on Crisis Management

Banking systems in emerging market countries have moved to center stage in resolving financial crises because the country's banks bear the brunt of the interest rate increases that are inevitably necessary to defend a currency.[14] It is not surprising, therefore, that solvency and liquidity problems in banking systems quickly move to the top of the agenda in countries that are experiencing financial stress.

The classical policy option for a central bank facing an attack on its pegged exchange rate is to use its foreign exchange reserves to buy its own currency and let domestic interest rates rise with the shrinking monetary base. The increase in short-term money market rates squeezes speculators by making them pay more for the funds they will need to deliver to make good on their short sales of the currency. The problem, however, is that the financial position of the banking system in many countries is such that authorities are frequently unable to let interest rates rise sufficiently to beat back the attack. It is common practice in most countries for banks to hold assets with longer maturities than their liabilities. To carry and manage such interest rate risk is, indeed, one of the main functions of the banking system. In practice, banks in developing countries may not be able to completely hedge such interest rate positions, and when short-term interest rates suddenly rise for a sustained period of time, the need to roll over the short-dated liabilities can seriously harm the income position of the banking system. In addition, other financial firms such as investment banks also tend to rely heavily on short-term borrowing to finance their trading positions.

A second and more indirect effect of a sudden increase in short-term rates is the increase in nonperforming loan assets on banks' balance sheets. Because bank debt is a key source of funding for industry in developing countries, any sustained increase in rates is likely to have a strong contractionary effect, which will bring with it an increase in the volume of nonperforming loans. Real estate and other asset prices often weaken with interest rate increases; thus, interest rate increases also reduce the value of the collateral against which loans were made. Similarly, household debt, for example, mortgages and credit cards, tends to be indexed to short-term rates, and, depending on its size and duration, an increase in rates will increase the rate of default on such debt. In Mexico, for example, most mortgage loans and consumer credit carry interest charges that are tied to the banks' short-term cost of funds. The growth in nonperforming assets and the decline in interest margins are all the more painful when the banking system is already struggling with poor asset quality, such as when the economy is in recession. Under such circumstances, the central bank's hands may be tied by the political unpopularity and economic effects of interest rate increases.

The recent Mexican experience is a case in point. The Mexican banking system began experiencing an increase in nonperforming loans well before the crisis. From 4.6 percent at the end of 1991, the ratio of past-due loans to total loans increased steadily, peaking at 8.5 percent in mid-1994. In response to the weakening of the banking sector following the devaluation, the Mexican authorities introduced in early 1995 a measure to strengthen the capital position of the banking system.[15] At the time of the exchange

---

[12]These data should be interpreted with caution as the breakdown by residents versus nonresidents is subject to uncertainty.

[13]Most of the world's major currencies are traded in over-the-counter forward foreign exchange markets. In the absence of such a forward market, investors have to liquidate their long positions in domestic securities and sell the proceeds in the spot foreign exchange market to avoid losses due to devaluation. On April 26, 1995, the Chicago Mercantile Exchange opened trading in a futures contract in Mexican pesos. It is still too early to tell whether this effort will succeed in providing a liquid market in which to hedge peso exposures.

[14]For further details, see the background paper "Financial Sector Constraints on Crisis Management," pp. 120–27.

[15]Banks with capital below 8 percent of risk-weighted assets can borrow funds from the deposit guarantee fund, the Fondo Bancario de Protección al Ahorro (FOBAPROA), by issuing five-year convertible subordinated debt with explicit conversion rules. The funds so obtained are held in blocked accounts at the Banco de Mexico to neutralize their effect on the monetary base. As of the end of March 1995, six banks had obtained assistance from FOBAPROA equal to about 15 percent of total end-of-1994 commercial bank assets.

rate crisis at the turn of the year, the banking system had already been sufficiently weakened by a growing stock of nonperforming loans that the authorities were reluctant to let the contractionary impact of its foreign exchange intervention be reflected fully in short-term interest rates. The need to stabilize the exchange market, however, as well as to achieve a contraction in domestic absorption, forced the Mexican authorities to let short-term interest rates rise to unprecedented levels. As the share of nonperforming loans continued to worsen in February and March 1995, and the risk of large-scale insolvencies increased, a plan to remove and restructure nonperforming loans totaling about MexN$148 billion was introduced.[16] A bank restructuring of such a magnitude also has fiscal and monetary implications that go beyond the immediate concern of how to recapitalize the banking system.

Where necessary, as in Mexico, a recapitalization of banking systems can be accomplished in three ways. First, loan losses can be monetized; inflation will reduce the real value of the bad loans relative to assets. In this case, the bank's creditors, mostly its depositors, would bear most of the losses. But the adjustment in inflationary expectations is likely to increase the pressure on the exchange rate, and further increases in real interest rates might be necessary. If loan losses are large, this solution might not produce a stable outcome. Second, the banking system can be recapitalized by exchanging nonperforming claims with explicit or implicit government claims in sufficient quantities to allow the bank to meet regulatory capital requirements. For this scheme to work, depositors must be persuaded that the economy will be able to generate sufficient real tax revenues to service the debt held by the banking system. Recapitalization of this form is usually accompanied by restrictions on banks: downsizing of balance sheets, streamlining of operations, reduced operating costs, possibly new management, and write-downs of equity positions. Third, a country can borrow from abroad to recapitalize its banking system. For example, in March 1995, Argentina and Mexico borrowed $2.5 billion and $2.25 billion, respectively, from the Inter-American Development Bank and the World Bank to finance bank recapitalization.[17]

An additional challenge exists under a currency board arrangement, such as in Argentina, Estonia, and Hong Kong. In these cases, the central bank cannot easily act as the lender of last resort. Because, at a minimum, central bank liabilities in domestic currency have to be backed one-for-one by foreign exchange reserves, the central bank is restricted in the amount of liquidity it can provide to the banking system by the amount of reserves it holds over and above what is necessary to back the currency.[18] Hence, for a currency board arrangement to work effectively, the banking system has to be able to tolerate significant movements in domestic interest rates. Indeed, a weak banking system in a currency board arrangement may well carry the seed of destruction: it will induce a conversion of deposits into foreign exchange, shrink the monetary base further, and cause interest rates to rise higher, thereby making the banking problem worse.

The Argentine banking system came under pressure immediately after the Mexican crisis, as investors fled the currency by converting their peso-denominated bank deposits into dollar-denominated bank deposits in Argentina. The currency board in Argentina converted commercial bank reserves into foreign currency so that capital outflows—that is, increased demand for foreign currency—quickly led to pressure on the interbank interest rate, as banks tried to replenish their reserves by borrowing in the interbank market. As demand for domestic currency increased, banks replenished their liquid reserves with sales of domestic assets. Interest rates rose automatically, initiating all of the negative effects on the financial system discussed above. Moreover, concerns about the ability of banks to meet cash demands led depositors to reduce their exposure to domestic banks by converting peso and dollar deposits held in Argentina into foreign currency deposits abroad, thereby producing further pressure on interest rates. Following recent increases in interest rates, 33 small financial institutions have requested credit assistance from the central bank in Argentina.

Stability of Global Banking and Payment Systems

The progressive integration of the major developing countries into the global financial system has also meant that disturbances in any other market, industrial or emerging, are transmitted more rapidly to developing country markets. Empirical evidence confirms that the growth of gross cross-border capital

---

[16]Under this new plan, banks would restructure some of their nonperforming loans into new instruments based on units of investment (UDIs) and transfer these new instruments to special off-balance-sheet trusts that would purchase, and then administer, the newly created UDIs. The trusts would pay for them by using the proceeds from sales of long-term UDI-indexed bonds to the Federal Government. The principal of UDI instruments would be indexed to the rate of inflation, while monthly payments would be the real interest rate applied to the indexed principal.

[17]It is also possible to recapitalize a banking system that is still solvent by borrowing in private capital markets. Argentina borrowed $1 billion from foreign, and $1 billion from domestic, private capital markets.

[18]Foreign exchange reserves of the Hong Kong Exchange Fund are more than five times the amount of currency in circulation, which provides the HKMA with greater latitude in providing liquidity assistance to banks.

flows over the past ten years has bound national equity and bond markets more closely together and that the transmission of disturbances occurs at a greater speed. This was amply demonstrated by events in the aftermath of the Mexican crisis: almost all of the major markets experienced major price adjustments and an increase in volatility as well as in trading volume. Even countries with sound fundamentals, for example, Singapore and Hong Kong, experienced significant, albeit temporary, exchange market turbulence in January, and in some countries this turbulence lasted for the better part of January. However, although the spillover from the Mexican exchange rate crisis was global in nature, and severe in many instances, the changed nature of capital flows to emerging markets implied that, unlike the 1982 debt crisis, the stability of the global banking and payments system in the major international financial centers was not as much at risk as it had been during the 1982 crisis.

The large exposure of the international banking system to developing countries in 1982 meant that Mexico's moratorium on debt-service payments in September 1982 posed a serious threat to the stability of the system. It became necessary for the major central banks to reassure markets and to press for an orderly resolution of the crisis. The stress was vividly apparent in the international interbank markets.

Today, a large volume of claims on developing countries takes the form of securitized lending by institutional investors, while the international banking system has a relatively small exposure in the form of syndicated loans to emerging market countries, and much of that tends to be in the form of short-term trade credits and project financing. Losses in mutual funds, however large, take time to work their way through the system and are likely to be only a small part of the end-investors' portfolios, and in any event such widely dispersed losses would not have any systemic implications for the global banking and payment systems.[19]

Furthermore, the equity and bond markets in the developing countries worked well. Although market liquidity became impaired in some countries, there was no evidence of a freezing up, despite the fact that a number of equity markets were confronted with historically large price declines and large volumes. Many of the major emerging market countries have undertaken significant reforms to strengthen op-

erational capabilities, (e.g., settlement and clearance systems, trading mechanisms) of their capital markets, and these reforms are now paying dividends. Finally, the international support packages for Mexico, assembled during January, forestalled further price declines and thus limited the potential risk of a breakdown in one of the major emerging markets.

Resolution of Debt-Service Problems

The changes in the nature of the financial claims and in the investor base, which have occurred as a consequence of the growing integration of emerging markets into global capital markets, are likely to have important implications for the restructuring and burden sharing in the resolution of sovereign debt-service problems. In this regard, the most relevant change in developing country financing is the shift in the composition of cross-border investments from syndicated bank loans to tradable securities—bonds, equities, and money market instruments. Reflecting this change, outstanding commercial bank loans to developing countries declined as a share of total developing country private debt, from 62 percent in 1980 to 46 percent in 1993. During this same period, the share of securitized debt increased from 8 percent to 32 percent. The ascendancy of international institutional investors—replacing the banking syndicates of earlier years and ranging from conservative pension funds to speculative hedge funds—has become a major factor in this development. Indeed, it would be very difficult to replicate the concerted debt restructuring of 1982 given the growing dispersion of creditors and their differences in attitudes toward risk and liquidity and the absence of a facilitator with influence over these investors, such as the major central banks in 1982. In contrast, the relatively small number of creditor banks made it possible, though by no means easy, to negotiate restructuring agreements during the debt crisis in the 1980s.[20]

In the absence of a voluntary and comprehensive restructuring agreement, a country with debt-servicing difficulties has two options. First, it can initiate a credible economic adjustment program in return for official financing. This is the approach adopted by the Mexican authorities. The adjustment program is designed to convince private external lenders that the country will be able to generate sufficient future export earnings to service its external obligations. Multilateral financial institutions have

---

[19]Nevertheless, market participants told of a significant volume, estimated in excess of $20 billion of notional value, of options-like contracts with payoffs related to the future value of the peso that had been written by U.S. investment houses. These contracts are dollar bets on the peso/dollar exchange rate and are cash-settled in dollars without any immediate impact on the peso/dollar exchange rate, and again, the losses on these contracts are fairly widely dispersed.

[20]The 1982 debt crisis was resolved through a concerted restructuring of commercial debt, and new external financing provided from the official sector and from commercial bank creditors was used to facilitate the economic adjustment programs. Most countries with debt-servicing difficulties in the early 1980s regained full access to international capital markets within eight years after the onset of the crisis.

traditionally played the role of the lender of last resort in these situations. The benefit of this approach to the country is that the economic program and the associated official funding allow a lengthening of the period of adjustment, while at the same time helping to avoid unnecessary or excessive damage from an overly hasty and disorderly adjustment process. External obligations to private creditors that fall due before full access has been restored are replaced with external obligations to official creditors. Because official funding will necessarily tend to be limited by budgetary and political considerations, in most cases it will still be necessary for the country to undertake an adjustment program that is sufficiently stringent to produce rapidly a current account surplus to signal its creditworthiness and to facilitate its return to private markets.

Second, when a country's debt-servicing capacity has been sufficiently impaired so that there is little prospect that an economic adjustment program cum official financing could restore financial stability any time soon—even with drastic compression of domestic absorption and a substantial devaluation—then countries might decide to resort to an involuntary restructuring of their external debt. Involuntary restructuring can take the form of a lengthening of maturities and a lowering of interest rates, as well as debt-reduction operations. Such debt restructuring may or may not be accompanied by official financial support. Because there exists no well-defined and accepted legal process that is applicable in such cases, the process of debt resolution by involuntary restructuring is necessarily ad hoc with an uncertain outcome. Bond holders may try to seek redress, on an individual or coordinated basis, by attempting to seize the assets of the borrowers or by threatening to disrupt their trade and payments systems. This threat will be more effective the greater the size and importance of the countries' export sector. "Free riders" may also undermine any negotiated solutions by trying to attempt to enforce their individual claims. In addition, involuntary debt restructuring will damage creditworthiness and may increase the cost of accessing international capital markets in the future.[21] Nevertheless, there may be sound economic and political reasons for an involuntary restructuring supported by an economic calculus that trades off higher future financing costs against the deadweight loss of rapid and deep domestic economic adjustment.

The fact that a major country with debt-service difficulties will in all likelihood face one of these two choices, rather than be able to secure a voluntary restructuring, places a premium on successful macroeconomic and macroprudential management.

Managing the Risks from Volatile Capital Flows

The increase in capital flows to emerging markets from 1990 to 1994 was a welcome global financial development. It helped recipient countries finance the current account deficits associated with domestic investment in export-enhancing infrastructure and it provided diversification opportunities to industrial country investors. However, flows that are large relative to GDP carry with them certain risks that, when managed properly, do not seriously diminish the economic advantages of greater integration into global capital markets. One of the risks is that a surge in capital inflows produces an appreciation of the real exchange rate, an inflationary expansion of domestic money and credit, an unsustainable current account deficit, and a more vulnerable banking system.[22] Likewise, as the Mexican case demonstrates, a sudden and large outflow can, inter alia, produce an exchange rate crisis, a liquidity problem brought on by the need to refinance a large volume of short-term external debt, and difficulties in the banking system caused by the increase in domestic interest rates. The management of these risks is the key challenge associated with capital inflows.

Macroeconomic Risks

To manage the macroeconomic risks associated with large inflows and sudden outflows, many developing countries have found it desirable to attempt to limit the impact of inflows. The menu of policy responses to capital inflows includes intervention in foreign exchange markets—with or without sterilization of the monetary impact of such intervention—fiscal consolidation, and capital controls. In countries with a flexible exchange rate regime, an appreciation of the nominal exchange rate during periods of heavy capital inflows can insulate the money supply, domestic credit, and the banking system from such inflows. Abrupt movements in the real exchange rate, however, may impose substantial adjustment burdens on the economy, particularly if such an appreciation is reversed as capital exits.[23] Even if the real exchange rate appreciation turns out to be

---

[21]Recall that countries that restructured their debt in the 1980s have not yet received investment grade credit ratings.

[22]The policy problem of how to deal with the exchange rate impact of capital inflows is akin to the so-called Dutch disease policy problem of preventing an erosion of the manufacturing base as a result of the discovery of natural resources.

[23]In practice, most developing Western Hemisphere countries have witnessed marked appreciation of the real exchange rate during periods of capital inflows, while for most Asian countries real exchange rates have remained largely unchanged.

Table 3. Policy Responses to Capital Inflows, 1988–94

Country	Fiscal Restraint	Revaluation	Increased Exchange Rate Variability	Sterilized Intervention	Controls on Capital Inflows	Liberalization of Capital Outflows	Trade Liberalization Accelerated
Argentina (1991)[1]	No[2]	No	No	No	No	No	No
Chile (1990)	Yes	Yes	Yes	Yes	Yes	Yes	No
Colombia (1991)	No	Yes	Yes	Yes	Yes	Yes	Yes
Indonesia (1990)	No	No	No[3]	Yes	Yes	No	No
Malaysia (1989)	Yes	No	Yes	Yes	Yes	Yes	Yes
Mexico (1990)	No[2]	No	No[3]	Yes	No[5]	Yes	Yes
Philippines (1992)	No	No	Yes[4]	Yes	No	Yes	No
Sri Lanka (1991)	No[2]	No	No[4]	Yes	No	No	Yes
Thailand (1988)	Yes	No	No	Yes	No	Yes	Yes

Source: Staff analysis in the background paper "Policy Responses to Previous Surges of Capital Inflows," pp. 80–94.

[1]The year next to the country name denotes the first year of the surge in inflows.

[2]Fiscal consolidation (including privatization efforts) was a part of the inflation stabilization program and not a response to the rise in capital inflows per se. The Convertibility Plan in Argentina began in April 1991, while the Mexican plan predates the surge in inflows and began in December 1987.

[3]Despite announcements of broader intervention bands, exchange rate variability does not change appreciably.

[4]The Philippines and Sri Lanka already had a relatively flexible exchange rate system at the start of the inflow episode.

[5]Caps on foreign currency liabilities of banks are not binding until 1994.

temporary, it may have long-lived hysteresis effects on trade and investment.[24]

Most of the developing economies that received sizable inflows during the early 1990s have tried to resist the nominal appreciation that might accompany such inflows, even within a regime of floating or managed exchange rates (Table 3). The policy most often used for this purpose (Chile, Colombia, Indonesia, Korea, Malaysia, Mexico, the Philippines, Sri Lanka) was sterilized intervention. The advantages of this policy are readily apparent: intervention avoids the nominal appreciation (Table 4), and sterilization avoids the monetary expansion associated with the central bank's accumulation of foreign exchange. The most straightforward way to sterilize is through open market operations. In effect, the intervening central bank obtains the capital inflow in exchange for an increase in the holdings of domestic assets by foreigners, and it avoids a change in the monetary base by reducing its holdings of domestic assets in the form of public sector obligations to residents. Increases in reserve requirements, which reduce the money multiplier, have also been used to sterilize the monetary expansion associated with foreign exchange market intervention (Chile, Colombia, Costa Rica, Malaysia, Peru, Sri Lanka).

The difficulty with this policy is that sterilized intervention has proved to be neither fully effective nor free of negative side effects. Sterilization through

open market sales of government securities or central bank bills prevents the interest rate differential from narrowing, and in some cases increases the domestic-international interest rate spread sufficiently so as to attract more short-term capital. This occurs because the domestic-currency assets that investors want to hold (e.g., bank CDs, equities, bonds) are imperfect substitutes for the short-term central government or central bank paper being supplied through the sterilization operation by the central bank. In addition, sterilization often involves significant quasi-fiscal costs resulting from the difference between the yield on foreign exchange acquired by the central bank and the higher interest rate paid on government or central bank securities. In fact, sterilization policies had to be scaled back in Chile, Colombia, Indonesia, and Malaysia as it became clear that high domestic interest rates were attracting more short-term inflows and were changing the composition of inflows toward the short end.

Fiscal consolidation is another possible response to capital inflows: the deflationary impulse will offset the expansionary impact of the unsterilized portion of foreign exchange intervention, which may put downward pressure on interest rates, particularly if the government borrowing requirement is perceived to be declining. The use of contractionary fiscal policy in response to capital inflows is most clear in Thailand, which over 1988–91 turned a modest fiscal deficit into a surplus of 5 percent of GDP. Chile and Malaysia have also initiated fiscal restraint as a means of dealing with capital inflows.

There are limits, however, on the use of fiscal policy in this context—fiscal policy may be less

---

[24]A detailed discussion and analysis of monetary and fiscal policy responses to capital inflows is contained in the background paper "Policy Responses to Previous Surges of Capital Inflows," pp. 80–94.

flexible than other policy instruments. Most capital-importing countries have not explicitly employed fiscal consolidation as a response to inflows, but as part of medium-term adjustment programs. More problematically, fiscal consolidation may also encourage capital inflows by easing concerns about possible future liquidity problems.

It is, therefore, not surprising to find that in addition to altering monetary, fiscal, and exchange rate policies in response to large swings in international capital flows, many countries have employed measures that discourage capital inflows or seek to influence their character. These measures are often generically referred to as "capital controls." In fact, such measures range from prudential controls on the banking system, to market-based measures, all the way to quantitative controls on inflows and outflows (Box 1). In particular, these measures have included imposing or tightening prudential limits on banks' offshore borrowing and foreign exchange transactions (Indonesia, Malaysia, and the Philippines), as well as taxing some types of inflows by requiring non-interest-bearing reserves deposits against foreign currency borrowing by firms (Brazil, Chile, and Colombia). For example, in Chile, the measures have taken the form of non-interest-bearing 30 percent reserve deposits placed at the Central Bank for a period of one year on direct foreign currency borrowing by firms.

In some instances, measures have taken the form of quantitative restrictions. For example, Colombia restricts foreigners from investing in the domestic bond market. Malaysia responded to the inflow of speculative short-term bank deposits with the imposition of several quantitative measures. The most successful of these measures was the prohibition on domestic residents selling short-term money-market instruments to foreigners. In this case, abandoning the sterilization of foreign exchange intervention and imposing capital controls appear to have been successful in reducing domestic interest rates and short-term inflows. A number of countries, particularly Asian developing countries, have restrictions on foreign borrowing by domestic companies and some have maintained prudential restrictions on financial institutions, such as restrictions on the open foreign exchange positions of banks.

It is dangerous to draw general conclusions about the consequences of "capital controls" without reference to the nature of such measures and the circumstances under which they were employed. On the one hand, comprehensive and detailed restrictions on capital inflows and outflows can have highly distorting effects, and such restrictions tend to erode over time. As the effectiveness of controls becomes weaker, authorities may be tempted to intensify them, increasing their distortionary effect.

Table 4. Reserve Accumulation and Capital Inflows

(Changes in reserves as a percent of the balance in the capital account)[1]

Country	First Year	Second Year	Third Year	Fourth Year	Fifth Year	Average
Argentina (1991)	82	42	46	12	...	46
Chile (1990)	77	167	86	22	110	92
Colombia (1991)	263	13,261	9	4	...	3,384
Indonesia (1990)	48	63	23	−9	...	31
Malaysia (1989)	92	126	18	67	121	85
Mexico (1990)	43	34	12	21	−159	28[2]
Philippines (1992)	13	9	17	...	...	13
Sri Lanka (1991)	17	29	37	59	30	34
Thailand (1988)	75	34	39	41	47	47

Sources: International Monetary Fund, *International Financial Statistics* and *World Economic Outlook*.

[1]The year in parentheses next to each country represents the first year of the surge in inflows. A minus sign indicates reserve losses.

[2]Does not include 1994.

On the other hand, measures to discourage excess short-term, foreign currency denominated borrowing by banks, such as increased reserve requirements, can be justified on prudential grounds—bank failures can have significant real effects, as well as fiscal consequences, when deposits are de facto guaranteed. Such measures also tend to have a more permanent effect. Some strong measures, such as taxes on short-term capital flows and bans on the purchase of particular types of securities, may be justified only as temporary measures until domestic financial markets and institutions become well established and resilient, while some other types of prudential measures and reserve requirements can be justified as more permanent features of the regulatory framework.

For example, a review of the Chilean and Malaysian experiences reveals that, in the short run, the volume of inflows was reduced by capital controls during episodes of higher exchange rate volatility and little or no sterilization, in 1991 and 1994, respectively. Furthermore, capital controls were undoubtedly less important than sound fundamentals in explaining the long-run success of several countries cited above in dealing with capital inflows.

In this regard, it should be noted that both Hong Kong and Singapore have managed large capital inflows without recourse to capital controls. Therefore, although capital controls may be helpful at times, they are not the distinguishing feature characterizing countries that have dealt successfully with capital inflows and outflows. Imposing capital controls on outflows during a crisis is interpreted as a measure of despair and hence is counterproductive. Furthermore, market participants tend to view the control of capital outflows as a confiscatory measure, which can be expected to increase future borrowing costs,

---

Box 1. Restrictions on Capital Inflows and Prudential Requirements[1]

Brazil (1992)

October 1994. A 1 percent tax was imposed on foreign investment in the stock market. It was eliminated on March 10, 1995.

The tax on Brazilian companies issuing bonds overseas was raised from 3 percent to 7 percent of the total. Eliminated on March 10, 1995.

The tax paid by foreigners on fixed interest investments in Brazil was raised from 5 percent to 9 percent, and reduced back to 5 percent on March 10, 1995.

The Central Bank raised limits on the amount of dollars that can be bought on foreign exchange markets.

Chile (1990)

June 1991. Nonrenumerated 20 percent reserve requirement to be deposited at the Central Bank for a period of one year on liabilities in foreign currency for direct borrowing by firms.

The stamp tax of 1.2 percent a year (previously paid on domestic currency credits only) was applied to foreign loans as well. This requirement applied to all credits during their first year, with the exception of trade loans.

May 1992. The reserve requirement on liabilities in foreign currency for direct borrowing by firms was raised to 30 percent. Hence, all foreign currency liabilities have a common reserve requirement.

Colombia (1991)

June 1991. A 3 percent withholding tax was imposed on foreign exchange receipts from personal services rendered abroad and other transfers, which could be claimed as credit against income tax liability.

February 1992. Banco de la República increased its commission on its cash purchases of foreign exchange from 1.5 percent to 5 percent.

June 1992. Regulation of the entry of foreign currency as payment for services.

September 1993. A nonrenumerated 47 percent reserve requirement to be deposited at the Banco de la República on liabilities in foreign currency for direct borrowing by firms. The reserve requirement is to be maintained for the duration of the loan and applies to all loans with a maturity of 18 months or less, except for trade credit.

August 1994. Nonrenumerated reserve requirement to be deposited at the Banco de la República on liabilities in foreign currency for direct borrowing by firms. The reserve requirement is to be maintained for the duration of the loan and applies to all loans with a maturity of five years or less, except for trade credit with a maturity of four months or less. The percentage of the requirement declines as the maturity lengthens; from 140 percent for funds that are 30 days or less to 42.8 percent for five-year funds.

Indonesia (1990)

March 1991. Bank Indonesia adopted measures to discourage offshore borrowing. It began to scale down its swap operations by reducing individual banks' limits from 25 percent to 20 percent of capital. The three-month swap premium was raised by 5 percent.

October 1991. All state-related offshore commercial borrowing was made subject to prior approval by the government and annual ceilings were set for new commitments over the next five years.

November 1991. Further measures were taken to discourage offshore borrowing. The limits on banks' net open market foreign exchange positions were tightened by placing a separate limit on off-balance-sheet positions.

Bank Indonesia also announced that future swap operations (except for "investment swaps" with maturities of more than two years) would be undertaken only at the initiative of Bank Indonesia.

September 1994. Bank Indonesia increased the maximum net open position from 20 percent of capital to 25 percent, on an average weekly basis. Individual currency limits were no longer applied.

Malaysia (1989)

June 1, 1992. Limits on non-trade-related swap transactions were imposed on commercial banks.

January 17, 1994–August 1994. Banks were subject to a ceiling on their non-trade- or non-investment-related external liabilities.

January 24, 1994–August 1994. Residents were prohibited from selling short-term monetary instruments to nonresidents.

February 2, 1994–August 1994. Commercial banks were required to place with Bank Negara the ringgit funds

---

[1]The year next to the country name denotes the first year of the surge in inflows.

---

whereas preannounced taxes on short-term inflows avoid this stigma.[25]

In sum, shifting international capital flows can represent large shocks to small open economies, occasionally amounting to more than 10 percent of GDP in one year. The policy response to large and volatile capital flows may require multiple instruments, including measures that seek to discourage capital inflows or change their character, and coordination of policies, monetary, fiscal, and exchange rate, to ensure that recipient countries can derive benefits without incurring much of the costs.

---

[25]For further discussion of capital controls, see the background paper "Controls on Capital Flows: Experience with Quantitative Measures and Capital Flow Taxation," pp. 95–108.

of foreign banking institutions (Vostro accounts) held in non-interest-bearing accounts. However, in the January–May period, these accounts were considered part of the eligible liabilities base for the calculation of required reserves, resulting in a negative effective interest rate in Vostro balances.

February 23, 1994–August 1994. Commercial banks were not allowed to undertake non-trade-related swap and outright forward transactions on the bid side with foreign customers.

Mexico (1990)

April 1992. A regulation that limited foreign currency liabilities of commercial banks to 10 percent of their total loan portfolio was passed. Banks had to place 15 percent of these liabilities in highly liquid instruments.

Philippines (1992)

July 1994. Bangko Sentral ng Pilipinas began discouraging forward cover arrangements with nonresident financial institutions. The Central Bank also required prior approval for all forward foreign exchange transactions.

November 1994. Banks' minimum oversold foreign exchange position was reduced from 15 percent of unimpaired capital to 5 percent.

Approvals for foreign loans were granted only to cover foreign exchange costs, with the exception of exporters and the public sector.

Liabilities of banks to their head offices were counted as unimpaired capital only if converted into pesos.

Thailand (1988)

May 1980. Banks and finance companies' net foreign exchange positions cannot exceed 20 percent of capital.

Residents were not allowed to hold foreign currency deposits except only for trade-related purposes.

April 1991. Banks and finance companies' net foreign exchange positions limit raised to 25 percent of capital.

Sources: Alfiler (1994); Banco Central de Chile, *Evolución de la Economía* (1991 and 1992); Banco de la República, Colombia (1993 and 1994); Banco de México (1992); Bank Indonesia, *Annual Report*, various issues; Bank Negara Malaysia, *Annual Report*, various issues; and Conselho Monétario Nacional, Brazil (1994 and 1995).

Financial Sector Risks

Financial systems in many emerging market countries have only recently been liberalized or privatized, and the ability of banks to manage financial risk is still relatively limited. Resilient and liquid capital markets that could absorb shocks are frequently not fully developed. The accounting and legal infra-

structure may not be sufficiently developed to monitor and enforce loan contracts effectively. In many developing countries, credit- and market-risk management in the banking system is still in the early stages of development. At the same time, it is likely that the bank supervisory and regulatory agency has not yet grown into an independent, highly competent agency. The legal framework for effective banking supervision also may not be well established. In some countries, supervisors are hampered by a lack of political independence and an inability to close delinquent institutions or to implement prompt corrective actions. Finally, market discipline over bank management may be weakened by the fact that banks are frequently benefiting from extensive implicit solvency guarantees from the public sector; that is, the public sector is more likely to recapitalize a bank than to allow losses to depositors.

In this environment, capital inflows generate a number of risks in the banking sectors of recipient countries. Foreign exchange market intervention that is not fully sterilized exposes the banking system to the additional credit risk generated by the expansion of bank balance sheets.[26] Experience suggests that a rapid expansion in banks' loan books can easily be accompanied by slippage in credit quality, even with effective regulatory and supervisory control over banking systems. Fast growth in credit tends to be concentrated in only a few sectors and a cyclical reversal will frequently lead to a deterioration of the credit quality of such sectors. In Mexico, the ratio of past due loans to total loans increased from 4.6 percent at the end of 1991 to 8.5 percent in mid-1994. The ratio of past due loans to capital increased sharply, from 46 percent to 97 percent over the same interval. It should be noted that periods of rapid expansion in bank lending also have led to problems in some Group of Ten countries' banking systems.[27] For example, extensive lending to real estate has on several occasions resulted in major banking problems in a number of well-regulated industrial countries.[28]

In addition to the increased credit risk, banks in emerging market countries frequently assume market risks—exchange rate, interest rate, equity price risks—that cannot be fully hedged. For example, there are frequent instances where banks, as major

---

[26]Examples of rapid credit expansion during periods of strong capital inflows include Mexico, where commercial bank loans to the private sector increased from 27 percent of GDP in 1991 to 47 percent in 1994. The same ratio increased in Indonesia from 25 percent in 1988 to 53 percent in 1994, and in Thailand from 51 percent to 89 percent over 1988–94.

[27]Group of Ten countries consists of the United States, Japan, Germany, France, Italy, the United Kingdom, Canada, the Netherlands, Sweden, Belgium, and Switzerland.

[28]See the discussion below on the continuing resolution of banking problems in several industrial countries, pp. 21–25; and in previous capital markets reports.

foreign borrowers, carry a significant foreign exchange exposure,[29] and where banks are exposed to volatility in equity prices by holding sizable equity portfolios.[30]

If a banking system practices adequate risk management and is financially resilient, and if the supervisory and regulatory agencies are well equipped to enforce prudential requirements, then the internationally active banking system may not be adversely affected by its enlarged intermediary role. This can be seen from the experiences in Hong Kong and Singapore, where international-quality supervisory and regulatory agencies have been established and where banking systems can cope with large capital inflows and outflows, as well as with large swings in asset prices. Recent history, however, provides ample evidence that these conditions are not always fully met, and the need to ensure that banking systems can safely intermediate capital flows remains an important policy challenge.[31]

Debt Management and Liquidity Risk

The recent events in Mexico illustrate how reliance on short-term debt finance indexed on foreign currency can make a country vulnerable to liquidity crises. As mentioned above, Mexican Tesobono liabilities had expanded rapidly since April 1994. By the end of November, they totaled $24 billion (MexN$83 billion, or about 6 percent of 1994 GDP) and comprised 50 percent of Mexico's domestic government debt. The depreciation of the peso in December and January meant that the peso value of these dollar-indexed liabilities skyrocketed, reaching MexN$149 billion, or 66 percent of total domestic debt. Investors' concern that Mexico might not be able to service its Tesobono obligations made them reluctant to roll over these bonds as they fell due in the early part of 1995, forcing significant increases in yields, as well as the outright cancellation of some Tesobono refinancing auctions. This in turn meant that scarce foreign exchange reserves had to be used to redeem the issues that were falling due. Domestic rates had to be raised to prevent a further capital outflow to halt the drain of reserves. The knowledge that of the $28.7 billion in Tesobono debt outstanding at the end of December $9.9 billion was scheduled to mature in the first quarter of 1995 put significant pressure on interest rates and on the exchange rate. The lesson here is that a longer maturity structure could have provided more breathing space for an orderly resolution of the crisis after the decision to float the peso in December. The exchange rate crisis may not have turned into a debt-service crisis had the maturity of the foreign currency indexed debt been longer.

The need to refinance a substantial volume of short-term debt at a turbulent time in exchange markets creates significant additional market pressure. Investors' doubts about the ability of the authorities to service their external debt is quickly translated into higher debt-servicing costs for the fraction of debt that is being rolled over during the turbulent period, and the larger the share of short-term debt, the more debt will have to be rolled over during that time, and the larger will be the increase in the debt-service burden. The increase in debt-servicing costs itself will also contribute to doubts about the countries ability to service debt. At some point, further increases in yields will lead investors to avoid the market altogether, and refinancing will become impossible.

The events in Mexico and the rest of the emerging markets during 1994 demonstrated that the existing market mechanisms can absorb significant losses owing to declines in the value of equity and longer-term bonds. Major additional challenges arise, however, when, during periods of extreme turbulence—such as in the wake of a devaluation—a large volume of short-term debt must be refinanced. In the case of Mexico, the postdevaluation financial stress would have been easier to resolve without the necessity to refinance a large volume—relative to the existing stock of foreign exchange reserves—of maturing Tesobonos.

---

[29]The gross foreign liabilities of commercial banks have expanded rapidly in many capital importing countries. In Malaysia, foreign liabilities as a percentage of GDP increased from 7 percent to 19 percent between 1990 and 1993. In Indonesia, banks' external liabilities increased from 2 percent of GDP in 1989 to 6 percent the following year. The same ratio increased from 8 percent in 1991 to 13 percent in 1994 in Mexico, and in Thailand it increased from 4 percent in 1988 to 20 percent in 1994.

[30]The pattern of inflows into the emerging securities markets has tended to be associated with increased volatility of equity prices. Equity markets in developing countries tend to lack sufficient liquidity to absorb and release such sizable flows of capital. For example, foreign investors' net purchases of Mexican shares declined from the high levels of $1.8 billion in January and $1.4 billion in February 1994, to purchases of $292 million in March and then net sales of $321 million in April. Over that period, equity prices in dollar terms rose by 13 percent between December 31, 1993 and February 8, 1994, and then declined by 24 percent by the end of April 1994.

[31]For further details, see the background paper "Role of Domestic Financial Institutions in Intermediating Foreign Capital Inflows," pp. 109–19.

III

Financial Supervisory and Regulatory Issues

Policy Challenges Posed by Derivatives

The dramatic collapse of Barings, a mid-sized, blue-chip investment bank established in 1762, which occurred with little warning and great speed, involved the extensive proprietary use of derivatives in establishing large, highly leveraged Nikkei 225 futures positions on the futures exchanges in Singapore and Osaka. The multinational nature of the firm's activities obscured its consolidated risk position sufficiently that neither the relevant supervisors nor the firm's counterparties acted in time to discipline its activities. Hence Barings' failure, coming on the heels of other financial tremors involving derivatives, for example, Orange County,[32] and Metallgesellschaft,[33] added new urgency to the initiatives now under way to strengthen the supervisory and regulatory infrastructure governing global derivative markets.

The good news is that the supervisory and regulatory arrangements currently in place proved adequate in containing any possible systemic spillovers from these accidents. The internal risk management systems of the major banks and securities houses had been effective in keeping their financial exposure to the failed entities well within tolerable limits. Indeed, the crisis involving Barings and its subsidiaries was resolved without a lasting negative effect on global markets. Moreover, the risk-management systems of the futures exchanges in Singapore and Osaka, where most of Barings' positions had been established, prevented a threat to the financial integrity of the exchanges.

The resolution of Barings, which ultimately involved the purchase of a significant share of Barings' assets by the Dutch bank ING, was helped by favorable circumstances. Markets were at the time not subject to disturbances and uncertainties from other sources, and Barings' problems were quickly recognized by market participants as firm specific. The sequence of events involving the collapse of Barings and its resolution is a textbook case of the failure of financial institutions: the management of a major global institution fails to control its risk positions; it loses capital; and the central bank is able to close the institution without negative consequences for the stability of the financial system. The resolution of Barings will undoubtedly have a profound effect on market discipline; the swift and resolute reaction of the Bank of England will be a milestone in the containment of moral hazard in financial markets.

Nevertheless, the fact a failure of this size caught supervisors by surprise suggests that renewed efforts to strengthen the existing international supervisory and regulatory infrastructure are called for. In broad terms, these efforts should be aimed at fostering a competitive market environment in which international financial activity can evolve efficiently, where market discipline induces firms to control their risk, and where the failure of major institutions can be managed in such a way as to limit spillovers to other markets. To this end, it will be necessary to introduce better internal risk-management methods to a larger number of the major financial institutions; to set the size of capital requirements governing market risk sufficiently high to offset the benefits flowing from explicit or implicit official financial guarantees for the affected institutions; to improve accounting and disclosure standards to increase the transparency of markets; to reduce risk in wholesale payments systems to limit the spillover of market disturbances; to

---

[32]Orange County lost $1.5 billion, due to a high-leverage strategy involving reverse repurchase agreements that allowed the county to leverage its assets up from $7.5 billion to $20 billion. When interest rates increased, the value of these instruments dropped significantly. The county was forced into bankruptcy when dealers refused to roll over the reverse repurchase agreements.

[33]MG Corporation, a U.S. subsidiary of Metallgesellschaft AG, Germany, lost almost $1.3 billion through the use of petroleum derivative products. MG had contracted to supply petroleum products to retail distributors at fixed prices, and it had taken a long position in short-term oil futures contracts to hedge its forward commitments. When oil prices dropped significantly in 1993, MG incurred large losses on these hedges, and had to meet margin calls on its outstanding futures contracts. However, while U.S. accounting principles allowed the losses on the futures contracts to be offset by the unrealized gains on the forward contracts, German accounting did not recognize such gains. As a result, and because of doubts about the creditworthiness of the counterparties to the forward contracts, MG's parent did not use the gains in the forward contracts as collateral for borrowing the necessary margin money. In the event, MG Corp. had to close out the futures positions at significant losses. Culp and Miller (1994) argue that the hedging strategy of MG Corp. was correct, but that the unwillingness of its parent to continue financing margin calls led to a disorderly liquidation of the futures positions, which greatly increased losses on these contracts.

reform legal codes relating to netting and bankruptcy of multinational financial firms; and to improve international coordination among regulators. Previous capital markets reports have dealt with many of these subjects in detail. Some of the more recent developments are summarized here.

Growth in Derivative Markets

The spectacular growth of derivative markets since the late 1980s and the rapid expansion of banks' involvement in these activities constitute perhaps the most worrisome aspect of recent developments in this area. Financial history contains many examples of rapid expansions in certain types of financial exposures that result in major losses during periods of consolidation. The expansion of bank lending in particular sectors, such as lending to developing countries in the 1970s and early 1980s, to real estate in the mid 1980s, and for highly leveraged transactions in the late 1980s, are some of these examples.

Derivative markets have continued to grow in recent years. The notional principal[34] of all outstanding exchange-traded and over-the-counter derivative contracts increased from less than $2 trillion at the end of 1986 to more than $20 trillion at the end of 1994, an average annual growth rate of 140 percent.[35] The replacement value of these products[36] is estimated to have remained at around 2.5 percent of notional value. Hence, at the end of 1994, approximately $500 billion of replacement value was outstanding, compared with the capital base of less than $200 billion of the 12 largest dealers, who together are responsible for the vast majority of over-the-counter transactions in derivatives.

The development of derivative markets has been accompanied by a dramatic change in the activities of many of the major international money-center banks, which together are responsible for more than three fourths of all derivatives activities. The financial activities of these banks have moved considerably away from their traditional lending role toward fee-based financial services and proprietary position taking. One of the main activities of banks now is the management of market risk, liquidity risk, and the credit risk associated with derivative activities. These changes, which have occurred in all major countries, are seen most clearly in the behavior of U.S. banks.

Among the seven major U.S. money-center banks, interest income declined as a share of total revenue from nearly 70 percent at the end of 1987 to less than 50 percent at the end of 1993. In addition, during the same period, trading income doubled to 14 percent of total revenue. Finally, the volume of over-the-counter transactions in derivatives has also become large relative to total assets. At year-end 1992, the notional principal value of interest rate and currency swaps held off balance sheet by the seven major U.S. money-center banks was 2.3 times the value of their balance sheet assets; the replacement value of the derivatives book of the seven major U.S. money center banks was well in excess of their paid-in equity (Tier I).

Recent Supervisory and Regulatory Initiatives

Regulatory Capital Requirements

The cornerstone of supervisory and regulatory efforts to deal with the developments in international financial markets in recent years has been a rethinking of the role of regulatory capital requirements. It has been recognized for some time that the risk-weighted, ratio-based approach to determining the appropriate amount of regulatory capital is out of step with modern risk-management methodology. The Basle Committee of Banking Supervision, representing supervisory authorities from 12 major countries, and operating under the auspices of the Bank for International Settlements (BIS), is currently developing a very different approach to the determination of regulatory capital required for market risk. It is likely that the new approach to capital requirements is going to affect banking as profoundly as did the 1988 Basle Capital Accord.

As discussed in previous capital markets reports, the focus on credit risk of the 1988 Basle Capital Accord soon came to be viewed by supervisors as too narrow to deal with the market, liquidity, and operational risks inherent in the growth of banks' trading and derivatives books. In response to this development, the European Union (EU) introduced the Capital Adequacy Directive (CAD) in March 1993, and the Basle Committee introduced a similar proposal for a revised framework for the supervisory treatment of market risk in April 1993. Market developments, however, outpaced regulatory developments, and it became clear during 1994 that the proposed framework had sufficiently serious shortcomings to put into question its usefulness. In response, the Basle Committee abandoned the April 1993 proposals in favor of a more radical approach (slated for adoption by the end of 1995 with full implementation by the end of 1997).

Under this new approach, banks would be allowed, if they choose, to use their own internal risk-management models to estimate the bank's

---

[34]Notional principal amount is the number by which the interest rates or exchange rates in a derivative contract are multiplied to calculate the settlement amount.

[35]This outstanding balance includes interest rate futures and options, currency futures and options, and stock market index futures and options.

[36]The replacement value is the unrealized capital gain or loss of the contract at current market prices; that is, it is the amount that would have to be paid to a third party to induce them to enter into a transaction to replace the contract.

value-at-risk.[37] To determine a bank's new capital adequacy requirement, supervisors would then multiply the bank's estimate of its value-at-risk by a "safety factor" greater than or equal to three. Supervisors will have the discretion to increase a bank's safety factor if its internal model is revealed, through time, to be inaccurate. Smaller banks that choose not to use internal models are required to follow a revised version of the standards proposed in April 1993.[38]

This new approach has the obvious advantage of providing banks with incentives to improve continuously their risk-management systems, and banks will incur no further administrative costs in calculating their regulatory capital requirements. A disadvantage, however, observed during a dry run conducted by the Basle Committee, is that different banks may arrive at different requirements for the same portfolio of derivative instruments, even after controlling for the choice of a confidence interval and the holding period.[39] It is expected that validation of the models by the supervisors will lead to a convergence of key aspects of risk-management models, including estimation techniques and possibly common data sets.[40] One challenge has been that the model-validation process has required that supervisors retool and become proficient in the use of rather sophisticated modeling techniques in order to be able to engage in this new process of validation. The approach, therefore, is only as effective as

supervisors' ability to judge the adequacy of banks' risk-management models. It is certain, however, that the calculation of regulatory capital cover for market risk and the process of private risk assessment and risk management have become inextricably bound.

Accounting Standards and Disclosure Requirements

It is widely acknowledged by market participants that current financial accounting systems used for valuing assets and liabilities are not adequately recording the current values of derivatives contracts. This is an important area of concern not only for regulators, but also for market participants that are potential counterparties in derivative contracts. In addition, differences in the accounting treatment of derivatives in national accounting systems are posing significant problems in cross-border counterparty risk assessment. Current financial technology and a high degree of market liquidity, however, allow institutions, and individuals, to change large market positions sufficiently rapidly—in minutes rather than days—to cast doubt on the usefulness of accounting data in providing an up-to-date picture of the financial position of the financial intermediary. Hence, the need for reliable internal position control is not addressed by improvements in disclosure and accounting data.[41]

A major improvement in accounting standards is under way in the United States. An important feature of the new standards is that derivative positions are disclosed differently if they are traded than if they are used solely for hedging purposes. Further, the standards call for the disclosure of more information about the value of, and the gains and losses from, traded derivatives. The standards also recommend that firms report their value-at-risk. The U.S. accounting standards are rapidly becoming the international reporting norm for those major financial institutions that are active in the dollar markets.

The improvement of accounting standards is also high on the agenda of the BIS. In September 1994, the Euro-Currency Standing Committee of the BIS issued a report on the public disclosure of market and credit risk that emphasizes the importance of quantitative measures of risk. The report recommends that banks disclose enough information for market participants to judge the bank's average risk exposure. For this purpose, the report suggests that banks disclose summary statistics on their value-at-risk over different holding periods. The report also recommends that ex-ante estimates of value-at-risk be compared with actual outcomes to identify the historical performance of an institution's risk-management system.

---

[37]*Value-at-risk* is an estimate of the maximum loss that a portfolio could generate with a given level of confidence and during a given period into the future. For example, a one-day value-at-risk of $100 million at a 95 percent confidence interval means that there is a 95 percent chance that the loss in portfolio value during the next day will be less than $100 million. In order to estimate value-at-risk it is necessary to estimate the parameters of the probability distribution of the portfolio return.

[38]For further analysis of the capital requirements controversy and this new approach, see the background paper "Capital Adequacy and Internal Risk Management," pp. 135–49.

[39]In September 1994, the Basle Committee asked a number of banks, active in the over-the-counter derivative markets, to compute risk exposures and capital requirements for four hypothetical portfolios with and without options. There are several reasons why banks might arrive at different estimates of value-at-risk for the same portfolio. First, different parametric and nonparametric approaches to estimate the probability distribution might be used. Second, options risk might be treated differently. Third, different dynamic models of the asset returns might be used. Finally, different sample periods might be used for estimation.

[40]While a bank will be free to choose its own model and its own estimation and simulation procedures, estimates of value-at-risk will be subject to certain quantitative standards and assumptions: a 99 percent confidence interval; a ten-day holding period; a sample period of not less than one year; data set updates at least every three months; and certain aggregation rules. Banks also will have to satisfy some qualitative standards: the maintenance of an independent risk control unit; the integration of its model into day-to-day risk management; the use of stress testing; and the adoption of a periodic review process for its risk measurement and risk-management system.

[41]For proposals to improve transparency and disclosure in derivatives markets see the background paper "Initiatives Relating to Derivatives," pp. 150–57.

International Cooperation

Although globally integrated capital markets are rapidly becoming a reality, the legal, accounting, and, to some extent, the supervisory and regulatory infrastructure have remained national in outlook and application. Capital markets in general, and derivative markets in particular, are global markets. Barings, headquartered in London, established futures and options positions on exchanges in Osaka, Singapore, and Tokyo. Although the resolution of the Barings debacle was made easier by the active cooperation among the regulatory authorities in London, Osaka, Singapore, Tokyo, and other major financial centers, there is much room for improvement. Efforts toward greater global cooperation[42] are required in areas such as coordination between the Basle Committee and the International Organization of Securities Commissions (IOSCO) in harmonizing financial regulation for banks and securities houses; the exchange of information among securities regulators; and, to some extent, coordination between the Basle Committee and the European Commission on capital requirements for banks.

In the area of capital requirements, the EU has tried to accommodate the new internal model-based approach proposed by the Basle Committee by allowing top European banks to follow the Basle approach to some extent. In April 1995, the commission's directorate-general agreed that daily value-at-risk models can be used in conjunction with the CAD provided that the capital requirement according to the firm's estimate of value-at-risk is no less than the capital requirement according to the CAD. In any event, should the Basle proposal be adopted, the EU has to amend its CAD sometime after its implementation on January 1, 1996. Without full harmonization, EU banks and non-EU banks will be competing on somewhat unequal grounds. Full harmonization between the EU and the Basle Committee is challenging because of their different approaches to banking and banking supervision between European and non-European regulators.

The Basle Committee and IOSCO have attempted to coordinate their efforts in supervising the derivative activities of banks and securities firms, respectively. This coordination effort has proven to be difficult, in part because many European countries have a universal banking system under which banks can perform securities activities directly, while the U.S. and Japan still separate much of the banking and securities business. Furthermore, capital requirements for U.S. securities houses, imposed by the U.S. Securities and Exchange Commission and the U.S. Commodities Futures Trading Commission, focus primarily on

liquid capital—defined as capital minus illiquid assets (called haircuts)—with the aim to ensure that registered broker-dealers have adequate liquid assets to meet their obligations to investors and creditors. Little progress has been made in this area to date. The Basle Committee and IOSCO have been able to coordinate their efforts on improving risk management, however, and they have jointly issued guidelines on risk management related to derivatives.

A final concern relates to the coordination among futures and options exchanges and among the authorities with regulatory responsibilities for the exchanges. Most exchanges compete across countries for international business, and how international futures and option exchanges can coordinate the sharing of information regarding clients and market activity without losing their competitive edge is an important challenge in the period ahead (see Box 2). One of the lessons of the Barings collapse is that had there been greater information sharing among regulatory authorities in Singapore and the United Kingdom, and between the futures exchanges in Singapore, Osaka, and Tokyo, the problems experienced by Barings may have surfaced early enough to prevent the collapse. For example, SIMEX, the futures exchange in Singapore, did not have access to information regarding Barings' positions in Nikkei futures contracts on the futures exchange in Osaka (OSE). Thus, officials at SIMEX could not determine if Barings' SIMEX position was in fact hedged by offsetting positions on OSE, as was claimed by Barings. Had officials at SIMEX and OSE been able to view Barings' consolidated position in Nikkei futures contracts in real time, it is likely that both exchanges would have required greater variation margin and prevented Barings' open position from becoming so large. When the same financial contracts—such as futures and options on the Nikkei 225 index—are cross-listed internationally, as they are on the exchanges in Osaka and Singapore, competition for international business will often put the exchanges in the difficult position of striking the proper balance between gaining a competitive edge, efficiency, and prudential concerns. The importance of this issue in Europe is reflected by the intense competition among the futures exchanges in Frankfurt, London, and Paris.

Strengthening Risk Management at Futures Exchanges

During the past five years, organized futures exchanges have become sufficiently important to the financial system that a disruption in one of the major futures exchanges—as occurred in Hong Kong in 1987—would likely have serious repercussions. As a result, and in the wake of the Barings' failure, their risk-management practices have come under increased scrutiny.

---

[42]Regional cooperation in the financial area is advancing within the EU under the Single Market legislation.

Under current institutional arrangements, the clearinghouses of futures exchanges are the central counterparties to all trades and guarantee execution of all transactions executed on their exchanges. The daily procedure of marking-to-market and collecting margins (even intraday if necessary) together, reduce the credit exposure of the clearinghouse to not more than one day's worth of losses on a counterparty's position. In addition, a guarantee fund maintained by the exchange absorbs potential losses if a counterparty defaults. Exchanges also establish loss-sharing rules that are used to allocate losses among clearinghouse members in the event of a default. Finally, some exchanges impose a number of prudential requirements on their members, including minimum capital requirements and limits on the size of clearing members' net positions to reduce the risk that any single member can assume and consequently minimize the risk exposure of the clearinghouse.

In the aftermath of the Barings failure, the futures exchanges in Singapore, Osaka, and Tokyo were able to liquidate Barings' positions quickly enough so that the exposure of clearing members of the exchanges was limited. However, the Barings episode exposed uncertainties in the loss-sharing formulas of the exchanges. These uncertainties are currently being resolved. In addition, the multinational nature of Barings' business raised questions about the treatment in bankruptcy courts of margins and guarantee funds held by the exchanges.

Continuing Resolution of Banking Problems in Several Industrial Countries

A number of industrial countries have experienced more traditional on-balance-sheet loan losses in their banking sector in recent years. Deregulation of banking in the early 1980s permitted banks in, inter alia, Japan, the Nordic countries, the United States, and the United Kingdom to tap new sources of funds and enter new types of activities—often in areas where they had little prior experience—in an increasingly competitive environment. In addition, rapid asset price inflation and an expansion of lending into real estate tend to reinforce each other. The increased risk taken by banks was exposed by the onset of a worldwide recession in the late 1980s and early 1990s. The usual cyclical decline in asset quality was made worse by a relatively large deflation of commercial and residential real estate values. As a result, the losses incurred by banks in a number of industrial countries were sufficiently large that banks had to slow the growth of their loan portfolios to meet regulatory capital requirements, thus contributing at times to the so-called credit crunch. In some instances, resolution of the nonperforming loans problem required direct intervention of the public sector. In retrospect, it seems that the supervisory infrastructure did not adapt quickly enough to the new competitive environment.

In most of the countries that experienced banking problems in the late 1980s and early 1990s, the situation has improved significantly. While the recovery of profits has been strong in the United Kingdom and the United States, it has been stronger still in Norway and Sweden. In these countries, banks wrote off large portions of their loan books, sold other assets and subsidiaries, sharply reduced noninterest expenses, and, in some cases, achieved consolidation through mergers. Banks in these countries were recapitalized, in some cases by the government and in others by raising private capital. Operating profits increased sharply in 1994, mostly reflecting the decline in provisions. Indeed, the recovery in profits has been so strong that it has raised questions about whether the extent of government assistance to the industry was excessive. The current state of profitability in the industry is such, however, that the authorities in both Sweden and Norway expect to recover a large proportion, perhaps all, of the funds they made available to the banking sectors.

The different resolution strategies employed in dealing with banking losses imply different allocations of losses among the involved parties. Two extreme examples of burden sharing can be identified. The first is a policy of forbearance, under which banks are permitted to carry on with their impaired capital positions in the expectation that they will be able to "earn their way out of trouble" through wider intermediation spreads and improved cash flow generated by the eventual economic recovery. Such an approach broadly characterizes the initial response to problems in the U.S. savings and loan industry and to the problems among major banks in Japan.

The alternative, more radical, approach involves a determined effort to identify problem assets, and devise a work-out program including, in most cases, significant use of public money to recapitalize the banks, while at the same time, strengthening the supervisory and regulatory infrastructure. Norway, Sweden, and Finland followed this approach, with banks in Finland and Sweden creating separately capitalized work-out units ("bad banks") to which the nonperforming assets were transferred.[43] The worst affected banks were made whole by injections of public funds from the government, specialized government agencies, or

---

[43] For details on the restructuring programs in each country see International Monetary Fund (1993c) and (1994). In November 1993, the Finnish government established an asset-management company, Arsenal Ltd., to which the nonperforming assets of the Savings Bank of Finland were transferred at the time of the sale of the bank to a consortium of private banks. The initial capital injection of Fmk 5 billion by the state and the Government Guarantee Fund was augmented by Fmk 6 billion in September 1994.

Box 2. Competition and Cooperation Among Futures Exchanges

Financial centers have emerged throughout the world either to provide financial services to a large and growing economy, such as in London, New York, and Tokyo, or to intermediate financial transactions between a region and other geographic sources of financing, such as in Hong Kong and Singapore in the southeast Asian region. Many of the financial services provided by these financial centers—including foreign exchange transactions, underwriting and syndication services, equity trading, over-the-counter derivative activities—in effect have no natural geographic home. These activities tend to migrate to markets that offer advantages of location, reflecting either a concentration of economic and financial activity or fiscal, regulatory, and cost advantages.[1]

One area where competition has been fierce and where cooperation is important is on the futures exchanges. The instruments traded on futures markets—stock index futures, currency futures, and bond futures—can be characterized as not having "a natural home," as their underlying instruments are often "foreign" to those markets. For instance, the London International Financial Futures and Options Exchange (LIFFE) trades German and Italian government bonds futures, and the Singapore and Chicago futures exchanges trade Japanese stock index futures and options. When financial instruments are standardized and cross-listed on several exchanges, the exchanges compete primarily on the basis of transactions costs (commissions, transactions taxes, and margin requirements), and on the basis of liquidity, the efficiency of clearing and settlement systems, and the sophistication of trading mechanisms. To strengthen their competitive position and establish themselves as global players, futures exchanges have been forging alliances to extend their trading activity across different time zones and to enlarge the geographical distribution of their products. For instance, in 1993, the Marché à Terme International de France (MATIF) and the Deutsche Terminbörse (DTB) signed a cooperation agreement that would allow members from one

Comparison of Trading Value of the Nikkei 225 Futures Between OSE and SIMEX

	Trading Value in		Trading Value in SIMEX
	OSE	SIMEX	Trading Value in OSE
	(In billions of Japanese yen)		(In percent)
1989	188,560	14,960	7.9
1990	394,871	12,781	3.2
1991	536,730	8,337	1.6
1992	219,872	29,383	13.4
1993	162,367	49,541	30.5
1994	124,219	58,124	46.8

Source: Osaka Securities Exchange.

exchange to have direct access to selected products of the respective partner exchange. The exchanges signed the agreement primarily to consolidate their positions within the European time zone, and because of the complementarity of their products, clients, and technologies. A recently announced trading link between LIFFE and the Chicago Board of Trade (CBOT) is another example of how futures exchanges have attempted to increase the global distribution of their products. The trading link would allow LIFFE's products (e.g., Bunds and Gilts futures and options) to be traded on CBOT's floor, thereby extending LIFFE's products to both the U.S. and Asian markets, as the time zones of both regions overlap. Similarly, CBOT's products (e.g., futures and options on U.S. Treasury bonds) would benefit from the European trading hours. Other exchanges are also considering expanding the distribution of their products through bilateral linkages, including the Hong Kong Futures Exchange and the Philadelphia Stock Exchange, and LIFFE and SIMEX.

The competition between the Osaka Securities Exchange (OSE) and SIMEX is a particularly revealing example of how derivatives exchanges compete. Both exchanges trade a similar futures contract on the Japanese Nikkei 225 stock index.[2] In 1989, the first full year of trading in the OSE, turnover of Nikkei 225 futures on

[1]For instance, London and New York's stock markets alone account for 90 percent of equities traded outside their home countries; the market for Japanese warrants is more developed in London than in Japan; 90 percent of the world's outstanding Eurobonds are listed in Luxembourg; and Singapore is the world's fourth largest foreign exchange center.

[2]The OSE and SIMEX are the most important exchanges for Nikkei 225 futures trading. The Chicago Mercantile Exchange (CME) also trades Nikkei futures, but its share of the total volume is about 3 percent.

the central bank. In some cases, these funds were used to facilitate mergers. However, since the rehabilitation efforts covered only banks that were insolvent, this approach raised concerns about competitive equality in the banking industry, and the authorities took care not to give the recapitalized bank an advantage over its competitors. In addition, there were concerns about the moral hazard generated by such blanket rescue plans; however, this event was viewed as unique in the financial history of the countries concerned, and a strengthened supervisory regime was put in place to forestall any further risk taking by depository financial intermediaries.

The resolution of the problems in the U.S. savings and loans industry followed the second approach after the initial forbearance approach proved to be ineffective. The Resolution Trust Company, a liquidation agency established to assume the nonperforming assets of institutions that could not meet the regulatory capital standards, required in the end a total of

Comparison of Trading Cost of the Nikkei 225 Futures in OSE and SIMEX, February 15, 1995[1]

(In thousands of Japanese yen)

	OSE		SIMEX	
	Member	Customer	Member	Customer
Margin				
Customers	...	45,000.0	...	18,750.0
Members	30,000.0	...	15,000.0	...
Trading costs	5.4	203.0	0.9	87.5
Brokerage commission	—	200.0	—	87.5
Fixed rate fees	2.4	—	0.9	—
Exchange tax	3.0	3.0	—	—

Source: Osaka Securities Exchange.

[1]Based on contract value of ¥ 300 million (OSE: 15 units and SIMEX: 30 units).

the OSE was ¥ 189 trillion, compared with ¥ 15 trillion on SIMEX—or less than 8 percent of the OSE's volume (see table on the left). By 1991, trading on SIMEX had declined to less than 2 percent of the OSE's volume. Since 1991, however, SIMEX's share of trading in Nikkei 225 futures has increased significantly, reaching about 47 percent of OSE's trading in 1994.

The shift of trading activity from the OSE to SIMEX during this period can be attributed to two factors. First, between the beginning of 1990 and the end of 1991, the OSE tripled its margin requirements, from 9 percent of the futures contract value to 30 percent, to limit volatility spillovers from the futures market to the cash market. The OSE also doubled the size of its commissions in 1993 to protect the fixed commission structure in the Japanese cash markets. Second, SIMEX reduced its margin requirements during this period, to reflect a reduction in price volatility.[3] As a result, the transactions cost differential between the two futures exchanges has widened significantly. By early 1995, OSE transactions costs for customers were more than twice those on SIMEX, with commissions accounting for most of the difference (see table above). The difference in

[3]Margins were also cut to bring them in line with those of other exchanges, as SIMEX had initially set them well above what standard practice required.

transactions costs between the two exchanges also led to a segmentation of the market for stock index futures, whereby Japanese retail investors are largely confined to trading on the OSE, while all other investors, including Japanese institutional investors and securities companies, trade on SIMEX.

Concerns have been expressed that competition between futures exchanges will inevitably lead to a weakening of prudential regulations to the lowest common denominator ("a regulatory race to the bottom"), thereby increasing the potential for systemic problems. Experience, however, suggests that competition between exchanges in the United States, Europe, and Asia has not led to a relaxation of prudential regulations and risk controls to capture financial activity from competing exchanges. SIMEX has been able to gain market share from OSE because it offered more competitive transactions costs without compromising on the quality of its prudential regime. In fact, Singapore has been promoting the quality of its regulatory environment and the related greater security and stability as one of the attractive aspects of its financial center. Similarly, competition among the European futures exchanges has tended to concentrate on offering higher liquidity and greater security of transactions, rather than competing with lower margins or looser risk controls.

Competition between futures exchanges for international business has not, however, encouraged widespread cooperation and sharing of information among the exchanges. Yet, as exchanges have been determined to avoid regulatory arbitrage, there is no reason to believe that there is an inherent contradiction between competing on transactions costs and exchanging information for prudential reasons. The recent Barings collapse is a clear case where greater coordination of information between the OSE and SIMEX might have raised early warning signals that could have averted the collapse of the securities firm. In particular, as officials at SIMEX did not have access to information regarding Barings' positions in Nikkei futures contracts on the OSE, they were unable to determine whether Barings' position on the Singapore exchange was in fact hedged by offsetting positions on the OSE, as was claimed by Barings. Had officials at SIMEX and OSE been able to view Barings' consolidated position in Nikkei futures contracts, both exchanges would have probably required higher margins and forced Barings to reduce its open position.

almost $200 billion of public funds to contain the savings and loans problem. In Japan, an asset liquidation company, the Cooperative Credit Purchasing Company (CCPC), was established by banks to take over their bad debts and thereby allow them to take advantage of tax write-offs by realizing losses. This balance-sheet operation overstates the extent to which the banks have resolved their nonperforming loans problems, because the banks remain liable for the losses incurred by the CCPC in the sale of the

assets it acquired from them. So far, in Japan, no direct subsidies have been provided by the government (aside from deposit insurance) to the major banks or the CCPC.

The experience with banking problems and their resolution in industrial countries offers a number of generally applicable lessons. First, the bank supervision structure has to evolve quickly in response to financial deregulation. Second, while the goal of bank supervision should be to identify and resolve problems in individual institutions early on, including through bank restructuring, sale or merger, it is highly desirable to set up a clear regulatory rule for closing an institution whose problems cannot be resolved before it becomes insolvent. Alternatively, if it is decided to let a bank with insufficient capital continue to operate in the hope that it may earn its way out of its predicament, then regulatory scrutiny of its activities should be increased. Insolvent or nearly insolvent institutions have strong incentives to undertake high-risk lending strategies with insured deposits in the hope that they might earn their way back into solvency. Third, it is important to establish a clear rule on how to share the nonperforming loans burden among the stake holders without increasing the risk of a systemic disturbance. Once significant losses have accrued on a bank's balance sheet, they sooner or later have to be shared among the bank's shareholders, its liability holders,[44] its borrowers, and the public sector.

The importance of addressing problems in the banking sector at an early stage is illustrated by two examples, one from Japan and one from France. In Japan,[45] the risk in the forbearance approach is evidenced in the most recent failures of two credit cooperatives in Tokyo. The authorities[46] were alerted through a special examination in 1993 of a significant nonperforming loans problem but did not close the insolvent credit cooperatives. Instead, a policy of forbearance was adopted. As a consequence of the policy, the two credit cooperatives rapidly expanded their balance sheets—attracting

deposits with above-market interest rates and lending to high-risk projects—and with it the volume of their nonperforming loans.

The lack of a clear rule for sharing the burden of recapitalizing weak banks became apparent in the episode of the two failing credit cooperatives. In the past, it had been common to resolve problems through a merger between an insolvent institution and a stronger one, at times supported by an injection of deposit insurance funds.[47] However, the condition of the banking system is now such that it is becoming more difficult to persuade the larger banks, which are beset by their own problem loans, to acquire insolvent banks.[48] In addition, the failure to deal early on with problems at the smaller institutions may have increased significantly the number of cases where intervention is needed.

The problems among some of the smaller Japanese depository institutions (credit cooperatives) and other specialized financial institutions (especially housing financing companies, commonly known as *jusen*) also remain a source of concern. In the second half of the 1980s, the housing finance companies (nonbank subsidiaries of banks) greatly expanded their lending to real estate companies with funds borrowed from city banks, agricultural cooperatives, and other financial institutions. A large portion of their loans became nonperforming in the early 1990s.[49] All seven *jusen* negotiated a ten-year plan for interest payment relief in 1993 in order to avoid default on interest payments to their creditors. To date, however, it has not been possible to devise a scheme to reduce the stock of nonperforming assets in the *jusen*.

The elimination of problem loans from the smaller institutions in Japan has been made more difficult by inadequate disclosure and poor supervision of the smaller institutions. For example, credit cooperatives are formally under the supervision of the local governments, which in some cases are not well equipped to conduct financial examinations, and, unlike the larger banks, they are not required to disclose nonperforming loans. Poor disclosure has meant that market discipline could not play its role because depositors and investors were unable to distinguish between the relatively strong institutions and the weaker ones.

---

[44]Attempts to share losses with depositors run the risk that deposits will be withdrawn from the banks perceived as weak, which is desirable from the point of view of market discipline but raises the specter of a general run on deposits in other, including solvent, institutions.

[45]For detailed discussions of the causes of balance sheet fragility in the Japanese banking system see International Monetary Fund (1993c) and (1994), and for a detailed analysis of the asset price cycle see International Monetary Fund (1992) and (1993b). The volume of nonperforming loans in the 21 leading banks decreased slightly in 1994 to around ¥ 13 trillion (about 3 percent of total loans), as banks were more aggressive in disposing of bad assets (mostly to the CCPC) and increased the rate at which they added to loan-loss reserves.

[46]When Tokyo Kyowa and Anzen Credit Unions failed, the Tokyo metropolitan government, along with the Bank of Japan and the Ministry of Finance, arranged a scheme to set up a new bank, which was to acquire all business of these two credit cooperatives—called Tokyo Kyodo Bank—with an injection of capital from the Bank of Japan and private financial institutions, along with financial assistance provided by the Tokyo metropolitan government, the Deposit Insurance Corporation, the Long-Term Credit Bank, the National Federation of Credit Cooperatives, and other private financial institutions. The Japanese authorities announced that the scheme was indispensable for closing the two credit cooperatives without causing a systemic disturbance under the current conditions surrounding the Japanese financial system. They also stressed that they would see to it that the management and shareholders of the two credit cooperatives should be held responsible for the failure, in order to minimize concern for moral hazard.

[47]There have been six cases in which the Deposit Insurance Corporation has provided financial assistance to mergers.

[48]Contributing to this difficulty is the fact that as a result of recent deregulation of financial institutions, banks and securities companies can now move into new lines of business by establishing subsidiaries rather than through mergers.

[49]As of September 1994, the total borrowing of the seven *jusen* companies was about ¥ 13 trillion, of which ¥ 6 trillion was owed to banks, and about ¥ 5.5 trillion was owed to the financial institutions for agriculture and forestry. The *jusen* companies are widely reported to hold ¥ 6 trillion in nonperforming loans.

The failure to respond quickly to resolve banking problems is also observed in France, on a scale comparable with that of the *jusen* problem in Japan. Problems with nonperforming assets and weak capital support have continued at the state-owned Crédit Lyonnais. The sources of these problem loans at Europe's largest bank were its very aggressive expansion into real estate, cross-border lending, and other nontraditional areas, which began in the late 1980s. The subsequent recession in France in the early 1990s led to a significant increase in nonperforming loans. Four features of Crédit Lyonnais's balance sheet appear to have made it particularly vulnerable to problem loans: the speed with which it expanded its operations exceeded management's capacity to monitor and control them; lending to the small and medium-sized firms increased significantly as a proportion of total lending; it became heavily exposed to real estate; and its loan portfolio was heavily concentrated in a few borrowers. The magnitude of the recession in France and the crisis in the property market, in which Crédit Lyonnais was one of the main participants, contributed to aggravating the situation. The bank's reliance on the implicit guarantees of the state, its main shareholder, may also have contributed to its aggressive lending policy.

While the bank's problems had been recognized as early as mid-1991 by the bank's supervisor, Commission Bancaire, these problems were not made public until late 1993 and became critical in early 1994 when the government injected capital to maintain the bank's risk-weighted capital above the Basle minimum of 8 percent. The rescue operation entailed a F 4.9 billion capital injection and the decision to ring-fence, in a Crédit Lyonnais fully owned subsidiary, F 43 billion of nonperforming loans; of this total, F 18.4 billion was guaranteed by the government. Problems at the bank contin-

ued to mount in 1994, and at the end of the year, a F 12 billion loss was reported. In March 1995, a second rescue operation was proposed. Crédit Lyonnais will lend F 155 billion to the state-controlled Societé de Participations Bancaires et Industrielles (SPBI), which will use that amount to finance a new special purpose vehicle, Consortium de Réalisation (CDR), and purchase zero-coupon government bonds with a face value of F 35 billion in 20 years. CDR will acquire from Crédit Lyonnais about F 135 billion in assets of which roughly two thirds were nonperforming—including the F 43 billion segregated in 1994—and one third were performing assets, including the bulk of Crédit Lyonnais's large portfolio of industrial shares. SBBI, which is fully liable for the F 145 billion loan (plus interest), will receive the income from the asset sales carried out by CDR and direct injections from the state. These injections are expected to be repaid by special dividends and a fee of 34 percent of the pretax profits of Crédit Lyonnais if profits are under 4 percent of shareholder funds, or 60 percent of pretax profits if the latter are above the 4 percent return, and capital gains from future privatization of the bank.

The continuing difficulties, and the costly rescue of Crédit Lyonnais, might have been averted had the bank conducted a less expansionary policy and strengthened its internal control procedures, including risk management and controls over its subsidiaries, and had the authorities acted sooner to deal with these problems. A belief that loan quality would improve as the economy recovered seems to have convinced all parties that drastic action was not required. The modalities of the rescue of Crédit Lyonnais have generated serious concerns on the part of its French competitors. This issue is currently under scrutiny by the EU Commission.

IV

Conclusions

Turbulence in Emerging Markets

The recent turbulence in emerging financial and foreign exchange markets has to be seen in the context of the broader trends that have been shaping developments in international financial markets during the past ten years. Principal among these are the growth of securitized global capital markets and the increasing dominance of performance-oriented institutional investors in these markets. The ongoing international diversification of institutional portfolios, the return of flight capital, and the cyclical developments in industrial countries combined to generate a significant volume of capital flows into emerging markets in the developing world. In keeping with developments in global markets, these flows have increasingly been in the form of purchases of tradable bonds, equities, and money market instruments—securities that can readily be sold when sentiments change. These developments have brought with them a number of important implications—some of which surfaced during the recent crisis in Mexico—for the macroeconomic and financial sector policies of the emerging market countries.

First, the liberalization of cross-border financial transactions of emerging market countries, along with the modernization and gradual internationalization of domestic banking systems in many of these countries, has meant that domestic investors can now far more easily sell domestic assets to acquire foreign assets, and vice versa, than was the case only a few years ago. Indeed, the pressure on Mexico's foreign exchange reserves in the run-up to the devaluation came primarily from residents rather than foreign investors selling their holding of Mexican securities. The volume of financial wealth that can flee a developing country is now sufficiently large that it can overwhelm any attempt to maintain an exchange rate incompatible with fundamentals. Thus the possibility for investors—domestic and foreign—to exert discipline over policy has strengthened significantly. The room for policy maneuvers not in line with fundamentals has shrunk, and the challenge is to adjust policies before investors force a more costly resolution.

Second, the increasing integration of developing countries into global capital markets has meant that emerging markets can expect to be more vulnerable to external developments, such as cyclical swings in industrial countries and disturbances in any of the major markets. The experiences with the 1987 equity market crash and now with the Mexican crisis demonstrate that disturbances in one market will spread across regional and global markets. Most countries were tested in the wake of Mexico's devaluation, particularly in Latin America, but even financially strong markets with sound fundamentals, such as Hong Kong, Singapore, Chile, and Malaysia, faced pressure. The massive international financial support package for Mexico, put together in January 1995, prevented further erosion of confidence and forestalled stronger contagion. Recent events suggest that once the panic trading subsided, markets discriminated, albeit imperfectly, among countries according to the quality of their economic fundamentals.

Third, the resolution of sovereign debt-servicing difficulties has become more complicated with the changes in instruments and participants in international markets. In particular, the shift away from syndicated bank lending toward securitized capital flows has made voluntary restructuring of external debt more difficult to complete now than during the negotiations in the early 1980s. An international investor base with a diversity of investors with different risk-reward preferences and different legal arrangements will make it difficult to secure agreement among creditors. Furthermore, the threat of legal action from external claimants has become more credible with the expansion of international trade and payments in recent years. It is likely, therefore, that if a major emerging market country is experiencing debt-servicing difficulties, it will be forced to seek official funding to allow it to continue servicing its external debts in full, rather than force creditors to the table to renegotiate its obligations. The recent Mexican experience is an example of this approach.

The limited scope to achieve a negotiated debt restructuring with private creditors adds urgency to the need for emerging market countries with significant foreign currency debt to manage the macroeconomic and financial risks that are part and parcel of becoming integrated into global capital markets. If properly managed, such risks need not diminish the substantial benefits that come with increased access to international capital in any significant way.

Macroeconomic Risks

Macroeconomic policy in emerging market countries will have to be used to mitigate the adverse effects of capital inflows on the real exchange rate and on inflation. First, intervention can be employed to smooth excessively volatile real exchange rates. Intervention can be sterilized to limit the impact on domestic credit. Full and prolonged sterilization, however, may distort domestic interest rates sufficiently to invite more capital inflows, create a quasi-fiscal deficit, and, worse yet, distort the composition of capital inflows toward short-term assets. In this respect, tightening fiscal policy can offset the expansionary effect of the unsterilized part of capital inflows. Finally, during times of surges in inflows a country might consider measures to influence the level and characteristics of capital inflows, such as taxes on short-term bank deposits and other financial assets, reserve requirements against foreign borrowing, prudential limits on banks' offshore borrowing, and limits on consumption credit. In this regard, the experiences of Chile, Colombia, and Malaysia have been revealing. It should be noted, however, that comprehensive restrictions on capital flows can be highly distorting and their effectiveness tends to erode over time. Capital controls on outflows are generally viewed as confiscatory taxes and, if applied during periods of exchange market stress, may aggravate a crisis of confidence. In countries facing large and potentially unsustainable capital flows, a mix of intervention, sterilization, fiscal consolidation, and some direct measures to discourage short-term portfolio flows or to influence their composition may be appropriate. The mix of policies will, naturally, vary from country to country.

Financial Risks

Prudential policies have to be geared to containing the increased risks coming from greater integration into global markets. An expansion of bank credit in emerging markets due to partial sterilization has in some instances led to a decline in credit quality, particularly in banking systems that have recently been liberalized. Financial liberalization combined with capital inflows and without strengthened supervision and increased monitoring produce fertile ground for a future banking crisis. The authorities will need to make sure that there are sufficient prudential requirements to limit the interest rate, exchange rate, and equity price exposures of banking systems in recipient countries. In addition, the domestic banking system will need to be strong enough to absorb the interest rate increases

that might be necessary to defend the exchange rate. In this regard, the experiences of Mexico and Argentina illustrate vividly how a fragile banking system can become a constraint on the ability of the authorities to raise domestic rates in response to exchange market pressure.

Debt Management and Liquidity Risk

Mexico's experience with short-term debt demonstrates that emerging markets will need to manage the maturity structure of their debt in such a way as to minimize the risks of a liquidity crisis. The longer is the maturity of debt, the less likely it will be that major refinancing operations will coincide with periods of market turbulence, and the smaller will be the volume of debt that will need to be refinanced during a turbulent period. The need to refinance a significant volume of Tesobonos greatly contributed to the financial stress in the wake of the devaluation of the Mexican peso. With this in mind, emerging market countries should favor direct foreign investment over long-term portfolio investment, and long-term portfolio investment over short-term debt. If short-term exposures are necessary, then the rollover risk will need to be reduced through sufficient reserves and access to liquidity facilities, either official or private.

Supervisory and Regulatory Issues

The supervision and regulation of international capital markets continue to be challenged by the possible spillovers from the string of major failures and losses in the expanding derivatives industry. However, the efforts undertaken by the key industrial countries in strengthening the regulatory and supervisory infrastructure in derivative markets have been largely successful. A significant abatement in the risk inherent in the large intraday credit positions in wholesale payment systems has been achieved with the ongoing shift toward real-time gross settlement. A proposal for fundamental redesign of the capital requirement regime for the off-balance-sheet and trading activities of international banks, the key players in international markets, has been put out for comments by the Basle Committee on Banking Supervision and is likely to be adopted by year-end. The new approach marks a radical departure from established procedures. It will create incentives for international banks to refine their own risk-management models, since the ability of these models to reduce overall risk will determine their regulatory capital requirements. The supervisors' role would be to validate the process of risk management in banking institutions, rather than to determine whether the bank's trading book satisfies certain regulatory ratios. It is likely that the new system of regulatory capital requirements will have a profound effect on how financial institutions manage risk, and, indeed, on what activities they will undertake.

Serious challenges remain, principally in the area of international cooperation and coordination of regulatory and supervisory, legal, accounting, and disclosure rules. Although capital markets are becoming increasingly global, the rules under which these markets and institutions operate remain largely national. The failure of Barings illustrates this point. If information about Barings' activities had passed freely among its five supervisors—the Bank of England, the Securities and Futures Association, the Monetary Authority of Singapore, and the futures exchanges in Osaka and Singapore—then it would have been possible to obtain a consolidated picture of Barings' exposure and the failure may well not have occurred.

A further example is given by the differences in approach of the Basle Committee and the EU Commission in the important area of capital requirements for financial institutions. The EU is now proceeding with the implementation of its own capital adequacy rules for credit institutions, while the Basle Committee is proposing a new and significantly different set of rules for international banks for adoption by year-end. It is likely that there will be two different capital regimes in effect for some time, one for European banks and one for international banks. Similarly, the coordination among securities regulators in the area of information sharing and the harmonizing of disclosure standards are progressing only slowly.

One key lesson emerges from the recent experience with resolving banking difficulties in several industrial countries. In the event that significant losses are incurred, the supervisory authority should act decisively to limit the activities of institutions that have an impaired capital base. It is essential that capital-impaired institutions not be allowed to operate without very close supervision, particularly if the government explicitly or implicitly insures deposits, lest they continue to put depositors' money at risk. The danger is that the incentives facing insolvent or nearly insolvent institutions are radically different—such as collecting deposits with high interest rates and investing in high-risk projects—from those facing institutions that meet capital standards. The recent case of two failed credit cooperatives in Japan illustrates this lesson.

Although a policy of regulatory forbearance, waiting for a gradual write-down of losses, may have fewer direct costs, it has potentially greater indirect costs. The drawn-out resolution of credit problems at the housing finance companies in Japan, and the case of state-owned Crédit Lyonnais in France, illustrates the difficulties that can arise with a forbearance policy. The weakness of the financial system, burdened by nonperforming loans, may become a drag on the economy, thereby prolonging the problem further. Moreover, the losses may not be recovered with forbearance, but may snowball instead. Once the institution's balance sheet is clearly beyond repair, a burden-sharing scheme—among management, depositors, other creditors, shareholders, and taxpayers—should be put in place quickly, while paying due attention to containment of a systemic disturbance and moral hazard.

Bibliography

Alfiler, F. Enrico, "Monetary and Exchange Rate Policy Responses to Surges in Capital Flows: The Case of the Philippines" paper prepared for the Eleventh Pacific Basin Central Bank Conference held in Hong Kong, October 31–November 2, 1994.

Banco de la República, Colombia, *Annual Report*, various issues.

Banco de México, *Informe Anual* (1992).

Conselho Monétario Nacional, "Medidas na Area Cambial" (mimeograph, Brazilia: Conselho Monétario Nacional, October 1994).

————, "Medidas na Area Cambial" (mimeograph, Brazilia: Conselho Monétario Nacional, March 1995).

Culp, Christopher, and Merton H. Miller, "Hedging a Flow of Derivatives of Commodity Deliveries with Futures: Lessons from Metallgesellschaft," *Derivatives Review*, Vol. 1, No. 1 (1994).

Dooley, Michael, Eduardo Fernández-Arias, and Kenneth Kletzer, "Recent Private Capital Inflows to Developing Countries: Is the Debt Crisis History?" NBER Working Paper, No. 4792 (Cambridge, Massachu-setts: National Bureau of Economic Research, July 1994).

International Monetary Fund, *World Economic Outlook: A Survey by the Staff of the International Monetary Fund*, World Economic and Financial Surveys (Washington: International Monetary Fund, October 1992).

———— (1993a), *International Capital Markets: Part I. Exchange Rate Management and International Capital Flows*, World Economic and Financial Surveys (Washington: International Monetary Fund, April 1993).

———— (1993b), *World Economic Outlook: A Survey by the Staff of the International Monetary Fund*, World Economic and Financial Surveys (Washington: International Monetary Fund, May 1993).

———— (1993c), *International Capital Markets: Part II. Systemic Issues in International Finance*, World Economic and Financial Surveys (Washington: International Monetary Fund, August 1993).

———— (1994), *International Capital Markets: Developments, Prospects and Policy Issues*, World Economic and Financial Surveys (Washington: International Monetary Fund, September 1994).

I. Background Papers

Turbulence in Emerging Markets

I

Capital Flows to Developing Countries

The 1990s have witnessed a dramatic revival and expansion in capital flows to developing countries and significant changes in the composition of these flows. Many Asian countries, building on their strong economic performances of the latter half of the 1980s, attracted increasing levels of inflows. Major countries in the Western Hemisphere experienced a reversal of previous outflows of flight capital and renewed access to international capital markets, as debt problems of the 1980s were resolved and strong economic adjustment programs and structural reforms created opportunities and suitable climates for investment and growth. At the same time, the external environment for developing country financing improved, with the slowdown in economic activity in the industrial countries and regulatory changes that facilitated developing country access to capital markets. Foreign direct investment flows surged, accounting for a large part of the increase in inflows to developing countries, particularly those in Asia.

The most significant development was the sharp rise in portfolio capital flows. A new term "emerging markets" entered the lexicon of investors, as growing amounts of funds were placed in the bonds and stocks of developing countries, especially Western Hemisphere countries. Commercial bank loans, which were the main financing vehicle during the last surge in capital inflows in the 1970s, have picked up somewhat during the early 1990s, but they account for a small portion of total inflows. Net capital inflows to developing countries reached a peak in 1993, and although maintaining a high level, they declined in 1994 with the change in the external environment prompted by the strengthening of economic recovery in the industrial countries. Rising U.S. interest rates in early 1994 triggered considerable turmoil in financial markets worldwide. The Mexican devaluation in December 1994 prompted a sell-off of developing country securities and continues to influence developments in these markets.

Total Capital Flows

With the onset of the debt crisis in 1982, net capital inflows to developing countries as a group fell sharply. Average annual inflows dropped from around $30 billion in 1977–82 to less than $9 bil-

Table I.1. Capital Flows to Developing Countries[1]
(Annual averages, in billions of U.S. dollars)

	1977–82	1983–89	1990–94
All developing countries[2]			
Total net capital inflows	30.5	8.8	104.9
Net foreign direct investment	11.2	13.3	39.1
Net portfolio investment	−10.5	6.5	43.6
Other[3]	29.8	−11.0	22.2
Asia			
Total net capital inflows	15.8	16.7	52.1
Net foreign direct investment	2.7	5.2	23.4
Net portfolio investment	0.6	1.4	12.4
Other[3]	12.5	10.1	16.3
Western Hemisphere			
Total net capital inflows	26.3	−16.6	40.1
Net foreign direct investment	5.3	4.4	11.9
Net portfolio investment	1.6	−1.2	26.6
Other[3]	19.4	−19.8	1.6
Other developing countries[2]			
Total net capital inflows	−11.6	8.7	12.7
Net foreign direct investment	3.2	3.7	3.8
Net portfolio investment	−12.7	6.3	4.6
Other[3]	−2.1	−1.3	4.3

Source: International Monetary Fund, World Economic Outlook data base.

[1]Flows exclude exceptional financing. A number of countries do not report assets and liabilities separately. For these countries, it is assumed that there are no outflows, so that liabilities are set equal to the net value. To the extent that this assumption is not valid, the data underestimate the gross value. Adjustments are also made to the World Economic Outlook data to net out the effects of bonds exchanged for commercial bank loans in debt and debt service reduction operations and to provide additional detail on selected private capital flows.

[2]Excludes capital exporting countries, such as Kuwait and Saudi Arabia.

[3]Includes bank lending.

lion in 1983–89 (Table I.1).[1] Experiences with capital flows during 1983–89 differed markedly across geographic regions (and individual developing countries). Western Hemisphere countries experienced a shift to substantial net capital outflows, reflecting the difficulties that many of them encountered in servicing commercial bank debts. In sharp contrast, net capital inflows to Asia increased slightly, led by a rise in foreign direct investment flows. This development

---

[1]These figures exclude net capital flows of capital exporting countries, such as Kuwait and Saudi Arabia.

reflected measures taken by a number of developing countries in Asia to correct for overvalued exchange rates; to open up their economies; to remove structural impediments to economic efficiency; and to establish a stable macroeconomic policy environment to foster sustained economic growth.

At the end of the 1980s, the stage was set for a new surge in capital flows to developing countries. Continued sound macroeconomic policies and strong economic growth in the dynamic Asian economies were accompanied by broadened economic reforms in other countries of the region (most notably China). Around this time as well, major debtor countries in the Western Hemisphere were moving to complete the normalization of their relationships with creditors, and countries across the region initiated economic adjustment programs and comprehensive structural reforms. Similar adjustment and reform programs were put in place in several major developing countries in Europe. With these policy actions came improvements in the domestic economic climates of a broad spectrum of developing countries. Adding significantly to these improved climates was a range of measures taken to strengthen local financial systems, including banking sector and stock market reforms, the rationalization of regulatory regimes, and the tightening of financial regulation and accounting standards. These developments increased opportunities for investment by foreigners and lowered perceptions of country risk, thus triggering strong interest in developing country assets among investors in industrial countries.

Moreover, the external environment for developing country financing improved in the early 1990s. The slowdown in economic activity in the industrial countries and the decline in interest rates, particularly in the United States, stimulated investor interest in developing country securities where returns were higher. Lower international interest rates, through their impact on the debt-servicing costs of developing countries, also contributed to reducing perceptions of country risk. Regulatory changes in industrial countries, notably the relaxation of restrictions on private security placements in the United States, also facilitated access by developing countries to international capital markets, while trends toward global diversification of portfolios boosted investor demand.[2] In addition, increasing international integration of production, led by multinational corporations seeking cost and geographical advantages, heightened interest in foreign direct investment in developing countries, particularly favoring countries in Asia and the Western Hemisphere.

Over the period 1990–94, average annual net capital inflows to developing countries amounted to $105 billion, with inflows increasing from about $40 billion in 1990 to a peak of $155 billion in 1993. During this period, there was a marked surge in foreign direct investment flows, which accounted for a significant portion of the increase in net inflows to developing countries. The most dramatic change, however, was the rise in portfolio capital flows, in terms of both absolute levels and the share of total inflows. Not since the opening decades of the twentieth century have portfolio capital inflows been a significant source of financing for these countries.

In Asia, the rise in net inflows was largely accounted for by foreign direct investment, although this was accompanied by a significant rise in portfolio flows. The data on net foreign direct investment flows mask one important development that took place in the region. Increasingly, some of the more economically advanced economies in Asia (Taiwan Province of China, Hong Kong, and, to a lesser extent, Korea) became sources of foreign direct investment flows to other countries in the region. In the Western Hemisphere, while foreign direct investment flows rose substantially, most of the shift from net capital outflows in 1983–89 to inflows in 1990–94 was accounted for by portfolio capital inflows.

The international economic climate began to change in 1994, as economic recovery in the industrial countries strengthened. The major impact of this development was seen in net portfolio capital flows to developing countries. Early in the year, increases in interest rates triggered considerable turbulence in financial markets worldwide. As a result, interest in developing country investments waned, and new issues of securities in international markets by borrowers in developing countries fell dramatically. With the restoration of relative calm in the markets after May 1994, developing countries returned to international bond and equity markets, but the terms on new issues were less favorable and only the better credit risks maintained access. The Mexican devaluation in December 1994 precipitated a broad sell-off of developing country securities by foreign investors in late December and early January 1995. While selling pressures were concentrated in Western Hemisphere markets, they temporarily spread to Asian markets in mid-January. Western Hemisphere markets generally remained under pressure until mid-April. In contrast, Asian markets recovered and appear to be experiencing some renewed inflows of portfolio capital. Since December 1994, issuing activity in international bond markets has been weak and equity issuance has come to a virtual halt. Most bonds issued in international markets have been placed by Asian entities.

---

[2]For further discussion of portfolio diversification, see the background paper "Increasing Importance of Institutional Investors," pp. 165–74.

Portfolio Capital Flows

Portfolio capital flows to developing countries consist of international placements of bonds, issues of equities in international markets, and purchases by foreigners of stocks and financial market instruments in developing countries' domestic markets. Over the period 1990–94, international bond issues have been the main source of external funding for developing countries. International equity issues have also been an important funding source, but to some extent they may have simply served to spark the interest of investors in developing country stocks. The fastest growing segment of portfolio flows appears to have been direct purchases of securities in domestic markets. Data on these flows are limited; however, the rapid growth (both in terms of numbers and net asset holdings) of mutual funds dedicated to investing in developing country securities (so-called emerging markets mutual funds) suggests that by 1994 inflows generated by direct securities purchases were at least on a par with funds raised through bond issues.

International Bond Placements

Bond issuance by developing countries in international capital markets grew from $6.3 billion in 1990 to $59.3 billion in 1993, before declining slightly to $57.6 billion in 1994 (Annex Table A1 and Chart I.1). In relation to total bond issuance in international markets, the share of developing country issues rose from 2.8 percent in 1990 to 12.4 percent in 1993. Most of the proceeds of developing country bond issues over the period represented net capital inflows, as maturing bonds issued by developing countries amounted to about $32 billion during 1990–94. Although the range of borrowers widened significantly, most of the bonds were issued by borrowers from a limited number of Asian and Western Hemisphere countries and a few issuers in Europe. Private sector borrowers accounted for nearly half the bond issues by developing countries.

With unsettled conditions in international bond markets early in 1994, access to the market during the year tended to be restricted to better quality developing country borrowers. Nonetheless, developing countries placed almost as many bonds as in 1993. Asian entities became the largest issuers, placing roughly half of the total bonds issued by developing countries in 1994. Entities in the Western Hemisphere continued to be major issuers, although total bond placements by borrowers in the region declined significantly. Mexico remained the single largest borrower among developing countries, despite the fact that its issuance activity fell off sharply during the year. Bond issues by Argentina and Brazil, while remaining quite large, also were down significantly from their 1993 levels. In other regions, South Africa and Israel stepped up bond issuance in 1994, while

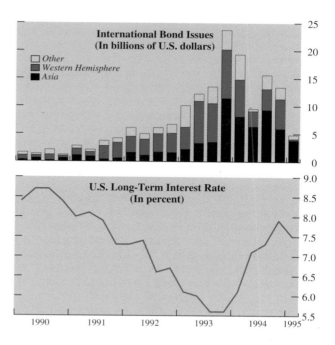

Chart I.1. International Bond Issues by Developing Countries and U.S. Long-Term Interest Rate

Sources: Eurobondware data base; *Financial Times; International Financing Review;* and International Monetary Fund, *International Financial Statistics.*

issuance by Hungary and Turkey declined sharply, reflecting deteriorating economic conditions in these countries. Following the Mexican devaluation, only a small number of developing countries, primarily Asian countries, have issued bonds in international markets, with total issues in the first quarter of 1995 amounting to $4.8 billion, only one third of the quarterly average rate of issues in 1994.

The terms of new issues by developing countries improved significantly during the early 1990s. The average yield spread at launch for U.S. dollar-denominated issues declined from over 400 basis points in 1991 to 187 basis points in the first quarter of 1994 (Annex Table A2).[3] The narrowing of spreads reflected a general improvement in credit ratings for developing countries, with several sovereign borrowers achieving investment grade ratings in the past few years.[4] Over the period, Mexico set the tone for much of the market. The spread on

---

[3]The yield spread is a proxy for the riskiness of developing country bonds. It is measured as the difference between the yield on a developing country bond issue and the yield on a risk-free asset, proxied by the yield on a U.S. Treasury security of comparable maturity.

[4]Including Chile, China, Colombia, the Czech Republic, Indonesia, Israel, and South Africa.

Mexican sovereign issues narrowed from 800 basis points in 1989 to around 200 basis points at the end of 1993. As the first debt-restructuring country to re-establish access to international financial markets, Mexico tended to set a benchmark for measuring the riskiness of sovereign debt issues by other developing countries in the Western Hemisphere and other regions, particularly those with subinvestment grade ratings. Asian countries with good debt-servicing records have generally commanded lower spreads, reflecting the high credit ratings that generally have been assigned to them by major credit-rating agencies. Sovereign borrowers continued to pay lower spreads than private sector borrowers, although private entities have achieved notable improvements in spreads in recent years.

In the second quarter of 1994, spreads began to widen, reflecting the unsettled market conditions triggered by the increase in U.S. interest rates. The widening of the average spread during this period may not fully reflect the deterioration in market conditions, as bonds were issued primarily by higher-rated borrowers and carried shorter maturities. In the fourth quarter of the year, the average spread rose to 255 basis points following additional increases in U.S. interest rates. After the devaluation of the Mexican peso, activity in the new issue market dropped off sharply, but a deterioration in spreads was evident in an increase in secondary market yield spreads on developing country Eurodollar bonds and in stripped yield spreads on Brady bonds (Charts I.2 and I.3). After lengthening through the early 1990s, the average maturity of bonds issued by developing countries shortened from seven years in the first quarter in 1994 to five years in the fourth quarter.

The U.S. dollar has been the dominant currency for developing country bond issues, accounting for about 70 percent of the total over the period 1990–94 (Annex Table A3), before declining to 55 percent in the first quarter of 1995. The large share of the U.S. dollar sector partly reflected U.S. investors' greater interest in high-yielding securities. The yen sector's share in the total rose from 7 percent in 1990 to 13 percent in 1994, and further to 34 percent in the first quarter of 1995. Asian borrowers continued to dominate the yen sector owing to close economic relations with Japan and preferences of Japanese investors. Nonetheless, several non-Asian borrowers (notably Hungary, Mexico, and Argentina) have placed yen issues. Bond issues in deutsche mark, principally by European borrowers and some borrowers in the Western Hemisphere, remained relatively small and tended to be focused on investors in Germany. Issues in other currencies were minor over the period, although some European and Western Hemisphere borrowers more actively tapped smaller currency markets, including the Austrian schilling, Swiss

Chart I.2. Secondary Market Yield Spreads on Selected Eurobonds, January 1994–March 1995[1]
(In basis points)

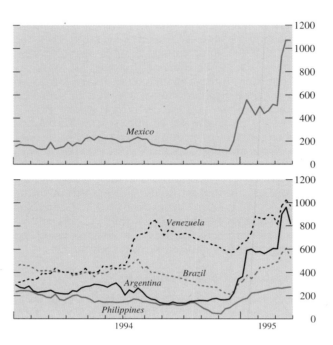

Sources: Reuters; and Salomon Brothers.
[1]Based on weekly average yields.

franc, Danish krone, and Spanish peseta, as financial market conditions tightened in 1994.

Regarding the composition of bond issuers, nonsovereign borrowers accounted for the vast majority of bonds placed during 1990–94. The principal exceptions were Hungary and Turkey where virtually all bonds were government issues (Annex Table A4). Financial institutions have been the leading borrowers in many countries. Among the 12 largest borrowers, the financial sector's share was particularly high in several countries, ranging from around 60 percent in Brazil and China to 40–50 percent in Hong Kong, Indonesia, Korea, and Mexico.[5] Other nonsovereign issuers tended to be well-established companies with large domestic market shares or strong export potential. Petroleum, telecommunications, and public utility companies were major issuers in Argentina, Brazil, and Mexico; real estate companies led issuers in Hong Kong; and steel

---

[5]Large foreign placements of bonds raises important questions as to the capacity of the financial sector in a developing country to intermediate capital flows effectively and efficiently. The background paper "Role of Domestic Financial Institutions in Intermediating Foreign Capital Inflows," pp. 109–19, looks at the implications of large capital inflows on developing countries' financial systems.

Chart I.3. **Secondary Market Stripped Yield Spreads on Selected Brady Bonds, January 1994–March 1995**[1]
(In basis points)

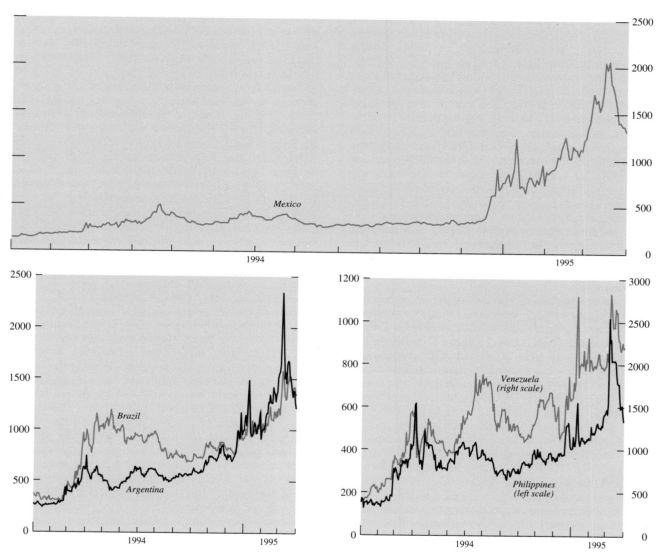

Sources: Reuters; and Salomon Brothers.
[1]Based on daily yields.

and electrical companies were the largest issuers in Korea.

International Equity Placements

Placements of new equity issues in international markets by developing country companies also grew rapidly over the 1990–94 period, in part reflecting the privatization of public sector companies by several countries. Funds raised over this period totaled nearly $46 billion, with the value of issues rising from $1.3 billion in 1990 to $17.9 billion in 1994 (Annex Table A5). Developing countries' share in total international equity issues increased from 16 percent in 1990 to 41 percent in 1992, but declined to 19 percent in 1994, as issuance by companies in industrial countries picked up. New placements of developing country equities trailed off sharply in December 1994, and total issues amounted to only $601 million in the first quarter of 1995.

Like bonds, international equity placements have been dominated by Asian and Western Hemisphere companies. Placements by Asian companies totaled nearly $25 billion in 1990–94, with roughly half of such issues taking place in 1994 alone. The leading issuers were Chinese companies ($5.6 billion), followed by companies in India ($3.6 billion, most of which was placed in 1994) and in Hong Kong and Indonesia ($3 billion each). Western Hemisphere companies placed equity valued at nearly $19 billion during 1990–94. Mexican firms led all issuers with $11 billion placed; however, new equity placements were at their highest level in 1991 and declined subsequently, partly reflecting the completion of some major privatizations. In 1993, issuing activity by Mexican firms was subdued in the first three quarters of the year owing to uncertainties regarding passage of the North American Free Trade Agreement (NAFTA); and with the agreement's passage, new issues rose sharply in the final quarter of the year. In 1994, Mexican equity placements in the first quarter were less than half of their fourth quarter 1993 level and proceeded to decline further over the year. Argentine equity issues amounted to $4.3 billion in 1990–94, with most of these funds being raised in 1993 with the partial privatization of the state-owned oil company.

An increasing share of developing country equities has been placed in international markets through equity-based instruments, such as American Depository Receipts (ADRs) and Global Depository Receipts (GDRs). In 1994, ADRs and GDRs accounted for 78 percent of total equity issues by developing countries. These facilities permit shares to be traded on industrial country exchanges, with the potential for raising liquidity, reducing settlement time, lowering settlement risk, and thus broadening the investor base. Most Western Hemisphere companies have placed international equity issues almost exclusively through ADR-GDR programs in 1993–94.

International equity placements by developing country companies have been concentrated in the telecommunications, banking, electrical, and petroleum industries in 1990–94 (Annex Table A6). On an individual country basis, telecommunications companies accounted for a significant share of issues by Indonesia, Mexico, Pakistan, and Thailand. Financial institutions were major issuers in Hong Kong, Indonesia, and Mexico. The electrical equipment and electronics industries in Hong Kong and Korea, and the transport industries (including shipbuilding) in China, India, and Korea were important issuers. The government privatization program made the petroleum company the largest issuer in Argentina.

Direct Portfolio Investment in Developing Country Markets

The information available suggests that direct purchases by foreigners of developing country securities in domestic markets have become an increasingly important source of portfolio flows to developing countries. In particular, emerging markets mutual funds have expanded rapidly in recent years.[6] The number of such funds reached 594 by the end of 1993 with a total net asset value of $90 billion (Annex Table A7). In 1994, despite turbulent market conditions in many developing country markets, the growth of those funds picked up significantly, probably reflecting the time lag involved in establishing these funds; the number of funds increased to 908, and their total net asset value rose to $132 billion. Much of the increase in the net assets took place in the second half of the year despite declines in stock prices in most developing countries (Charts I.4 and I.5). It was largely accounted for by open-end equity funds domiciled in the United States (Annex Tables A8 and A9). Net purchases of bonds and equities through emerging markets' mutual funds are estimated to have amounted to $100 billion in 1990–94, with $18 billion in purchases taking place in 1993, and $64 billion in 1994 (Annex Table A10).[7]

Emerging markets mutual funds have focused on equities in Asia, with the net asset value of those funds dedicated to Asian markets accounting for 58 percent of the net asset value of all emerging markets mutual funds in 1994. In contrast, mutual funds dedicated to the Western Hemisphere increased more moderately, with their share remaining at about 12 percent of total net asset value. Among dedicated country funds, Korean funds are the largest on the basis of net asset value, followed by India, Taiwan Province of China, Thailand, and China. The fastest growing segment of the market has been the global emerging markets mutual funds, which do not exclusively target specific countries or regions; the net asset value of these funds rose to 28 percent of the total in 1994. Global mutual funds (which invest in foreign securities but are not dedicated to emerging market investments) have also become major holders of developing country securities; however, comprehensive data on the activities of these funds are not readily available.

---

[6]An emerging market mutual fund is defined as one that holds at least 60 percent of its assets in developing country securities. Data on the activities of these funds provide only an indicator of direct security purchases. Information on other major investors, including global mutual funds, other institutional investors (such as pension funds and hedge funds), and high net worth individuals, is limited.

[7]An approximation for net purchases of developing country equities by emerging markets mutual funds can be obtained by adjusting the changes in the funds' net assets for share price changes. To the extent that emerging markets mutual funds hold part of their portfolios in cash, industrial country assets, or equities issued by developing countries in international capital markets, net purchases estimated in this way may misstate actual purchases of emerging markets securities in domestic markets. Moreover, changes in the indices used to measure share prices (the IFC investible indices) may not accurately proxy actual changes in the value of the portfolios of the emerging markets mutual funds.

Chart I.4. Share Price Indices for Selected Markets in Latin America, January 1993–March 1995
(IFC weekly investable price indices, December 1988 = 100)

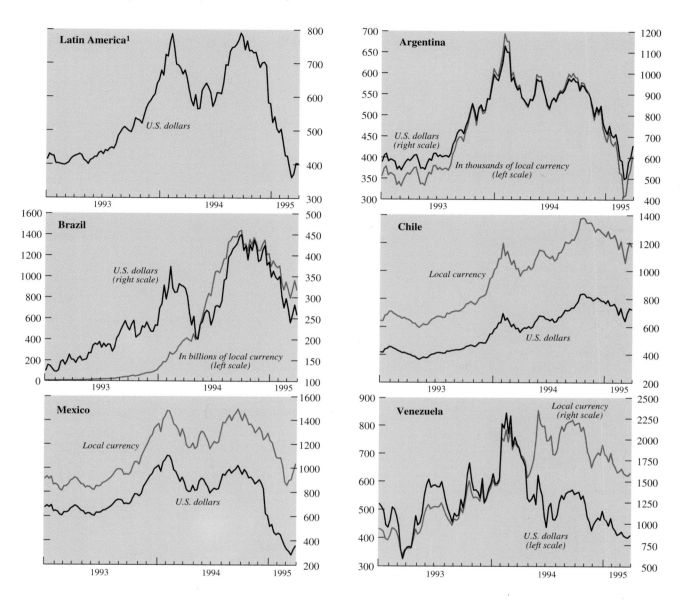

Source: International Finance Corporation (IFC), Emerging Markets Data Base.
[1]Argentina, Brazil, Chile, Colombia, Mexico, and Venezuela.

Events in Mexico in December 1994 prompted a sell-off of equities on developing country markets worldwide, with pressures being concentrated and sustained only in major Western Hemisphere markets. Actual or anticipated redemptions by shareholders led mutual funds to sell equities across Western Hemisphere markets and, on a more limited and temporary scale, in some Asian markets. Global mutual funds are reported to have been the largest sellers, while selling by emerging markets mutual funds has been more limited. This picture may change, however, since it is anticipated that the dedicated emerging markets funds will post significant losses in their net asset values in the first quarter of 1995. Such losses could induce redemptions and further selling into Western Hemisphere markets where market liquidity is already strained.

Investment in bonds by emerging markets mutual funds has been small, compared with equity investment. The total net asset value of emerging market

Chart I.5. Share Price Indices for Selected Markets in Asia, January 1993–March 1995
(IFC weekly investable price indices, December 1988 = 100)

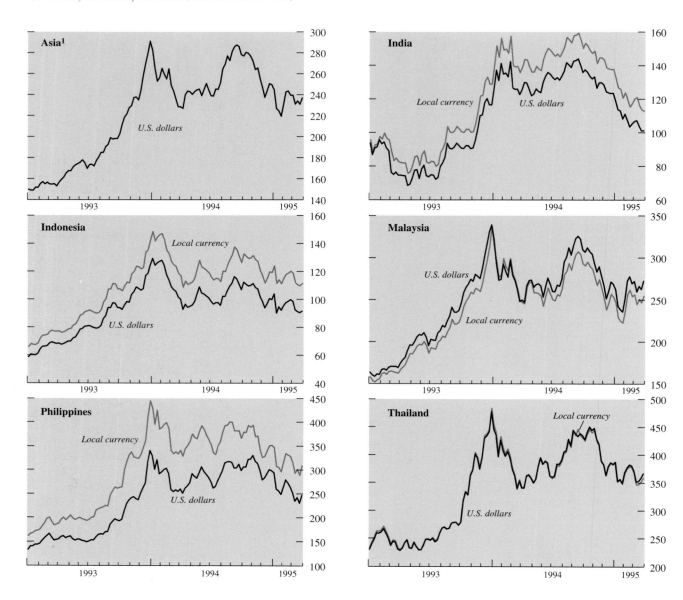

Source: International Finance Corporation (IFC), Emerging Markets Data Base.
[1]India, Korea, Malaysia, Pakistan, Philippines, Taiwan Province of China, and Thailand.

bond funds was only $8 billion at the end of 1994, compared with $6 billion at the end of 1993. Market participants reported that non-dedicated general mutual funds, such as short-term bond funds, have heavily invested in short-term developing country government securities. These funds were reported to have invested a substantial share of their assets in Mexican Tesobonos prior to the devaluation in December 1994 and to have sold off a significant part of their holdings in the aftermath of the crisis. Their hold-

ings, while large, relative to the total assets of the funds, nonetheless, were only a small fraction of all Tesobonos held by nonresidents of Mexico.

Investor Base

Comprehensive statistics are not available on the composition of the investor base in developing country securities. A crude picture, however, emerges from an examination of the partial information available and from anecdotal evidence. In the late 1980s and early 1990s, institutional investors (principally, pension funds and insurance companies in the United States and the United Kingdom) began to show interest in the securities of developing countries in Asia—particularly the dynamic economies—as part of efforts by these investors to diversify their portfolios.[8] In contrast, market participants report that, in the early stages of the resurgence of inflows to developing countries in the Western Hemisphere, the largest source of inflows was returning flight capital.

In the early 1990s, mutual funds began to expand their investment activities in developing country securities. At the same time, an increasing number of emerging markets mutual funds were established, first in the form of closed end funds and then increasingly as open-end funds. The majority of these mutual funds are located in the United States and the United Kingdom—traditional locations for fund managers—but they attract money from investors throughout the world.[9] By the end of 1994, there were at least 260 closed end mutual funds and 648 open-end mutual funds dedicated to investing in emerging markets. Pension funds also expanded their holdings of developing country securities, moving beyond Asia to invest in Western Hemisphere assets. While these investors have significantly increased their holdings, they still place only a fraction of their portfolios in international investments, and of this amount only a small portion in developing country securities. Emerging market securities as a distinct asset class developed over the early 1990s and were firmly established by 1993.

The 1993–94 period witnessed a rather rapid expansion in the number of investors in developing country securities; however, there was a distinct tendency for these investors to have similar characteristics (for example, mutual funds). In particular, they tended to have similar risk-return preferences and methods of operation. Moreover, since securities markets in developing countries generally are not very deep, there was a concentration of investments in the largest markets and in the biggest issues. Moreover, in the face of actual or anticipated redemptions, the mutual funds sold securities across a range of countries outside of Mexico, especially those in the Western Hemisphere, in order

to maintain the relative shares of the various assets in their portfolios roughly in line with their targeted allocations. Because of the concentration of investments, markets in Argentina and Brazil were strongly affected.

Bank Lending

Thus far in the 1990s, the level of bank lending to developing countries has remained relatively unchanged and a relatively small source of financing for these countries (Annex Table A11).[10] In relation to total medium- and long-term bank commitments, the share of developing countries also has declined, falling from a high of 24.6 percent in 1991 to 12 percent in 1994. The weighted average spread on bank loans over the London interbank offered rate (LIBOR) has risen steadily from 64 basis points in 1990 to 107 basis points in 1994. At the same time, the average maturity of loans shortened from 9.5 years in 1990 to 6.8 years in 1994. The U.S. dollar remained the most important currency of denomination, accounting for nearly 80 percent of total bank loans to developing counties in 1994, followed by the pound sterling.

The bulk of medium- and long-term bank commitments to developing countries continued to be concentrated in Asian countries, which had not experienced debt-servicing difficulties in the past. New commitments to Asian developing countries increased over the 1990–94 period, particularly after a small decline in 1992. Loan commitments rose to $15.7 billion in 1993 and to $20.4 billion in 1994, largely reflecting increased borrowing by private entities in Indonesia and Thailand. Indonesia was the largest Asian borrower in 1990–94, receiving loans totaling $16.6 billion; it was followed by China ($14.1 billion), Thailand ($13 billion), and Korea ($11.8 billion).

Bank commitments to Western Hemisphere countries have remained relatively small and widely disbursed across major countries in the region. Mexico was the largest borrower over the 1990–94 period but has borrowed very little from banks in the last two years. In contrast, all new loan commitments to Argentina have occurred in 1993 and 1994. Bank lending to Europe also has remained relatively small, declining somewhat in recent years. Turkey was the largest borrower until 1994, when its access to bank credits was sharply reduced reflecting its economic difficulties. Bank loan commitments to other European countries remained small, although some Eastern European countries, including Hungary, increased their recourse to bank borrowing over the 1990–94 period.

---

[8]For further details on the changing role of institutional investors see the background paper "Increasing Importance of Institutional Investors," pp. 165–74.

[9]For example, Japanese investors placing money in U.S. dollar-denominated funds investing in developing country securities tend to have their transactions cleared through New York. Thus, a portion of Japanese portfolio investment abroad recorded in the balance of payments accounts as an outflow to the United States may actually be flows through the United States to developing countries.

[10]These data cover commitments that are not insured by export credit agencies.

Annex

Table A1. International Bond Issues by Selected Developing Countries and Regions[1]
(In millions of U.S. dollars)

	1990	1991	1992	1993	1994	1994 1st qtr.	1994 2nd qtr.	1994 3rd qtr.	1994 4th qtr.	1995 1st qtr.
Developing countries	6,335	12,838	23,780	59,337	57,597	19,040	9,562	15,627	13,369	4,779
Africa	90	236	725	—	2,492	1,247	—	320	925	408
Congo	—	—	—	—	600	600	—	—	—	—
South Africa	—	236	725	—	1,615	370	—	320	925	158
Tunisia	—	—	—	—	277	277	—	—	—	251
Asia	1,630	3,000	5,917	20,401	29,639	8,066	6,290	9,346	5,936	3,830
China	—	115	1,359	3,047	4,077	1,650	876	888	668	154
Hong Kong	66	100	185	5,887	5,850	1,570	791	1,706	1,781	491
India	274	227	—	546	884	439	195	250	—	—
Indonesia	80	369	494	—	2,266	699	750	717	100	20
Korea	1,105	2,012	3,208	5,864	6,348	1,193	1,209	2,250	1,695	2,994
Macao	—	—	—	—	155	—	155	—	—	—
Malaysia	—	—	—	954	2,345	330	735	580	700	—
Pakistan	—	—	—	—	195	—	45	—	150	—
Philippines	—	—	—	1,293	1,144	154	385	345	261	—
Singapore	—	—	—	—	358	—	86	272	—	—
Taiwan Province of China	—	160	60	79	2,062	318	658	896	191	71
Thailand	—	17	610	2,247	3,955	1,713	407	1,442	391	100
Europe	1,856	1,960	4,561	9,638	3,542	1,055	439	921	1,127	254
Czech Republic	—	—	—	697	400	—	250	—	150	—
Czechoslovakia	375	277	129	—	—	—	—	—	—	—
Hungary	888	1,186	1,242	4,796	1,728	69	189	668	802	254
Malta	—	—	—	205	205	205	—	—	—	—
Russia	—	—	—	—	75	—	—	—	75	—
Slovak Republic	—	—	—	240	275	21	—	254	—	—
Turkey	593	497	3,190	3,905	859	760	—	—	99	—
Middle East	—	400	—	2,002	3,201	1,958	—	1,243	—	—
Israel	—	400	—	2,002	2,521	1,958	—	563	—	—
Lebanon	—	—	—	—	400	—	—	400	—	—
Saudi Arabia	—	—	—	—	280	—	—	280	—	—
Western Hemisphere	2,760	7,242	12,577	27,296	18,723	6,714	2,833	3,796	5,381	287
Argentina	21	795	1,570	6,233	5,319	1,460	900	879	2,080	—
Barbados	—	—	—	—	50	—	20	—	30	—
Bolivia	—	—	—	—	10	10	—	—	—	—
Brazil	—	1,837	3,655	6,679	4,036	1,180	100	595	2,161	50
Chile	—	200	120	433	155	—	—	155	—	—
Colombia	—	—	—	566	955	250	83	300	322	100
Costa Rica	—	—	—	—	50	50	—	—	—	—
Guatemala	—	—	—	60	—	—	—	—	—	—
Jamaica	—	—	—	—	55	—	—	55	—	—
Mexico	2,477	3,782	6,100	10,683	7,394	3,623	1,690	1,393	688	137
Panama	—	50	—	—	250	—	—	250	—	—
Peru	—	—	—	30	100	40	40	20	—	—
Trinidad and Tobago	—	—	100	125	150	—	—	150	—	—
Uruguay	—	—	100	140	200	100	—	—	100	—
Venezuela	262	578	932	2,348	—	—	—	—	—	—
Total bond issues in international bond markets	226,556	297,588	333,694	480,997	523,381	157,143	118,215	127,190	120,833	112,416
Shares of developing countries in global issuance	2.8	4.3	7.1	12.4	11.0	12.1	8.1	12.3	11.1	4.3

Sources: *Euromoney* data base; *Euroweek*; *Financial Times*; and *International Financing Review (IFR)*.
[1]Including note issues under European medium-term notes (EMTN) programs. Data for 1994 are based on *Euromoney* data base and are not strictly comparable with data for 1991–93, which are estimated on the basis of data from *Euroweek*, *Financial Times*, and *IFR*.

Table A2. Yield Spread at Launch for Unenhanced Bond Issues by Developing Countries and Regions[1]
(In basis points)

	1990	1991	1992	1993	1994	1994 1st qtr.	2nd qtr.	3rd qtr.	4th qtr.	1995 1st qtr.
Sovereign borrowers	211	271	239	262	184	107	450	212	272	...
Argentina	...	375	294	277	248	120	...	190	350	...
Barbados	...	...	...	...	420	...	450	...	400	...
Chile	...	150	150	...	...	...	...	...	...	...
China	...	...	...	88	94	94	...	...	...	...
Colombia	...	...	...	215	153	148	...	160	...	...
Czech Republic	...	...	...	270	...	...	...	...	...	...
Czechoslovakia, former	...	300	...	...	...	...	...	...	...	...
Hungary	...	300	275	266	160	...	...	160	...	...
Lebanon	...	...	...	...	325	...	...	325	...	...
Mexico	...	...	215	208	...	...	...	...	...	...
Pakistan	...	...	...	...	385	...	...	...	385	...
Philippines	...	...	...	320	...	...	...	...	...	...
Saudi Arabia	...	...	...	...	25	...	...	25	...	...
South Africa	...	...	...	...	193	...	...	...	193	...
Thailand	...	...	100	74	...	...	...	...	...	...
Trinidad and Tobago	...	...	565	...	425	...	...	425	...	...
Turkey	211	...	219	...	...	...	...	...	...	...
Uruguay	...	...	275	228	158	158	...	...	...	...
Venezuela	...	235	...	385	...	...	...	...	...	...
Public sector	317	357	261	193	151	171	172	85	142	64
Argentina	...	...	...	440	338	...	333	...	344	...
Brazil	...	480	428	481	450	450	...	...	...	...
Chile	...	...	...	...	138	...	...	138	...	...
China	...	...	69	82	135	...	229	...	100	...
Colombia	...	...	...	217	180	...	...	...	180	...
Costa Rica	...	...	...	...	395	395	...	...	...	...
Czech Republic	...	...	...	...	116	...	120	...	110	...
Guatemala	...	...	...	605	...	...	...	...	...	...
India	160	...	...	...	...	...	...	...	...	...
Indonesia	...	...	...	...	150	158	...	144	...	...
Korea	...	...	89	83	46	68	...	34	38	68
Malaysia	...	...	...	100	...	...	...	...	...	...
Malta	...	...	...	...	115	115	...	...	...	...
Mexico	375	285	220	196	151	154	126	...	...	42
Philippines	...	...	...	250	167	...	...	...	167	...
Slovak Republic	...	...	...	...	325	325	...	...	...	...
Thailand	...	...	...	43	85	...	...	83	103	...
Turkey	...	...	...	205	...	...	...	...	...	...
Venezuela	...	275	265	212	...	...	...	...	...	...
Private sector	650	540	389	348	283	281	406	207	287	75
Argentina	730	447	409	375	379	310	411	420	430	...
Bolivia	...	...	...	...	428	428	...	...	...	...
Brazil	...	530	512	519	374	377	465	335	378	350
Chile	...	...	...	194	125	...	...	125	...	...
Colombia	...	...	...	310	641	...	641	...	...	...
Hong Kong	...	...	180	118	95	...	103	93	97	130
India	...	...	...	110	285	...	...	285	...	...
Indonesia	...	...	...	410	477	...	467	515	325	160
Korea	...	...	121	82	55	79	...	44	46	39
Mexico	613	593	414	359	305	253	498	235	322	...
Panama	...	...	...	...	60	...	...	60	...	...
Peru	...	...	...	706	680	680	...	...	...	...
Philippines	...	...	...	375	293	...	340	190	...	...
Thailand	...	...	43	43	132	157	81	141	147	98
Uruguay	...	...	...	300	...	...	...	...	...	...
Venezuela	693	362	375	469	...	...	...	...	...	...
All borrowers	355	405	322	282	225	187	343	187	255	70

Sources: Staff estimates based on *Euromoney* data base; *Euroweek*; *Financial Times*; and *International Financing Review (IFR)*.

[1]Excluding issues denominated in non-U.S. dollars. Yield spread measured as the difference between the bond yield at issue and the prevailing yield for industrial country government bonds in the same currency and of comparable maturity. All figures are weighted averages. Data for 1994 are based on *Euromoney* data base and are not strictly comparable with data for 1990–93, which were estimated on the basis of data from *Financial Times*, *Euroweek*, and *IFR*.

Table A3. International Bond Issues by Developing Countries by Currency of Denomination[1]

(In millions of U.S. dollars)

	1990	1991	1992	1993	1994	1994 1st qtr.	1994 2nd qtr.	1994 3rd qtr.	1994 4th qtr.	1995 1st qtr.
U.S. dollar	3,890	8,755	16,991	44,192	44,049	15,696	6,782	11,901	9,671	2,621
Africa	—	—	—	—	1,845	600	—	320	925	—
Asia	960	1,683	4,143	16,700	21,342	6,249	4,059	6,751	4,284	2,334
Europe	550	300	1,014	1,395	1,115	291	250	250	324	—
Middle East	—	400	—	2,002	3,201	1,958	—	1,243	—	—
Western Hemisphere	2,380	6,372	11,834	24,095	16,546	6,598	2,473	3,337	4,139	287
Deutsche mark	1,693	1,618	2,013	4,521	1,560	141	540	129	749	203
Africa	89	236	408	—	—	—	—	—	—	—
Asia	283	96	125	—	270	26	180	64	—	203
Europe	983	961	1,063	3,285	425	—	—	—	425	—
Western Hemisphere	337	326	417	1,236	864	115	360	65	324	—
Japanese yen	450	1,458	3,554	7,965	7,403	1,611	1,532	2,391	1,869	1,633
Africa	—	—	—	—	277	277	—	—	—	251
Asia	259	1,001	1,306	3,099	4,849	638	1,532	1,774	905	1,128
Europe	190	457	2,247	4,078	1,562	695	—	558	309	254
Western Hemisphere	—	—	—	787	715	—	—	60	655	—
European currency unit (ECU)	127	423	630	—	—	—	—	—	—	—
Africa	—	—	318	—	—	—	—	—	—	—
Asia	127	—	—	—	—	—	—	—	—	—
Europe	—	242	186	—	—	—	—	—	—	—
Western Hemisphere	—	181	126	—	—	—	—	—	—	—
Other	175	585	593	2,759	4,622	1,592	708	1,206	1,116	322
Africa	—	—	—	—	370	370	—	—	—	158
Asia	—	221	342	602	3,178	1,153	519	758	748	164
Europe	132	—	51	880	439	69	189	114	67	—
Western Hemisphere	43	364	200	1,278	635	—	—	335	301	—
Total	6,335	12,838	23,780	59,437	57,634	19,040	9,562	15,627	13,406	4,779
Memorandum items										
Share in total issues by developing countries *(in percent)*										
U.S. dollar	61	68	71	74	76	81	71	76	72	55
Deutsche mark	27	13	8	8	3	1	6	1	6	4
Japanese yen	7	11	15	13	13	8	16	15	14	34
ECU	2	3	3	—	—	—	—	—	—	—
Other	3	5	2	5	8	9	7	8	8	7
Share in total issues in global bond market *(in percent)*										
U.S. dollar	32	30	39	36	15	36	21	34	40	37
Deutsche mark	8	7	11	13	3	9	1	6	8	13
Japanese yen	14	14	13	12	5	7	15	21	19	14
ECU	9	11	7	1	1	2	1	1	1	3
Other	38	40	34	38	17	36	28	27	24	35

Sources: IMF staff estimates based on *Euromoney* data base; *Euroweek; Financial Times*; and *International Financing Review (IFR)*.
[1]Data for 1994 are based on *Euromoney* data base and are not strictly comparable with data for 1991–93, which were estimated on the basis of *Euroweek, Financial Times*, and *IFR*.

Table A4. International Bond Issues by Country or Region, and Sector, 1990–94

	Argentina	Brazil	China	Hong Kong	Hungary	Indonesia	Korea	Malaysia	Mexico	Thailand	Turkey	Venezuela
(In millions of U.S. dollars)												
Financial sector	2,790	9,827	5,263	4,912	359	1,801	9,085	320	13,034	3,674	577	75
Banks	2,740	9,587	2,500	2,459	359	1,476	8,985	100	12,083	3,658	577	75
Other	50	240	2,763	2,453	—	325	100	220	951	16	—	—
Petroleum	1,330	2,318	—	—	—	—	727	954	3,927	392	—	2,389
Transport	172	55	—	343	—	—	—	—	675	—	—	—
Real estate	50	—	—	3,763	—	22	—	—	325	899	—	—
Utility	1,365	150	—	—	—	—	2,572	600	350	141	—	—
Cement	—	—	—	7	—	—	115	—	150	—	—	—
Manufacturing	100	70	—	150	—	30	255	—	1,190	—	—	35
Steel	280	720	—	251	—	—	1,566	—	363	154	—	100
Telecommunications	1,780	1,000	—	—	—	—	100	735	1,130	—	—	50
Electrical	—	—	—	150	—	—	1,675	—	235	45	—	—
Construction	100	191	—	138	—	245	502	225	4,658	40	—	75
Sovereign	5,336	100	3,013	—	9,480	—	300	—	1,388	1,134	8,467	1,276
Other	636	1,813	323	2,372	—	1,596	1,640	465	3,110	350	—	120
Total	13,938	16,243	8,599	12,088	9,839	3,694	18,537	3,299	30,536	6,829	9,044	4,120
(In percent of total)												
Financial sector	20.0	60.5	61.2	40.6		48.8	49.0	9.7	42.7	53.8		1.8
Banks	19.7	59.0	29.1	20.3	3.6	40.0	48.5	3.0	39.6	53.6	6.4	1.8
Other	0.4	1.5	32.1	20.3	—	8.8	0.5	6.7	3.1	0.2	—	—
Petroleum	9.5	14.3	—	—	—	—	3.9	28.9	12.9	5.7	—	58.0
Transport	1.2	0.3	—	2.8	—	—	—	—	2.2	—	—	—
Real estate	0.4	—	—	31.1	—	0.6	—	—	1.1	13.2	—	—
Utility	9.8	0.9	—	—	—	—	13.9	18.2	1.1	2.1	—	—
Cement	—	—	—	0.1	—	—	0.6	—	0.5	—	—	—
Manufacturing	0.7	0.4	—	1.2	—	0.8	1.4	—	3.9	—	—	0.8
Steel	2.0	4.4	—	2.1	—	—	8.4	—	1.2	2.3	—	2.4
Telecommunications	12.8	6.2	—	—	—	—	0.5	22.3	3.7	—	—	1.2
Electrical	—	—	—	1.2	—	—	9.0	—	0.8	0.7	—	—
Construction	0.7	1.2	—	1.1	—	6.6	2.7	6.8	15.3	0.6	—	1.8
Sovereign	38.3	0.6	35.0	—	96.4	—	1.6	—	4.5	16.6	93.6	31.0
Other	4.6	11.2	3.8	19.6	—	43.2	8.8	14.1	10.2	5.1	—	2.9

Sources: *Euromoney* data base; *Euroweek; Financial Times;* and *International Financing Review.*

Table A5. International Equity Issues by Developing Countries and Regions[1]
(In millions of U.S. dollars)

| | | | | | | 1994 | | | | 1995 |
	1990	1991	1992	1993	1994	1st qtr.	2nd qtr.	3rd qtr.	4th qtr.	1st qtr.
Developing countries	1,262	5,437	9,259	11,865	17,959	3,802	3,647	4,626	5,884	601
Africa	—	143	270	8	574	—	539	—	35	—
Ghana	—	—	—	—	398	—	398	—	—	—
Morocco	—	—	—	8	—	—	—	—	—	—
South Africa	—	143	270	—	176	—	141	—	35	—
Asia	1,040	1,022	4,732	5,673	12,039	2,097	1,855	3,273	4,814	587
Bangladesh	—	—	—	19	—	—	—	—	—	—
China	—	11	1,049	1,908	2,644	437	250	491	1,466	—
Hong Kong	—	140	1,250	1,264	318	—	133	145	40	147
India	—	—	240	331	3,028	1,185	424	696	723	138
Indonesia	633	168	262	604	1,329	95	15	201	1,018	—
Korea	40	200	150	328	1,168	150	208	210	600	150
Malaysia	—	—	382	—	—	—	—	—	—	—
Pakistan	—	11	48	5	1,183	20	—	918	245	—
Philippines	53	159	392	64	839	142	107	181	409	42
Singapore	214	125	272	613	300	35	—	190	75	—
Sri Lanka	—	—	—	—	33	33	—	—	—	—
Taiwan Province of China	—	—	543	72	438	—	220	218	—	110
Thailand	100	209	145	466	759	—	498	23	238	—
Europe	124	91	67	202	568	330	145	63	30	14
Czech Republic	—	—	—	—	10	—	—	—	10	—
Estonia	—	—	—	—	7	—	7	—	—	—
Hungary	68	91	33	17	201	—	138	63	—	—
Poland	—	—	—	1	—	—	—	—	—	14
Romania	—	—	—	—	1	—	—	—	1	—
Turkey	56	—	34	184	349	330	—	—	19	—
Middle East	—	60	127	257	89	32	8	—	49	—
Israel	—	60	127	257	89	32	8	—	49	—
Western Hemisphere	98	4,120	4,063	5,725	4,689	1,343	1,100	1,290	956	—
Argentina	—	356	372	2,793	735	194	380	—	161	—
Bolivia	—	—	—	10	—	—	—	—	—	—
Brazil	—	—	133	—	1,028	300	—	616	112	—
Chile	98	—	129	271	597	96	97	279	125	—
Colombia	—	—	—	91	393	—	86	68	239	—
Mexico	—	3,764	3,058	2,493	1,680	753	455	276	196	—
Panama	—	—	88	—	100	—	—	—	100	—
Peru	—	—	—	26	133	—	82	51	—	—
Uruguay	—	—	—	—	23	—	—	—	23	—
Venezuela	—	—	283	42	—	—	—	—	—	—
Memorandum items										
Total equity issues in international equity market	8,152	15,546	22,632	51,654	95,541	36,893	25,422	16,682	16,544	4,138
Share of developing countries in global issuance *(in percent)*	15.5	35.0	40.9	23.0	18.8	10.3	14.3	27.7	35.5	14.5
GDR/ADR *(in percent of developing countries' total equity issuance)*	7.8	74.4	52.9	54.6	77.6	83.9	68.3	85.5	73.2	11.8

Sources: IMF staff estimates based on *Euromoney* data base; *Euroweek; Financial Times*; and *International Financing Review (IFR)*.
[1]Data for 1994 are based on *Euromoney* data base and are not strictly comparable to data for 1992–93, which are estimated on the basis of data from *Euroweek, Financial Times,* and *IFR*.

Table A6. International Equity Issues by Country or Region, and Sector, 1990–94

	Argentina	China	Hong Kong	India	Indonesia	Korea	Mexico	Pakistan	Thailand
	(In millions of U.S. dollars)								
Financial sector	292	142	1,146	230	489	—	2,055	25	127
Banks	292	—	246	—	229	—	1,166	25	96
Other	—	142	900	230	260	—	889	—	31
Petroleum	2,711	185	—	—	44	90	—	—	211
Transport	—	703	145	400	—	414	246	6	47
Real estate	31	246	250	—	281	—	—	—	129
Utility	—	1,008	—	—	—	—	—	—	54
Cement	—	—	—	—	—	—	622	—	—
Manufacturing	56	539	—	150	36	—	—	—	4
Steel	—	541	251	76	—	300	215	—	86
Telecommunications	622	82	—	35	925	—	4,830	898	508
Electrical	208	63	712	362	169	890	—	145	23
Construction	—	20	—	—	—	95	1,165	143	52
Sovereign	—	—	—	—	—	—	—	—	—
Other	335	2,083	717	2,348	1,052	77	1,860	29	438
Total	4,255	5,612	3,221	3,601	2,996	1,866	10,993	1,246	1,679
	(In percent of total)								
Financial sector	6.9	2.5	35.6	6.4	16.3	—	18.7	2.0	7.6
Banks	6.9	—	7.6	—	7.6	—	10.6	2.0	5.7
Other	—	2.5	27.9	6.4	8.7	—	8.1	—	1.8
Petroleum	63.7	3.3	—	—	1.5	4.8	—	—	12.6
Transport	—	12.5	4.5	11.1	—	22.2	2.2	0.5	2.8
Real estate	0.7	4.4	7.8	—	9.4	—	—	—	7.7
Utility	—	18.0	—	—	—	—	—	—	3.2
Cement	—	—	—	—	—	—	5.7	—	—
Manufacturing	1.3	9.6	—	4.2	1.2	—	—	—	0.2
Steel	—	9.6	7.8	2.1	—	16.1	2.0	—	5.1
Telecommunications	14.6	1.5	—	1.0	30.9	—	43.9	72.1	30.3
Electrical	4.9	1.1	22.1	10.1	5.6	47.7	—	11.6	1.4
Construction	—	0.4	—	—	—	5.1	10.6	11.5	3.1
Sovereign	—	—	—	—	—	—	—	—	—
Other	7.9	37.1	22.3	65.2	35.1	4.1	16.9	2.3	26.1

Sources: *Euromoney* data base; *Euroweek; Financial Times;* and *International Financing Review.*

Table A7. Emerging Markets Mutual Funds[1]

	1988		1989		1990		1991		1992		1993		1994	
	Net assets	Number of funds	Net assets	Number of funds	Net assets	Number of funds	Net assets	Number of funds	Net assets	Number of funds	Net assets	Number of funds	Net assets	Number of funds
Equities	5,857	91	9,975	142	13,320	225	19,180	290	29,531	448	84,102	547	123,849	820
Global	900	15	1,350	18	2,300	29	3,750	39	5,040	35	18,033	52	34,977	118
Asia	4,437	72	7,435	112	9,240	174	11,575	211	18,823	344	55,472	418	71,889	554
Regional	1,750	35	3,100	50	4,000	75	5,350	92	10,673	193	38,509	228	51,113	308
China	47	2	50	2	60	3	110	4	783	19	2,360	30	2,731	30
Hong Kong	...	...	...	...	...	...	...	...	47	6	728	19	636	27
India	270	3	300	4	830	6	970	6	1,083	6	1,817	7	3,849	30
Indonesia	35	1	260	7	525	18	400	18	455	19	808	19	708	20
Korea	990	10	1,215	13	1,205	17	1,310	24	1,690	29	2,987	40	4,268	43
Malaysia and Singapore	75	3	240	7	505	17	600	17	824	28	1,559	27	1,238	27
Pakistan	—	—	—	—	—	—	65	2	31	2	220	3	377	6
Philippines	45	3	280	7	240	8	290	8	343	8	661	8	654	9
Taiwan Province of China	80	4	600	4	475	5	890	13	785	10	2,273	13	3,262	19
Thailand	845	11	1,390	18	1,400	25	1,580	26	2,109	24	3,458	22	2,761	22
Viet Nam	—	—	—	—	—	—	10	1	—	—	92	2	272	5
Latin America	520	4	985	9	1,455	16	3,525	33	4,862	55	9,741	65	14,706	105
Regional	—	—	175	2	380	5	1,510	18	2,169	36	5,951	48	10,571	75
Brazil	220	3	320	3	165	3	380	4	391	5	506	4	1,354	19
Chile	—	—	160	2	380	4	740	4	1,110	6	1,397	6	1,739	5
Mexico	300	1	330	2	530	4	780	5	1,192	8	1,887	7	1,042	6
Europe	—	—	205	3	325	6	330	7	806	14	757	10	1,430	32
Regional	—	—	90	2	210	4	240	5	541	8	433	6	917	21
Hungary	—	—	—	—	—	—	—	—	210	4	180	2	199	3
Russia	—	—	—	—	—	—	—	—	—	—	—	—	197	5
Turkey	—	—	115	1	115	2	90	2	55	2	144	2	117	3
Africa/Middle East	—	—	—	—	—	—	—	—	—	—	99	2	847	11
Bonds	275	...	500	...	900	...	1,700	...	3,750	...	5,954	47	8,149	88
Total funds	6,132	...	10,475	...	14,220	...	20,880	...	33,281	...	90,056	594	131,998	908

Sources: Emerging Market Funds Research, Inc; and Lipper Analytical Services, Inc.
[1]Data for 1992–94 are based on Lipper Analytical Services, Inc. and are not comparable with data for 1988–91, which were estimated by Emerging Market Fund Research, Inc. Net assets are shown in millions of U.S. dollars.

Table A8. Emerging Markets Open-End Mutual Funds

	December 1993		March 1994		June 1994		September 1994		December 1994	
	Number of funds	Net assets[1]	Number of funds	Net assets[1]	Number of funds	Net assets[1]	Number of funds	Net assets[1]	Number of funds	Net assets[1]
Overseas open-end funds	357	36,408	402	36,244	423	37,183	497	48,829	511	43,632
Equities	325	34,352	361	33,571	379	34,653	450	46,043	459	39,635
Global	20	3,161	28	4,238	32	4,232	43	7,211	47	7,097
Pacific Basin	80	8,791	87	8,314	87	8,845	91	9,567	94	8,892
Africa	—	—	—	—	—	—	—	—	—	—
Asia	195	20,619	211	18,254	219	19,000	257	25,666	251	20,671
Southeast Asia	95	14,680	103	12,508	104	12,807	116	15,092	120	14,060
China	10	413	12	263	12	247	13	296	15	257
Hong Kong	19	728	20	591	21	526	24	597	27	636
India	2	627	6	925	8	938	13	2,136	16	948
Indonesia	7	75	7	58	6	57	9	259	7	160
Korea	23	1,426	23	1,686	27	2,141	37	3,601	25	2,055
Malaysia/Singapore	9	262	10	218	10	227	9	247	9	214
Malaysia	7	349	7	277	7	223	8	386	7	283
Philippines	3	49	3	26	4	42	4	110	3	57
Singapore	4	62	4	44	4	55	5	135	4	70
Taiwan Province of China	8	1,367	8	1,332	8	1,390	10	2,050	10	1,469
Thailand	8	581	8	326	8	347	9	757	8	462
Europe	—	—	—	—	—	—	10	207	11	142
Latin America	30	1,781	35	2,765	41	2,576	49	3,392	56	2,833
Regional	26	1,592	31	2,597	31	2,033	40	2,600	39	2,103
Brazil	—	—	—	—	6	384	6	658	14	647
Mexico	4	189	4	168	4	159	3	134	3	83
Bonds	32	2,056	41	2,673	44	2,530	47	2,786	52	3,997
Global	5	266	6	415	7	366	8	397	13	399
Pacific Basin	2	14	2	14	2	14	2	14	2	13
Africa	—	—	1	9	1	9	1	7	1	7
Asia	2	12	3	69	4	89	4	96	3	101
Southeast Asia	1	1	2	59	3	79	3	88	2	93
Philippines	1	11	1	10	1	10	1	8	1	8
Latin America	23	1,764	29	2,166	30	2,052	32	2,272	32	3,365
Regional	12	650	13	1,062	11	1,039	13	1,280	13	2,477
Brazil	—	—	—	—	3	190	3	230	4	274
Mexico	11	1,114	16	1,104	16	823	16	762	15	614
U.S. open-end funds	47	14,137	78	20,604	95	22,235	114	28,124	137	46,582
Equities	43	13,655	70	19,997	83	21,284	102	26,841	122	45,363
Global	1	101	15	6,691	23	6,925	32	9,349	42	16,110
Pacific Basin	34	11,312	40	10,143	49	11,378	58	13,142	65	23,420
Latin America	8	2,242	15	3,163	11	2,981	12	4,350	15	5,833
Bonds	4	482	8	607	12	951	12	1,283	15	1,219

Source: Lipper Analytical Services, Inc.
[1] In millions of U.S. dollars.

Table A9. Emerging Markets Closed End Mutual Funds

	December 1993		March 1994		June 1994		September 1994		December 1994	
	Number of funds	Net assets[1]	Number of funds	Net assets[1]	Number of funds	Net assets[1]	Number of funds	Net assets[1]	Number of funds	Net assets[1]
Closed end funds	178	33,450	214	36,476	227	36,806	234	44,847	260	41,784
Equities	167	30,034	196	33,522	204	33,837	213	41,678	239	38,851
Global	19	8,710	23	10,516	24	10,288	26	12,810	29	11,770
Africa	—	—	5	387	7	413	7	592	7	611
Asia	109	14,750	125	15,360	126	16,008	129	19,410	144	18,906
Regional	19	3,726	27	4,124	27	4,115	26	5,079	29	4,761
China	20	1,947	21	1,665	22	1,651	23	2,643	23	2,474
India	5	1,190	8	2,477	11	2,836	12	3,101	14	2,901
Indonesia	12	733	13	641	13	588	13	619	14	548
Korea	17	1,561	17	1,595	17	1,865	17	2,145	18	2,213
Malaysia/Singapore	7	886	7	663	7	688	7	823	7	671
Pakistan	3	220	3	226	—	—	—	—	—	—
Philippines	5	612	6	509	6	535	6	602	6	597
Taiwan Province of China	5	906	7	1,308	7	1,415	7	1,621	9	1,793
Thailand	14	2,877	14	2,059	14	2,197	14	2,535	14	2,299
Viet Nam	2	92	2	93	2	118	4	242	5	272
Europe	10	757	13	1,055	12	998	16	1,255	21	1,288
Regional	6	433	9	795	10	743	8	814	10	775
Hungary	2	180	2	195	2	185	2	180	3	199
Russia	—	—	—	—	—	—	3	131	5	197
Turkey	2	144	2	65	2	70	3	130	3	117
Middle East	2	99	2	212	3	193	3	202	4	236
Latin America	27	5,718	28	5,992	32	5,937	32	7,409	34	6,040
Regional	14	2,117	16	2,458	19	2,470	20	3,142	21	2,635
Brazil	4	506	5	724	5	604	4	885	5	707
Chile	6	1,397	4	1,279	5	1,435	5	1,669	5	1,739
Mexico	3	1,698	3	1,531	3	1,428	3	1,713	3	959
Bonds	11	3,416	18	2,954	21	2,969	21	3,169	21	2,933
Global	7	2,806	9	2,325	11	2,321	11	2,502	11	2,319
Africa/Middle East	2	28	2	25	2	26	2	25	2	25
Europe	—	—	1	18	1	19	1	18	1	19
Latin America	2	582	6	586	7	603	7	624	7	570

Source: Lipper Analytical Services, Inc.
[1] In millions of U.S. dollars.

Table A10. Net Bond and Equity Purchases by Emerging Markets Mutual Funds[1]

(In millions of U.S. dollars)

	1990	1991	1992	1993	1994
Equities	6,464	2,511	8,448	17,559	58,150
Global	1,076	457	3,908	5,243	22,449
Asia	4,632	1,798	3,385	11,355	26,039
Regional	1,976	876	1,577	9,177	20,524
China	26	40	1,016	790	2,165
Hong Kong	—	—	271	290	168
India	412	2	−77	377	1,851
Indonesia	285	146	30	−74	66
Korea	407	352	342	791	544
Malaysia and Singapore	331	54	−64	−62	−11
Pakistan	—	25	34	82	190
Philippines	302	−69	3	−80	67
Taiwan Province of China	368	427	388	461	350
Thailand	525	−64	−150	−445	−73
Viet Nam	—	9	16	47	198
Latin America	652	36	678	1,362	7,587
Regional	185	267	446	1,625	6,574
Brazil	244	−60	108	−120	475
Chile	124	−13	7	−219	686
Mexico	99	−158	117	76	−148
Europe	103	199	393	−448	1,085
Regional	102	141	313	−336	803
Hungary	—	—	—	−125	104
Russia	—	—	—	—	183
Turkey	1	58	80	13	−5
Africa/Middle East	—	—	24	47	990
Bonds	400	323	827	248	5,482
Total funds	6,864	2,834	9,275	17,807	63,632

Sources: Emerging Markets Fund Research, Inc.; Lipper Analytical Services, Inc.; and IMF staff estimates.

[1]Estimated by deflating changes in the stock of fund net assets by International Finance Corporation (IFC) investable share price indices for equities and by the J.P. Morgan Eurobond price index for bonds. Data for 1993–94 are based on Lipper Analytical Services, Inc. and are not comparable with data for 1989–92, which are estimated on the basis of data provided by Emerging Market Funds Research, Inc.

Table A11. Bank Credit Commitments by Country or Region of Destination[1]
(In billions of U.S. dollars)

	1990	1991	1992	1993	1994
Developing countries and regions	24.6	28.5	18.5	21.2	24.4
Africa	0.6	0.2	0.6	0.2	0.1
Algeria	—	0.1	—	—	—
Angola	—	—	0.3	—	—
Ghana	0.1	0.1	0.1	—	0.1
Morocco	0.1	—	—	—	—
Tunisia	—	—	0.1	0.1	—
Zimbabwe	—	0.1	—	0.1	—
Other	0.4	—	0.1	—	—
Asia	13.4	14.6	11.9	15.7	20.4
China	1.5	2.3	2.7	3.6	4.0
Hong Kong	1.1	0.7	1.0	2.0	1.3
India	0.7	—	0.2	—	0.6
Indonesia	3.9	5.0	1.8	1.9	4.0
Korea	2.0	3.5	1.8	1.9	2.6
Malaysia	0.5	0.2	1.2	1.6	1.8
Pakistan	0.4	0.1	—	—	—
Philippines	0.7	—	—	—	—
Singapore	0.3	0.4	0.4	0.4	1.1
Taiwan Province of China	0.8	0.7	0.8	0.9	—
Thailand	1.3	1.6	2.0	3.4	4.7
Other	0.2	0.3	—	—	0.3
Europe	4.9	1.9	2.1	2.6	1.6
Czech Republic	—	—	—	0.2	0.2
Hungary	—	0.1	0.2	0.3	0.8
Turkey	1.8	1.6	1.8	1.9	0.2
Slovak Republic	—	—	—	0.1	0.1
U.S.S.R., former	3.0	—	—	—	—
Other	0.1	0.2	0.1	—	0.3
Middle East	1.7	10.7	3.0	0.4	1.3
Bahrain	1.6	0.4	0.1	0.1	0.5
Kuwait	—	5.5	—	—	—
Saudi Arabia	0.1	4.5	2.9	0.2	0.2
Other	0.1	0.3	—	0.1	0.6
Western Hemisphere	4.0	1.0	0.9	2.2	1.0
Argentina	—	—	—	0.4	0.6
Brazil	—	—	0.2	0.2	—
Chile	0.3	—	0.4	0.3	—
Colombia	—	0.2	—	0.1	0.3
Mexico	1.6	0.6	0.2	0.4	—
Uruguay	—	0.1	—	—	—
Venezuela	1.4	—	0.2	0.8	—
Offshore banking centers (The Bahamas and Cayman Islands)	—	—	—	0.1	—
Other	0.7	0.1	—	—	0.1
Memorandum items					
Total bank credit commitments	124.5	116.0	117.9	136.7	202.8
Share of bank credit commitments to developing countries in total *(in percent)*	19.8	24.6	15.7	15.5	12.0
Weighted average spread[2]	64	75	86	100	107
Weighted average maturity *(in years)*	9.5	7.6	6.7	5.5	6.8

Source: Organization for Economic Cooperation and Development, *Financial Statistics Monthly.*
[1]Excludes medium- and long-term loans that are insured by export credit agencies.
[2]Over LIBOR in basis points.

II

Evolution of the Mexican Peso Crisis

On December 20, 1994, the Mexican peso was devalued by about 15 percent. Two days later, market pressures led to the free float of the Mexican peso, and in the months that followed, the peso reached a level less than half of its predevaluation rate. With the benefit of hindsight, the Mexican peso crisis reflected several factors, including the size of its net capital inflows in the early 1990s, the emergence of internal and external macroeconomic imbalances, the concentration of its government debt at the short end of the maturity spectrum, the currency composition of its debt, and problems in the banking system.[11] The situation in Mexico did not stabilize until a package of multilateral and bilateral assistance was provided and until a credible program of adjustment was put in place. Before the Mexican crisis was resolved, however, financial market pressures had spilled over into several other countries, and the countries most affected were in the Western Hemisphere (namely, Argentina and Brazil).

Capital Inflows, 1990–93

In the period 1990–93, Mexico received $91 billion in net capital inflows, or roughly one fifth of all net inflows to developing countries. Annual net inflows to Mexico reached a peak of $30 billion in 1993, representing 20 percent of developing country inflows. In part as a result of these inflows, foreign exchange reserves increased rapidly in Mexico, from a level of $6.3 billion at the end of 1989, to $25.1 billion at the end of 1993. Foreign exchange reserves continued to increase in Mexico in early 1994.

A large portion of the net capital inflows to Mexico consisted of net portfolio investment. Over the 1990–93 period, net portfolio inflows amounted to $61 billion, reaching an annual peak of $28 billion in 1993. Net foreign direct investment totaled $16.6 billion over the period 1990–93.

The Mexican equity market received much of the net portfolio investment inflows. Over 1991–93, $22 billion of foreign investment flowed into the Mexican stock market, including nearly $11 billion in 1993. On the strength of these net portfolio inflows, the Mexican stock market boomed. The Bolsa index rose 436 percent in dollar terms over the period 1990–93. The most rapid rise occurred at the end of 1993 and the beginning of 1994, as markets reacted to the ratification of the NAFTA.

Buildup of Pressures in Mexico in 1994

Domestic and International Events

As described in Box I.1, a series of domestic and international events affected Mexican financial markets in 1994. The first such event was the unrest in the state of Chiapas in January. This was soon followed by a period of turbulence in international bond markets that came after the 25 basis point increase in the U.S. federal funds rate, to 3¼ percent, on February 4. This relatively small increase was widely, and apparently correctly, seen as the first in a series of interest rate increases in the United States, and in the industrial countries generally. The rise in interest rates reflected the improved economic conditions and prospects in the industrial countries, which had entered a period of expansion after years of low growth or recession. For the two-month period following the 25 basis point increase, world interest rates increased sharply.[12] During 1994, U.S. official interest rates were raised five times, and the Federal funds rate reached 5.5 percent by the end of November.

Other political events in Mexico also affected financial markets. On March 23, 1994, Luis Donaldo Colosio, the presidential candidate of the Partido Revolucionario Institucional (PRI), the ruling party, was assassinated. The political situation stabilized in Mexico during the summer, culminating in the victory of PRI candidate Ernesto Zedillo in the presidential election on August 21. Political difficulties surfaced again, however, on September 28 when PRI secretary general Jose Francisco Ruíz Massieu was assassinated. Shortly after the newly elected President Zedillo took office on December 1, 1994, violence occurred again in Chiapas on December 19, just before the devaluation of the peso.

---

[11]The Mexican crisis was also discussed in Annex I of International Monetary Fund (1995).

[12]For a detailed description of this turbulence and its implications for international capital markets see International Monetary Fund (1994a).

Box I.1. Chronology of Major Events in Mexican Crisis and Its Spillover Effects

1994

January 1. Chiapas rebels seize six towns.

February 4. Federal Reserve raises federal funds rate 25 basis points after having left the rate at 3.0 percent since September 1992.

March 22. Federal Reserve raises rates another 25 basis points.

March 23. Mexican presidential candidate Colosio assassinated.

April 18. Federal Reserve raises rates another 25 basis points.

April 26. Permanent swap arrangement of Mexico with Canada and the United States announced, replacing a temporary facility that had been announced on March 24.

May 17. Federal Reserve raises interest rates by 50 basis points.

August 16. Federal Reserve raises interest rates by 50 basis points.

August 21. Victory of PRI candidate Ernesto Zedillo in the election for president of Mexico.

September 28. Jose Francisco Ruíz Massieu, Secretary General of Mexico's ruling party, Partido Revolucionario Institucional, assassinated.

November 15. Federal Reserve raises interest rates by 75 basis points.

November 23. Mexican Deputy Attorney General Mario Ruíz Massieu resigns, alleging a cover-up of the murder of his brother.

November 30. Cabinet of Mexican President Zedillo is announced.

December 1. New Mexican government takes office.

December 19. Violence in Chiapas.

December 20. Mexico shifts intervention limit for peso by 15 percent.

December 21. Mexican authorities announce tightening of monetary and fiscal policies.

December 22. Mexico allows peso to float; Finance Minister Serra meets with U.S. investors in a stormy session at the Federal Reserve Bank of New York; Mexico announces a 60-day wage-and-price freeze; $7 billion in swap lines with Canada and the United States are activated.

December 27. Mexico announces that the authorities are formulating a new economic plan, which is to be announced in a presidential speech on January 2; weekly auction of Tesobonos fails and the peso hits its December low of 5.7.

December 28. Discussions reported between the Mexican authorities and both the IMF and the U.S. Treasury Department; unconfirmed press reports that the Federal Reserve intervened to support the peso; Mexico announces liberalization measures, including permitting faster expansion by foreign banks, and land reform measures in Chiapas.

December 29. Mexican President Zedillo announces a new finance minister, Guillermo Ortiz.

December 30. Chiapas rebels declare a temporary truce.

1995

January 7. Argentina relaxes reserve requirements.

January 9. Mexico announces scheme to recapitalize banks.

January 11. U.S. President Clinton vows to provide

In addition to these political and international events, macroeconomic fundamentals in Mexico could be interpreted as having contributed to financial market stress in Mexico during 1994. One factor that contributed to the internal imbalances was that the Bank of Mexico followed a policy of sterilized intervention in 1994 when the peso came under pressure, first in the April–March period and later in November and early December. This sterilized intervention had the effect of maintaining the stock of base money in the presence of a decline in the demand for pesos; in effect, the decline in foreign exchange reserves in Mexico were offset by an increase in the Bank of Mexico's net domestic assets. This policy maintained relatively low interest rates early in the year when industrial country interest rates increased, and later in the year in the presence of heavy selling pressures on the Mexican peso. In addition, domestic credit expanded rapidly in Mexico, and the current account deficit widened from 6.4 percent of GDP in 1993 to 8.0 percent

in 1994. The rise in Mexico's external deficit reflected a sharp rise of 20 percent in the value of imports, compared with a 14 percent rise in the value of exports. This rise in imports reflected, in part, a 35 percent appreciation of the real effective value of the Mexican peso in the four-year period ended February 1994. During the period from February through November 1994, the real effective value of the peso declined 9 percent, however. Counterbalancing the emergence of these apparent macroeconomic imbalances in 1994 were some positive developments, including a reduction in inflation and the maintenance of balanced government fiscal accounts.[13]

---

[13]For a more detailed discussion of the macroeconomic events in Mexico in 1994 see International Monetary Fund (1995), Annex I.

more financial support to Mexico if necessary; IMF team was reported to be commencing meetings with the Mexican authorities.

January 12. U.S. authorities propose a program to guarantee Mexico's debt.

Argentina eliminates a small differential between its buy and sell rates for pesos, unifying the rates at one peso per dollar; it also mandates that banks may maintain their required reserves in either currency, unifies the reserve ratios for the two currencies, and creates a fund of approximately $1 billion to assist troubled banks.

Rumors of a baht devaluation sweep Thai markets.

Hungary cancels a privatization deal and removes the privatization commissioner.

January 13. Thai authorities arrange temporary swap facility to defend the baht.

A temporary, automatic halt to trading in the Philippine peso is called on January 13 after a large depreciation that day.

Hong Kong Monetary Authority raises interbank rates more than 6 percentage points in response to pressure on Hong Kong dollar.

January 14. Indonesia leaves the foreign exchange window open on Saturday.

January 15. Direct talks between Mexican government and Zapatista rebels begin.

January 16. Indonesian authorities raise official discount rate 50 basis points.

January 17. Canada raises rates for third time in nine days.

January 26. Mexico signs a letter of intent on a $7.8 billion IMF stand-by arrangement.

January 31. U.S. authorities withdraw their loan guarantee proposal and in its place announce a direct loan package of $50 billion, including $20 billion from the United States, $18 billion from the IMF (including the previously agreed $7.8 billion), $10 billion from the Bank for International Settlements, and $3 billion from commercial banks.

February 15. Grupo Sidek, a Mexican conglomerate, announces that it will suspend payments on $19.5 million in U.S. dollar commercial paper owed by three of its affiliates.

February 21. Mexico and the United States sign loan agreement.

February 22. Mexican authorities tighten their prudential standards for banks by mandating that loan-loss reserves should cover at least 60 percent of past-due loans or 4 percent of total loans.

February 24. The Philippine peso again breaches its daily trading band, and the authorities respond by raising domestic overnight interest rates and tightening restrictions on short-term peso borrowing by foreign banks.

March 3. Mexico takes over holding company for BANPAIS.

March 6. Brazil shifts fluctuation bands for real and slates further adjustment for May.

March 10. Brazil shifts real bands again and institutes several measures aimed at increasing capital inflows and decreasing outflows.

March 9. Mexican economic program announced.

March 10. Mexican authorities announce a program to restructure bank loans to small and medium-sized companies.

Financial Market Developments in 1994

Flows and Reserve Changes

Equity Flows. Foreign investment in the Mexican stock market peaked in late 1993 and early 1994, with the passage of NAFTA (see Chart I.6). Equity inflows fell off sharply in March, reflecting pressures following the increase in interest rates in the United States in February and later in other industrial countries. Following the assassination of presidential candidate Colosio in March 1994, there was a net outflow of capital in April, the first such outflow since July 1992. Net foreign investment turned positive again in the period between the end of April and the end of the summer, but outflows resumed again in the fall, when there was a net outflow of $744 million in the three-month period of September through November.

Government Debt Restructuring. Mexican public finances also came under pressure in 1994. As a result of the events early in the year and the ensuing financial pressures, the Mexican government altered its financing strategy and shifted from standard, peso-denominated debt (principally Cetes) to debt indexed to the peso-dollar exchange rate (Chart I.6). The government began to make heavier use of Tesobonos, which are short-term debt securities paid in pesos but indexed to the U.S. dollar. In April 1994, the government reduced peso debt by MexN$17 billion, at the same time it increased Tesobono debt by MexN$22 billion. As a share of total Mexican debt, Tesobonos continued to increase in the period after April until the end of November, when they accounted for 50 percent of the value of all Mexican government securities outstanding; Tesobonos had accounted for 6 percent of Mexican government debt at the end of February 1994.

The attractiveness of Tesobonos relative to Cetes increased with the exchange market pressures that resulted from the Colosio assassination in March. These pressures led to a sharp increase in interest rates on Cetes (Chart I.7). As yields on Cetes

Chart I.6. Mexico: Stock Market Flows and Government Debt Outstanding

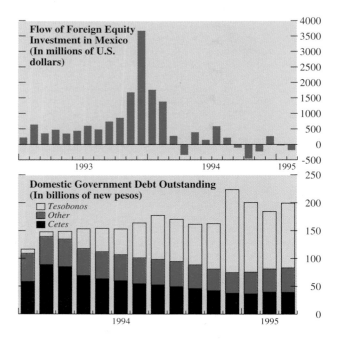

Sources: Banco de México; and Comisión Nacional de Valores.

Chart I.7. Mexico: Yields on Cetes and Tesobonos, December 31, 1993–March 31, 1995[1]

(In percent)

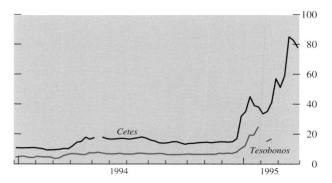

Source: Bloomberg Financial Markets.

[1]Weekly auction data for 91-day Cetes (Mexican government treasury bills) and 91-day Tesobonos. The break in the Cetes series reflects the fact that there was no auction during the week of May 11, 1994. The break in the Tesobonos series is due to cancellation of the January 31, 1995 auction by the Banco de México.

increased, the spread between yields on Cetes and Tesobonos increased from 437 basis points in mid-March to 735 basis points at the beginning of April and then to 870 basis points by the end of April. The spread between the yields on these two instruments reflects, in part, investor perceptions of exchange rate risk.[14]

Reserve Changes. In retrospect, foreign exchange reserves in Mexico clearly reflected these growing concerns in financial markets (Chart I.8). Reflecting successful macroeconomic adjustment in the early 1990s and sizable net capital inflows, foreign exchange reserves reached a peak of $29.3 billion in Mexico by the end of February 1994. Financial pressures on the Mexican peso following the Colosio assassination led to a decline in reserves of $3.4 billion in March and a further decline of $8.2 billion in April. With these financial market pressures subsiding temporarily beginning in May, the stock of foreign exchange reserves remained fairly stable until the end of October. In November, selling pressures on the Mexican peso increased again, and foreign exchange reserves in Mexico declined $4.8

billion. This reduced the stock of reserves to $12.9 billion by the end of November. The decline in reserves in November was not publicly announced until after the devaluation of the Mexican peso in December.

Evolution of Financial Prices

In the eleven months leading up to December 1994, Mexican interest rates, Mexican stock prices, and the peso-dollar exchange rate all experienced periods of turbulence. Up until the devaluation of the peso, the peso-dollar exchange rate was allowed to fluctuate in a band consisting of a fixed lower limit (on the peso appreciation) and an upper limit that increased by MexN$0.0004 a day. At the beginning of 1994, the peso-dollar exchange rate fluctuated within a narrow trading range until February 22, when it began a 4 percent decline over the next two months. At the end of this two-month period, the peso had reached the lower end of the intervention band.

Short-term peso interest rates increased significantly after the Colosio assassination; interest rates on 91-day Cetes rose from 10.1 percent on March 23 to 17.8 percent one month later. In the period from April to December, the peso-dollar rate mostly remained near the upper intervention limit, appreciating away from the intervention limit only twice, at the end of April and again in August. Likewise, short-term interest rates remained fairly steady until July, with rates on Cetes fluctuating between 16 and 18 percent. In early August, as the peso strengthened

---

[14]See the background paper "Mexican Foreign Exchange Market Crises from the Perspective of the Speculative Attack Literature," pp. 70–79.

temporarily, interest rates declined, and from then until the end of November rates fluctuated in the range of 13 to 15 percent.

The Mexican stock and bond markets also showed signs of pressure. Spreads on Mexico's Brady bonds over comparable U.S. Treasury bills began to widen in January as violence flared up in Chiapas. Between the beginning of the year and the week of the Colosio assassination in March, spreads on Mexican (par) Brady bonds increased about 140 basis points. After the Colosio assassination, spreads increased an additional 220 basis points, and reached a peak of 528 basis points on April 21. From May through November, Brady spreads fluctuated in the 300–460 basis points range, well above their levels before the Colosio assassination.

Prices on the Mexican stock market increased in January 1994, reflecting in part the perception that the NAFTA agreement would improve corporate performance in Mexico (Chart I.9). Stock prices began to decline, however, with the increase in interest rates in February. The Bolsa reached a 1990's high on February 8, but by April 20, the Bolsa had declined 37 percent in dollar terms. The stock market recovered in May and was especially strong in August, but then began a gradual decline in September.

The Crisis in Mexico

As is typical of crises, the financial situation in Mexico unfolded rapidly. As a result of the financial pressures in the first two weeks of December 1994, the peso was devalued on December 20. Reflecting continuous pressure during the next two days, and a steep decline in reserves, the peso was allowed to float on December 22, after which Mexican financial markets experienced heavy selling pressures. These pressures were exacerbated by two factors. First, the value of Mexico's dollar-linked Tesobono debt increased sharply as the peso depreciated. Second, the depreciation of the peso and the associated rapid rise in domestic interest rates increased the amount of nonperforming loans in the Mexican banking system, in part because most loans in Mexico have floating interest rates that quickly reflect market rates. The immediate crisis was resolved during the early part of 1995: on January 31 the United States announced a lending program; on February 1 the IMF approved the largest stand-by arrangement in its history; and throughout the first quarter the Mexican government announced policy measures. The financial market pressures in Mexico spilled over into a number of other markets, including those of Argentina and Brazil, and led to a general re-evaluation and rebalancing of international portfolios by institutional investors, which affected countries in Asia as well.

Chart I.8. Mexico: International Reserves, 1994[1]
(In billions of U.S. dollars)

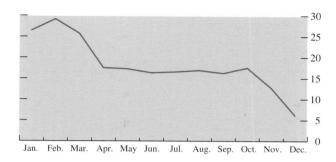

Source: International Monetary Fund, *International Financial Statistics.*
[1]Total reserves minus gold.

Financial Market Developments During Devaluation and Floating of the Peso

After a gradual decline in the Mexican stock market in the fall of 1994, downward pressures on prices intensified in early December. In dollar terms, the Mexican Bolsa declined 9 percent from December 1 to December 16 (Chart I.9). Violence erupted in Chiapas on Monday, December 19. In the early morning of December 20, the Mexican authorities announced that the intervention limit for the peso would be widened by 15 percent (from MexN\$3.4712 to MexN\$4.0016 per dollar), which allowed further room for the currency to depreciate. It was the stated objective of the authorities to maintain the value of the peso within the band and to continue to allow the band to change by MexN\$0.0004 a day.

Financial Market Reaction to Devaluation

The evolution of the peso in December and subsequent months is shown in Chart I.9. The widening of the intervention band resulted in an immediate 12 percent depreciation of the peso, from 3.47 pesos to the dollar (the close on December 19) to 3.88 (the opening) on December 20. During the course of the trading day on December 20, the peso depreciated an additional 3 percent and reached a low at the close of the market just below the new intervention limit. On December 21, the peso remained in a narrow range, opening at 3.9870 and then closing at 3.9965, near that day's intervention limit of 4.0020. During this two-day period, December 20 and 21, however, foreign exchange reserves in Mexico declined by \$4 billion.

Short-term interest rates rose in reaction to the devaluation. In the secondary market for Mexican government securities, the rate on 28-day Cetes repurchase agreements increased from 14.7 percent on December 19 to 17 percent on December 21. At the

Chart I.9. Mexico: Exchange Rate and Stock Market Index

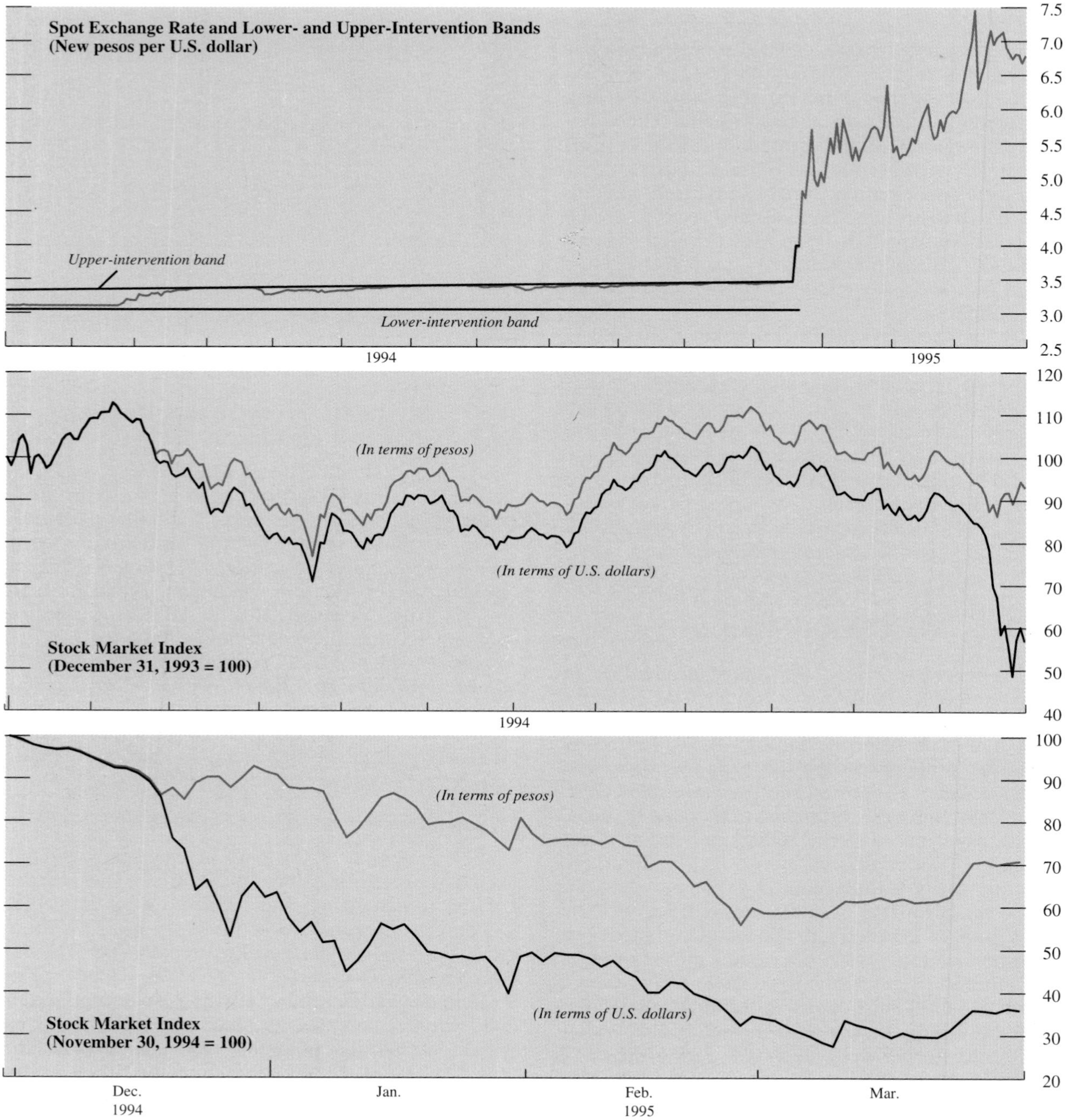

Sources: Bloomberg Financial Markets; and International Monetary Fund.

Cetes auctions on December 21, the average interest rates on Cetes increased from 14.8 percent in the previous week's auction to 16.2 percent. This rise was sufficient for the auctions to be reasonably successful; almost all of the Cetes that were offered were sold

(Table I.2). At the December 20 Tesobono auction, average interest rates increased by 38 basis points above the previous week's auction rates.

The dollar value of Mexican equity securities declined sharply after the devaluation. Although the

Table I.2. Mexico: Cetes and Tesobonos Auctions

	Yield[1]	Amount Sold	Amount Offered	Amount Bid	Bid-Cover Ratio
Cetes	*(In percent)*		*(In millions of new pesos)*		*(In percent)*
Dec. 7, 1994	14.25	1,100	1,100	4,314	392.18
Dec. 14, 1994	14.80	897	1,100	1,371	124.64
Dec. 21, 1994	16.22	1,066	1,100	1,773	161.18
Dec. 28, 1994	31.41	586	1,100	645	58.64
Jan. 4, 1995	32.46	1,403	1,500	1,921	128.07
Jan. 11, 1995	40.91	1,425	2,800	2,332	83.29
Jan. 18, 1995	38.80	3,306	2,800	6,252	223.29
Jan. 25, 1995	36.33	2,800	2,800	10,610	378.93
Feb. 1, 1995	31.74	4,000	4,000	10,540	263.50
Feb. 8, 1995	33.70	3,805	4,200	7,942	189.10
Feb. 15, 1995	38.58	2,967	3,400	3,698	108.76
Feb. 22, 1995	53.00	2,865	3,400	3,747	110.21
Mar. 1, 1995	48.98	3,200	3,200	8,180	255.63
Mar. 8, 1995	57.13	1,867	3,200	2,628	82.13
Mar. 15, 1995	83.13	1,400	1,400	3,220	230.00
Tesobonos			*(In millions of U.S. dollars)*		
Dec. 6, 1994	8.39	420	420	1,071	255.00
Dec. 13, 1994	8.23	375	375	865	230.67
Dec. 20, 1994	8.61	416	600	868	144.67
Dec. 27, 1994	10.23	28	600	28	4.67
Jan. 3, 1995	12.31	52	500	72	14.40
Jan. 10, 1995	19.63	63	400	129	32.25
Jan. 17, 1995	19.75	400	300	941	313.67
Jan. 24, 1995	21.40	50	50	147	294.00
Jan. 31, 1995	24.98	155	150	164	109.33
Feb. 7, 1995	21.01	240	270	439	162.59
Feb. 14, 1995[2]	17.81	210	210	427	203.33

Source: Bloomberg Financial Markets.

[1]Yield averaged across maturities auctioned, weighted by amounts sold of each maturity.

[2]Most recent auction held.

Mexican Bolsa rose 2 percent in peso terms on December 20 and then fell by 3 percent the next day, the dollar value of the index fell a total of 14 percent. Meanwhile, spreads on Mexican Brady bonds over interest rates on similar U.S. Treasury securities increased 143 basis points.

Impact of Decision to Float on December 22 on Financial Markets

Before markets opened on December 22, an announcement was made that the Mexican peso would be allowed to float against the dollar. Also announced were the activation of a $7 billion swap line with Canada and the United States, and agreements between business and labor leaders in Mexico to restrain wage and price increases. Selling pressures on Mexican assets generally followed these announcements. By the close of the foreign exchange market in Mexico on December 22, the peso had declined by an additional 20 percent to MexN$4.80 to the dollar. Prices of shares on the Mexican stock market increased 5 percent in peso terms, but fell 13 percent in dollar terms. Meanwhile, spreads on

Mexican Brady bonds increased an additional 103 basis points from the previous day. Reflecting these additional selling pressures and a loss of confidence, money market conditions in Mexico tightened significantly as interest rates on 28-day Cetes repurchase agreements rose from 17 percent on December 21 to 24.5 percent on December 22.

Financial Developments During Week Following Float

In the days following the floating of the peso, selling pressure on Mexican assets continued. Following the Christmas weekend, the peso declined to a 1994 low of MexN$5.7 per dollar on Tuesday, December 27. Partly accounting for this decline was the weak demand for Tesobonos at the auction held on that day. At auction, bids were received for $28 million of the $600 million in Tesobonos offered for sale, a bid-cover ratio of only 5 percent. During this same period, the dollar value of Mexican stocks declined nearly one-for-one with the value of the peso. Overall, the dollar value of the Bolsa fell 17 percent between December 22 and December 27. Mexican Brady bonds spreads reached 936 basis points on December 27, an increase of 286 basis points from December 22 and 527 basis points from December 19.

After reaching this low, markets recovered before the end of the week (and year), with the peso recovering 11 percent of its value and the Bolsa 17 percent of its dollar value. Brady bond spreads declined 143 basis points before the end of the week. Policy measures contributed to this upswing. International support for a solution to the Mexican crisis began to crystalize on Wednesday, December 28, as discussions were widely reported to be taking place between the Mexican authorities and both the International Monetary Fund and the U.S. Treasury Department. That same day, the Mexican government announced liberalization measures. One of these permitted faster expansion by foreign banks, a measure that was designed to add capital to a banking system depleted by the depreciating currency, as well as to maintain an increase in capital inflows. The government also announced land reform measures in Chiapas, after which rebels in Chiapas declared a temporary truce.

Money market conditions remained tight in Mexico in the week following the decision to allow the peso to float. Interest rates on 28-day Cetes repurchase agreements increased from 21 percent on December 26 to 25 percent on December 30, indicating that conditions tightened in response to the selling pressures that peaked on December 27. Interest rates at the Cetes auctions on Tuesday, December 28, nearly doubled and reached an average of 31.4 percent, up from 16.2 on the previous Tuesday (see Table I.2). The bids received at the December 28 Cetes auctions amounted to slightly more than half of the Cetes offered for sale.

Evidence on Capital Outflows

Data on portfolio capital outflows during December 1994 is quite scant. According to stock market investment data, there was a small net inflow of $282 million of net foreign investment into the stock market.[15] Foreign holdings of Cetes declined by MexN$5.5 billion over the month, but foreign holdings of Tesobonos increased by about MexN$3.1 billion. On balance, there was a net outflow in the form of foreign holdings of Mexican domestic government securities (including Cetes, Tesobonos, and others) of about MexN$3.6 billion ($790 million). Despite net sales of foreign holdings of equity and government securities of about $510 million, the Banco de México sold $6.6 billion in foreign reserves during December.

---

[15]Data provided by the Comision Nacional de Valores. Data on foreign holdings of government securities are from the Banco de México.

Evidence on sales by foreign institutional investors is limited.[16] Net outflows of U.S. based mutual funds occurred in some categories, as did net inflows in other categories, with no specific information on the holdings of Mexican assets by these institutional funds. Before the crisis, U.S. mutual funds held Mexican bonds amounting to $1.5 billion, including sovereign bonds issued in international capital markets. Tesobonos held by U.S. mutual funds at that time are estimated to have been around $700 million, compared with $16 billion held by nonresidents in mid-December 1994. It appears unlikely, therefore, that U.S. mutual funds were a major source of selling pressure on Mexican fixed income markets.

Tesobono Problem

Operation of Tesobono Market

Until recently, Tesobonos were bought in a primary market operated by the Banco de México. Bids were submitted in dollars at 9:30 a.m. on Tuesday. At 11:00 a.m. the foreign exchange "fix" determined the peso value of these bids. This fix was also used to determine the peso value of maturing Tesobonos, which were settled on Thursday in pesos. The fix is an average market exchange rate that the central bank calculates daily, dropping the high and low observations from the prices quoted by the six largest market participants. For a fee (normally about 10–15 basis points), banks sell insurance that guarantees that customers will receive pesos indexed to the fix rate, for delivery two days later for the purchase of Tesobonos or the conversion of the proceeds of maturing Tesobonos into dollars. For this two-day settlement period, investors incur some exchange rate risk. Tesobonos were last sold in the primary market on February 14, 1995. In March, the government moved to permit the direct settlement of Tesobonos at maturity in dollars, at the option of investors.

Effects of Peso Depreciation on Tesobono Liabilities

Mexico's reliance on Tesobonos had increased during 1994, and by the end of November about 50 percent, or $24 billion, of domestic government debt was held in this form. By the end of December, Tesobonos comprised 66 percent of total domestic government debt, as the value of Tesobonos outstanding rose from MexN$82 billion at the end of November to MexN$149 billion at the end of December. As the crisis continued, market participants became increasingly concerned about the amount of Tesobonos that would mature in the first few months of 1995, and this created further pressure on financial markets in Mexico. A total of $3.3 billion in

---

[16]For details see Table II.10.

Table I.3. Mexico: Calendar of Total Maturing Cetes and Tesobonos, 1995

Month Maturing	Cetes	Cetes	Tesobonos	Cetes plus Tesobonos
	(In millions of new pesos)	(In millions of U.S. dollars)[1]	(In millions of U.S. dollars)	
January	5,142.37	1,142.75	3,290.37	4,433.12
February	3,186.67	708.15	3,495.68	4,203.83
March	5,238.47	1,164.10	3,087.88	4,251.99
April	2,272.61	505.02	1,852.23	2,357.25
May	1,264.35	280.97	2,634.96	2,915.93
June	3,498.64	777.48	1,942.07	2,719.54
July	682.99	151.78	3,631.16	3,782.94
August	1,824.43	405.43	4,143.18	4,548.61
September	2,184.56	485.46	651.35	1,136.81
October	1,481.35	329.19	865.31	1,194.50
November	1,560.80	346.84	2,206.55	2,553.40
December	1,201.94	267.10	855.97	1,123.07
By quarter				
January–March	13,567.51	3,015.00	9,873.94	12,888.94
April–June	7,035.60	1,563.47	6,429.26	7,992.72
July–September	4,691.98	1,042.66	8,425.70	9,468.36
October–December	4,244.09	943.13	3,927.83	4,870.97

Source: Banco de México.
[1]Converted by the Banco de México at MexN$4.5 to the dollar.

Tesobonos were expected to mature in January 1995, and a total of $9.9 billion were expected to mature in the first quarter; however, foreign exchange reserves in Mexico amounted to $6.3 billion at the end of December 1994 (Table I.3). At this time, market commentaries increasingly focused on the possibility that Tesobonos would be restructured, and there were rumors that discussions were under way in Mexico with investment bankers on how the Tesobonos could be refinanced.

Changes in Foreign and Domestic Holdings of Tesobonos After Devaluation

Available evidence indicates that investors retained their holdings of Tesobonos immediately following the devaluation. Foreign holdings of Tesobonos remained relatively constant (in dollar terms) in the weeks before the devaluation and then increased somewhat in the week following the devaluation, before falling off again (Chart I.10). Foreign holdings of Tesobonos amounted to $16.1 billion on December 19, the day before the devaluation, and peaked at $17.0 billion on December 27. Meanwhile, there appears to have been a portfolio shift out of Cetes after the devaluation, mirroring the rise in foreign holdings of Tesobonos. Holdings of Tesobonos by Mexican banks and nonbank residents also increased in the wake of the devaluation. Holdings by nonbank residents rose from $3.9 billion just before the devaluation to a peak of $5.1 billion on December 23.

Concerns about Tesobono liabilities intensified after December 27, and as a result, holdings of Tesobonos by foreigners and domestic nonbank residents decreased. Some of this slack was taken up by Mexican banks and the remaining slack was taken up by a reduction in the total outstanding. The falloff in holdings of Tesobonos by nonbank residents was particularly marked, as these holdings declined from $5.1 billion on December 23 to $2.4 billion at the end of January. Foreign holdings were more stable, falling by $0.9 billion at the end of January from a peak of $17.0 billion.

Auction Performance After Peso Float

Although the Tesobono auction on December 20 immediately following the devaluation was relatively successful, subsequent auctions were not (see Table I.2). For three successive weekly auctions between December 27, 1994 and January 10, 1995, the quantity of bids fell far short of the amount of Tesobonos offered at auctions for all maturities. Bid-cover ratios for all maturities ranged between 5 percent and 32 percent during these auctions. There was somewhat higher demand for Cetes, although bids at many of the Cetes auctions also fell short of the amount offered for sale.[17] In the weeks following mid-January,

---

[17]Auction results are difficult to interpret. The Banco de México can adjust the amount sold after receiving bids. This fact may lead to strategic behavior by bidders and make bid-cover ratios difficult to interpret. Winners' curse considerations might also complicate interpretation; see International Monetary Fund (1994a), p. 44.

61

Chart I.10. Mexico: Government Securities Holdings by Sector, December 2, 1994–January 27, 1995

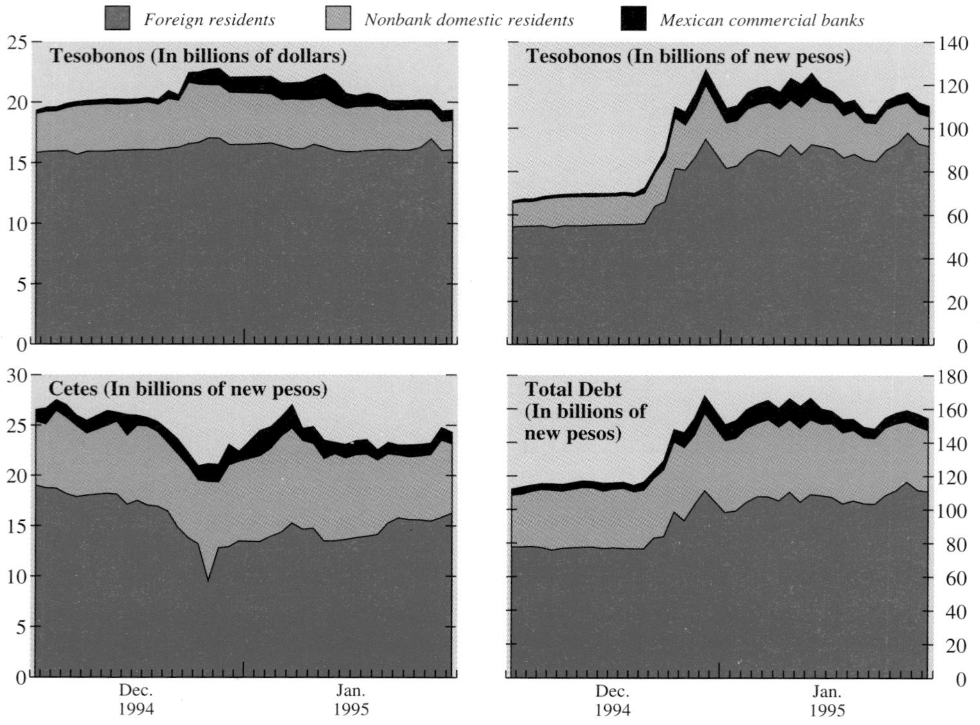

■ *Foreign residents*   ■ *Nonbank domestic residents*   ■ *Mexican commercial banks*

Source: Banco de México.

demand at auctions increased, although yields continued to rise for both Cetes and Tesobonos. After February 14, the authorities discontinued Tesobono auctions.

Financial Fragility in Banking System

Before the devaluation in late December, the Mexican banking system had already experienced a sharp increase in nonperforming loans: the ratio of past-due loans to total loans increased from 4.6 percent at the end of 1991 to 8.5 percent in March 1994.[18] The depreciation of the peso had an immediate, though modest, impact on the health of Mexican banks. Banks experienced losses on their securities portfolios in the wake of the devaluation, particularly in their fixed income portfolios. Losses from equity holdings may have been considerably smaller. After a 39 percent decline in peso terms

from the end of December 1994 to February 27, 1995, the Mexican stock market has recovered half of its losses.

The peso devaluation and the subsequent tightening of financial market conditions created asset quality problems in the peso-denominated and foreign currency loan books of Mexican banks. Foreign currency loans represented about a third of total loans made by Mexican banks as of December 1994, but many of these loans were extended to firms without sources of foreign currency income.[19] As the peso depreciated, borrowers encountered debt-servicing problems as the value of their liabilities increased in peso terms. The sharp rise in interest rates also affected the peso-loan portfolio. Most, if not all bank credits in Mexico have variable interest rates tied to the one-month Cetes rate or to interbank interest rates. When interest rates reached levels as high as 80 percent in the first quarter of 1995, payments ceased on a large proportion of loans of all types. Banks generally chose to restructure these

---

[18]For further details on both recent developments in the Mexican banking system and on the restructuring plans see the background paper "Financial Sector Constraints on Crisis Management," pp. 121–27.

[19]Moody's Investors Service.

loans, or simply to suspend interest payments, rather than be forced to recognize them as high-risk assets and write off a certain amount of their already declining capital by making provisions. Nevertheless, the deterioration in asset quality forced the risk-weighted capital ratios of several Mexican banks below the 8 percent minimum.

Banks in January 1995 faced severe dollar liquidity problems. Many had borrowed in dollars, using Tesobonos as collateral. These Tesobonos proved illiquid as concerns over the government's Tesobono liabilities grew. In response, the Banco de Mexico operated a dollar liquidity facility in January for banks needing to refinance maturing dollar liabilities.

On January 9, the authorities announced a scheme to recapitalize banks with capital ratios below the 8 percent minimum. As of the end of March 1995, six banks had obtained assistance totaling MexN$6.49 billion (equal to 14.5 percent of the net worth of all Mexican commercial banks at the end of 1994) from the deposit-guarantee fund (FOBAPROA) under the temporary capitalization program (PROCAPTE). On February 22, the National Banking Commission (CNB) changed prudential requirements for banks. It imposed on banks the requirement to maintain a minimum level of loan-loss reserves equal to the greater of 60 percent of their nonperforming loan portfolio or 4 percent of their total loan portfolio in an attempt to ensure that banks would have sufficient reserves to withstand a decline in asset quality. Finally, in March 1995 three additional facilities were introduced for restructuring loans, with additional funding totaling MexN$148 billion: one for small and medium-sized companies, another for mortgages, and another for dollar-denominated loans.

Continuation and Resolution of Crisis in First Quarter of 1995

Domestic and International Measures to Resolve Crisis

The first international effort to assist Mexico came early in January 1995. On January 2, it was announced that an $18 billion international credit package had been agreed, including $9 billion from the United States, $1 billion from Canada, $5 billion from the Bank for International Settlements (BIS), and $3 billion from U.S. banks. The next day, following intensive discussions with business and labor representatives, the Mexican authorities announced a stabilization plan, including commitments on the part of business and labor to restrain wage and price increases. The government also announced a privatization program, and opened the Mexican banking system to greater foreign investment by permitting 100 percent foreign ownership of Mexican banks.

After markets continued to deteriorate, and pressures spread to other emerging markets, the international loan package was replaced by a larger program. On January 12, a program guaranteeing Mexico's debt was proposed, but later in the month opposition to this proposal increased in the U.S. Congress.

The proposal was subsequently withdrawn on January 31 and a direct loan package of $50 billion was announced in its place. This involved $20 billion from the United States, $18 billion from the IMF, $10 billion from the BIS, and $3 billion from commercial banks. The $18 billion from the Fund included $7.8 billion on which Mexico had already signed a letter of intent on January 26, and an additional $10 billion in non-BIS central bank financing that was to be arranged. The IMF Executive Board approved the new credit on February 1. Negotiations between the United States and Mexico on the $20 billion credit, however, did not commence until February 16, and they were concluded five days later. The other parts of the loan proposals, from the BIS and from commercial banks, were never finalized.

The final stage in the resolution of the crisis occurred on March 9, when the Mexican government announced a new economic plan. The plan included substantial increases in government revenues, government spending cuts, and curbs on wage increases. In response to the plan, the United States authorized Mexico to draw the first $3 billion of the agreed loan.

Financial Market Developments in Mexico

Mexican financial markets continued to experience turbulence throughout January and February, until the announcement of the economic plan and the release of U.S. funds on March 9. From December 30, 1994 until March 9, 1995 the peso declined 32 percent against the dollar, reaching a low of MexN$7.45 to a dollar, which was 53 percent below its predevaluation level (see Chart I.9). Between March 9 and the end of April, the peso appreciated 20 percent and stood at MexN$5.925 per dollar at the end of April.

Throughout January and February, money market conditions continued to tighten, reflecting exchange market pressures. In the secondary market for Mexican government debt, the interest rate on 28-day Cetes repurchase agreements rose from 25 percent on December 30, 1994 to 47 percent on January 10, 1995. They subsequently declined after the announcement of the U.S. loan guarantee package. Interest rates remained between 30 percent and 40 percent until February 20, when they began to rise sharply, reaching a high of 80 percent on March 16. Since then (through April 26), rates have remained above 70 percent. Interest rates determined in Cetes auctions evolved in a similar manner (see Table I.2). Bid-cover ratios remained above 100 percent in most auctions, with the exception of the January 11 and March 8 auctions and several other scattered auctions (not shown in the aggregate numbers in the table).

Prices on the Mexican stock market also continued to decline throughout January and February (see Chart I.9). The Bolsa declined before the announcements of the support packages on January 12 and 31, rebounded when the programs were announced, and then declined steadily in February. In peso terms, the Bolsa reached its trough on February 27, when it was 39 percent below its end-1994 level. Since reaching this trough, the market has risen 35 percent. The flow of foreign investment in the stock market turned negative in January and February; the total outflow for these two months was $188 million (see Chart I.6).

Mexican Brady bonds also experienced sharp losses in the first quarter. Spreads on these instruments increased to a peak of nearly 21 percentage points (i.e., 2,094 basis points) on March 20, up from 409 basis points immediately before the devaluation. Since late March, spreads have recovered and recently (April 21) moved below 1,000 basis points again.

Spillovers to Other Markets

Direct, Short-Term Effects of Devaluation

The initial effects of the peso devaluation and subsequent floating of the peso were confined to a few markets. Among developing country stock markets, prices on the exchanges in Argentina and Brazil declined substantially, but other countries were relatively unaffected (see Charts I.11 and I.12). The Argentine market fell 14 percent in dollar terms from December 19 to December 27, and the Brazilian market fell 17 percent over the same period. Other emerging financial markets in the Western Hemisphere were less affected; the Chilean market gained 1 percent in dollar terms while the Colombian market rose 8 percent. Stock markets in Asian emerging markets increased after the devaluation; the largest increase occurred in the Malaysian market, which gained 3 percent in dollar terms between December 19 and December 27. During this period, stock markets in industrial countries generally gained ground, with the U.S. stock market (Standard and Poor's 500) gaining 1 percent, the Japanese market gaining 2 percent (in yen terms), and the German market rising 1 percent (in deutsche mark terms).

Brady bond markets also declined and spreads generally widened (Chart I.13). The spread on Argentine Brady bonds increased 389 basis points, and the spread on Brazilian Brady bonds rose 207 basis points. Although the stock market in the Philippines increased after the peso devaluation, Philippine Brady bond spreads increased 149 basis points. To some extent, Mexico had provided a baseline for emerging markets, especially for the pricing of fixed

income securities.[20] Correlations among Brady bond yields generally increased up to May 1994, then declined, but increased significantly after the crisis (Table I.4).

Effects on Other Western Hemisphere Markets

Argentina

Argentina was the first country to experience financial market pressures, probably because it had some of the macroeconomic features that characterized Mexico, including a fixed exchange regime, a low domestic savings rate, a weak banking system, and a significant current account deficit.[21] On December 28, the week after the Mexican peso was floated, Argentina sold $353 million of reserves, the largest amount since the start of the convertibility plan in 1991, and sold more than one third of its foreign exchange reserves during the next three months. Both the movement out of Argentine peso assets into dollar assets and the movement out of the domestic banking system increased funding costs for Argentine banks, as interbank interest rates rose from 9.5 percent on December 19 to 23 percent a week later.[22] A wholesale bank was closed during the week, and the financial condition of other banks was reported to have worsened. On December 28, reserve requirements on foreign currency deposits were reduced, and on January 12, reserve requirements on local currency deposits were lowered to the level on foreign currency deposits. Banks were allowed to maintain their required reserves in either currency, and the small differential between buying and selling rates for pesos was eliminated, thus reducing banks' transactions costs. At the same time, the authorities moved to strengthen fiscal policy by decreeing an Arg$1 billion cut in expenditure (0.3 percent of GDP) from the 1995 budget, vetoing all additional expenditures approved by Congress, and announced a delay in lowering employer social security contributions in 1995.

Following these measures and the announcement of the initial loan guarantee program for Mexico, pressures in financial markets in Argentina subsided for the next month and a half. In the second half of February, however, the interbank peso interest rate increased from 12 percent on February 17 to 17 percent a week later and then to 65 percent the following week (March 3). Between February 17 and March 9, prices on the Argentine stock market fell 25 percent. Responding to these pressures, the authorities took strong action to reinforce public finances (equal to

---

[20]See International Monetary Fund (1994a).
[21]Under the "convertibility plan," Argentina maintains a currency board arrangement, whereby the monetary base is backed one-for-one by central bank dollar reserves.
[22]During that period, total deposits in the banking system fell by $313 million.

Chart I.11. Stock Market Performance and Nominal Exchanges Rates in Selected Latin American Countries

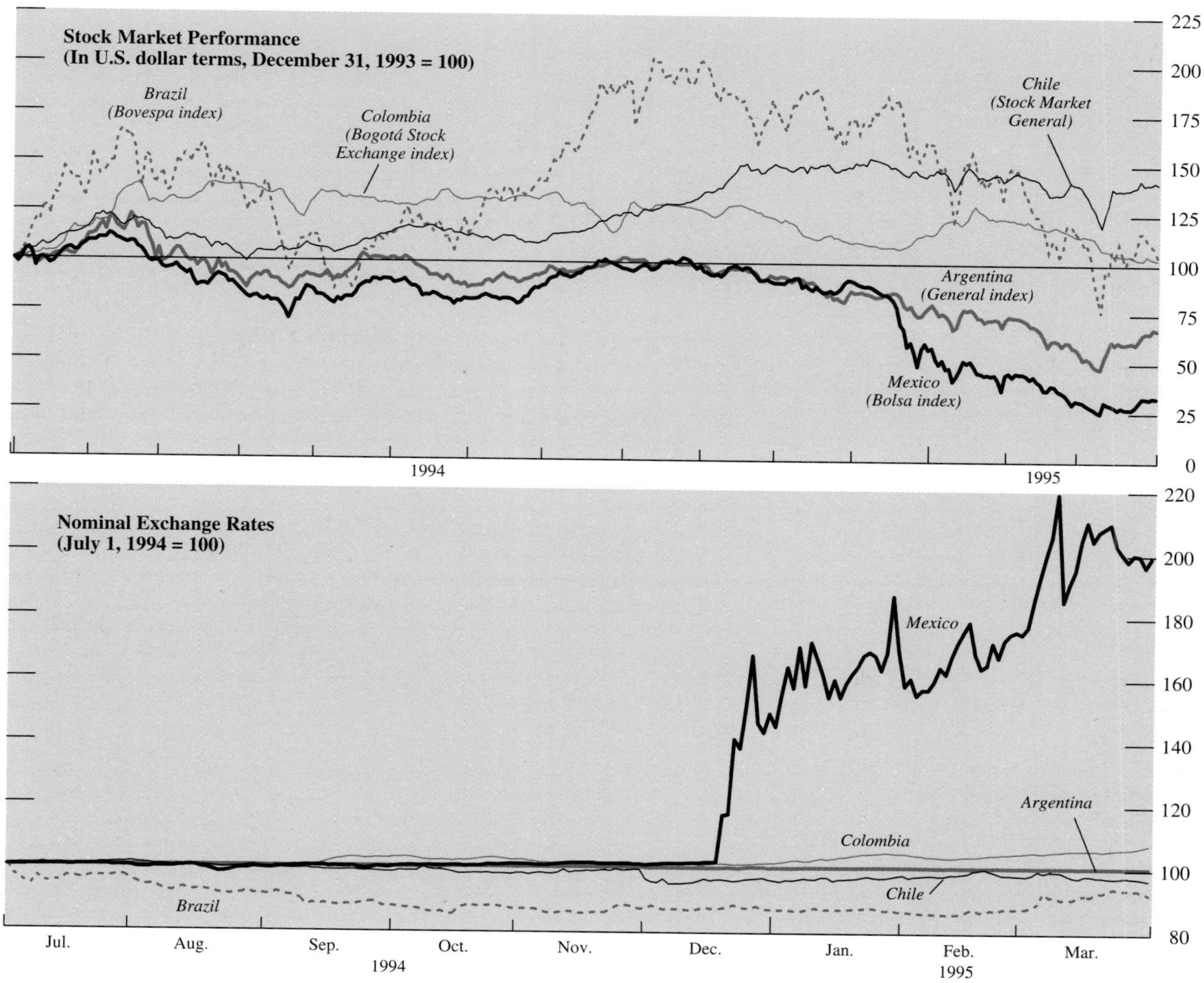
Stock Market Performance
(In U.S. dollar terms, December 31, 1993 = 100)
Brazil
(Bovespa index)
Colombia
(Bogotá Stock
Exchange index)
Chile
(Stock Market
General)
Argentina
(General index)
Mexico
(Bolsa index)
225
200
175
150
125
100
75
50
25
0
1994
1995
Nominal Exchange Rates
(July 1, 1994 = 100)
Mexico
Argentina
Colombia
Chile
Brazil
220
200
180
160
140
120
100
80
Jul.
Aug.
Sep.
Oct.
Nov.
Dec.
Jan.
Feb.
Mar.
1994
1995

Source: Bloomberg Financial Markets.

2¾ percent of GDP at an annual basis); set up a deposit insurance scheme and two special funds for the privatization of provincial banks and the restructuring of the banking system; and arranged international financial assistance (including through a one-year extension of the extended arrangement from the IMF). The markets reacted positively to these measures, reflected, inter alia, in a noticeable recovery in the prices of bonds and stocks, and the stabilization of the level of deposits in the banking system.

Brazil

Financial markets in Brazil also came under pressure. The Brazilian stock market fell 25 percent in dollar terms over January and February, and the authorities had to intervene in the foreign exchange market to maintain the exchange rate around R$0.85 per U.S. dollar.[23]

In March 1995, however, pressures on the real increased. On Monday, March 6, the authorities switched their exchange rate policy to a system of adjustable exchange rate bands. The initial band was set at R$0.86–0.90 per U.S. dollar, and it was announced that the band would be widened to

[23]In principle, the real was floating freely subject to a floor of parity with respect to the U.S. dollar. In effect, however, the exchange rate has been managed to remain close to R$0.85 per U.S. dollar since October 1994.

Chart I.12. Stock Market Performance, Nominal Exchanges Rates, and Interest Rates in Selected Asian Countries

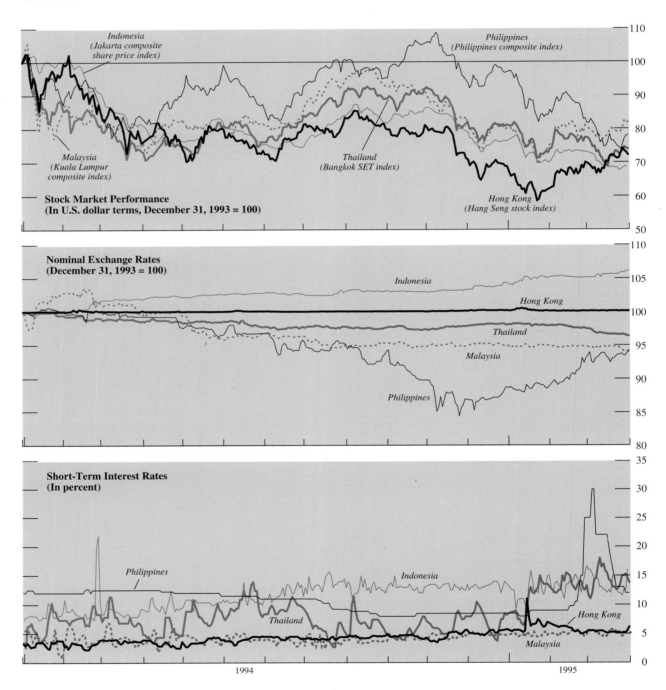

Source: Bloomberg Financial Markets.

Chart I.13. Brady Bond Spreads
(In basis points)

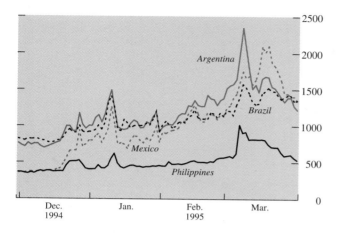

Sources: Reuters; Salomon Brothers; and IMF staff estimates.

R$0.86–0.98 per U.S. dollar on May 2, 1995, for an undetermined period of time. This led to strong pressures on the real, and the central bank intervened heavily, as reflected by the decline in foreign reserves. On Friday, March 10, the authorities established a new exchange rate band (R$0.88–0.93 per U.S. dollar), increased interest rates (the overnight market interest rate rose from 46 percent to 65 percent), and took steps to increase capital inflows and to increase outflows. As a consequence, the attack on the currency was halted.

Other Western Hemisphere Countries

Other developing countries in the Western Hemisphere generally experienced less turbulence in financial markets than in Argentina and Brazil. The Chilean stock market fell 3 percent in dollar terms in the first quarter of 1995, and the Chilean peso was unchanged against the dollar over the quarter; the peso depreciated 4 percent up to February 21, but then appreciated during the remaining weeks (Chart I.11). Prices on the Colombian stock market declined 11 percent in dollar terms over the quarter, after gaining 7 percent at the end of December after the devaluation. The Colombian peso depreciated 6 percent during the first quarter.

Effects on Asian Markets

After declining in the first half of December, most Asian stock markets rebounded in dollar terms in the wake of the Mexican devaluation (see Chart I.12). These markets did not begin to experience price declines until the beginning of January, when pressures

on Mexico began to intensify. Price declines in Asian emerging stock markets in January ranged from 7 percent in Malaysia to 13 percent in the Philippines. Asian markets felt the greatest pressure during the week of January 9 to 13. Most markets recovered in February, although the Philippine market fell an additional 1 percent in dollar terms as the Philippine peso continued to depreciate.

Thailand

Perhaps the most pronounced event occurred in Thailand, which took successful measures in January to defend its currency. While many Asian markets felt pressure during this same week (January 9–13), the baht came under greater pressure because traders had built up large positions in the domestic money market to arbitrage the peg of the baht against the basket of the dollar, yen, and mark.[24] On Thursday, January 12, rumors of a devaluation swept through the markets, causing selling pressure against the baht. The authorities responded by announcing that they would sell any amount of dollars that banks needed and by assuring market participants that they would maintain the peg. The next day, the Bank of Thailand instituted a swap facility with foreign banks that allowed it to borrow dollars from foreign banks through a swap of bahts for dollars, so it could continue to buy bahts for dollars from domestic banks. This facility was replaced a week later with a more flexible swap facility, and it was finally closed in February. Domestic short-term interest rates rose in January as the central bank tightened conditions; Bangkok overnight rates rose from 6.5 percent on January 11 to 12.0 percent on January 16 (see Chart I.12). In the event, the defense of the baht was successful, and the peg held. Thai foreign exchange reserves fell $400 million in January.

The Philippines

The Philippine peso also came under pressure in early 1995. In contrast to Thailand and the major countries in the Western Hemisphere, however, the Philippines did not have a pegged or target zone exchange rate system. The peso depreciated 7 percent against the dollar from December 19 to February 28 (see Chart I.12). A temporary, automatic halt to trading in the peso was called on January 13 after a large depreciation that day, the same day that pressures in Thailand peaked. Pressure on the peso persisted in February, despite intervention in the foreign exchange market and increases in the central bank overnight rate and the benchmark 91-day

[24]"Tequila Slammers" (1995).

Table I.4. Correlation Among Total Returns on Brady Bonds

	Argentina	Brazil	Mexico	Nigeria	Philippines	Venezuela
			January 1993–January 1994			
Argentina	1.00					
Brazil	0.23	1.00				
Mexico	0.56	0.22	1.00			
Nigeria	0.41	0.11	0.58	1.00		
Philippines	0.29	0.22	0.32	0.33	1.00	
Venezuela	0.53	0.19	0.55	0.38	0.28	1.00
Thirty-year U.S. Treasury bonds	0.36	0.04	0.51	0.26	0.16	0.31
			February–May 1994			
Argentina	1.00					
Brazil	0.57	1.00				
Mexico	0.84	0.51	1.00			
Nigeria	0.57	0.63	0.59	1.00		
Philippines	0.21	0.40	0.22	0.44	1.00	
Venezuela	0.72	0.58	0.65	0.75	0.35	1.00
Thirty-year U.S. Treasury bonds	0.74	0.42	0.63	0.40	0.18	0.46
			Mid-May 1994–mid-December 1994			
Argentina	1.00					
Brazil	0.58	1.00				
Mexico	0.77	0.45	1.00			
Nigeria	0.42	0.33	0.35	1.00		
Philippines	0.26	0.11	0.25	0.09	1.00	
Venezuela	0.48	0.31	0.47	0.29	0.15	1.00
Thirty-year U.S. Treasury bonds	0.55	0.24	0.55	0.18	0.11	0.28
			Mid-December 1994–early March 1995			
Argentina	1.00					
Brazil	0.80	1.00				
Mexico	0.89	0.73	1.00			
Nigeria	0.68	0.55	0.70	1.00		
Philippines	0.34	0.38	0.43	0.38	1.00	
Venezuela	0.83	0.80	0.78	0.80	0.42	1.00
Thirty-year U.S. Treasury bonds	0.06	0.04	−0.01	−0.10	−0.13	—

Source: IMF staff estimates based on Salomon Brothers data.

treasury bill rate. After the peso again breached its daily trading band on February 24, the central bank responded with a sharp and temporary increase in its overnight rate to 30 percent, and the treasury bill rate was allowed to rise by two percent. Since mid-March, the treasury bill rate has risen by about another 1 percent, and the peso has stabilized.

It is unclear why the Philippines experienced these pressures. Possible explanations are the expansion of liquidity and the sharp decline in interest rates during 1994, and the low level of foreign exchange reserves by Asian standards. However, the weakening of the exchange rate in February 1995 does not appear to have reflected an unsustainable strengthening of the peso during 1994. Both the Philippines

and Thailand have high current account deficits compared with other Asian countries (Table I.5).

Hong Kong

Hong Kong also experienced financial pressures in January. After a 0.23 percent fall in the Hong Kong dollar against the U.S. dollar and signs of a speculative attack on the currency, the Hong Kong Monetary Authority tightened liquidity, which led to an increase in interbank rates of more than six percentage points during January 13, and the currency, which is pegged to the dollar, was stabilized. A speculative attack on the Hong Kong dollar led to a tightening of rates in

Table I.5. Current Account Balances for Selected Developing Countries

(In percent of GDP)

	1989	1990	1991	1992	1993
Argentina	−1.60	3.22	−0.34	−2.86	−2.91
Brazil	0.23	−0.79	−0.36	1.63	−0.15
Chile	−2.50	−2.13	0.03	−1.74	−4.58
Colombia	−0.51	1.35	5.53	1.87	...
Mexico	−2.82	−3.05	−5.19	−7.53	−6.45
Indonesia	−1.17	−2.82	−3.65	−2.17	−1.64
Malaysia	0.68	−2.14	−8.99	−3.16	−3.89
Philippines	−3.46	−8.50	−7.71	−5.75	−5.60
Thailand	−3.41	−6.11	−2.28	−1.89	−6.05

Sources: International Monetary Fund, *Balance of Payments Statistics* and *World Economic Outlook*.

the interbank market in order to make it difficult for speculators to cover their short positions.

Other Asian Markets

Other Asian emerging markets, including Indonesia and Malaysia, also experienced brief pressures in mid-January. Indonesian overnight interbank interest rates rose from 10.0 percent on January 13 to 15.8 percent on January 17, while Malaysian rates remained stable. The Indonesian authorities also sought to strengthen confidence by leaving the foreign exchange window open on Saturday, January 14, and they tightened the official discount rate by 50 basis points on January 16.

III

Mexican Foreign Exchange Market Crises From the Perspective of the Speculative Attack Literature

When a country pursues the policy of a fixed exchange rate or controls its rate of depreciation, it is widely understood by market participants that the exchange rate policy will continue as long as it does not impinge on other, more important, economic or political constraints. If investors believe that the exchange rate policy will be altered eventually, their actions can precipitate a series of events, a speculative attack, that tests the credibility of the commitment, and the ability, to maintain the exchange rate policy. This section examines, from the perspective of the speculative attacks literature, some of the developments in Mexican financial markets surrounding the devaluation of the Mexican peso in December 1994, and the subsequent floating of the peso. Data on the key economic and financial variables suggest that developments in Mexico surrounding the devaluation were consistent with the classic properties of a speculative attack driven by investor perceptions of deteriorating fundamentals, with some variations that might have created uncertainty in the postattack, floating rate regime.

Speculative Attacks Are Not Market Pathologies

A speculative attack on a fixed or managed exchange rate is a sudden and massive restructuring of portfolios in which market participants attempt to reap gains or prevent losses from an expected change in the exchange rate regime.[25] It was once thought by economists that speculative attacks were market pathologies that would not be present or possible in healthy markets. Recent research has considered that a speculative attack is a market's rational response to a perceived inconsistency in economic policies.[26] In this research, a country tries to sustain a fixed exchange rate using a limited quantity of reserves and pursues other, higher priority, objectives, such as inflation objectives, that might be inconsistent with the fixed exchange rate. Private market participants—called speculators—who recognize the

policy inconsistency and the limited availability of reserves, come to realize that the fixed exchange rate cannot be sustained. In foreseeing the unsustainability of policies, market participants anticipate profits and losses and enter into foreign exchange transactions that ultimately hasten the collapse of the exchange rate regime.

A Simple, Rarefied Example of a Speculative Attack

As an example, consider a small country that fixes its exchange rate to the currency of a single large trading partner and suppose that the small country is following a domestic policy that implies a higher inflation rate than its partner. Further suppose that speculators can foresee perfectly the future collapse of the exchange rate regime and know that a flexible exchange rate will be adopted once the fixed rate becomes unsustainable. While the exchange rate is fixed, the short-term domestic interest rate will be equal to the foreign interest rate for very short-term interest rates (e.g., overnight rates); after the devaluation, the domestic interest rate will rise above the foreign rate to reflect the higher domestic rate of inflation.

In this simple model, the increase in domestic interest rates reduces the demand for non-interest-bearing domestic currency assets and leads to the depreciation of the currency. A well-financed single speculator can successfully attack the fixed exchange rate regime, if, after correctly anticipating the exchange rate devaluation, the speculator buys the entire stock of international reserves from the authorities, at the fixed exchange rate, and consequently reaps a capital gain equal to the exchange rate depreciation multiplied by the stock of reserves. The earlier the attack takes place, the larger would be the stock of reserves that can be purchased and the smaller would be the depreciation at the time of the attack because the attack absorbs domestic currency assets.

Unfortunately for the wealthy single speculator in this rarified example, other speculators also can foresee the opportunity for risk-free profits. This recognition, in effect, begins the process of a concerted speculative attack on the currency. The process ends when

---

[25]The exchange rate is defined as the domestic currency price of foreign currency.

[26]See Salant and Henderson (1978), Krugman (1979), and Flood and Garber (1984).

the reduced demand for domestic currency assets owing to the interest rate increase exactly matches the decrease in supply of these assets owing to the purchases of reserves. At such a time, the exchange rate need not jump at all and speculators, in their frenzy to obtain profits at the expense of the exchange authority, will have competed away all profits.

The example illustrates that a speculative attack need not be viewed as a market pathology. Instead, it can be seen and modeled as a competitive market's response to perceived inconsistencies in economic policies. The essential feature of the speculative attack example is the sudden and massive restructuring of portfolios as market participants react to their knowledge of the unsustainable economic policies. Such a sudden and massive restructuring of portfolios can just as easily occur when investors sell foreign exchange in spot markets to avoid losses, as when speculators sell foreign exchange short in forward markets to reap profits.

Kinds of Speculative Attacks and Shadow Exchange Rate

In the economics and finance literature, speculative attacks arise from three sources: (1) an attack due to misaligned fundamentals; (2) a pre-emptive attack by the government to alter its policies before the market attacks; and (3) an attack based on multiple equilibria.[27] Of these three types, only the last one might be considered a market pathology, and it will be seen below to be irrelevant for explaining recent events involving the Mexican peso.

Each type of attack can be modeled as evolving according to the relationship between the actual exchange rate and a hypothetical construct known as the shadow exchange rate, which is defined as the floating exchange rate that would prevail immediately after a successful attack in which reserves are exhausted and base money contracts by the domestic currency value of the attack.[28] A speculative attack is worthwhile only if the shadow rate is above the controlled rate (i.e., if the shadow rate is depreciated relative to the actual rate). At the time of the attack, market participants buy all available foreign exchange at the controlled rate from the authorities and resell it at the depreciated shadow rate, thereby

reaping a profit equal to the shadow rate less the controlled rate on each unit of foreign currency. Before an attack, the shadow rate is below the controlled rate and rises toward the controlled rate as reserves decline.

The shadow exchange rate provides a means of quantifying the compensation investors demand for holding assets denominated in domestic currency prior to the attack; its value depends on expectations about the effects of the attack on reserves and future monetary and exchange rate policies. The compensation is related to the probability of an attack during an asset's holding period and the size of the currency depreciation in the event of an attack. The literature on speculative attacks primarily addresses the estimation of the probability of an attack in the future and the determination of the shadow rate.[29]

Relevant Arbitrage Condition

Much of the literature is organized around one measure of the financial market's perception of the health of a controlled exchange rate regime, namely, "the" short-term, domestic currency interest rate on domestic treasury securities. As a matter of definition investors are in equilibrium when[30]

$$i = i^* + E\Delta s + \epsilon. \qquad (1)$$

According to the equation the domestic currency interest rate, i, must equal the comparable foreign interest rate, i^*, plus two additional elements. The first element is the expected percent change in the exchange rate, $E\Delta s$, with E indicating the expectation and Δs the percent change in the exchange rate. The second element, ϵ, is a residual that can incorporate a risk premium that investors demand as compensation for undiversifiable risk.

The term $E\Delta s$ is usefully divided into two conditional parts:

$$E\Delta s = (1 - \pi)E\Delta \bar{s} + \pi E\Delta \hat{s}. \qquad (2)$$

The first term combines the probability of its occurrence, $(1 - \pi)$, with the expected change in the exchange rate if the current exchange rate policy stays in place, $E\Delta \bar{s}$. In the second term, π is the probability of an attack over the holding period and $E\Delta \hat{s}$ is the expected movement of the exchange rate if the current policy is abandoned either in a regime-ending attack or in a pre-emptive adjustment in policies by the authorities.

---

[27]The literature also recognizes the possibility of attacks due to speculative bubbles in the postattack exchange rate. That possibility is ignored here since rational bubble models are consistently rejected in the foreign exchange market. See background paper "Bubbles, Noise, and the Trading Process in Speculative Markets," pp. 175–85.

[28]These methods were first applied to Mexico by Blanco and Garber (1986); some of their analysis is illustrated in the next section.

[29]In models, the probability that an attack will occur during a given interval of time in the future is equal to the probability that the shadow rate will exceed the controlled rate during that same period of time because currency speculators would then find it worthwhile to restructure their portfolios at the controlled price.

[30]For simplicity, dating has been suppressed in the equations.

Chart I.14. Probability of Devaluation Next Quarter

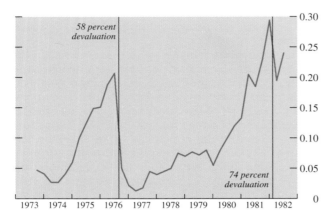

Source: Blanco and Garber (1986).

While the equations summarize the effects of exchange market arbitrage, they do not explain the determination of the crucial variable $\hat{s}$. To determine $\hat{s}$, it is necessary to refer to a model of government and private behavior that addresses four questions: What triggers an attack? How does the government behave during and after an attack? Will the government engage in a pre-emptive attack on its own policy? How does the private sector behave during and after an attack?

To demonstrate how useful these ideas have been, consider the following application of them to Mexico.[31] Chart I.14 presents estimates of the one-quarter-ahead devaluation probabilities for the Mexican peso—that is, the values for π in equation (2) for the period 1973–82. The estimated probability increases from less than 4 percent in early 1974 to more than 18 percent just before the devaluation of 58 percent in August 1976. It then declines precipitously in the third quarter of 1976 and begins to rise—albeit with a few dips—until it reaches devaluation in February 1982. The peak reached in 1982 is a convincing application of this approach, because the peak was projected "out of sample" using only data that were available at the time.

In the literature, a speculative attack usually begins with an expansionary policy that is given higher priority than the exchange rate policy so that the policy mix is unsustainable. Prior to the attack, the unsustainability of the policy mix becomes clear to investors who recognize that the exchange rate policy will likely be abandoned in a crisis. Investors know neither the precise timing of the regime change nor the successor policy.

In the speculative attacks literature, in the period just before the "crisis," three fundamental indicators move in anticipation of the crisis. First, international reserves are slowly depleted under the controlled exchange rate policy as a reflection of the expansionary policy. Reserve losses end with a large, final portfolio reallocation reflecting the exchange of reserves between the authorities and private market participants.

Second, in most of the literature, the country that suffers the attack is a price taker, so that domestic inflation matches foreign inflation. In actual experience, however, the country often has higher inflation than its trading partners and experiences a large increase in the real exchange rate, which increases the speed with which reserves are depleted.

Third, domestic currency interest rates rise, at all maturities, as the attack becomes more likely. The larger is the expected depreciation rate of the shadow exchange rate relative to the controlled rate and the more likely it is that reserves will reach some limit, the larger is the spread between the domestic interest rate and the foreign rate.[32] In the models in the literature, the usefulness of these indicators depends on the prompt release of information on reserves and prices.[33]

Peso Devaluation and Modifications of Standard Attack Model

The developments involving the Mexican peso in late 1994 and early 1995 do not conform precisely to the conditions hypothesized in these simple speculative attack models in two respects: the monetary

---

[31]See Blanco and Garber (1986). Two shadow exchange rates are relevant: the shadow floating rate corresponding to expectations that the postattack regime will be a floating rate regime; and the same shadow rate plus an increment to allow for the devaluation. Current interest rates are determined by the possibility of a shift to the second shadow rate. The shadow rate provides the lower bound for the devaluation of the peso. Blanco and Garber use a model of the shadow rate and its stochastic behavior to estimate the probability distribution of next period's shadow rate, which provides an estimate of probability that the shadow rate will be above the fixed rate (i.e., that a devaluation will occur).

[32]The effort to preserve a regime may involve other policy instruments also. In the 1992 European exchange rate mechanism (ERM) crisis, some countries were able to mount temporary interest rate defenses of their currencies, for example. Such a defense boosts short-term, domestic currency interest rates temporarily above that suggested by equality in equation (1), draws capital into the country, and makes speculation against the currency expensive. Such a defense is limited by the vulnerability of the private sector to high domestic currency interest rates. Private floating rate financing of mortgages and inventories, for example, is particularly sensitive to the interest rate defense and political pressures arising from such sources can limit a government's ability to mount such a defense.

[33]Information delays in the models can postpone an attack at the cost of postattack credibility.

Chart I.15. Mexico: International Reserves
(In billions of U.S. dollars)

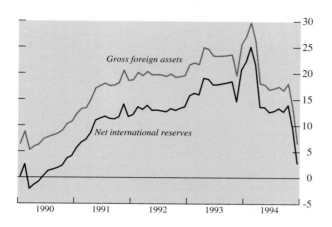

Source: Banco de México.
Note: Net international reserves exclude short-term, foreign currency liabilities.

Chart I.16. Mexico: Current Account Balance
(In percent of GDP)

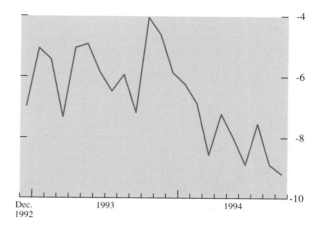

Sources: Banco de México, *Indicadores Económicos*, various issues; and International Monetary Fund, *International Financial Statistics;* and IMF staff calculations.

policy response to reserve losses and movements in the real exchange rate.

Mexican International Reserves and Monetary Base

The first important element of a successful attack is the large portfolio reallocation that exhausts the ability or desire to defend the controlled parity. The amount of reserves used in the defense also influences the shadow exchange rate. The nature of a reserve defense is that reserves are exchanged for domestic currency at the controlled parity. Following a successful attack, speculators end up holding reserves and the exchange authority holds the amount of domestic currency acquired at the controlled exchange rate. How soon an attack occurs in the presence of exchange market pressures depends on the amount of reserves expended in the defense of the fixed parity and the anticipated postattack interest rates and prices.

Chart I.15 presents gross and net Mexican international reserves since 1990. There was initially a long period of increasing net reserves, which reached a peak of more than $25 billion in February 1994. The subsequent decline in reserves was dramatic and rapid; more than $3 billion in reserves was lost in March; more than $8 billion, in April; there was a lull until November, when $4.5 billion was lost; and then finally $6.5 billion was lost in December.

The pattern of reserve losses mirrors the current account balance less external financing (Chart I.16).

While external financing was robust in the early 1990s, the large current account deficit was overfinanced by external sources and allowed a massive buildup of net international reserves. In early 1994 external financing began to dry up, requiring current account deficits to be financed more directly by accumulated reserves. In the period 1990–93, the current account deficit averaged about 5 percent of GDP, but by February 1994, it had risen to more than 8 percent of GDP. To provide some perspective on this pattern, in the period 1990–93, current account deficits averaged 1.9 percent of GDP in Argentina, −0.1 percent in Brazil, and 1.1 percent in the United States.

In the speculative attack literature, economic policy ensures that (1) the net domestic credit component of the monetary base is unaffected by the foreign exchange market; and (2) foreign exchange reserves are residuals that balance the domestic money market at the policy-designated exchange rate. The events in Mexico followed a different course between January 1992 and December 1994. Reserve losses and gains during this period usually were sterilized so that the monetary base, rather than domestic credit, proceeded on a smooth growth path with some acceleration in the final months of 1994 (Chart I.17).

Mexican Real Exchange Rate

The second departure from the standard model in the recent events in Mexico involves the real

Chart I.17. Mexico: Base Money by Component, January 1992–December 1994
(In billions of new pesos)

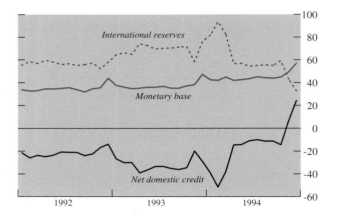

Source: Banco de México, *Indicadores Económicos*, February 1995.

Chart I.18. Mexico: Real Effective Exchange Rate, January 1979–January 1995
(1980 = 100)

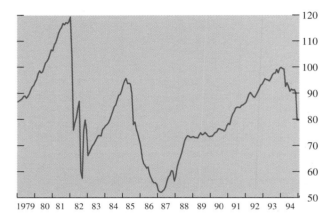

Sources: International Monetary Fund, Effective Exchange Rates data base and *Annual Report on Exchange Arrangements and Exchange Restrictions,* various issues.

exchange rate. In the literature, the country that experiences an attack is a price taker and its real exchange rate, the domestic price level divided by its trading partner's price level multiplied by the controlled exchange rate, is presumed to be fixed (say, at unity).[34] In reality, real exchange rates are not controlled by exchange rate policies: they can change dramatically when nominal exchange rates are flexible, because goods prices respond relatively slowly. When the nominal exchange rate is fixed, large and extended movements in the real exchange rate will occur if there is inflation; this can have important real economic effects and influence the shadow rate indirectly by changing the current account balance.

During the 15-year period ended in 1994, the real effective exchange rate (REER) in Mexico changed significantly (Chart I.18).[35] The three long cycles that can be seen in the chart correspond to major changes in exchange rate policy.[36] They involve long periods during which the REER increased fairly smoothly followed by precipitous declines. The declines are as-

sociated with either large peso devaluations or the floating of the peso.

An increase in the REER makes domestic goods less competitive in international markets (unless matched by productivity gains), which exacerbates the rate of reserve loss, raises the shadow rate over time, and, thereby, raises estimates of the future shadow exchange rate. In addition, because a rise in the REER is normally correlated with low and declining reserves, foreign investors anticipate a future peso depreciation and make intertemporal substitutions that further depress exports. The other side of trading suffers equally. Imports are as attractive to Mexicans as exports are unattractive to foreigners. While reserves were rising in Mexico, up until early 1994, as a result of foreign investment, the high and rising REER was not an immediate problem, but, it may have served as a warning, along with the rise in the current account deficit, that the underlying trade and competitiveness conditions in Mexico were unsustainable.

Model Adjustments Relevant to Mexican Experience

In models of speculative attacks, reserve losses mirror domestic credit increases until the time of the attack. During the attack, reserve losses are not sterilized and the monetary base declines by the size of the attack. In Mexico, however, before and during the exchange market turbulence, the authorities ster-

---

[34]Speculative attack models where the real exchange rate is not fixed are reviewed by Agenor and Flood (1994).

[35]The Mexican REER as calculated in IMF, *International Financial Statistics (IFS)*, is equal to the Mexican CPI multiplied by the U.S. dollar price of the peso, for example, ⅛ dollar/peso, divided by a trade-weighted average of trading partner CPIs multiplied by their respective dollar currency prices. The REER is indexed at 1980 = 100.

[36]Box I.2 recounts all of the events surrounding the major changes in the real exchange rate during this period.

ilized reserve losses, which kept the monetary base on a relatively smooth trend. Reserve losses that are sterilized do not affect the money supply. When sterilization occurs, a speculative attack becomes a portfolio adjustment in the markets for domestic and foreign securities rather than the markets for domestic money and foreign securities.[37]

With this model adjustment, the introduction of securities markets, the attack is set up by the shift in wealth from domestic to foreign residents associated with the current account deficit. The wealth transfer increases the overall demand for foreign securities, which requires the monetary authority to expend international reserves to accommodate demand at an unchanged exchange rate. The process ends, as before, in a final speculative attack that has the domestic monetary authority exchanging domestic securities for foreign securities to keep the monetary base constant. The portfolio reallocation is accommodated by a shift in domestic interest rates and in the expected change in the exchange rate.

Mexican Interest Rates in 1994

The third element of an attack involves the movement of the interest rate before the attack and the jump in the interest rate after the attack.[38] According to equation (1), movements in the pre-attack interest rates should reflect two elements: during 1994, U.S. short-term interest rates increased by 263 basis points;[39] and, the probability of collapse, π, increased as reserves were depleted. The expected rate of change of the exchange rate in the event of an attack would be above the depreciation rate of the controlled rate; and an increase in π will increase domestic interest rates.[40]

Chart I.19 presents 91-day Cetes, Tesobonos, and U.S. treasury bill rates. Cetes are peso-denominated government securities; Tesobonos are peso-denominated government securities with the principal indexed to the U.S. dollar exchange rate. The evolution of Mexican interest rates and interest rate differentials relative to U.S. interest rates conveys useful information about market perceptions about the exchange rate regime in Mexico. In early 1994, Cetes interest rates were around 10 percent. They then shot up to the 14–17 percent range in April, reflecting an increased spread over Tesobono rates and U.S. treasury bill rates. Despite the decline in

the REER, reserve losses, and the increase in the current account deficit during the remainder of 1994, the markets apparently did not demand a very large increase in premium for peso lending.

Following the 15 percent devaluation on December 20 and the subsequent floating of the peso against the dollar, both Cetes and Tesobono interest rates rose dramatically. Cetes rates rose to more than 30 percent in January 1995 and then jumped temporarily to more than 40 percent. Tesobono rates rose dramatically as well, despite being indexed to the dollar. As emphasized above, the final element of an attack is an upward jump in domestic currency interest rates that reflects perceptions about the postattack inflation rate and that is consistent with the postattack portfolio allocation.

Postattack Policy

In the speculative attack literature, the shadow exchange rate depends on anticipations of reserve losses during an expected attack and expected policies after the attack. Thus, the policy options that can be expected after the collapse of the exchange rate regime are important for fully implementing the concept of the shadow exchange rate. Four options, which are not mutually exclusive, are typically considered: (1) a freely floating exchange rate; (2) a step devaluation followed by a new fixed rate; (3) the imposition of capital controls or some other default; and (4) changes in other government policies.

The shift to a freely floating exchange rate is the most commonly analyzed option in the literature.[41] The domestic currency interest rate rises, possibly dramatically, as reserves are depleted and the probability of an impending attack rises. Domestic currency interest rates rise to compensate investors for the possibility that an attack will force the abandonment of the exchange rate regime during the life of a loan denominated in domestic currency. Following the attack, domestic interest rates are free to reflect the domestic inflation rate. Real domestic currency balances decline because of the portfolio shift at the time of the attack and the increased opportunity cost of holding currency.[42]

The second option is, in some ways, a special case of the first option.[43] The devaluation may reflect a pre-emptive policy adjustment to avoid having to mount an expensive defense. The devaluation is effective only if it reduces the value of the currency by more than the currency would have been devalued in a move to a free float. Otherwise, it still would be

---

[37] In this case there would be an adjustment in the risk premium in equation (1).

[38] If the authorities mount an interest rate defense then interest rates drop after the attack.

[39] Increase in Federal Funds rate from December 12, 1993 to December 28, 1994.

[40] In addition, policy uncertainty reflected in contradictory announcements concerning the regime may increase the risk premium which is embedded in ϵ in equation (1).

[41] This is the option used by Salant and Henderson (1978), Krugman (1979), and Flood and Garber (1984).

[42] In the Mexican case, both domestic credit and the overall monetary base increased at the time of the crisis.

[43] This is the option studied by Blanco and Garber (1986).

Box I.2. Mexico: Exchange Market Developments, 1982–94[1]

1. February 18, 1982. The Banco de México announced a temporary withdrawal from the foreign exchange market. On February 19, the peso depreciated by 30 percent and continued to depreciate another 19 percent during February.

2. June 5, 1982. The Banco de México announced that it would intervene again and would let the peso depreciate at 0.04 pesos per dollar a day.

3. August 5, 1982. A two-tier exchange rate system was announced. A preferential rate was to apply to service on public debt, interest on private external debt, and "certain priority imports." The proceeds of petroleum exports and foreign borrowing by the public sector were to be converted through this market. All other transactions were to take place at a freely floating rate. Commercial banks were required to surrender to the Banco de México their net foreign exchange holdings, including gold and silver.

August 13, 1982. All foreign currency deposits in Mexican banks were made eligible for conversion at maturity into pesos at a rate of 69.5. The foreign exchange market was closed temporarily.

August 16, 1982. Commercial banks were authorized to open accounts in foreign currencies for embassies, consulates, and international organizations and their foreign personnel.

August 18, 1982. A Presidential Decree established that public sector agencies (including enterprises) surrender their foreign exchange holdings and their foreign currency time deposits at maturity. Petroleos Mexicanos was allowed to open a special foreign currency account at the Banco de México for its deposits and was permitted withdrawals for specified payments. Private enterprises were required to register their foreign debt obligations with the government. The decree authorized the sale of foreign exchange at the dollar rate applicable to local deposits denominated in foreign currency (69.5) for obligations payable abroad by local financial entities and offset by foreign currency liabilities payable in Mexico by other Mexican residents. This rate also applied to obligations in foreign currency resulting from forward cover arrangements (*reportos*), loads with fiduciary guarantees in local currency, and deposits held by embassies, consulates, and international agencies located in Mexico and their personnel. The rate also applied to payments of deposits in foreign currency made by foreign financial institutions in the Mexican banking system.

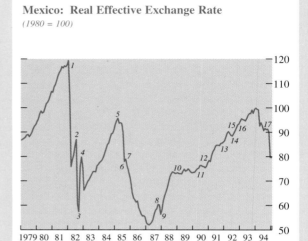

Mexico: Real Effective Exchange Rate
(1980 = 100)

Sources: International Monetary Fund, Effective Exchange Rates data base and *Exchange Arrangements and Exchange Restrictions*, various issues.

August 19, 1982. The foreign exchange market was reopened, and banks were authorized to transact foreign exchange at a free market rate.

September 1, 1982. Exchange controls were established by Presidential Decree, with supplementary rules issued by the Secretariat of Finance and Public Credit (SFPC) on September 14. All foreign exchange transactions were subject to control, and exports and imports of foreign currency could take place only through the Banco de México or its designated agents. Two exchange rates (ordinary and preferential) would be maintained; other special rates might be introduced later. Exports or imports of more than 5,000 pesos in foreign currency by individuals were prohibited, and exports of gold or silver required prior authorization. A foreign exchange budget was established to help establish priorities in the distribution of foreign exchange. Sales at the preferential rate were to apply principally to the foreign obligations of the public sector and domestic credit institutions, interest and principal on private sector obligations contracted before September 1, 1982, and "specified imports." Unless otherwise authorized by the Banco de México, all other exchange transactions were to be effected at the ordinary rate.

Mexican Private Banks Nationalized by Presidential Decree

All capital transferred and held abroad prior to September 1, 1982 could be repatriated at the ordinary rate.

---

[1]The information is collected from International Monetary Fund, *Annual Report on Exchange Arrangements and Exchange Restrictions*, various issues. This box should be read with the accompanying chart. The numbers at the beginning of a paragraph correspond to those shown in the chart.

Accounts opened in Mexican banks and loans granted by Mexican banks could not be denominated in foreign currency, with exceptions for foreign service and press correspondents, exporters, and tourist industries.

September 6, 1982. Two exchange rates were announced, a preferential rate (50) and an ordinary rate (70). Banco Internacional, SA, was authorized by the Banco de México as the only bank that could open accounts in foreign currency for the foreign service, international organizations operating in Mexico, and their foreign personnel.

September 14, 1982. Rules and regulations pertaining to the exchange arrangement were issued by SFPC.

September 20, 1982. The issuance of payments and other transactions in pesos abroad by Mexican credit institutions was prohibited.

4. *December 13, 1982.* A decree established two foreign exchange markets, a controlled market and a free market. The decree envisioned that specified foreign obligations could be repaid through a special coverage exchange system with a fixed exchange rate plus a forward premium. The new arrangement would come into effect on December 20. The exchange rate in the controlled market was to be officially established and would apply to (1) all merchandise export receipts, net of any required payment abroad by the exporter (unless specifically exempt); (2) payments by in-bond industries for wages, salaries, rent, and the purchase of Mexican goods and services other than fixed assets; (3) principal, interest, and related expenses on foreign obligations of public and private sectors (with proceeds from such loans to be surrendered); (4) payments for authorized imports; (5) payments to the Mexican foreign service and to international organizations; and (6) other transactions authorized by the SFPC.

All Mexican credit institutions and existing exchange houses could operate in the free market. This market would apply to all transactions not specifically designated for the controlled market. Initially (and temporarily) individual transactions would be limited to $1,000 for a person and $5,000 for an enterprise (though no limits were imposed on the number of transactions). No limitations would be applied to the determination of the rate or sales, ownership, or transfer of foreign exchange, including imports and exports.

December 17, 1982. Banco de México banned intervention in forward transactions by Mexican credit institutions linked to transactions in local currency. In addition, banks were limited to free-market foreign exchange positions (short or long) not exceeding 10 percent of total capital and reserves.

December 18, 1982. Banco de México issued regulations governing the functioning of the controlled foreign exchange market and foreign currency deposits held by enterprises in free trade zones and border areas. Transactions in foreign currency related to the expenses of the enterprise were permitted. Payments could also be made at the relevant rate in pesos.

December 20, 1982. The exchange arrangement announced on December 13, 1982 came into effect, with ask and bid rates of 95.1/95 in the controlled market and 150/148.5 in the free market.

5. *March 6, 1985.* The rate of depreciation of the Mexican peso in the controlled and free markets was raised to 0.21 per dollar a day.

6. *July 25, 1985.* The midpoint exchange rate in the controlled market was changed from 233.1 to 279.7, representing a devaluation of 16.7 percent.

August 5, 1985. Managed floating was begun, with daily fixing sessions.

7. *November 5, 1985.* The Banco de México issued regulations prohibiting credit institutions from receiving peso deposits from foreign financial institutions or non-Mexican money exchange establishments.

8. *November 18, 1987.* Banco de México discontinued intervention in the free market.

December 14, 1987. The exchange rate in the controlled market was depreciated by 18 percent, reducing the spread between the controlled and free rates to about 1.5 percent.

9. *March 1, 1988.* The government undertook to fix the exchange rate for the dollar for a period of three months, within the context of the anti-inflation pact. The period of the fixed rate was subsequently extended through the end of the year.

10. *January 1, 1989.* Daily preannounced amounts of depreciation against the dollar were initiated.

11. *May 28, 1990.* The preannounced rate of depreciation was set at 0.80 per dollar a day.

12. *November 12, 1990.* The rate of depreciation was changed to 0.40 per dollar a day.

13. *November 11, 1991.* The controlled exchange rate market was eliminated.

14. *June 22, 1992.* The government announced that the new peso, equivalent to 1,000 former pesos, would be introduced January 1, 1993.

15. *October 21, 1992.* The daily depreciation of the selling intervention point was changed to 0.40.

16. *January 1, 1993.* New peso introduced (equal to 1,000 old pesos).

17. *December 20, 1994.* Upper band devalued by 15 percent.

December 22, 1994. Fixed regime abandoned for a floating regime.

Chart I.19. Yields on Mexican and U.S. Government Securities, January 1994–February 17, 1995[1]

(In percent)

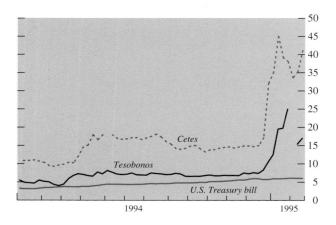

Sources: Bloomberg Financial Markets; and Board of Governors of the Federal Reserve System.

[1]Weekly auction data for 91-day Cetes (Mexican government treasury bills) and 91-day Tesobonos. The break in the Cetes series reflects the fact that there was no auction during the week of May 11, 1994. The break in the Tesobonos series is due to cancellation of the January 31, 1995 auction by the Banco de México.

worthwhile to attack the fixed exchange rate regime. Consequently, the interest rate must rise before the devaluation by even more for a step devaluation than for a freely floating regime. This second option appears to characterize reasonably well the 15 percent devaluation of the Mexican peso that occurred on December 20, 1994, which was then followed by a freely floating exchange rate after reserves continued to decline.

The third option, the imposition of capital controls, is a form of default because capital controls, in effect, usurp, without compensation, either the rights of investors to freely move capital across borders or a portion of the invested proceeds. As an example of such an option, suppose that, after the attack, convertibility of current and capital account transactions are treated differently, by maintaining the old regime for current account transactions but using a floating rate for capital account transactions. Investments in securities are capital account items, and the capital proceeds of investments must then be repatriated at the lower floating rate. Investors would perceive this as a tax on their investment returns. In 1982, Mexico imposed a two-tier market, and in 1994, investors might have given some weight in the formation of the shadow exchange rate to the possibility that such a policy might be pursued again.[44]

_____

[44]See Box I.2.

The potential importance of this option in the formation of investor views about the Mexican peso shadow exchange rate is underscored by changes in the interest rate on Tesobonos in late 1994. Although Tesobonos are nominally indexed to the dollar, Tesobono contracts were, in principle, potentially subject to some form of capital controls or some other form of direct or indirect "default," including restructuring, involuntary conversion, and other options. The observed increase in Tesobono yields in December 1994 and January 1995 can be viewed, therefore, as the compensation demanded by investors for incurring the risk of these various potential forms of taxes.

Finally, consider the fourth option—other policy changes in addition to exchange rate policy changes at the time of an attack. This option opens up the possibility that an attack on a fundamentally sound, fixed rate regime could create a change in policies that inadvertently validates the attack and leads to a devaluation. For example, consider a country in which a fixed exchange rate regime provided the nominal anchor that effectively contained inflationary pressures, and in which in the absence of the anchor the economy would have moved to an equilibrium with significantly higher inflation and a less valuable currency. In such a situation, an attack that provokes the policy response of floating the exchange rate would in effect lead to higher inflation and a lower exchange rate. Thus, by acting as a policy-switching trigger the attack is self-validating. In the academic literature, such a possibility is referred to as multiple equilibria, but so far, actual examples of this possibility have not been documented.

The fourth option does not appear to be a reasonable characterization of what occurred in Mexico, because of the losses in reserves, the rising current account deficit, and the rise in the real exchange rate.

Conclusions

Events in Mexico in late 1994 and early 1995 appear to conform to some of the elements of the first three postattack options including foreign investor misperceptions. In 1994, both internal and external imbalances emerged and yet for quite some time domestic interest rates did not rise to fully reflect these imbalances. The devaluation on December 20, 1994 can be interpreted as a pre-emptive strike against speculation that the Mexican peso was overvalued in the presence of a persistent decline in reserves from $25 billion in February 1994 to $10 billion by the end of November 1994. The 15 percent devaluation was followed by further pressure on the peso, after which the peso was allowed to float freely. Immediately following the move to a floating rate, Cetes interest rates jumped to almost 32 percent on December 30, 1994 and continued to rise to more than

Chart I.20. Mexico: Daily Exchange Rate, November 1, 1994–March 6, 1995

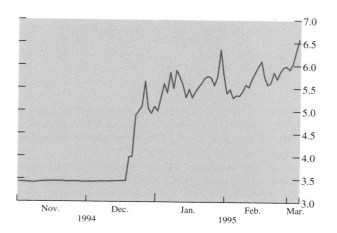

Source: Reuters.

40 percent by January 13, 1995. Models of speculative attacks would predict this reaction in the presence of expectations by market participants of a continuation of downward pressure on the exchange rate. In addition, the rise in interest rates on Tesobonos to 25 percent by January 30, 1995, also is consistent with the predictions of models of speculative attacks in situations when investors expect the imposition of capital controls, as in 1982, or some other form of "default."

In short, the devaluation of the Mexican peso and the events that followed during the weeks of the freely floating peso are consistent with all of the classic elements of a speculative attack in the economics literature, with two interesting twists. First, reserve losses were sterilized at the time of the attack, and this may have inhibited the normal tendency in such circumstances for monetary tightening to stabilize financial markets. Second, there was a reporting lag for Mexican reserves that may have prevented investors from observing the decline in reserves and interest rates from rising to reflect the problems of the exchange rate regime. The devaluation of the Mexican peso, by most accounts, caught many investors by surprise and later precipitated a re-evaluation of economic conditions in Mexico. In such a climate, it is natural for investors to demand a greater interest rate risk premium for holding peso-denominated assets. It is a prediction of models of speculative attacks that such a risk premium would be reflected in the value of the peso once it was allowed to float (Chart I.20).[45]

---

[45]The foreign exchange market in Mexico is dominated by a few big banks. Banamex has about 30 percent of the market with Bancomer and Serfin with about 10 percent each. Nafinsa, the government development bank, is also a large player. Since the market is concentrated in the hands of a few large participants, volume is more than proportionately lower than in U.S.-based dollar markets. The volatility in the foreign exchange market was minimal during most of 1994 and foreign exchange bid-ask spreads were 25–50 basis points. Since December 29, 1994, however, when volatility increased enormously (see Chart I.20) spreads increased by an order of magnitude sometimes reaching 500 basis points.

IV

Policy Responses to Previous Surges of Capital Inflows

Most developing countries that experienced heavy capital inflows in the early 1990s took measures to limit the impact of the inflows on their economies. One approach was simply to allow the exchange rate to respond to the pressures created by the capital inflows, either through a revaluation of the fixed exchange rate or an appreciation of the exchange rate in a flexible exchange rate system. Another approach was to use monetary or fiscal policy to offset the pressure on the currency to appreciate. The motivation for the macroeconomic policy response was either that an appreciation jeopardized the effectiveness of the fixed exchange rate policy or that the inflows and, hence, the pressure on the exchange rate, were only temporary. In either case, appreciation of the currency was considered to have an adverse effect on international competitiveness, and, therefore, it was worthwhile to attempt to offset the pressures on the exchange rate associated with capital inflows. In addition to the reluctance to allow the exchange rate to appreciate, there have been concerns that the volatile nature of these flows could add to the vulnerability of the financial sector, particularly if the banking system plays a dominant role in intermediating these flows.

Monetary Policy: Sterilized Intervention

Sterilized intervention seeks to accomplish two things. First, foreign exchange market intervention aims to reduce pressure on the nominal exchange rate. Second, sterilizing the intervention aims to avoid the monetary expansion that intervention creates (when there are heavy capital inflows).[46] Although sterilization policies have been used extensively in developing countries, relatively little is known about the impact they have had on domestic interest rates, monetary growth, and the volume and composition of capital flows.

The scope for using sterilization policy hinges on the cross-border mobility of capital. Specifically, if capital is perfectly mobile internationally, the scope for sterilization is limited.[47] Although the evidence

is somewhat mixed, it generally suggests that capital mobility is less than perfect in the short run, implying that there is some scope for short-run sterilization policies in developing countries.[48]

Sterilization policies affect capital flows through their impact on domestic interest rates. Domestic interest rates would likely rise if the domestic currency assets investors (including domestic banks) want to hold (i.e., loans, bank CDs, stocks, bonds) are poor substitutes for short-term central bank paper or treasury bills being supplied by the central bank. Another reason why interest rates might rise is that money demand may increase owing to lower inflation or a higher level of income; the latter often accompanies large capital inflows. Hence, there are two disadvantages with using sterilized intervention. First, the rise in domestic interest rates may stimulate further short-term inflows. Second, the wider domestic and foreign interest rate spread entails larger quasi-fiscal costs because the interest rate paid on debt issued by the central bank exceeds earnings by the central bank on international reserve holdings. Overall, the evidence presented in this section suggests that sterilized intervention is not very effective on a sustained basis and may even create problems.

Sterilization policies have taken a variety of forms, and country experiences with these policies can best be understood by examining each of these forms. There are three main types of sterilization policies: open market operations, changes in reserve requirements, and the management of government deposits.[49]

Open Market Operations

Sterilization through open market operations usually takes place through the sale, by the central bank, of either government or central bank securities. The objective of these sales is to remove the liquidity generated by central bank purchases of foreign currency. Mexico, for instance, sterilized inflows by selling government debt, including Cetes and Tesobonos. In

---

[46]Sterilized intervention may also influence the exchange rate by "signaling" policy intentions; see Mussa (1981).

[47]Indeed, the empirical evidence on the effectiveness of sterilized intervention in industrial countries is mixed. Some studies ar-

gue that intervention has not played an important role in currency realignments in recent years. See Obstfeld (1990), Dominguez and Frankel (forthcoming), and Taylor (1995).

[48]See Schadler and others (1993).

[49]See Folkerts-Landau and others (1995).

Box I.3. Sterilization Through Open Market Operations[1]

Chile (1990)

January 5, 1990. Large-scale sterilization efforts begin with the Central Bank increasing its long-term real interest rate on its bonds from 6.9 percent to 9.7 percent and its 90-day paper from 6.8 percent to 8.7 percent.

August 17, 1990. Short-term rates begin a moderate decline (from 8.7 percent to 8.2 percent).

March 18, 1991. Further easing of policy with 90-day paper reaching 5.7 percent and 360-day paper declining from 9.2 percent to 5.9 percent.

April 2, 1992. Further easing with bond rate reducing from 9.7 percent to 6.6 percent.

August 20, 1992. Policy begins to tighten with short-term rate rising to 5.7 percent.

November 2, 1992. Further tightening with short-term rate rising to 6.5 percent and long-term rate rising to 7.7 percent.

September 1993. Yield curve becomes inverted with ten-year bond rate at 6.4 percent and short-term rate remaining at 6.5 percent.

November 2, 1992. Further tightening.

Colombia (1991)

January 1991. Heavy sterilization of inflows begins.

October 1991. Sterilization policies are abandoned.

Indonesia (1990)

February 1991. Significant monetary tightening. Sales of Bank Indonesia certificates (SBIs) increase sharply.

March 1991. State enterprises are instructed to convert Rp 10 trillion in bank deposits to SBIs.

May 1993. Monetary policy begins to ease and sterilization efforts diminish.

Korea (1992)

April 1993. Korea begins to sterilize through auctions of monetary stabilization bonds (MSBs). Previously open market operations consisted of a mandatory allocation scheme whereby the Bank of Korea allocated securities at controlled, below-market interest rates.

Malaysia (1989)

1990. Bank Negara begins to borrow in interbank market.

1992. Heavy open market operations begin as Bank Negara steps up sales of treasury bills and borrows heavily in the interbank market.

February 10, 1993. Bank Negara begins to issue Bank Negara Bills (BNBs), which are similar to Malaysian

government treasury bills. This move is prompted by the need to have an instrument through which to conduct open market operations, since treasury issuance is dwindling in line with the shrinking government deficit. During the first half of 1993, issuance is RM 9,300 billion, and during the second half, issuance tapers off to RM 4,300 billion.

February 16, 1993. Bank Negara sells the first issues of the Malaysia Savings Bond (MSB) for RM 1 billion.

Mexico (1990)

1990–93. Partial sterilization of inflows through sales of government paper, mostly Cetes denominated in domestic currency.

Philippines (1992)

1992. Sterilization efforts intensify through issuance of central bank bills and borrowings under the central bank reverse repurchase facility. Furthermore, in view of the central bank's lack of holding of treasury bills, the government was called to issue government securities and deposit the proceeds with the central bank.

Mid-1993. Sterilization efforts diminish and the government shifts its deposits out of the central bank to commercial banks. More adjustment comes through allowing the nominal exchange rate to appreciate.

Sri Lanka (1990)

1991–mid-1993. Intense sterilization efforts through open market operations of treasury bills.

October 1993. After depleting its holdings of treasury bills, the central bank begins to issue paper to conduct open market operations. Sterilization efforts moderate considerably.

Thailand (1988)

1989–91. Heavy sterilization period. During this period the Bank of Thailand increases its rediscount rate from 8 percent at the end of 1989 to 12 percent at the end of 1990.

Late 1989. The Bank of Thailand reduces commercial banks' access to refinancing facilities. The amount of refinancing is reduced from 100 percent to 50 percent of the face value of qualifying notes.

Mid-1993. Sterilization efforts cease.

Sources: Alfiler (1994); Aziz (1994); Banco Central de Chile, *Memoria Anual* and *Evolución de la Economía*, various issues; Banco de México, *Informe Anual 1993*; Bank Negara Malaysia, *Annual Report*, various issues; Harinowo and Belchere (1994); Hettiarachchi and Herat (1994); Kang (1994); *Laporan Mingguan Weekly Report*, various issues; Nijathaworn and Dejthamrong (1994); and Rodríguez (1991).

[1]The year next to the country name denotes the first year of the surge in inflows.

many countries (Chile, Colombia, Indonesia, Korea, and the Philippines), the central bank issued its own debt to conduct open market operations. In some countries (Malaysia and Sri Lanka), open market operations were initially conducted by selling public sector debt and then subsequently by selling central bank debt, as the central bank depleted its own holdings of government debt (Box I.3).

A key advantage of sterilization via open market operations is that it limits the monetary-credit expansion of intervention without imposing the additional burdens on the banking system that other forms of sterilization impose, such as reserve requirements.[50] Furthermore, sterilization by open market operations may limit the involvement of domestic banks in intermediating inflows. This limit can be desirable when there are concerns about the resiliency of the banking system or when inflows are considered to be temporary. The main disadvantage of sterilization is that it may entail sizable central bank financial losses, even in a relatively short period of time.[51] Sterilization efforts also might increase the domestic-international interest rate spread and thereby attract additional short-term capital.

The intensity of these open-market policies has varied considerably across countries and across time (see Box I.3). One can gauge the intensity of the sterilization efforts by examining the stock of central bank bills relative to the monetary base, or by analyzing changes in net domestic assets. Chile during the first half of 1990, Colombia in most of 1991, Indonesia during 1991–92, Malaysia from mid-1991 through early 1993, and Sri Lanka in 1991–93, attempted to conduct open market operations on a scale that would almost fully sterilize capital inflows.[52] Chile (mid-1991 to the present), Korea, Mexico, the Philippines, and Thailand used sterilized intervention throughout much of the inflow period to sterilize a portion of the inflows. For example, Mexico sterilized about 25 percent of the inflows in 1993, the year when capital inflows peaked.[53]

Reserve Requirements

An increase in reserve requirements can be used to reduce the money multiplier and thereby curtail the monetary expansion associated with central bank intervention in the foreign exchange market. Some countries have simply increased the statutory reserve requirement on all domestic currency deposits. Leading examples of this policy are Costa Rica, Malaysia, and Sri Lanka. For instance, when inflows began to accelerate in Malaysia in 1989, the statutory reserve requirement was 3.5 percent; by early 1994 it had been increased (in multiple steps) to 11.5 percent (Box I.4). Other countries (e.g., Colombia 1991) imposed high marginal reserve requirements. In several countries where banks received foreign currency

deposits—Chile, Peru, and Sri Lanka—reserve requirements on the accounts were either newly imposed or increased. While this latter measure does not affect the narrow-money multiplier, it reduces the expansion of the broader aggregates.

In other countries, the period of heavy capital inflows coincided with reductions in reserve requirements. For example, in April 1989, Mexico eliminated reserve requirements and instituted in their place a 30 percent liquidity ratio that could be held in the form of interest-bearing government paper.[54] Argentina also reduced reserve requirements during the inflow period. In the Philippines, the central bank announced a reduction in reserve requirements in August 1994 with the objective of decreasing domestic interest rates and therefore capital inflows.[55]

Reserve requirements are a tax on the banking system. As banks are likely to pass on all or a part of any tax to its clients, an interesting issue is whether an increase in reserve requirements reduces deposit rates or increases loan rates. Lower domestic deposit rates will discourage capital inflows, but increased loan rates may induce firms to borrow abroad, and therefore further stimulate inflows. The empirical evidence suggests that in most of the cases mentioned above, much of the adjustment took place through higher lending rates.[56] Therefore, just as open market operations may increase interest rates and have the opposite effect of what was intended, increasing reserve requirements may in fact increase borrowing costs and further increase inflows. In addition, if disintermediation is significant, and leads to a shift of funds to the nonbank financial sector (which is not subject to reserve requirements), then this too could mean that a reserve requirement will not have the desired effect.[57]

Management of Public Sector Deposits

Several developing countries and regions (e.g., Indonesia, Malaysia, Taiwan Province of China, and Thailand) sterilized the effects of capital inflows by shifting deposits of the public sector or of pension funds from the banking system to the central bank (Box I.5).[58] During 1991, the Mexican government also placed the proceeds of privatizations in the central bank to assist sterilization efforts.

If government deposits are counted as part of the money stock, then their transfer to the central bank

---

[50]For instance, increased reserve requirements tend to promote disintermediation (see Calvo, Leiderman, and Reinhart (1994)).

[51]Rodríguez (1991) suggests that the central bank losses associated with Colombia's sterilization efforts during 1991 amounted to 0.5–0.7 percent of GDP. Kiguel and Leiderman (1994) indicate that during 1990 to mid-1992 Chile's central bank losses due to sterilization policies were about 1.4 percent of GDP. Gurria (1993) estimates that the quasi-fiscal losses for Mexico were in the 0.2–0.4 percent a year range during 1990–92. Central bank losses in Indonesia, Malaysia, and Sri Lanka have also not been trivial.

[52]In addition to open market operations, Indonesia and Malaysia used other forms of sterilization, which will be discussed later in the section.

[53]Banco de México (1992).

[54]See Coorey (1992).

[55]See Alfiler (1994).

[56]For example, in Malaysia deposit rates rose during the period in which reserve requirements were raised (see Box I.5 and Table I.6); a similar pattern emerges in Sri Lanka (see Hettiarachchi and Herat (1994)).

[57]See Calvo, Leiderman, and Reinhart (1994), and Folkerts-Landau and others (1995).

[58]See Reisen (1993), and Folkerts-Landau and others (1995).

Box I.4. Changes in Reserve Requirements[1]

Chile (1990)

January 1992. Nonrenumerated 20 percent reserve requirement on deposits and loans in foreign currency held by commercial banks. The reserve requirement must be maintained for one year.

May 1992. Reserve requirement on foreign currency deposits and loans held by commercial banks is increased to 30 percent. The requirement is designed to make the tax rate fall as the maturity increases.

A 30 percent marginal reserve requirement on interbank deposits is introduced.

Colombia (1991)

January 1991. Marginal reserve requirement of 100 percent is imposed on all new deposits. The reserves are held as interest-bearing central bank bonds.

September 1991. The marginal reserve requirement is replaced by an increase in reserve requirements on most deposits.

Malaysia (1989)

May 2, 1989. Reserve requirement is increased to 4.5 percent from 3.5 percent for commercial banks and 3.0 percent for finance companies.

October 16, 1989. Reserve requirement is increased from 4.5 percent to 5.5 percent.

January 16, 1990. Reserve requirement is increased from 5.5 percent to 6.5 percent.

August 16, 1991. Reserve requirement is increased from 6.5 percent to 7.5 percent.

September 16, 1991. All outstanding ringgit received through swap transactions with nonresidents, including offshore banks, is to be included in the eligible liabilities base and be subject to the statutory reserve requirements.

May 2, 1992. Reserve requirement is increased from 7.5 percent to 8.5 percent.

January 3, 1994. Reserve requirement is increased from 8.5 percent to 9.5 percent.

The reserve requirement is extended to cover foreign currency deposits and transactions (such as foreign currency borrowing from foreign banking institutions and interbank borrowing). Previously it had only applied to ringgit-denominated transactions.

1994. Reserve requirement is increased in two steps to 11.5 percent.

Mexico (1990)

April 1992. A compulsory liquidity coefficient for dollar liabilities is set at 15 percent. This coefficient must be invested in liquid securities denominated in the same currency.

Philippines (1992)

August 15, 1994. The reserve requirement is reduced from 19 percent to 17 percent (excluding reserves held in the form of government securities) with the objective of inducing a decline in domestic interest rates.

Sri Lanka (1990)

November 1, 1991. Reserve requirement is raised to 13 percent.

January 24, 1992. Reserve requirement is raised to 14 percent from 13 percent.

September 4, 1992. Reserve requirement is extended to include foreign currency deposits.

September 24, 1992. Reserve requirement is lowered back to 13 percent.

January 29, 1993. Reserve requirement is raised to 13.5 percent.

April 16, 1993. Reserve requirement is increased to 14 percent.

May 21, 1993. Reserve requirement is raised to 15 percent.

August 1993. Reserve requirement on foreign currency deposits is increased to 15 percent.

Sources: Aziz (1994); Banco Central de Chile, *Memoria Anual* and *Evolución de la Economía*, various issues; Bank Negara Malaysia, *Annual Report*, various issues; Gurria (1993); Hettiarachchi and Herat (1994); and Rodríguez (1991).

---

[1]The year next to the country name denotes the first year of the surge in inflows.

---

works in the same way as an increase in reserve requirements (the reserve requirement on those deposits is effectively increased to 100 percent). If the deposits are not counted as part of the money stock, then the shift is more akin to a liquidity-draining, open market operation; the key difference is that the central bank may not have to pay a market rate of interest on its deposits as it would on its sterilization bonds.

This type of sterilization operation has several advantages. It does not act like a tax on the banking system, and it does not appear to increase short-term interest rates as much as sales of sterilization bonds. Further, if the deposits are not remunerated, then there are no quasi-fiscal costs associated with sterilization operations; if they are remunerated at below-market interest rates, there is a quasi-fiscal cost, but it is below the cost of sterilization via open market operations.[59]

---

[59]Quasi-fiscal costs are reduced or eliminated by transferring these costs to the government (i.e., by making them explicit fiscal costs).

Box I.5. Sterilization Through Management of Government Funds[1]

Malaysia (1989)

April 1990. The Money Market Operations (MMO) account of the accountant general maintained at Bank Negara is reactivated. Government deposits that are placed with the banking system maturing that year (about RM 3.7 billion) have been withdrawn from the system and are deposited in the MMO account.

1992–94. Transfer of government deposits and Employee Provident Fund (EPF) deposits to Bank Negara.

Philippines (1992 and 1994)

The national government issues securities and deposits proceeds with the Central Bank.

Singapore

Savings of Central Provident Fund (CPF) are heavily invested in government bonds.

Taiwan Province of China

Postal savings are transferred from the domestic banks to the central bank.

Thailand (1988)

1987–mid-1992. Government deposits held at the Bank of Thailand increased from 25 percent of total deposits at the end of 1987 to 82 percent in mid-1992.

—————

Sources: Aziz (1994); Bank Negara Malaysia, *Annual Report*, various issues; and Folkerts-Landau and others (1995).

[1]The year next to the country name denotes the first year of the surge in inflows.

There are some drawbacks to the shifting of public sector deposits, however. Large and unpredictable changes in bank deposits make it difficult for banks to manage their cash positions. For example, when Indonesia forced state enterprises to move their deposits out of the state banks, these banks not only lost liquidity but they also had to reduce their amount of loans outstanding. In addition, some of the deposits are not strictly public sector deposits (e.g., Malaysia's Employee Provident Fund (EPF) or Singapore's Central Provident Fund (CPF)). In these cases, the cost of shifting deposits may be borne by those who contribute to the fund, depending on whether payouts from the funds are tied to the return on the funds. Finally, the shifting of deposits may be limited in scope by the availability of eligible funds. For example, government deposits held at the Bank of Thailand increased from 25 percent of total government deposits at the end of 1987 to a peak of 82 percent in mid-1992. In this case, the scope for further ster-

ilization operations via deposit shifting was clearly limited.

Effects on Interest Rates and Capital Flows

This section documents some of the experiences with sterilization efforts discussed above in order to gauge the macroeconomic effects of these policies. The episodes examined include Chile during the first half of 1990, Colombia in most of 1991, Indonesia during 1991–92, and Malaysia from mid-1991 through early 1993.

Several conclusions can be drawn from these case studies. First, there is a particularly marked accumulation of international reserves, which points to significant central bank intervention (Chart I.21). Second, despite heavy foreign exchange market intervention by central banks, in all of these countries either the rate of devaluation slows down, or there is a revaluation (Malaysia) (see Chart I.22). Although this may seem puzzling in light of the objectives of intervention, these two observations together highlight the limitations of sterilized intervention in the presence of very large capital inflows.

A third conclusion is that the magnitude of central bank note issuance (in both absolute terms and relative to the monetary base) has been dramatic over a relatively short period of time in all countries; the scale of open market operations was substantial. In Colombia, the ratio of open market paper to the monetary base increased from less than 30 percent in late 1990 to over 80 percent by October 1991. In Chile, this ratio increased by more than 100 percent in a period of six months. In Indonesia, there was a similar surge in outstanding Bank Indonesia certificates (see Chart I.23).

In Malaysia, the central bank sold treasury bills and Bank Negara bills (BNB) and it borrowed heavily in the interbank market. A more comprehensive indicator of the sterilization effort is, therefore, required. Chart I.23 presents a broad measure of central bank liquidity operations. In 1990, during the first year of heavy inflows, Bank Negara increased liquidity by RM 6.5 billion; by 1993, the last year of the heavy sterilization effort (capital controls were imposed at the beginning of 1994), Bank Negara was draining liquidity at a rate of RM 40.3 billion a year.

A fourth general conclusion from these four episodes is that domestic short-term interest rates increased when the sterilization efforts began (Table I.6). Short-term interest rates also increased during sterilization efforts in Korea (1988–89), Sri Lanka (1992–93), and the Philippines (1992–93).[60]

—————

[60]See Hettiarachchi and Herat (1994) for Sri Lanka, and Alfiler (1994) for the Philippines. The Colombian experience is detailed in Rodríguez (1991). For a comprehensive study of the Indonesian case see Harinowo and Belchere (1994). For the Malaysian experience see Aziz (1994).

Chart I.21. Sterilization Policies and International Reserves
(In billions of U.S. dollars)

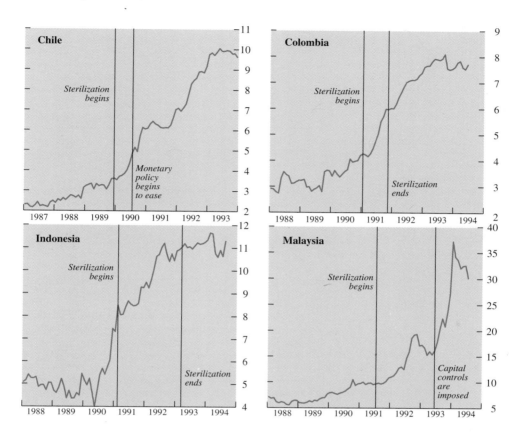

Source: International Monetary Fund, *International Financial Statistics.*

In all of these countries, interest rates increased during sterilization operations despite heavy capital inflows. Furthermore, in several of these countries (including Chile and Colombia), the country risk premiums appear to have declined during these episodes, which should have contributed to the downward pressure on domestic interest rates.[61]

The evidence shows that the rise in interest rates often was pronounced and, given the reduced rate of devaluation (or in the case of Malaysia an appreciation), the rise in ex post dollar interest rates was even greater (see Table I.6). Further, interest rates fell when sterilization policies were abandoned. One explanation for this is that higher capital inflows were due to an increased demand for corporate securities and direct investment but not for short-term government paper. That is, to entice investors to hold more

government securities, interest rates had to increase. Further, capital inflows often coincided with strong economic activity and, therefore, possibly an increase in money demand. The result of sterilization operations may have been that there was an unintended tightening of monetary policy.

A fifth conclusion is that ex post interest rate spreads (in dollars) were large during the period of sterilization. This suggests that sterilization policies do have an impact, at least in the short run, on how quickly domestic interest rates converge to international levels.[62] In all of the countries considered, domestic short-term interest rate spreads remained high relative to those countries (e.g., Argentina) that did not undertake any form of sterilization (Chart I.24). Although sterilization policies appear to have slowed the convergence of domestic interest rates to

---

[61]An indication of the evolution of country risk is given by the behavior of secondary market prices for loans, which were increasing sharply during these episodes (see Calvo, Leiderman, and Reinhart (1993)).

[62]Frankel (1994b), for instance, has suggested that expected devaluation can fully account for observed interest differentials. However, his result would not be inconsistent with a steady-state offset coefficient of unity.

Chart I.22. Sterilization Policies and Exchange Rates
(Three-month percent change, annualized)

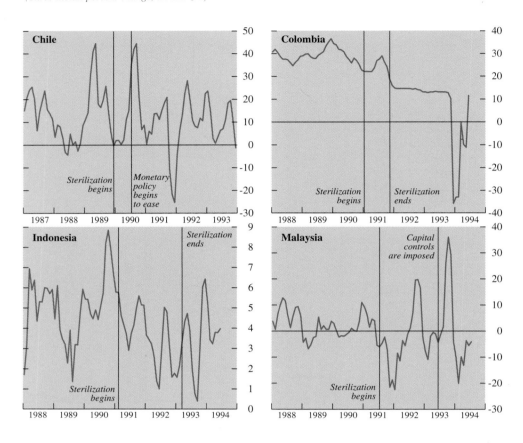

Source: International Monetary Fund, *International Financial Statistics.*

international levels, the ability to affect domestic interest rates and control the money supply appears to have eroded over time.[63] In all four countries considered, sterilization policies were either abandoned altogether, scaled back, or complemented by capital controls, because the high domestic interest rates were attracting more inflows.

The effect of sterilization policies on the size and composition of capital flows is illustrated in Chart I.25.[64] Sterilization policies in several of the rapidly growing economies in Southeast Asia in the late 1980s coincided with rising interest differentials and large inflows of short-term capital. In Thailand, the interest rate differential narrowed when sterilization efforts were scaled back and the exchange rate was allowed to appreciate. Short-term inflows subsequently slowed in 1991–92.[65] In Indonesia, although the interest rate differential widened further in 1991–92, short-term capital inflows declined in part owing to steps taken by the government to limit short-term foreign borrowing by public sector enterprises and new limits imposed on the open foreign currency positions of commercial banks. In Malaysia, short-term inflows continued to rise in 1991–92 as the interest differential widened further. After 1991, the authorities reduced intervention and allowed the exchange rate to appreciate. Despite a narrowing of the differential in 1993, short-term inflows

[63]This is consistent with the findings of Schadler and others (1993). See Alfiler (1994), Aziz (1994), Harinowo and Belchere (1994), Hettiarachchi and Herat (1994), and Rodríguez (1991).

[64]The charts show for each country (Argentina, Chile, Indonesia, Malaysia, and Thailand) the composition of capital flows, split between total and short-term flows; differentials between interest rates on domestic deposits and U.S. Treasury bills, adjusted for actual exchange rate changes; and international reserves and exchange rates. A widening of interest rate differentials in conjunction with rising international reserves and a relatively constant exchange rate would suggest that the authorities were at least partially sterilizing capital inflows.

[65]The sharp rise in short-term flows in 1993 primarily reflected a reclassification of foreign loans from long-term to short-term flows when they were rebooked in the Bangkok International Banking Facility after the center was opened.

Chart I.23. Indicators of Sterilization Efforts

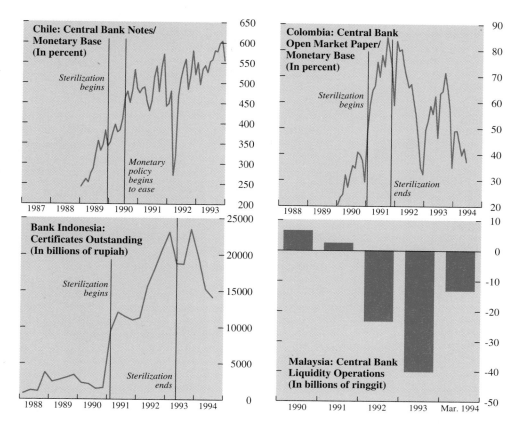

Sources: Banco Central de Chile; Banco de la República, Colombia; Bank Indonesia; and Bank Negara Malaysia.

rose, and the authorities imposed capital controls in early 1994. In Chile (Chart I.25), short-term inflows moved closely with the interest differential throughout 1989–93.[66]

In all of the countries that pursued sterilization policies, short-term capital flows rose at least initially during the period of sterilization. There does not appear, however, to have been any pronounced or sustained shift in the composition of capital inflows as a result of such intervention, owing possibly to the fact that the periods of sterilization were relatively brief or that other mitigating factors (principally those influencing foreign direct investment behavior) were present.

In comparison with the experiences of countries that pursued sterilization policies, Argentina provides an interesting comparison because it did not sterilize over the period 1989–92 (Chart I.25). In this case, there was a change from sizable outflows in 1989 to significant inflows in 1992 following the introduction of the currency board—or "Convertibility Plan"—in April 1991. In the absence of sterilization policies, interest rates converged to world levels and short-term capital inflows leveled off by 1993.

Exchange Rate Policy and Large Capital Flows

There are several advantages to allowing the nominal exchange rate to appreciate when there are heavy capital inflows.[67] First, an appreciation tends to insulate the domestic money supply from the expansionary effects of capital inflows. This advantage may be particularly desirable if the inflows are perceived to be easily reversible, banking supervision is weak, or there are inefficiencies in pricing risk. Second, if economic "fundamentals" warrant a real exchange rate

---

[66]Note that Chile introduced a tax on short-term flows in mid-1991. This makes it difficult to distinguish whether short-term flows declined during that period because of the easing in monetary policy, the introduction of new capital controls, or both.

[67]See Calvo, Leiderman, and Reinhart (1994).

Table I.6. Interest Rates and Sterilization Policies[1]

(In percent, annualized rates)

	In Domestic Currency			Converted into U.S. dollars[1]		
Chile	Loans 30–89 days	Deposits 30–89 days		Loans 30–89 days	Deposits 30–89 days	
Pre-inflow: 1988:1–1989:12	28.54	21.41		16.83	10.39	
Capital inflows and heavy sterilization: 1990:1–1990:7	46.58	37.80		35.16	27.01	
Capital inflows and partial sterilization: 1990:7–1994:5	27.93	21.76		18.91	13.17	
Colombia	Prime loans	Deposits 90-day	Central bank paper	Prime loans	Deposits 90-day	Central bank paper
Pre-inflow: 1989:1–1990:12	44.14	34.41	33.79	3.74	3.29	11.25
Capital inflows and heavy sterilization: 1991:1–1991:11	47.16	36.61	42.08	10.31	14.70	18.85
Capital inflows and moderate sterilization: 1991:12–1993:12	36.95	26.20	24.31	11.08	9.42	20.53
Indonesia	Prime loans	Deposits 90-day		Prime loans	Deposits 90-day	
Early stages of inflow: 1989–1990:12	22.54	17.99		17.03	13.24	
Capital inflows and heavy sterilization: 1991–1992:12	25.27	21.88		20.84	17.58	
Capital inflows and moderate sterilization: 1993:1–1994:6	19.22	13.66		15.30	9.93	
Malaysia	Deposits			Deposits		
Early stages of inflow: 1989:1–1991:6	6.21			5.52		
Capital inflows and heavy sterilization: 1991:7–1993:6	7.92			13.07		
Capital inflows, moderate sterilization, and heavy foreign exchange intervention: 1993:7–1993:12	6.74			−4.87		
Capital controls and currency appreciation: 1994:1–1994:6	5.30			18.19		

Sources: Bloomberg Financial Markets; International Monetary Fund, *International Financial Statistics*; and various central bank bulletins.

[1]The following formula is used to convert the domestic interest rate into U.S. dollars: $\dfrac{(1+i)_t e_t}{e_{t+3}}$ where e_t is the spot exchange rate and i_t is the nominal interest rate.

appreciation, the adjustment comes via the exchange rate and not via higher inflation. Third, but related to the previous point, because of a pass-through from the exchange rate to domestic prices, an appreciation may help reduce inflation.

Revaluation

If the exchange rate is flexible, an appreciation of the nominal exchange rate in response to capital inflows can occur without any policy action. In contrast, if the exchange rate is set by the authorities (i.e., peg, crawling peg, and narrow band), then a realignment decision is the event that triggers an appreciation. Revaluations in fact have been relatively uncommon; sterilized intervention has been the preferred

course of action. Chile and Colombia are the two countries of those discussed above in which revaluations have been used. But even in these countries, the realignments were initiated only after it became clear that the inflows were larger than first anticipated. Between April 1991 and June 1991, Chile's exchange rate band was revalued by a cumulative 3.4 percent (Box I.6). Larger revaluations followed in January 1992 (5 percent) and November 1994 (9.5 percent) because the exchange rate persistently stuck to the bottom of the band.[68] In Colombia— where a crawling peg system had been in place for about twenty-five years[69] —the exchange rate was

---

[68]See Budnevich and Cifuentes (1993).
[69]See Carrasquilla (1995).

Chart I.24. Deposit Rate Spreads[1]

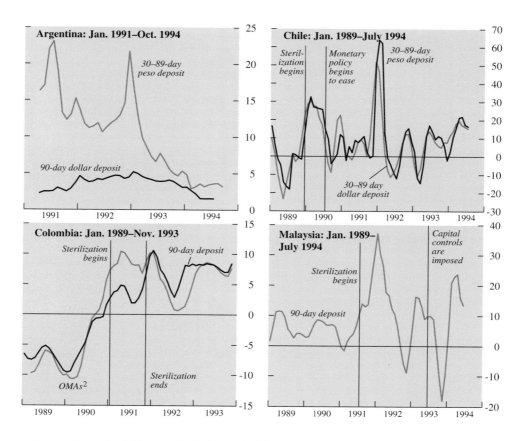

Sources: International Monetary Fund, *International Financial Statistics;* Reuters; and various central bank bulletins.

[1]The spreads are defined as the domestic interest rates converted into U.S. dollars minus the dollar-LIBOR rate of comparable maturity.

[2]OMA refers to central bank open market paper.

revalued by 2.6 percent in June 1991. More substantial realignments occurred in 1994 (5 percent and 7 percent in January and December, respectively), in the context of a newly established exchange-rate band.

Greater Exchange Rate Flexibility

Rather than simply revaluing the exchange rate in response to capital inflows, there are reasons why it is beneficial to allow the exchange rate to fluctuate freely. One reason is that exchange rate flexibility introduces uncertainty that could discourage some inflows, especially speculative (easily reversible) inflows. Exchange rate uncertainty creates a bias toward domestic assets, dampens the sensitivity of the current account to most types of shocks, and reduces net capital flows.[70] Indeed, greater exchange rate

uncertainty has the same effect as a Tobin-type transaction tax.[71] Furthermore, in the event of capital outflows, exchange rate flexibility takes pressure off foreign exchange reserves to accommodate the outflows. Finally, exchange rate flexibility grants the monetary authorities a greater degree of independence and permits them to exercise more control over monetary aggregates.

A main disadvantage of exchange rate flexibility is, however, that heavy capital flows could induce abrupt and large movements in the real exchange rate. In turn, this could impose a substantial adjustment burden on the economy. Concern with strategic sectors of the economy (e.g., the nontraditional export sector) has indeed been a key motivation in many developing countries for not allowing much

---

[70]See Bacchetta and Van Wincoop (1994).

[71]See background paper "Controls on Capital Flows: Experience with Quantitative Measures and Capital Flow Taxation," pp. 95–108.

Chart I.25. Capital Flows and Interest Rate Differentials of Selected Countries

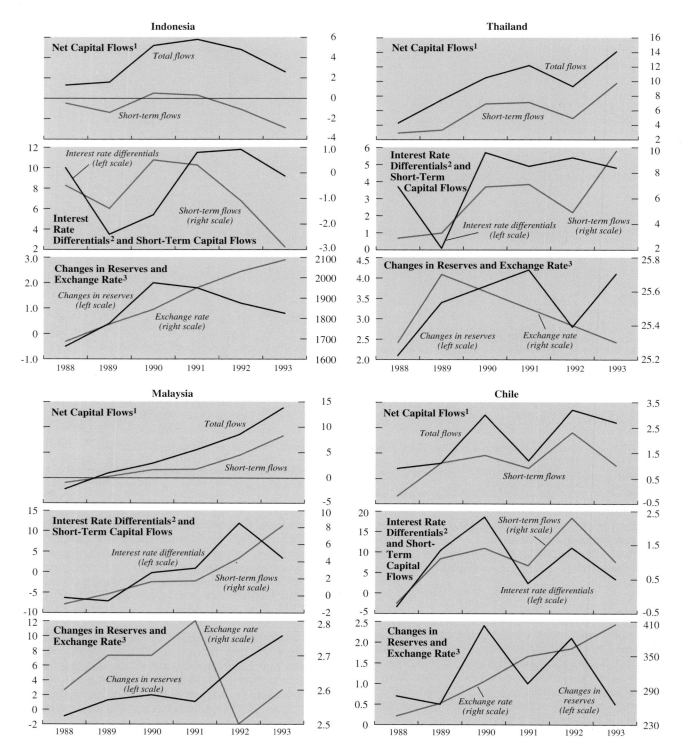

Chart I.25 (concluded)

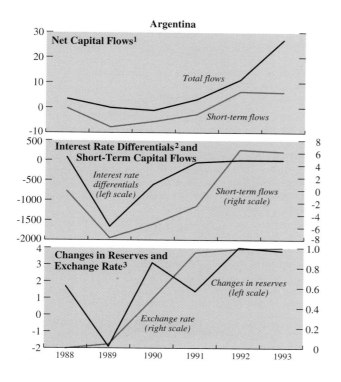

Argentina

Sources: International Monetary Fund, *Balance of Payments Statistics* and *International Financial Statistics.*

[1]In billions of U.S. dollars; short-term capital flows include net errors and omissions.

[2]In percentage points, measured as domestic deposit rates adjusted for actual exchange rate changes minus the three-month U.S. Treasury bill rate.

[3]Reserves are in billions of U.S. dollars; the exchange rate is expressed in units of domestic currency per U.S. dollar.

flexibility in the nominal exchange rate.[72] Moreover, empirical evidence does suggest that greater real exchange rate volatility may have negative effects on tradable goods sectors.[73] One explanation for this finding is that there are incomplete markets to hedge exchange rate fluctuations. Another disadvantage of greater exchange rate flexibility is that it may also deter medium-term capital flows, such as foreign direct investment, in addition to deterring the growth of nontraditional exports.

In practice, there is a wide variation in the degree of exchange rate flexibility across capital importing countries. Although some countries (such as Peru and the Philippines) have a float, the common ground is

---

that all central banks intervene in the foreign exchange market to some degree, and no country has operated a pure float. Among the Asian countries, Indonesia widened its intervention band twice in 1994 (Box I.7) and Malaysia and the Philippines have allowed greater variability of the exchange rate, particularly since 1992 (Table I.7). The Korean authorities have stated publicly their intention to further widen the margins for daily exchange rate fluctuations, with the aim of moving toward a free float in two to three years.[74] Among the Western Hemisphere countries, Chile, Mexico, and, more recently, Colombia, have permitted some exchange rate flexibility because of their operation of exchange rate bands. Both Chile and Mexico widened their bands (Box I.7), and in Chile the exchange rate has been allowed to fluctuate considerably within the band.[75]

Despite the fact that many countries have implemented wider bands and therefore presumably greater exchange rate flexibility, the variance of monthly exchange rates has shown little change (see Table I.7). The variance of monthly exchange rates in Indonesia, for example, did not change after the band was widened twice in 1994. Similarly, during 1992 and 1993, and most of 1994, the variance of the Mexican peso was small prior to the exchange market turbulence in December 1994—about the same as Argentina's exchange rate variability under the Convertibility Plan. In contrast, there was a marked

---

[72]Krugman (1987) points out that, if the inflows are temporary and if there are hysteresis effects on exports from the real exchange rate appreciation, then there may be reasons for avoiding or dampening the real exchange rate adjustment.

[73]See, for instance, Grobar (1993).

[74]In 1993 and 1994, however, Korea's exchange rate policy has been characterized by exchange rate intervention in response to a sizable increase in capital inflows.

[75]On various aspects of exchange rate bands in Chile and Mexico, see Helpman, Leiderman, and Bufman (1995).

Box I.7. Increasing Exchange Rate Flexibility[1]

Chile (1990)

January 1992. The central parity is revalued by 5 percent, and the exchange rate band is widened from 10 percent to 20 percent, 10 percent on each side.

July 1992. The exchange rate ceases to be pegged exclusively to the dollar, and a peg to a basket of currencies (50 percent in dollars, 30 percent in deutsche mark, and 20 percent in Japanese yen) is introduced.

November 30, 1994. The central parity is revalued by 9.5 percent. The weights of the currency basket are changed to 40 percent in dollars, 35 percent in deutsche mark, and 25 percent in Japanese yen.

Colombia (1991)

January 25, 1994. An exchange rate band is introduced. The width of the band is 15 percent, and the rate at which the band is to be devalued is equal to 11 percent a year.

Indonesia (1990)

January 1994. Intervention band is widened from Rp 10 to Rp 20.

August 1994. Intervention band is widened from Rp 20 to Rp 30.

Malaysia (1989)

Mid-1991. Greater degree of flotation allowed.

Mexico (1990)

November 11, 1991. An exchange rate band is introduced. The upper limit of the band was depreciated at the rate of 20 cents a day, and the floor remained fixed. Its total width increased from 1.2 percent in November 1991 to 4.3 percent in December 1992.

October 1992. The rate of crawl of the upper limit is increased to 40 cents a day. The band width reaches 8.7 percent by the end of 1993.

Philippines (1992)

Mid-1992. Foreign exchange intervention is reduced, allowing for a nominal appreciation of the peso.

Sources: Alfiler (1994); Aziz (1994); Carrasquilla (1995); Gurria (1993); Harinowo and Belchere (1994); Helpman, Leiderman, and Bufman (1995); and Schadler and others (1993).

---

[1]The year next to the country name denotes the first year of the surge in inflows.

---

jump in the variance of the exchange rate in Colombia after the introduction of the band in January 1994 and a more moderate increase in exchange rate variability in Malaysia.

It is difficult to determine the impact of greater exchange rate variability on short-term capital flows even in the cases where the variance changed considerably. In Chile, where short-term flows as a proportion of total flows have declined, there were other impediments to short-term inflows (i.e., capital controls).[76] In Colombia, the composition of flows

---

[76]See background paper "Controls on Capital Flows: Experience with Quantitative Measures and Capital Flow Taxation," pp. 95–108.

displays a pattern similar to Chile's, but the introduction of the band coincided with the imposition of a tax on short-term borrowing. Finally, in Malaysia, the effects of increased exchange rate variability may have been offset by the effects of tight monetary policy.

Fiscal Policies

A different policy reaction to capital inflows is to tighten fiscal policy. In practice, this could be accomplished by either reducing expenditure, increasing taxes, or both (Box I.8). This approach uses fiscal restraint so as to lower aggregate demand and curb the potentially inflationary impact of capital in-

Table I.7. Exchange Rate Variability, 1988–94[1]

(Variance of monthly exchange rate changes, in percent)

	Argentina (1991)	Chile (1990)	Colombia (1991)	Indonesia (1990)	Malaysia (1990)	Mexico (1989)	Philippines (1992)	Thailand (1988)
1988	54.18	0.91	0.05	0.07	0.65	0.56	0.21	0.40
1989	12,788.58	2.66	0.01	0.07	0.80	0.01	0.16	0.41
1990	3,768.23	2.22	0.07	0.03	0.17	0.07	6.16	0.27
1991	358.61[2]	1.22	0.05	0.02	0.76	0.02	0.58	0.37
1992	0.06	5.21	0.01	0.03	2.69	0.40	12.38	2.43
1993	0.07	0.76	0.01	0.02	2.95	0.09	6.43	0.15
1994	0.01	0.75	13.95	0.02	2.63	3.61	2.69	0.14

Source: International Monetary Fund, *International Financial Statistics.*
[1]The years in parentheses indicate the year in which capital inflows began.
[2]Convertibility Plan began in April 1991.

Box I.8. Fiscal Austerity Measures[1]

Chile (1990)

1990–94. Moderation of expenditure. Nonfinancial public sector surplus averages 2.5 percent during this period.

Mid-1990. An increase in the value-added tax rate to 18 percent. An increase in the corporate tax rate to 15 percent, and an increase in the progressiveness of the personal income tax.

Malaysia (1989)

1992–93. Fiscal consolidation. Real public consumption growth reduces significantly (0.4 percent in 1992). Public sector deficit is reduced to about 1.5 percent of GDP.

Thailand (1988)

1988–91. Moderation of government expenditure. Government budgetary balance (in percent of GDP) swings from a deficit of 1.4 percent to a surplus of 4.9 percent in 1991.

1992. Introduction of a value-added tax.

Sources: Nijathaworn and Dejthamrong (1994); Schadler and others (1993); and IMF staff estimates.

[1]The year next to the country name denotes the first year of the surge in inflows.

---

flows. The manner in which the fiscal gap is closed is likely to determine the macroeconomic consequences of the fiscal policy response. For instance, if government expenditure is more heavily weighted toward nontraded goods than is private expenditure, then a cut in government spending may be more effective than increased taxation for alleviating pressure on the real exchange rate. Furthermore, if consumer credit is readily available—as it typically is during periods of heavy capital inflows—this could offset the reduction in disposable income associated with increased taxation, especially if the tax is perceived as temporary.

A contraction in government expenditure is usually a sensitive political issue and typically cannot be undertaken on short notice. Such delays increase the risk that, ex post, the policy is in fact procyclical. One more drawback is that fiscal policy is usually set on the basis of medium- or long-term considerations (e.g., infrastructure and social services), rather than in response to what may turn out to be short-term fluctuations in international capital movements.[77] Finally, there are also important asymmetries in using fiscal policy to deal with fluctuations in international capital flows. In particular, while a fiscal tightening has sometimes been suggested as a means of dealing

with inflows, a loosening of fiscal policy would not seem to be a prudent method to deal with outflows. But despite these drawbacks to using fiscal policy in reaction to heavy capital flows, the contribution of fiscal consolidation to the prevention of a liquidity crisis may be substantial. Also, the consequent lowering of interest rates may have a stabilizing effect on capital flows.

The clearest example of fiscal restraint as a central policy response to capital inflows occurred in Thailand during 1988–91.[78] A combination of moderation of government expenditure and a strong cyclical improvement in revenues (real GDP growth averaged 11.3 percent during 1988–91) resulted in changing the government's budgetary balance (as a percent of GDP) from a deficit of 1.4 percent to a surplus of 4.9 percent over the period. However, with significant infrastructure needs, the cost of reductions in government expenditures in Thailand in order to deal with capital inflows could be significant.

Chile, from mid-1990 to the present, has also initiated fiscal restraint through an increase in the value-added tax and corporate taxes in conjunction with expenditure restraint. By substantially limiting public consumption, Malaysia also began to downsize its public sector in 1992. In that year, the overall public sector deficit shrank by about 1 percent of GDP to around 1.5 percent of GDP. However, for most of the other capital importing countries, fiscal policy has not been a key tool in responding to rising capital inflows. Indeed, many of the fiscal austerity measures that were undertaken in a number of developing countries (e.g., Argentina, Mexico, and Sri Lanka) in the early 1990s were part of domestic inflation stabilization plans, privatization efforts, and adjustments associated with IMF programs and not a response to rising capital inflows per se.

Policy Mix

A review of the policy response to surges in capital inflows illustrates how individual policies interact to either magnify or reduce the volume of inflows, affect their composition, or alter their macroeconomic consequences. For example, a combination of little or no short-term exchange rate uncertainty (as is the case when there is an implicit or explicit peg), sterilized intervention (which tends to prevent domestic short-term interest rates from converging toward international levels), and no capital controls, is likely to maximize the volume of short-term capital inflows a country receives. This policy mix in conjunction with a substantial stock of government debt characterizes reasonably well the Mexican experience during 1990–93 (Table I.8). The pairing of little or no short-term

---

[77]See Bercuson and Koenig (1993).

[78]See also Schadler and others (1993) and Nijathaworn and Dejthamrong (1994).

Table I.8. Policy Mix in Response to Capital Inflows

Country	Fiscal Adjustment	Revaluation	Increased Exchange Rate Variability	Sterilized Intervention	Controls on Capital Inflows	Liberalization of Capital Outflows	Trade Liberalization Accelerated
Argentina	No[1]	No	No	No	No	No	No
Chile	Yes	Yes	Yes	Yes	Yes	Yes	No
Colombia	No	Yes	Yes	Yes	Yes	Yes	Yes
Indonesia	No	No	No[2]	Yes	Yes	No	No
Malaysia	Yes	No	Yes	Yes	Yes	Yes	Yes
Mexico	No[1]	No	No[2]	Yes	No[4]	Yes	Yes
Philippines	No	No	Yes[3]	Yes	No	Yes	No
Sri Lanka	No[1]	No	No[3]	Yes	No	No	Yes
Thailand	Yes	No	No	Yes	No	Yes	Yes

Sources: Boxes I.3–I.13.

[1]Fiscal consolidation (including privatization efforts) was a part of the inflation stabilization program and not a response to the rise in capital inflows per se. The Convertibility Plan in Argentina began in April 1991, while the Mexican plan predates the surge in inflows and began in December 1987.

[2]Despite announcements of broader intervention bands, exchange rate variability does not change appreciably.

[3]The Philippines and Sri Lanka already had a relatively flexible exchange rate system at the start of the inflow episode.

[4]Caps on foreign currency liabilities of banks are not binding until 1994 (see the background paper "Controls on Capital Flows: Experience with Quantitative Measures and Capital Flow Taxation," pp. 95–108).

exchange rate risk with relatively high domestic interest rates favors the short-term investor; the long-term investor always bears some exchange rate risk, even if the currency is not floating. Furthermore, longer-term investments (such as foreign direct investment) tend to be less interest sensitive. It would not be surprising, therefore, to find that this policy mix over the long run would skew the composition of inflows toward short maturities.

It is also possible that sterilized intervention in conjunction with controls on inflows and large government borrowing requirements will undermine the "individual effectiveness" of these policies. The comparatively high interest rate differentials that usually accompany sterilized intervention and large government borrowing may act as an inducement to circumvent the capital controls (i.e., firms and banks may find ways of borrowing offshore). To the extent that they are successful in dodging controls, this tends to offset some of the contractionary effects of the sterilization efforts. Similarly, liberalizing controls on outflows in order to reduce net capital inflows may backfire if domestic interest rates are high relative to international levels, or if it is interpreted as a positive signal of the future policy environment. Indeed, several countries (Chile, Malaysia, and Thailand) liberalized outflows while at the same time engaging in substantive sterilization efforts (see Table I.8).

V

Controls on Capital Flows: Experience with Quantitative Measures and Capital Flow Taxation

The measures discussed in the previous section are used in most capital importing countries to reduce the effect of capital flows on the exchange rate. A complementary approach taken in the past has been to employ measures that discourage capital inflows (and outflows) or seek to influence their character. These measures are often generically referred to as "capital controls." In fact, such measures range from prudential controls on the banking system, to market-based measures, all the way to quantitative controls on inflows and outflows. In practice, the usefulness of capital controls hinges on whether they are effective, that is, on whether they can be easily circumvented. This is a difficult question to answer because whether or not they are circumvented in practice depends on the types of controls as well as the incentives to evade them. The analysis presented here suggests that capital controls, if effective at all, appear to be most effective in the short term and are more effective on inflows than on outflows. This second implication is attributable to the fact that the incentives to evade controls on outflows are generally much greater than for controls on inflows.

The next section summarizes some of the benefits and costs of capital inflows, and reviews the measures taken in this direction during the 1990s by countries experiencing heavy capital inflows. Recent experiences with liberalizing controls on capital outflows as a measure to limit the impact of heavy inflows is also reviewed. The discussion then turns to capital outflows, and addresses the general policy issues regarding the use of controls on capital outflows during a crisis as well as reviews the experiences of selected countries. The subsequent section discusses some of the issues associated with the speed and sequencing of financial-sector and capital-account liberalization. The final section reviews some of the lessons from experiences with capital controls.

Measures to Influence Capital Inflows

Pros and Cons

Greater capital market integration and the associated capital flows can improve economic growth and macroeconomic performance. At the same time, however, capital flows can increase the potential costs of inappropriate domestic policies. Moreover, large capital inflows can pose problems of their own, including

an overheated economy, an appreciation of the real exchange rate, and an unsustainable current account deficit. On the other hand, large outflows could produce a decline in investment as well as a general recession. Large flows may also complicate the conduct of monetary policy: inflows may cause monetary and credit expansions that conflict with desired inflation objectives, and outflows may lead to high interest rates, placing additional strains on the banking sector. In the past, countries have attempted to avoid the instability associated with large inflows or outflows by first limiting the size of inflows, either through quantitative controls, explicit taxes (e.g., a transactions tax), or implicit taxes (e.g., a non-interest-bearing reserve requirement on foreign borrowing). However, recourse to restricting inflows or outflows with capital controls should be considered within the context of other policies.[79]

If inflows are perceived as temporary, then the motive to implement measures to reduce them may be especially strong.[80] For instance, the temporary real exchange rate appreciation that often accompanies a rise in capital inflows may have adverse long-lived effects on exports (so-called hysteresis). A further motive for restricting inflows exists when the inflows are purely speculative.[81]

With regard to reducing speculative inflows, one proposal that has acquired some recent popularity is the worldwide implementation of a tax on foreign exchange trading or on short-term, cross-border bank loans.[82] The benefits include increased domestic monetary policy autonomy, increased costs of speculative attacks on fixed exchange rate regimes and thus a reduced likelihood of an attack, and a shift in emphasis to longer-term investments rather than short-term speculative opportunities. This pro-

---

[79]It is common to label controls or restrictions on cross-border capital flows as controls on either inflows or outflows; this convention is used here. However, many types of controls influence both inflows and outflows. For example, the suspension of convertibility of a currency to curtail outflows will make the country less attractive to foreign investors and reduce inflows. Similarly, a liberalization of outflows might increase foreign investor confidence and therefore result in higher net inflows. See Bartolini and Drazen (1994) and Labán and Larraín (1994).

[80]See Krugman (1987).

[81]See Summers (1988).

[82]See Eichengreen, Tobin, and Wyplosz (1995).

posal is a modern vintage of James Tobin's proposal to tax foreign exchange transactions to throw sand in the wheels of international finance. Although there are a number of proposals of this sort that differ by the tax base or tax rate, they all aim to increase the cost of establishing short positions in foreign currencies, and therefore the cost of speculative activities. Some countries that have recently implemented these types of controls are discussed below.

There are a number of practical problems with a "Tobin tax" that may significantly limit its appeal.[83] First, to be effective it would probably need to be adopted worldwide and uniformly; if it were adopted by just the Group of Ten countries, say, it would likely cause the taxed activities to shift to untaxed countries. Second, the specific proposal to penalize cross-border bank loans may not be very effective in restraining speculative activity if banks do not engage in large position taking.[84] Third, it is becoming increasingly easy to create synthetic positions in derivative markets so that taxation of "foreign exchange transactions" is not a simple matter. Fourth, taxing foreign exchange trading is likely to remove significant liquidity from these markets.[85]

A more general practical problem with any type of capital control is provided by the empirical finding that capital controls tend to lose their effectiveness relatively quickly as individuals find ways of avoiding the controls.[86] However, this problem is proba-break bly more important for controls on outflows, because the benefits to foreign investors of gaining access to one particular country are probably not that large in comparison with the benefits to a resident of a financially repressed country of converting wealth into a foreign currency asset. Indeed, countries that have controls on outflows often have higher inflation and lower real interest rates than other countries.[87]

Short-Term Versus Long-Term Flows: Is There Much of a Difference?

It is currently popular in several countries to promote long-term capital inflows, but to discourage short-term inflows. The motivation for this policy stems from the fact that long-term capital inflows take a longer period of time to withdraw from a country. Therefore, the lower the share of short-term capital in total flows, the lower the probability of a sudden reversal in capital inflows. Further, long-term flows, such as foreign direct investment, might be more strongly guided by medium-term fundamentals and be less sensitive than short-term flows to cyclical fluctuations in domestic or international interest rates.[88]

In addition to the potential reversibility of short-term inflows, there may be other reasons why countries may wish to limit these types of inflows. Notably, a surge in short-term inflows often shows up as an expansion in short-maturity bank deposits; if the domestic banking sector is inefficient or poorly supervised the authorities may want to minimize the role played by banks in intermediating capital flows. In this case, it may be preferable to have a larger share of flows routed through bond and equity markets.[89]

The current practices of several developing countries amount to restricting either the types of external financing of domestic entities or the maturities of external financing. An example of the former approach is restricting the foreign issuance of securities by domestic entities, thereby encouraging instead direct investment. An example of the latter policy would be to restrict, say via a tax, short-maturity foreign bond issues or bank loans.

Just as there are practical problems associated with designing capital controls to target only inflows or only outflows, it may be quite difficult to design capital controls that distinguish between short-term and long-term capital flows. Specifically, it is often not clear whether certain brands of capital flows are short term or long term. Standard balance of payments classifications, direct investment, portfolio flows, short-term flows, and others, are in general not very informative about the volatility, effective maturity, and liquidity of the flows. Indeed, the distinctiveness of these flows may be significantly less clear than these categories suggest.[90] Furthermore, it seems likely that even if a set of controls is effective in limiting "short-term" foreign financing, if incentives are strong enough, even flows that are perceived by policymakers to be "long-term" flows may in fact be considerably more liquid. For example, selling direct investments may require time and significant transactions costs, but it is possible to create a "synthetic sale" by obtaining bank loans in the domestic currency that can be initiated rather quickly and with low transactions costs. In addition, to the extent that equity and long-term bonds—and to a much lesser degree, term deposits and bank loans—have reasonably liquid secondary markets, asset sales by foreigners can be expected to require an adjustment in the secondary market, rather than an adjustment in the primary market as is the case when

---

[83]See Garber and Taylor (1995).

[84]The experience of Spain during the 1992 ERM crisis highlights the importance of this point.

[85]For further analysis see Box I.9.

[86]See Mathieson and Rojas-Suárez (1993) for a comprehensive review.

[87]See Grilli and Milesi-Ferretti (forthcoming).

[88]See Edwards (1991).

[89]This point is reinforced by the fact that most countries view stability and solvency of the banking system as a much more important consideration than weakness in equity markets.

[90]See Claessens, Dooley, and Warner (1993).

short-term flows dry up. But since large-scale liquidation of "long-term" securities (equity, long-term bonds) positions may well have important spillover effects on primary markets, it is not clear that this sort of policy would be effective precisely at those times when it would be beneficial. Indeed, the sell-off in late 1994 and early 1995 of emerging markets securities has not only reduced securities prices but has also sharply contracted issuance activity in primary securities markets by developing countries.

Taxing Short-Term Flows

The above discussion suggests that one way to reduce net inflows is by taxing gross inflows, possibly in the form of a tax that falls more heavily on short-term inflows. This is the type of policy adopted by Chile in 1991 and Colombia in 1993 (Box I.10). In both countries, a nonremunerated, reserve-requirement deposit at the central bank was required on firms' liabilities associated with direct borrowing in foreign currency. In Colombia, the reserve requirement is to be maintained for the duration of the loan and applies to all loans with a maturity of five years or less, except for trade credit with a maturity of four months or less. The percentage of the requirement declines (at a decreasing rate) as the maturity lengthens; from 140 percent for funds that are 30 days or less to 42.8 percent for five-year funds. In Chile, the tax stems from a nonremunerated 30 percent reserve requirement for a period of one year.[91] Considering the tax rate for various maturities highlights how such a measure may act as a disincentive to borrow abroad, particularly at short maturities. In principle, these measures affect the household sector, nonfinancial businesses, and the financial sector. In practice, these policies have mainly served as a deterrent to banks from borrowing offshore.

Brazil has also recently implemented a tax on inflows (see Box I.10), but with greater variation across assets, rather than across maturities, than the above policies.[92] As in Chile and Colombia, the tax on foreign issuance of bonds falls on domestic borrowers. Some other taxes, however, are paid by foreign lenders in Brazil. Notably, foreigners investing in the stock market until recently had to pay a 1 percent tax, and a similar tax must be paid by foreigners on fixed income investments.[93] Notice that these taxes fall

more heavily on investors that have relatively short horizons and less heavily on longer-term investors. These measures are clearly designed to target the speculative, "hot money" capital inflows.

The main disadvantage of these measures is that flows are likely to be rerouted through other channels. For example, over- or underinvoicing of imports and exports might be used because trade credits are exempt from the tax.[94] Others have argued that, in the case of Chile, overinvoicing of imports is not likely to be an attractive alternative because imports are taxed at a comparable rate.[95] Indeed, inflows to Chile in 1991 were below those observed in 1990, possibly attesting to the success of this policy. While net inflows increased beginning in 1992, the increases were primarily in foreign direct investment and other long-term flows. A similar pattern emerged in Colombia during 1994, with short-term flows accounting for a declining share of total flows. However, total inflows to Colombia continued to increase in 1994.

Prudential Limits

Capital controls may alternatively be quantitative limits on inflows (see Box I.10). Measures implemented have included prudential limits on, or even prohibition of, non-trade-related swap activities, offshore borrowing, and banks' net open market foreign exchange positions (Indonesia, Malaysia, the Philippines, and Thailand); caps on banks' foreign currency liabilities (Mexico); or blanket measures that prohibited domestic residents from selling short-term money-market instruments to foreigners (Malaysia).

In Malaysia, a combination of large domestic-foreign interest rate differentials and widespread expectations of an appreciation of the ringgit during late 1993 led to a surge in short-term capital inflows that led the authorities to impose six measures to restrict inflows in January 1994. The response was based on the fact that the inflows were largely associated with short-term bank deposits and were therefore viewed as speculative in nature.[96] Consequently, most of the measures were directed toward controlling the activities of the financial sector, and most were announced as being only temporary; only two of the six measures remain in place.

One of the measures implemented by Malaysia that appears to have been effective was prohibiting domestic residents from selling short-term money-market instruments to foreigners. The result of this regulation was that maturing CDs could not be rolled over and, therefore, short-term inflows (and monetary aggregates) declined. The combination of

---

[91]The taxes in both Chile and Colombia follow a graduated schedule with decreasing tax rates for increasing maturities beginning with a rate of 95 percent and 140 percent for one-month securities in Chile and Colombia, respectively, and a rate of zero percent and 43 percent at a maturity of five years in each respective country.

[92]As capital inflows were reduced in the wake of the Mexican crisis, Brazil eased or eliminated some restrictions on inflows in March 1995.

[93]This was eliminated on March 10, 1995 to encourage inflows in the wake of the Mexican crisis.

[94]See Mathieson and Rojas-Suárez (1993).

[95]See Labán and Larraín (1994). However, some circumvention of the tax is effected by reclassifying loans as trade related.

[96]See Aziz (1994).

Box I.9. Financial Transactions Taxes

Recent volatility in world financial markets has generated interest in ways in which the tax system can be used to reduce destabilizing capital flows, and hence, to reduce securities price and exchange rate volatility. There has been a revival of interest in a proposal by Professor James Tobin to tax foreign currency conversions (now often referred to as the "Tobin tax"). The advisability of such taxes, however, is open to question. Many economists have discouraged their use, arguing that they would not reduce volatility in financial markets, but instead would impair the efficient functioning of financial markets, would be costly to implement, and would be easily avoided.[1]

Although domestic securities transactions taxes have been widely used in industrial and developing countries, taxes on international transactions have been less widely used.[2] Financial transactions taxes can take many different forms. In a domestic context, they are usually excises levied on transactions in financial assets, including stocks, bonds, futures, options, and other derivative instruments. In an international context, they are usually excises levied on transactions involving currency conversions.

Economic Effects of Financial Transactions Taxes

Financial transactions taxes may have pervasive effects on capital markets. One principal argument against financial transactions taxes is that they would reduce market efficiency. Since financial transactions taxes would increase transactions costs, they would impose an efficiency cost on financial markets, by creating an incentive for investors to hold on to financial assets rather than to trade them. Financial transactions taxes would also increase the taxation of income from capital, increasing before-tax rates of return and the cost of capital. In the long run, increasing the cost of capital could lead to lower rates of capital formation and economic growth.

If these taxes applied only to certain assets, they would shift investment to untaxed assets, adding to distortions present under existing tax systems. For instance, if only domestic transactions were taxed, transactions would quickly move offshore. In international markets, if transactions taxes applied only to certain currencies, traders would shift into other currencies.

Although financial transactions taxes would increase transactions costs, it has been argued that they would still improve the overall efficiency of financial markets because they would reduce trading, thus contributing to reduced volatility and therefore risk (which would reduce before-tax rates of return and the cost of capital). Yet the opposite has also been argued, that reduced trading would lead to less liquid markets, thus contributing to greater volatility.

The effect of transactions costs on the volatility of domestic and international financial markets thus becomes an important empirical issue. The key empirical questions are, How would financial transactions taxes influence the behavior of financial market participants and how would these changes in behavior affect the volatility of financial markets? Regarding the former, the evidence from financial markets is inconclusive: while such taxes appear to alter the composition of trading, it is less clear that they affect the overall volume of trading or of capital flows. Empirical relationships between the volume of trading and capital flows and market volatility are also uncertain, based on evidence from financial and real estate markets.

Some theoretical arguments have recently been offered that suggest that financial transactions taxes may reduce volatility in financial markets based on a new view of the behavior of financial markets in which investors have diverse motives for investing.[3] Summers and Summers (1990) hypothesize that financial transactions taxes would discourage destabilizing traders more than stabilizing traders and therefore reduce volatility in financial markets. There is, however, little empirical evidence to support such a hypothesis.

The distributional effects of financial transactions taxes are complex. Initially, their burden is likely to fall on the participants in financial markets, including investors and borrowers, and the financial services industry, making the incidence progressive. In industrial economies, however, institutional investors hold a considerable share of financial securities.[4] This would tend to reduce the progressivity of the tax. To the extent that the burden of these taxes is shifted through behavioral changes on to all assets or even other factors of production, the incidence could fall on an even broader cross-section of the population, including homeowners and others.

One appeal of financial transactions taxes has been their potential to raise large amounts of revenues with low tax rates, given the large tax base implied by the high level of financial transactions. Global net turnover in the world's foreign currency markets (spot, forward, and derivative contracts) is on the order of $1 trillion a day. A static revenue estimate of a tax on foreign currency transactions at a tax rate of .01 percent (i.e., 1 basis point) would raise about $25 billion a year (based on 250 business days a year).

The potential revenue from such a tax would depend, however, on the nature of the tax, the scope of its coverage, the tax rate chosen, and the behavioral effects on financial market participants induced by its imposition. Static revenue estimates would be misleading because these taxes would change financial markets in fundamental ways, probably reducing both the price and vol-

---

[1]For a discussion of these issues, see Greenaway (1995), Eichengreen, Tobin, and Wyplosz (1995), Garber and Taylor (1995), and Kenen (1995).

[2]Although, of course, various types of fees typically apply to both domestic and foreign financial transactions.

[3]See the background paper "Bubbles, Noise, and the Trading Process in Speculative Markets," pp. 175–82.

[4]See the background paper "Increasing Importance of Institutional Investors," pp. 165–74.

ume of the assets being traded (and thus the size of the tax base).

Issues in Design of Financial Transactions Taxes

In its broadest form, a financial transactions tax should apply to all financial transactions, regardless of whether they involve domestic or foreign financial instruments, and no matter with whom and where a particular transaction takes place. If the goal is, narrowly, to influence international capital flows, it may be desirable to limit the coverage of the tax to transactions involving currency conversions. There is no exact equivalence, however, between capital flows and foreign currency transactions.

There is no easy way to design a uniform financial transactions tax. Transactions taxes applied at a uniform rate on all financial instruments would have different effective tax rates depending on the maturities and holding period of the assets; with a single ad valorem rate, the effective burden on assets would be higher, the shorter the maturity. If assets were taxed before maturity, this would complicate the picture; a frequently traded long-term asset would face a higher tax burden than one with the same maturity held to maturity by a single investor.

Under a comprehensive transactions tax, transactions in derivatives should be taxed; otherwise, investors could construct equivalent positions with derivatives as they would with cash instruments.[5] It is difficult, however, to achieve equivalent taxation of cash and derivative instruments. Financial intermediaries pose another set of difficult problems in designing a financial transactions tax. Imposing transactions taxes on intermediaries can multiply the number of times a financial asset is taxed.

The increasing international integration of financial markets ensures that there would be international dimensions to any kind of financial transactions tax, even one focused only on domestic trade in financial assets. If transactions taxes applied to transactions only in domestic markets, investors could substitute foreign trading as a means to avoid the tax. Shifting the location of trade in financial assets is relatively easy, with trade shifting to other countries or to locations with established financial markets.

Taxes on International Transactions and Related Taxes

Tobin proposed the idea of imposing a tax on all transactions involving the currency conversions in 1978 (although the idea can be traced to earlier proposals by Keynes). His argument for the tax was that it would reduce speculative short-term capital mobility. Tobin envisaged an international tax, levied at a uniform rate, on all spot transactions in domestic security and foreign exchange markets involving currency conversions. For its success, the Tobin tax would require international policy coordination in tax policy, tax administration, and the sharing of the proceeds of the tax. The analytical shortcomings of the Tobin tax proposal are similar to any financial transactions tax. In addition, the low tax rate generally envisaged under the Tobin tax would only minimally inhibit speculative activities in foreign exchange markets when there are expectations of a change in exchange rates exceeding the tax. Financial market participants are likely to oppose even small tax rates in view of the narrow spreads that characterize foreign exchange markets transactions.

In terms of the effective implementation of the tax, the mobility of financial transactions would make the tax easy to avoid unless the tax were internationally agreed upon and administered by each government for taxable transactions carried out in its own jurisdiction. It has proven difficult to reach international agreement in other areas of taxation, even by relatively homogeneous groups of countries. The disposal of the proceeds from the tax would also have to be worked out by international agreement.

As originally conceived, the Tobin tax would appear impractical. Individual countries could impose various measures on a unilateral basis, as many have done with domestic securities transactions taxes and taxes on currency conversions. These measures may take different forms, including explicit and implicit taxes.

One approach would be a tax on capital outflows or inflows. A tax on capital outflows could take the form of a levy on purchases by residents of foreign investments. A tax on capital inflows could take the form of a levy on purchases by foreigners of domestic investments. Even nondiscriminatory forms of domestic securities transactions taxes would still tend to reduce capital inflows. Capital outflow taxes were used, for instance, by the United States during the 1960s. The tax was ultimately repealed because it was highly vulnerable to tax avoidance schemes through related party transactions and other means. Such taxes have proven unsuccessful in coping with underlying structural economic problems on a long-term basis, and they impair the free movement of capital.

Other variants of the Tobin tax could take the form of monetary policy measures. One scheme would work similarly to the mechanism used for exchange rate stabilization in the European Monetary System. A tax would apply to currency conversions that occur when the effective exchange rate moves beyond some band. The tax could also be applied to the difference between the band and the effective rate (see Spahn (1995)). Another approach would be to require banks to deposit a sum related to the foreigncurrency transaction, interest free, with the central bank for a period of time, thereby effectively raising the cost of these foreign currency transactions (see Eichengreen and Wyplosz (1993)). This scheme is being employed in Chile, where the Central Bank has introduced a reserve requirement on all new foreign loans.

---

[5]See the background paper "Initiatives Relating to Derivatives," pp. 150–57.

Box I.10. Restrictions on Inflows and Prudential Requirements[1]

Brazil (1992)

October 1994. A 1 percent tax was imposed on foreign investment in the stock market. It was eliminated on March 10, 1995.

The tax on Brazilian companies issuing bonds overseas was raised from 3 percent to 7 percent of the total. Eliminated on March 10, 1995.

The tax paid by foreigners on fixed interest investments in Brazil was raised from 5 percent to 9 percent, and reduced back to 5 percent on March 10, 1995.

The Central Bank raised limits on the amount of dollars that can be bought on foreign exchange markets.

Chile (1990)

June 1991. Nonrenumerated 20 percent reserve requirement to be deposited at the Central Bank for a period of one year on liabilities in foreign currency for direct borrowing by firms.

The stamp tax of 1.2 percent a year (previously paid on domestic currency credits only) was applied to foreign loans as well. This requirement applied to all credits during their first year, with the exception of trade loans.

May 1992. The reserve requirement on liabilities in foreign currency for direct borrowing by firms was raised to 30 percent. Hence, all foreign currency liabilities had a common reserve requirement.

Colombia (1991)

June 1991. A 3 percent withholding tax was imposed on foreign exchange receipts from personal services

rendered abroad and other transfers, which could be claimed as credit against income tax liability.

February 1992. Banco de la República increased its commission on its cash purchases of foreign exchange from 1.5 percent to 5 percent.

June 1992. Regulation of the entry of foreign currency as payment for services.

September 1993. A nonrenumerated 47 percent reserve requirement to be deposited at the Banco de la República on liabilities in foreign currency for direct borrowing by firms. The reserve requirement is to be maintained for the duration of the loan and applies to all loans with a maturity of 18 months or less, except for trade credit.

August 1994. Nonrenumerated reserve requirement to be deposited at the Banco de la República on liabilities in foreign currency for direct borrowing by firms. The reserve requirement was to be maintained for the duration of the loan and applied to all loans with a maturity of five years or less, except for trade credit with a maturity of four months or less. The percentage of the requirement declined as the maturity lengthened—from 140 percent for funds that were 30 days or less to 42.8 percent for five-year funds.

Indonesia (1990)

March 1991. Bank Indonesia adopted measures to discourage offshore borrowing. It began to scale down its swap operations by reducing individual banks' limits from 25 percent to 20 percent of capital. The three-month swap premium was raised by 5 percentage points.

October 1991. All state-related offshore commercial borrowing was made subject to prior approval by the government and annual ceilings were set for new commitments over the next five years.

---

[1]The year next to the country name denotes the first year of the surge in inflows.

---

abandoning sterilization policies and imposing capital controls was considered to have been successful in reducing domestic interest rates and short-term inflows. However, as with taxation of inflows, as the length of time these kinds of policies are kept in place increases, the competitiveness and development of the financial sector may be jeopardized.

Mexico imposed a regulation in April 1992 that limited foreign currency liabilities of commercial banks to 10 percent of their total loan portfolio. However, it is not clear to what extent this measure worked to reduce the size of capital inflows, because banks' total loan portfolios had been expanding rapidly and the initial share of loans in foreign currency was below the 10 percent limit. For example, bank assets in 1992 grew by 41 percent while foreign currency loans grew by 88 percent; a similar pattern emerged in 1993, with foreign currency loans increasing by 50 percent and total loans rising by

25 percent. Indeed, the constraint only appears to have been binding in 1994 when both total and foreign currency loans rose by 27 percent.

Based on the recent experiences of these selected countries with policies directed toward curbing short-term capital inflows, two conclusions can be drawn. First, reviewing the Chilean and Malaysian experience, it appears that these two distinctly different policies were successful in reducing the volume of inflows (at least in the short run) in a relatively brief period of time. If the inflows are seen largely as a temporary phenomenon, such policies could therefore be effective; the longer the inflows persist or the longer the policies remain in place, however, the greater the chances that the controls are less binding and potentially harmful to the financial system. Second, the effect of these policies on the composition of flows (this also applies to Colombia) was in fact the "desired" one of lengthening maturities.

November 1991. Further measures were taken to discourage offshore borrowing. The limits on banks' net open market foreign exchange positions were tightened by placing a separate limit on off-balance-sheet positions.

Bank Indonesia also announced that future swap operations (except for investment swaps with maturities of more than two years) would be undertaken only at the initiative of Bank Indonesia.

September 1994. Banks' maximum net open positions increased from 20 percent of capital to 25 percent on an average weekly basis. Separate limits for individual currencies were no longer applied.

Malaysia (1989)

June 1, 1992. Limits on non-trade-related swap transactions were imposed on commercial banks.

January 17, 1994–August 1994. Banks were subject to a ceiling on their non-trade- or non-investment-related external liabilities.

January 24, 1994–August 1994. Residents were prohibited from selling short-term monetary instruments to nonresidents.

February 2, 1994–August 1994. Commercial banks were required to place with Bank Negara the ringgit funds of foreign banking institutions (Vostro accounts) held in non-interest-bearing accounts. However, in the January–May period these accounts were considered part of the eligible liabilities base for the calculation of required reserves, resulting in a negative effective interest rate in Vostro balances.

February 23, 1994–August 1994. Commercial banks were not allowed to undertake non-trade-related swap and outright forward transactions on the bid side with foreign customers.

Mexico (1990)

April 1992. A regulation that limited foreign currency liabilities of commercial banks to 10 percent of their total loan portfolio was passed. Banks had to place 15 percent of these liabilities in highly liquid instruments.

Philippines (1992)

July 1994. Bangko Sentral ng Pilipinas began discouraging forward cover arrangements with nonresident financial institutions.

Central bank approval required for all forward transactions in foreign exchange.

November 1994. Banks' minimum oversold foreign exchange positions reduced from the equivalent of 15 percent of unimpaired capital to 5 percent.

Approvals for foreign loans granted only to cover foreign exchange costs, with the exception of exporters and the public sector.

Liabilities of banks to their head offices counted as unimpaired capital only if converted into pesos.

Thailand (1988)

May 1980. Banks and finance companies' net foreign exchange positions cannot exceed 20 percent of capital.

Residents were not allowed to hold foreign currency deposits except for trade-related purposes only.

April 1990. Banks and finance companies' net foreign exchange positions limit was raised to 25 percent of capital.

Sources: Alfiler (1994); Banco Central de Chile, *Evolución de la Economía* (1991 and 1992); Banco de la República, Colombia (1993 and 1994); Banco de México (1992); Bank Indonesia, *Annual Report*, various issues; Bank Negara Malaysia, *Annual Report*, various issues; and Conselho Monétario Nacional, Brazil (1994 and 1995).

Liberalization of Capital Outflows

A different approach to tempering the impact of large capital inflows is to remove controls on capital outflows. If existing controls are binding, this policy would likely increase outflows and therefore lower net capital inflows. In practice, these policies have usually meant that domestic investors (notably, pension funds) had greater freedom to acquire foreign assets. Chile, Colombia, Mexico, the Philippines, Sri Lanka, and Thailand are among those that have liberalized capital outflows (Box I.11).

Reducing barriers to outflows will lower net inflows only if several conditions are satisfied. First, existing controls on outflows must be binding, a proposition that may not be true.[97] Second, it requires that a greater ability by domestic residents to invest abroad will translate into greater investment abroad. This may not occur if rate-of-return differentials favor the domestic country. Finally, it requires that gross inflows will not be affected positively by the liberalization announcement. This last condition is probably the most tenuous. Specifically, both economic theory and insights based on the evidence from a number of well-documented country cases show that liberalization of outflows has actually induced heavier inflows. Examples include Italy and New Zealand in 1984, Spain in 1986, Yugoslavia in 1990, and Chile in the 1990s.[98] The reason for this is that lifting restrictions on capital outflows appears to send a positive signal that increases the confidence of foreign investors and further stimulates capital inflows.[99] In addition, the effectiveness of this policy may be further jeopardized

[97]See Mathieson and Rojas-Suárez (1993).

[98]See Bartolini and Drazen (1994) and Labán and Larraín (1994).

[99]See Bartolini and Drazen (1994).

Box I.11. Liberalization of Outflows[1]

Chile (1990)

April 1990. New measures liberalizing foreign exchange market operations were brought in. Previously, all foreign exchange market operations were prohibited unless they were done under the Central Bank's specific authorization. Under new rules, all transactions were permitted unless specifically restricted by the Central Bank.

1991. In a number of steps (February, April, May, and October), commercial banks were permitted to increase external trade financing and use up to 25 percent of foreign exchange time deposits for foreign trade financing. Joint venture rules were simplified, and the waiting period for remitting capital invested in Chile under the debt-conversion program was shortened. Procedures for enterprises to directly invest abroad were modified and made easier. (These types of transactions were already done through the legal informal market.)

March 1992. Pension funds were allowed to hold a portion of their portfolio in foreign assets (government bonds, certificates of deposit, and bankers' acceptances). The limit on these investments was increased gradually to 10 percent of investment portfolio.

The limit on net foreign exchange holdings of commercial banks was doubled. The share of export receipts exempt from surrender requirements was increased. Allocations of foreign exchange for a variety of payments abroad (including travel) were raised. The period for advance purchase of foreign exchange for debt service was extended.

Colombia (1990)

June 1990. The ceiling applicable to foreign currency deposits held by domestic commercial banks was increased to 15 percent (from 8 percent).

October 22, 1991. The foreign investment regime was liberalized (under Resolution 51) to expand existing guarantees and to ease the way to new investment. Foreign firms were allowed to remit up to 100 percent of net annual profits.

December 1991. Investors were permitted to buy up to 100 percent of locally listed companies. Restrictions on capital and income repatriation were abolished.

January 1992. Surrender requirement of export proceeds was eased: all exporters were allowed to retain part of export proceeds abroad. Previously, this was granted only to coffee growers and to state enterprises exporting oil and minerals.

Residents were allowed to hold foreign stocks and other foreign portfolio investments abroad up to $500,000. Higher amounts required approval of the National Planning Department.

February 1992. Minimum maturity on foreign loans was reduced from five years with two years' grace, to one year. Such loans were permitted only to finance working capital or fixed investment. Limit on contractual interest rate (LIBOR + 2.5 percent) was eliminated for the private sector.

April 1994. Limits on foreign investments of domestic pension funds, insurance companies, and mutual funds were raised from 3 percent to 4 percent.

The share of export proceeds subject to surrender requirements was reduced from 90 percent to 85 percent and the period of surrender of foreign exchange was extended from 150 days to 180 days.

October 1994. The share of export proceeds subject to surrender requirements was further reduced from 85 percent to 80 percent.

Mexico (1990)

November 1991. Foreign exchange surrender requirements and related exchange control measures were abolished, permitting unification of controlled and free market exchange rates.

Philippines (1992)

July 1994. Bangko Sentral ng Pilipinas raised the limit on outward investments from the banking system, from $1 million to $3 million.

Restrictions on repatriation of investments (and earning accruing therefrom) funded by debt-to-equity conversions under the old debt-restructuring program were lifted.

Sri Lanka (1990)

1993. Limits on foreign currency working balances of commercial banks were removed.

February 1994. The reserve ratio was lowered on foreign currency deposits to the extent that the funds were invested abroad.

Thailand (1988)

April 1991. Foreign exchange earners were allowed to open foreign exchange accounts with commercial banks in Thailand up to $500,000 for individuals and $2 million for corporations. Thai investors could freely transfer up to $5 million abroad for direct investment. Bank of Thailand approval requirement of repatriation of investment funds was eliminated.

February 1994. The amount of Thai baht that could be taken out to Viet Nam and bordering countries was raised to B 500,000.

The ceiling on the amount of foreign exchange that could be taken abroad for traveling expenses was eliminated (the previous ceiling was $20,000).

Sources: Alfiler (1994); Banco de la República, *Annual Report*, various issues; Hettiarachchi and Herat (1994); Labán and Larraín (1994); Nijathaworn and Dejthamrong (1994); and Schadler and others (1993).

[1]The year next to the country name denotes the first year of the surge in inflows.

if domestic interest rates are being kept high relative to international levels (say by sterilization polices).[100] Certainly, stock market returns (in dollars) during 1990–93 for several of the countries that liberalized (including Chile, Colombia, Mexico, and Thailand) far exceeded the returns available in major industrial countries.

Controls on Capital Outflows

There are a number of reasons why controls on capital outflows (e.g., a tax on purchases of foreign assets) may exacerbate problems in the financial sector and worsen a crisis. Paralleling the discussion above, failure to remove controls on outflows or imposing new controls may send an adverse signal about the future ability to move capital out of the country. In addition, foreign investors might require a higher-risk premium on their investment to compensate them for the implicit tax resulting from controls. Further, a tax on residents' holdings of foreign assets may result in a transitory trade deficit (or a widening of the existing one) as agents shift to domestic assets.[101] However, a large number of countries have imposed controls on capital outflows, and it is therefore useful to study more closely the types of controls imposed and whether they were effective.

Issues in Using Capital Controls to Slow a Crisis

Although controls on capital outflows may be effective in delaying a balance of payments crisis, the length of the delay is not obvious. On the one hand, restrictions that slow inflows of capital may prevent a crisis from occurring in the first place if the swing in the capital account is reduced by the controls. On the other hand, on the eve of a balance of payments crisis, the implementation of controls on outflows seems extremely unlikely to avert a crisis, and the amount of time that is bought is likely to be only a few months, and possibly less. However, it is difficult to determine precisely the benefits of controls on outflows during a crisis. The extent of the benefits depends on the types of controls imposed, how easily they are circumvented, the effect of leakage through the controls, and how divergent are actual policies from what market participants perceive to be "equilibrium" policies.

There may be important adverse consequences of capital controls from a policymaker's perspective. Chief among these is the effect of the temporary imposition of controls on foreign investors' preferences for investing in the domestic economy in the future. In addition, introducing temporary capital controls can have important effects during relatively normal times, even if they do not affect the ability to repatriate capital. Specifically, a rise in the perceived probability that capital controls will be imposed at any future moment could itself spark a run on a currency, even though one would not have occurred had this probability been much lower.[102] But notice that this then may introduce a time-inconsistency problem: if it is expected that controls on outflows will be implemented with high probability, then this could spark a run sooner, which could lead to controls being implemented sooner, leading to a possibly worst-case equilibrium. The implication is that if the authorities implement controls on capital outflows when a crisis appears imminent, then this results in an additional component of uncertainty for foreign investors, which may be central to speculative outflows. If this effect is important, then it leaves as options either not imposing controls or implementing pre-emptive controls on capital inflows, that is, controls on capital inflows before a crisis has occurred.

Evidence from the ERM Crisis

The crisis of the European exchange rate mechanism (ERM) in the summer and fall of 1992 provides a recent experiment for examining the role of capital controls in the aftermath of a sudden reversal of capital flows. After experiencing a wave of capital outflows, the authorities in Ireland, Portugal, and Spain relied on capital controls to slow speculative runs against their foreign exchange reserves. Of these three countries, only Spain implemented new controls, while Portugal and Ireland tightened existing ones (Box I.12). Although there were differences in the types of controls implemented, all three countries generally sought to restrict speculative portfolios— short positions in the domestic currency and long positions in foreign currency—much like the sand-in-the-wheels taxes discussed above are supposed to.

Since a run on a currency affects directly a central bank's foreign exchange reserves, an obvious way to measure the impact of imposing controls is to study the behavior of reserves around the time that the controls were imposed. Of course, reserves may not tell the whole story if central banks tap lines of credit. Although it is impossible to know what would have happened to reserves in the absence of the controls, it appears that during the ERM crisis those countries that implemented controls did not significantly reduce the pressure on their stock of reserves (Chart I.26). Indeed, if one takes into account the fact that lines of credit were tapped heavily during the crisis, reserve losses understate actual dollar losses. At best,

---

[100]See background paper "Policy Responses to Previous Surges of Capital Inflows," pp. 80–94.

[101]See Reinhart (1991).

[102]See, for example, Dellas and Stockman (1993).

Box I.12. Use of Capital Controls to Defend Currencies During the ERM Crisis

Ireland

September 1992. No new capital or foreign exchange controls were introduced; enforcement of existing controls tightened. Controls included (1) all credits to nonresident, Irish pound denominated accounts in excess of £250,000 must be reported to the Central Bank unless the credit was trade related; (2) residents were not allowed to make financial loans in Irish pounds for periods of less than one year to nonresidents without the permission of the Central Bank; (3) foreign currency accounts were available to residents with some restrictions. One such restriction was that deposits made with funds converted from Irish pounds must be for a fixed term of three months; (4) forward foreign exchange transactions in Irish pounds for speculative purposes were prohibited. The minimum maturity of allowable forward transactions was 21 days; and (5) on September 24, 1992 the delegated approval system for swap transactions was suspended. Henceforth, swaps required central bank approval.

January 1, 1993. All controls were eliminated.

Portugal

September 1992. No new capital or foreign exchange controls were introduced; enforcement of existing controls tightened. Controls included the following: (1) commercial banks were obligated to get approval from the Banco de Portugal for foreign currency exposures. Whereas formerly such approval was generally forthcoming; in September, the Banco de Portugal withheld approval; and (2) among other existing restrictions were prohibitions on the acquisitions of money market instruments by nonresidents, short-term, escudo-denominated lending to nonresidents, and forward foreign exchange transactions.

December 16, 1992. Controls were lifted.

Spain

September 24, 1992. A compulsory one-year, non-interest-bearing deposit to be held at the Bank of Spain was introduced against the increments from the September 22 level of long positions taken against the peseta in foreign exchange markets and in peseta-denominated lending to nonresidents.

The reserve requirement ratio on the increases in peseta-denominated liabilities of domestic credit entities (national or foreign) with their branches, subsidiaries, or parent companies abroad was raised to 100 percent.

October 5, 1992. The above controls were removed, and replaced by a compulsory non-interest-bearing deposit, to be held by commercial and savings banks or the Bank of Spain, against the increase in peseta lending to nonresidents through swaps on foreign exchange markets.

November 22, 1992. Controls were removed.

Sources: International Monetary Fund, *Annual Report on Exchange Arrangements and Exchange Restrictions*, various issues; and national authorities.

---

the controls may have temporarily slowed the rate of contraction of reserves. Moreover, all three countries eventually devalued their currencies; the Spanish peseta and Portuguese escudo were devalued by 6 percent on November 23, 1992 and the Irish pound by 10 percent on January 30, 1993. It is noteworthy that in Spain and Portugal, the currencies were devalued roughly a month after the controls were implemented or strengthened, whereas in Ireland, the devaluation occurred four months later.

Another way of gauging the effectiveness of controls is to study the spreads between onshore and offshore interest rates. Specifically, if controls are effective in limiting outflows of capital then this effectiveness should be reflected in the extent to which a domestic interest rate is lower than the comparable Eurocurrency rate. That is, the more costly it is to penetrate capital controls, the lower should be the required return on domestic deposits.[103] If controls

are effective in limiting domestic interest rates, then they may be of considerable value in such circumstances since the costs associated with high domestic interest rates (e.g., from stress on the banking system) may be avoided to a large degree relative to a pure interest rate defense of a currency.

The evidence suggests that the effectiveness of the controls varied widely across time, countries, and types of controls (Chart I.27).[104] The evolution of onshore-offshore spreads also suggests that the Portuguese controls were more effective than the Spanish controls, a belief that seems to have been widely held during the crisis. In addition, it has been shown that domestic interest rates in several Scandinavian countries during the ERM crisis were actually considerably higher than the corresponding Eurodeposit rates, which may reflect a credit risk premium for the domestic banking system.[105]

One problem with Tobin-type transactions taxes is that the incidence of the tax falls on all traders

---

[103]Grilli and Milesi-Ferretti (forthcoming) find evidence for industrial and developing countries that real interest rates tend to be lower in the countries that had capital controls in place relative to those that had liberal capital accounts.

[104]The unavailability of data for Ireland precludes studying interest rate spreads in that case.

[105]See Fieleke (1994).

Chart I.26. Foreign Exchange Reserves, 1991–93
(In billions of U.S. dollars)

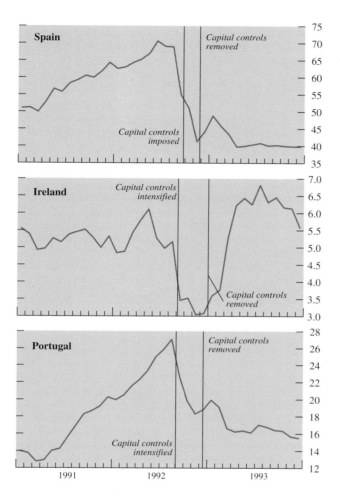

Source: International Monetary Fund, *International Financial Statistics.*

Chart I.27. Onshore and Offshore Deposit Rates, May 1992–April 1993
(In percent)

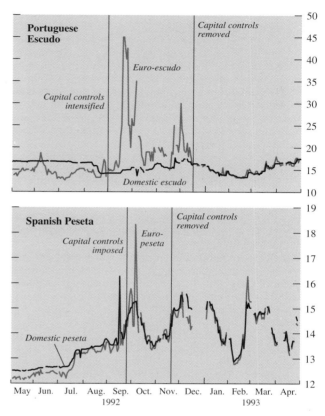

Source: Bloomberg Financial Markets.

and not just speculators. The question arises as to whether it is feasible to structure the policy to target only speculators. Although the answer to this question will in general depend on the specific policy measure, during the ERM crisis, France had some success with tailoring a policy in this manner. Specifically, as the attack against the franc gathered momentum, the French authorities increased interest rates in an attempt to squeeze speculators. However, to offset the adverse effects of higher interest rates on nonspeculative behavior, banks with normal commercial requirements received relatively cheap funding that could be passed through to customers, and therefore avoid a rise in the base rate. The effect was that many regular customers could obtain near-normal rates, while others had to pay higher rates. In contrast to the measures imposed by some of the other ERM coun-

tries discussed above, the French distinguished lending not by nationality of the borrower but by class of borrower. This is clearly a tactic that can only be used as a very short-term instrument of crisis management, as going beyond that could severely strain the banking system and introduce inefficiencies into the allocation of credit.[106]

Evidence from the 1982 Debt Crisis

The developing country debt crisis in the early 1980s provides a second natural experiment to study experiences with capital controls. Argentina, Mexico, and Venezuela are among the developing countries that implemented controls on outflows during this period. The details of the controls implemented in these cases varied widely, and the array of controls was often quite complex for many countries (Box I.13).

---

[106]See International Monetary Fund (1993) for further discussion of the tactics adopted by various countries during the ERM crisis.

Box I.13. Controls on Capital Outflows During the Debt Crisis of 1982

Argentina

April 5, 1982. Sales of foreign exchange were prohibited, except for imports and for principal repayments and interest payments on foreign loans.

April 20, 1982. The right to transfer profits and to repatriate investments under Argentina's foreign investment regulations was suspended. Henceforth, foreign obligations arising from profits, dividends, royalties, and technical assistance could only be paid with U.S. dollar denominated bonds issued by the Government of Argentina (Bonex bonds). Access to foreign exchange (at the official rate) was restored for these purposes on August 15, 1983.

April 30, 1982. Foreign exchange transactions and transactions abroad without the prior consent of the Central Bank were banned. Requirement lifted July 5, 1982 for imports and for principal repayments and interest payments on foreign loans.

August 2, 1982. Forward transactions were authorized only for imports and exports of goods and with a 180-day limit on maturity.

October 5, 1983. All foreign currency term deposits maturing through December 4, 1983 were to be extended for 60 days, and all foreign currency demand deposits were frozen until December 4, 1983.

Mexico

August 5, 1982. Commercial banks were required to surrender to the Banco de México their net foreign exchange holdings, including gold and silver.

August 13, 1982. Foreign currency deposits with Mexican banks were required to be converted into pesos at maturity and at a predetermined exchange rate. The foreign exchange market was closed. The foreign exchange market was reopened on August 19, 1982, and banks were authorized to deal foreign currencies at a free market rate.

September 1, 1982. By Presidential decree, additional exchange controls were imposed. All foreign exchange transactions were made subject to control, with the Banco de México (and its designated agents) being the only authorized foreign exchange supplier. A 5,000 peso limit was imposed on imports or exports of domestic currency, and limits were placed on the amount of foreign currency that could be taken out

of Mexico by each person depending on the nature of the trip. Exports of gold and silver required authorization. Deposits and loans of Mexican banks could not be denominated in foreign currency, with minor exceptions.

September 20, 1982. Issuance of payments and other transactions in pesos abroad by Mexican credit institutions was prohibited.

October 11, 1982. Profit and royalty remittances associated with foreign direct investment in Mexico were limited to 15 percent of equity, subject to foreign exchange availability.

October 22, 1982. Beginning November 1, 1982, repayment of foreign currency deposits held by foreign banks in local Mexican credit institutions was limited to monthly amounts not exceeding one sixth of the total amount outstanding on November 1, 1982.

December 1, 1982. Establishment of a controlled market and a free market for foreign exchange. Individual transactions in the free market were limited to $1,000 a person per transaction and $5,000 an enterprise per transaction.

December 17, 1982. Banks were restricted in forward exchange market, and short or long positions in foreign currency were limited to 10 percent of total capital and reserves.

December 20, 1982. Gold and silver markets were re-opened.

Venezuela

February 20, 1983. Foreign exchange market was closed; it remained closed until March 4, 1983.

February 22, 1983. Suspension of free convertibility of the domestic currency and establishment of a multiple exchange rate system. Foreign exchange surrender requirements were imposed on some firms.

February 28, 1983. Only firms of mixed or Venezuelan ownership were given access to the preferential exchange rate.

March 26, 1983. Irrespective of debt-rescheduling agreements, authorities would only authorize amortization payments for one third of principal starting from 1984 subject to the availability of foreign exchange.

Source: International Monetary Fund, *Annual Report on Exchange Arrangements and Exchange Restrictions*, various issues.

It is difficult in this case to draw firm conclusions from studying the behavior of foreign exchange reserves (Chart I.28). Reserves continued their slide for several months after controls were implemented in Mexico, whereas they rebounded in Argentina and Venezuela. Because of data limitations, it is not possible to examine onshore-offshore interest rate differentials for these countries for that time period. However, the behavior of interest rates denominated in the domestic currency and in U.S. dollars does suggest some reprieve from speculative pressures (Chart I.29). Specifically, interest rate spreads declined despite rising risk premiums, at least in the short run; drawing longer-run conclusions is difficult without having a useful benchmark interest rate (Table I.9).

Sequencing Issues

There is general consensus in the literature on sequencing of economic reform that the capital ac-

Chart I.28. Foreign Exchange Reserves, 1981–84
(In billions of U.S. dollars)

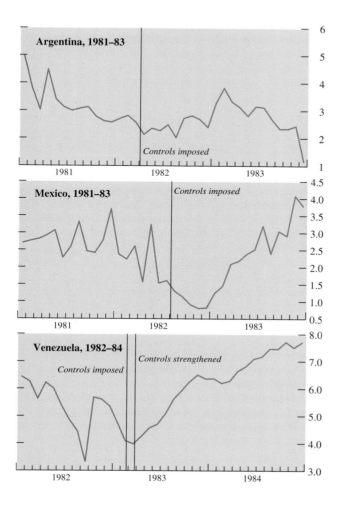

Source: International Monetary Fund, *International Financial Statistics.*

Chart I.29. Deposit Rate Spreads
(Domestic currency/U.S. dollar)

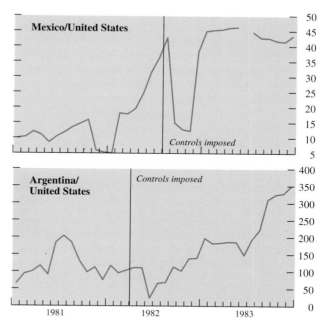

Sources: International Monetary Fund, *International Financial Statistics;* and The WEFA Group.

count should be liberalized last.[107] If the domestic financial system has not been liberalized, and there are interest rate controls and financial repression, then liberalizing the capital account will result in heavy capital outflows. Even if interest rate controls were removed and domestic interest rates were above world levels, if credit allocation does not adequately reflect economic fundamentals—say, because there is mispricing of risk or directed credits—the capital inflows induced by the capital account liberalization may lead to the financing of unproductive

activities.[108] If trade is not liberalized prior to the capital account, then the higher inflows may be funneled into inefficient protected sectors or industries. Alternatively, if the current and capital accounts are simultaneously liberalized, the capital inflow, and the potential real exchange rate appreciation that accompanies it, may adversely affect the tradable sector and generate an expansion in the nontradable sector. If the appreciation is large and persistent, it may jeopardize medium-term objectives, such as the development of a nontraditional export sector. Similar arguments apply to macroeconomic stabilization: if fiscal consolidation and reform have not taken place, the capital inflows will be funneled to an inefficient public sector and temporarily help finance an unsustainable accumulation of public sector debt.

This discussion suggests that countries already experiencing a surge in capital inflows, irrespective of whether these are primarily due to a favorable external environment, an attractive domestic investment environment, or both, may want to postpone liberal-

---

[107]See, for instance, Edwards (1984), McKinnon (1991), and Mathieson and Rojas-Suárez (1993).

[108]Mathieson and Rojas-Suárez (1993) and Galbis (1994) stress a further preliminary requirement for financial (and capital account) liberalization, namely, the establishment of prudential regulation and supervision. Without these, the increased availability of credit that accompanies a capital inflow could result in adverse loan selection and in eventual financial crisis.

Table I.9. Argentina: Interest Rates and Country Risk

Period		Interest Rate on BONEX (a)	180-day LIBOR Rate (b)	Implied Country Risk Premium (a)–(b)
1981	III	20.30	18.71	1.59
	IV	18.38	14.66	3.72
1982	I	18.41	15.33	3.08
	II	16.62	15.14	1.48
	III	23.88	12.85	11.03[1]
	IV	20.14	9.96	10.18
1983	I	15.48	9.50	5.98
	II	15.04	9.67	5.37
	III	23.27	10.44	12.83[2]
	IV	22.22	9.79	12.43
1984	I	21.34	10.52	10.82
	II	30.76	12.44	18.32
	III	23.01	12.12	10.89
	IV	19.11	9.73	9.38
1985	I	18.70	9.52	9.18
	II	20.73	8.46	12.27

Sources: Fanelli and Damill (1993); and IMF staff calculations.
[1]Capital controls were imposed.
[2]Capital controls were strengthened.

izing the capital account. A liberalization of the capital account may work further to stimulate inflows and reinforce the macroeconomic effects of the inflows (i.e., real exchange rate appreciation, wider current account deficits, reserve accumulation, and accelerating money and credit growth). As discussed above, it appears that for a number of countries, a liberalization of capital outflows induced further net inflows. In addition, as Box I.10 illustrates, in several countries that liberalized controls on inflows, the tendency during the capital inflow surge in the early 1990s was toward reinstating some controls or tightening prudential regulation.

Some Lessons

In light of the recent experiences of countries that adopted measures designed to curb short-term capital inflows, it appears that, at least in the short run, the policies were effective in either reducing the volume of capital inflows or affecting their composition, or both. A conclusion, therefore, is that, if the capital inflows are perceived as being temporary, these types of policies may be effective, not least because they reduce potential future outflows and the economic costs of such turbulence. Of course, the longer the inflows persist, or the longer the policies remain in place, the greater the chances that the controls become both ineffective and destructive to the development of the domestic financial system. But more generally, recourse to capital controls must be considered within the context of other policies.

With regard to controls on outflows, the existing empirical evidence on the effectiveness of capital controls in general, and the experiences of some of the countries that implemented capital controls during the recent ERM crisis and during the debt crisis in the early 1980s, suggests that controls on capital outflows offer only limited relief from market pressures. In most instances, central bank reserves continued to decline, despite the controls. In all these cases, there were either devaluations (the ERM countries) or a substantial depreciation. With regard to interest rate spreads, it does appear that temporary controls on outflows may alleviate upward pressure on interest rates and are therefore potentially most beneficial when the domestic banking system is fragile. However, given the magnitude and persistence of flight capital in the 1980s, due largely to repressed domestic interest rates, controls are never effective in the long run and may in fact make things even worse.[109]

Most of the empirical work on the effectiveness of capital controls concludes that controls lose their effectiveness relatively quickly. In most of this work, however, no distinctions are made between the "types" of capital controls. Specifically, little distinction is made between measures to discourage inflows and controls on outflows. Indeed, there may be reasons to believe that their "lack of effectiveness" is not symmetric and that controls on inflows may be more effective than controls on outflows and that market-based controls may be more effective than quantity constraints. Such differences may have little to do with the design of the measures per se but rather have more to do with incentives to circumvent the controls.

Controls on outflows are usually resorted to during balance of payments or financial crises. These episodes are characterized by large devaluations of the exchange rate, steep declines in the stock market, increased volatility in financial variables, a higher risk of default, and, in some cases, political instability. Imposing controls, in and of itself, may send a "signal" that worse times are to come. In such circumstances, domestic-foreign interest rate spreads usually reach levels (particularly on a risk-adjusted basis) that provide a powerful incentive for outflows. In contrast, as the experiences of several countries in the early 1990s shows, controls on inflows tend to emerge under more "normal" economic circumstances. While rate-of-return spreads may still provide an incentive to evade controls, the rate-of-return differentials tend to be smaller than those observed during crises, and thus the desire to circumvent controls may not be as great for controls on inflows. Further, from the viewpoint of an international investor, one can always redirect investments to countries where there are fewer impediments.

[109]See Dooley (1988).

VI

Role of Domestic Financial Institutions in Intermediating Foreign Capital Inflows

This chapter examines the effects that capital inflows can have on the domestic financial systems of recipient countries. A rapid expansion of liquidity in the banking system due to a sudden surge in capital inflows can result in a deterioration of bank balance sheets if these funds are not invested efficiently. In addition, portfolio capital inflows may affect the efficiency with which domestic financial assets are priced. Inflows may also lead to greater integration of securities markets, allowing shocks in one country to be transferred to other countries.

Role of Banks in Intermediating Capital Inflows

When capital flows into a country through an increase in foreign liabilities at domestic banks, the impact on the banking system is immediate: a local bank experiences an increase in foreign currency liabilities and obtains a foreign currency asset, usually in the form of a deposit in a bank chartered in another country. If the local central bank purchases the foreign currency from the recipient bank, domestic currency bank reserves will rise relative to the deposit base. If this transaction increases the reserve-deposit ratio above the legal minimum, and if the central bank does not sterilize the monetary base against the increase in liquidity, banks can use their excess reserves to increase credit (by a multiple of that surplus amount). Hence, an increase in foreign liabilities can lead to an expansion of bank balance sheets just as an increase in domestic currency deposits would. If the local authorities permit residents to hold foreign currency deposits, a similar expansionary process would take hold, although there would not necessarily be an increase in central bank holdings of foreign reserves. The local foreign currency deposit base will expand, which may allow an expansion of foreign currency loans.

Capital flows that enter a country through nonbank financial markets can have a similar impact on the banking system.[110] When a nonresident invests in a local nonbank financial asset, a local deposit must be used to pay for it, which involves exchanging a foreign currency deposit for a local currency deposit. In such transactions, the deposits and reserves of the domestic banking system increase, at least temporarily. Hence, regardless of whether foreign capital flows into the market as foreign direct investment, equity portfolio investment, bond issuance, or bank borrowing, the associated increase in deposits and bank reserves can potentially lead to an increase in bank lending.

Capital inflows need not necessarily result in a significant expansion of banking sector assets, however. If the capital inflow is used to finance an equivalent current account deficit, as when a nonresident purchases a domestic asset from a resident, who in turn uses the proceeds to import foreign goods, the funds flow out of the country, causing no further expansion in domestic credit.[111] When the local bank lends funds to the importer, it simultaneously books a foreign currency loan and a foreign currency deposit to the importer. The local bank executes the transaction by drawing on its deposit in the foreign bank. At the end of the transaction, the local bank has a liability to the foreign bank and a foreign currency loan to the importer, and no increase in domestic assets. Alternatively, the net capital inflow can be deposited in the banking system and completely sterilized by the central bank. In each of these cases, net capital inflows do not affect the level of private domestic currency credit, and only in the latter case will the composition of domestic currency financial assets and liabilities be altered.

Capital Flows, Sterilization, and the Banking System

Capital inflows to developing countries increased significantly in the early 1990s, and the composition of these flows changed from bank lending and foreign

---

[110] For example, most of the bond portfolio inflows, which have dominated portfolio inflows into developing countries in recent years, originated in the Euromarkets and are denominated in one of the major currencies. Thus, when nonresidents purchase Eurobonds issued by borrowers in developing countries, they transfer foreign currency deposits to these borrowers. If these borrowers hold their deposits in the local banking system, bond purchases have the same impact on the domestic financial system as a direct increase in domestic bank foreign liabilities.

[111] For example, foreign direct investment is often claimed to have little effect on bank liquidity as inflows frequently are accompanied by rising imports.

direct investment to portfolio investment. While a few countries experienced periods of significant capital inflows earlier in the period, net inflows increased in a large number of developing countries in the late 1980s and early 1990s, first in Asia and then in the Western Hemisphere (Table I.10).[112] Capital account surpluses, excluding changes in reserves and exceptional financing, have been particularly large since 1990 in Malaysia, Mexico, and Thailand, but have also been well above the 1983–89 averages in Argentina, Chile, Korea, the Philippines, and Turkey.

As discussed earlier, when net capital inflows exceed current account deficits, or are combined with current account surpluses, the result is an expansion in liquidity—denominated in either local or foreign currency—in the domestic banking system. In many countries, the central bank has acquired a large part of the net inflows to prevent an appreciation of the exchange rate. Such purchases lead immediately to an increase in commercial bank reserves at the central bank and, via the usual multiplier effect, to an expansion in the money supply. In fact, more than two thirds of the capital inflows to developing countries during 1991–94 were absorbed by central banks in recipient countries through increases in foreign currency reserves. The increase in foreign exchange reserves has been highest in Malaysia, where the central bank has aggressively defended the exchange rate. Reserves increased by 18 percent of GDP in 1993 alone. In countries where inflows were not as significant to begin with, and where current account deficits were often higher relative to inflows, there were much smaller increases in reserves.

Sterilization policies have been used aggressively in developing countries that experienced large net capital inflows, in part to insulate the banking system from the effects of these inflows.[113] Sterilization techniques have included open market operations, increases in reserve requirements, mandatory purchases of government or central bank securities by financial institutions, and transfers of government deposits, including those of government-owned enterprises, to the central bank or into holdings of government securities.[114]

The decision to sterilize capital inflows generally implies that the balance sheet of the central bank

will expand rather than that of the banking system. This effectively transfers risk from the banking system to the central bank.[115] Because of the high cost of sterilization, and the high potential public cost of financial losses, the allocation of risk between the private and public sectors is an important decision.

In countries where the banking system is sound and efficient and where there are effective regulatory and supervisory controls, capital flows are less likely to create additional risks to the financial system. In these countries, banks have the ability when extending loans to anticipate, at least to some extent, the effect of capital flows on their borrowers' ability to pay. This ability allows banks to price their loans accordingly, to accumulate reserves against potential loan losses, and to reduce the concentration of their loan portfolios to sectors that are more sensitive to capital flows.

In contrast, in countries where credit institutions are not well regulated and supervised and where there are poorly enforced penalties for misallocating credit and mismanaging balance sheets, capital inflows will create further opportunities for banks to expand lending and to expose the financial system to larger potential losses. In pursuing a policy of nonsterilization in such weak systems, the authorities run the risk of later having to provide liquidity to, or to recapitalize, banks that become illiquid or insolvent as a result of poor management. Moreover, in the event of a reversal of capital flows, weak banks would become especially vulnerable. Owing to poor credit ratings, weaker financial institutions would be unable to access interbank or capital markets and would need public support to remain viable. The history of bank crises, including recent crises in some industrial countries, clearly demonstrates how high the public costs can be of such rescue operations.[116]

Partly because of differences in sterilization policies, the link between changes in central bank reserves and bank balance sheet expansion is mixed across countries. In Thailand, for example, bank assets expanded rapidly after 1987, reaching 110 percent of GDP in 1994 (Table I.11). In Malaysia, the ratio of commercial bank assets to GDP increased from 118 percent in 1992 to 134 percent in 1993. The measures taken in 1994 to contain capital inflows and the consequent narrowing of interest differentials contributed to a relative decline in bank assets to 122 percent of GDP in October 1994. In some countries, the expansion in bank balance sheets has been very significant despite only modest

---

[112]Net errors and omissions and exceptional financing items are not included. Hence, the capital account and changes in reserves generally do not completely offset the current account position.

[113]The emphasis here is on the ability of sterilization to insulate the commercial banking system from capital inflows. Even when sterilized, capital flows can have real economic effects deriving from, for example, changes in the relative prices of traded and nontraded goods.

[114]Some countries have also attempted to curtail net capital inflows by imposing controls on capital inflows (Brazil, Chile, Colombia, Indonesia, Malaysia, and Mexico), or by liberalization of capital controls on outflows (Chile, Colombia, Malaysia, Mexico, and Thailand), or both.

---

[115]The use of sterilization as a prudential policy to prevent the accumulation of risk in the banking sector was explicitly recognized in Indonesia and Chile.

[116]Several industrial countries have recently experienced, or are still experiencing, costly banking problems, including Finland, Japan, Norway, Sweden, and the United States.

Table I.10. Balance of Payments Data for Selected Developing Countries and Regions[1]

(In percent of GDP)

	1980	1981	1982	1983	1984	1985	1986	1987	1988	1989	1990	1991	1992	1993
Argentina														
Current account balance	−2.3	−2.8	−2.8	−2.3	−2.1	−1.1	−2.7	−3.9	−1.2	−1.6	3.2	−0.2	−2.8	−2.9
Capital account balance	1.2	1.0	2.5	0.4	2.3	2.8	1.6	2.2	2.8	0.3	−1.3	1.9	4.8	3.9
Changes in reserves	1.2	1.9	0.8	2.4	−0.1	−1.2	0.8	1.8	−1.5	1.7	−2.4	−1.4	−2.0	−1.0
Brazil														
Current account balance	−5.5	−4.5	−5.9	−3.4	—	−0.1	−2.0	−0.5	1.3	0.2	−0.8	−0.4	1.6	−0.1
Capital account balance	4.2	4.9	4.1	2.8	2.4	0.1	0.8	1.1	−0.5	0.3	1.1	0.2	2.7	2.5
Changes in reserves	1.5	−0.2	1.9	0.9	−2.6	0.2	1.2	−0.7	−0.5	−0.4	−0.3	−0.1	−4.0	−2.1
Chile														
Current account balance	−6.9	−14.1	−9.2	−5.5	−10.7	−8.6	−6.7	−3.9	−0.7	−2.5	−2.1	—	−1.7	−4.6
Capital account balance	11.4	14.2	4.1	2.6	10.2	8.4	4.0	4.9	4.6	4.9	9.9	2.4	6.9	5.7
Changes in reserves	−4.7	−0.4	5.3	2.6	−0.5	0.6	1.4	−0.7	−3.4	−2.0	−7.7	−3.6	−6.0	−0.9
China														
Current account balance	...	...	2.1	1.5	0.7	−3.9	−2.5	0.1	−1.0	−1.0	3.1	3.3	1.3	−2.0
Capital account balance	...	...	0.1	−0.1	−0.3	3.1	2.1	2.0	1.9	0.9	0.8	2.0	−0.1	4.0
Changes in reserves	—	0.3	−2.3	−1.4	—	0.8	0.7	−1.6	−0.6	0.1	−3.1	−3.6	0.4	−0.3
Colombia														
Current account balance	−0.7	−6.9	−10.7	−10.4	−4.6	−5.7	1.1	0.9	−0.6	−0.5	1.3	5.5	1.9	...
Capital account balance	3.4	7.2	7.8	5.0	3.1	7.0	3.3	—	2.4	1.2	—	−1.8	0.3	...
Changes in reserves	−3.2	0.1	3.1	6.4	1.3	−0.5	−3.7	−1.1	−0.5	−1.1	−1.5	−4.3	−2.2	...
Indonesia														
Current account balance	3.7	−0.6	−5.6	−7.4	−2.1	−2.2	−4.9	−2.8	−1.7	−1.2	−2.8	−3.7	−2.2	−1.6
Capital account balance	1.6	2.0	6.0	7.1	3.9	2.0	5.2	4.6	2.6	3.1	4.2	4.9	4.8	3.9
Changes in reserves	−3.2	0.4	2.0	−0.2	−1.1	−0.6	1.3	−0.8	0.1	−0.5	−2.1	−1.3	−1.6	−0.4
Korea														
Current account balance	−8.4	−6.6	−3.5	−1.9	−1.5	−0.9	4.3	7.2	7.8	2.3	−0.9	−3.0	−1.5	0.1
Capital account balance	9.4	6.7	5.2	2.8	3.1	2.1	−3.7	−6.6	−2.3	−1.2	1.2	2.3	2.3	1.0
Changes in reserves	−0.5	0.5	—	0.3	−0.6	−0.2	−0.1	−1.5	−5.1	−1.4	0.5	0.4	−1.2	−0.9
Malaysia														
Current account balance	−1.2	−9.9	−13.4	−11.7	−4.9	−2.0	−0.4	8.0	5.2	0.7	−2.1	−9.0	−3.2	−3.9
Capital account balance	5.8	10.5	14.0	12.9	8.9	6.2	4.0	−4.8	−5.8	3.5	4.2	11.9	15.1	17.4
Changes in reserves	−1.9	1.8	1.0	—	−1.4	−3.7	−5.3	−3.6	1.3	−3.3	−4.6	−2.6	−11.5	−17.9
Mexico														
Current account balance	−5.2	−6.4	−3.5	3.8	2.3	0.4	−3.9	3.0	−1.4	−2.8	−3.1	−5.2	−7.5	−6.4
Capital account balance	5.8	10.5	5.7	−0.5	—	−0.3	5.7	−1.1	−0.6	0.7	3.5	8.8	8.2	8.8
Changes in reserves	−0.4	−0.5	2.1	−1.3	−1.2	1.5	0.3	−4.0	3.8	−0.1	−0.9	−2.8	−0.5	−2.0
Philippines														
Current account balance	−5.9	−5.8	−8.6	−8.3	−4.1	−0.1	3.2	−1.3	−1.0	−3.4	−6.1	−2.3	−1.9	−6.0
Capital account balance	8.3	6.2	7.7	3.2	4.5	−2.5	0.5	1.0	1.5	3.2	4.7	6.5	6.1	6.0
Changes in reserves	−2.8	0.9	1.9	6.1	−0.6	0.9	−3.8	0.2	−1.8	−0.7	0.1	−3.9	−3.2	−0.5
Sri Lanka														
Current account balance	−16.3	−10.1	−11.5	−9.0	—	−7.1	−6.5	−4.9	−5.7	−5.9	−3.7	−6.6	−4.7	−3.7
Capital account balance	8.6	8.4	12.2	8.7	4.7	6.3	5.6	5.9	3.6	8.3	6.6	7.7	5.0	9.2
Changes in reserves	7.3	1.1	−0.7	0.1	−4.1	1.5	1.4	0.8	1.5	−0.7	−1.4	−3.6	−2.1	−6.8
Taiwan Province of China														
Current account balance	−2.2	1.1	4.6	8.4	11.8	14.8	21.6	17.7	8.3	7.8	6.9	6.8	3.9	3.1
Capital account balance	5.4	10.0	−0.7	−1.4	−4.4	−5.1	9.2	10.2	−9.4	−8.3	−9.7	−1.3	−3.3	−2.2
Changes in reserves	−2.3	−10.4	−2.9	−6.4	−6.7	−10.5	−30.9	−27.7	1.1	−0.5	2.5	−5.5	−0.7	−0.7
Thailand														
Current account balance	−6.4	−7.4	−2.7	−7.2	−5.0	−4.0	0.6	−0.7	−2.7	−3.5	−8.5	−7.7	−5.7	−5.6
Capital account balance	6.3	7.1	3.9	5.3	6.1	4.0	−0.3	2.1	6.2	9.1	10.6	12.0	8.9	11.7
Changes in reserves	0.6	−0.1	0.2	0.4	−1.3	−0.3	−1.7	−1.9	−4.2	−7.0	−3.8	−4.7	−2.6	−5.8
Turkey														
Current account balance	−4.9	−2.7	−1.5	−3.1	−2.4	−1.5	−1.9	−0.9	1.8	0.9	−1.7	0.2	−0.6	−3.7
Capital account balance	2.9	1.7	1.8	2.4	1.8	2.6	2.8	2.2	−1.1	0.7	2.7	−1.6	2.3	5.1
Changes in reserves	−0.1	0.1	−0.2	—	−0.2	0.2	−0.7	−0.7	−1.3	−2.5	−0.6	0.8	−0.9	−0.2

Sources: Central Bank of China (Taiwan Province of China); and International Monetary Fund, *Balance of Payments Statistics* and World Economic Outlook data bases.

[1]For changes in reserves, a minus sign indicates an increase. Discrepancies between the combined current and capital account and changes in reserves are due to net errors and omissions.

net capital inflows. In Indonesia, commercial bank assets expanded as a share of GDP by more than 20 percentage points over 1988–94, although it is likely that much of that expansion resulted from the important deregulation measures implemented in 1988–90. In Mexico, the banking sector has expanded rapidly, from total assets equal to 45 percent of GDP in 1991 to 67 percent in 1994. This rapid expansion reflected both the effect of capital inflows and the injection of new capital into the industry since privatization in 1991: paid-in capital increased from MexN$1.5 billion in 1991 to MexN$10.2 billion in 1994, which, assuming an 8 percent ratio of capital to risk-weighted assets, could have accounted for half of the expansion in bank assets as a proportion of GDP.

Impact on Bank Balance Sheets

Virtually all developing countries that have received large capital inflows have, at different times and to different degrees, attempted to sterilize these inflows. As was noted earlier, open market operations sterilized almost all capital inflows to Chile in the second half of 1990, but were pursued less aggressively since early 1991. Similarly, Thailand during 1989–91, Indonesia and Malaysia during 1991–92, and Sri Lanka during 1991–93 attempted to sterilize almost all capital inflows through open market operations. Other countries engaged in less than complete sterilization throughout the period of high capital inflows.

The impact that large capital inflows can have on banking systems can be seen by examining elements of the consolidated balance sheets in selected banking systems (see Table I.11). The ratio of commercial bank assets to GDP is a measure of the size of a country's banking system, and this clearly has been affected in countries that have received high capital inflows. Moreover, one can also see in the balance sheet data the effect that sterilized intervention has had in those countries that pursued such strategies. In Indonesia, Malaysia, Thailand, and Sri Lanka, periods of aggressive sterilization have been associated with very low growth in bank assets, and the relaxation of sterilization coincided with rapid bank-asset expansions (see Table I.11). In Malaysia, the ratio of bank assets to GDP increased by more than 16 percentage points in 1993; the measures adopted in early 1994 to contain capital inflows contributed to a relative decline in bank assets to 122 percent of GDP in October 1994. In Indonesia and Sri Lanka, this same ratio increased by 7 percentage points between the end of 1992 and November 1994. In Thailand, bank assets grew slowly until the relaxation of sterilization efforts in 1991, after which bank assets increased from 87 percent of GDP to a peak of 102 percent in 1993.

In addition to affecting the size of the commercial banking systems in recipient countries, capital inflows have also changed the composition of bank balance sheets in important ways. Banks in recipient countries relied more heavily on foreign capital and used these funds to expand domestic lending and securities investments.

In the countries with the largest capital inflows, Malaysia, Mexico, and Thailand, there was a greater-than-two-fold increase in foreign currency denominated liabilities as a share of GDP during the periods of capital inflows (see Table I.11). In each country, the source of the greatest increase in liabilities was borrowing from foreign banks rather than the accumulation of foreign currency deposits. Foreign liabilities of commercial banks also increased sharply in the Philippines and Turkey during periods of high capital inflows, but in Sri Lanka, the expansion in commercial bank foreign liabilities was relatively small. In Chile, the use of capital controls reinforced the declining trend in foreign liabilities among commercial banks. In countries that imported less capital, foreign liabilities of the banking system expanded more slowly, if at all. In addition, the countries with the largest capital inflows also experienced the greatest expansions in nongovernment deposits in the commercial banking system.

Increases in foreign liabilities will be less expansionary if they result in an increase in foreign assets, as when banks invest in foreign securities or lend funds abroad. The experience suggests that funds were directed mostly toward domestic, rather than foreign investments (see Table I.11). Since 1988, net foreign assets declined sharply in the commercial banking systems in Chile, Indonesia, Malaysia, Sri Lanka, and Thailand. For example, in Malaysia, commercial bank's net foreign liabilities increased from 0.4 percent of GDP in 1990 to 12.7 percent in 1993. Similarly, in Thailand, the net foreign asset position went from near balance at the end of 1987 to a net foreign liability position of 15 percent of GDP in November 1994. Mexico and Turkey, however, are exceptions. In both cases, while foreign liabilities increased sharply with the onset of capital inflows, net assets rose even faster. In Mexico for example, net foreign assets rose from 2.2 percent of GDP in 1991 to 8.0 percent in 1994.

The increase in net foreign liabilities of commercial banks, if not sterilized, will lead to an expansion of domestic lending and consumption or investment. In Indonesia, Mexico, and Thailand, domestic lending to the private sector increased by more than 20 percentage points of GDP with the onset of high capital inflows—much more than the increase in foreign liabilities. In Malaysia, lending to the private sector expanded moderately and actually declined as a share of total assets. Banks in Malaysia invested funds in the interbank market by holding excess reserves at

Table I.11. Indicators of Banking Activity in Selected Developing Countries and Regions

(In percent of GDP)

	1985	1986	1987	1988	1989	1990	1991	1992	1993	1994[1]
Chile										
Assets of commercial banks	...	...	...	131.2	119.1	123.3	99.6	95.7	102.5	120.6
Loans[2]	...	...	...	52.8	55.5	53.6	50.7	53.8	58.5	57.2
Holdings of government securities	...	...	...	0.3	0.3	0.3	0.4	0.4	0.5	0.5
Holdings of nongovernment securities	...	...	...	29.9	24.3	27.4	25.3	18.7	16.9	16.9
Deposits	...	...	...	35.6	35.1	37.3	39.5	41.1	42.3	43.9
Foreign currency assets[3]	...	...	...	43.1	36.2	37.3	23.1	22.3	24.0	34.5
Foreign currency liabilities[3]	...	...	...	43.1	36.4	37.5	23.4	22.6	24.3	34.9
Indonesia										
Assets of commercial banks	32.0	36.7	35.7	41.0	51.3	62.6	61.0	61.0	63.5	68.3
Loans to private sector[2]	15.6	19.1	20.4	24.8	33.1	45.4	46.6	45.7	50.3	53.1
Nongovernment deposits	18.1	20.5	21.1	23.7	29.1	36.6	37.3	38.7	41.1	42.1
Foreign assets	6.4	7.9	6.1	5.8	6.3	5.8	4.7	4.8	3.8	3.7
Foreign liabilities	0.6	0.5	0.6	0.8	1.7	5.8	4.7	6.0	6.5	6.9
Korea										
Assets of commercial banks	70.4	63.9	62.2	59.1	61.2	75.5	74.9	75.1	73.4	72.0
Loans[2]	27.5	26.7	24.3	22.2	26.1	29.4	29.9	29.6	28.2	30.0
Nongovernment deposits	23.1	23.0	26.2	28.6	28.1	33.3	31.7	30.2	30.0	29.2
Holdings of government securities	1.1	1.2	1.2	1.3	1.2	1.6	1.6	1.0	1.0	1.0
Holdings of nongovernment securities	2.0	2.4	2.4	2.1	3.3	4.8	4.8	5.5	6.5	6.5
Foreign currency assets[3]	8.3	7.2	7.0	6.0	5.6	8.5	8.6	8.7	9.0	9.6
Foreign currency liabilities[3]	10.9	9.2	8.3	6.9	6.1	8.8	8.9	8.7	9.3	10.0
Malaysia										
Assets of commercial banks	95.7	110.8	106.4	106.5	109.8	111.6	117.3	117.6	134.0	122.4
Loans to private sector	62.5	72.4	64.6	61.4	64.4	68.8	74.2	70.9	69.8	67.3
Nongovernment deposits	59.1	67.7	62.4	58.0	58.4	53.8	58.9	62.7	71.8	68.6
Holdings of government securities	8.6	9.0	11.8	13.0	10.7	9.3	8.7	7.0	5.7	4.6
Holdings of nongovernment securities	2.1	3.2	4.6	5.5	4.3	6.2	8.3	8.9	11.0	10.8
Foreign assets	3.9	5.4	6.3	8.1	7.7	6.6	5.0	3.6	6.3	5.3
Foreign liabilities	8.2	8.6	6.3	5.6	6.2	7.0	9.1	12.6	19.0	9.2
Mexico										
Assets of commercial banks	...	...	...	...	...	...	45.3	45.9	52.4	67.4
Loans to private sector	...	...	...	...	...	...	27.5	33.1	37.3	47.5
Nongovernment deposits	...	...	...	...	...	...	38.2	38.6	44.2	53.7
Holdings of government securities	...	...	...	...	...	...	6.5	2.2	0.3	1.0
Holdings of nongovernment securities[4]	...	...	...	...	...	...	5.5	5.4	8.1	12.1
Foreign assets[3, 5]	...	...	...	...	...	...	10.4	10.5	12.3	21.5
Foreign liabilities[3, 5]	...	...	...	...	...	...	8.1	7.6	8.2	13.4
Philippines										
Assets of commercial banks	51.8	43.5	42.1	42.8	45.4	50.1	48.0	51.1	58.9	...
Loans to private sector	19.3	13.9	15.3	15.6	16.7	18.6	17.4	20.0	25.7	24.4
Nongovernment deposits	22.1	20.3	20.5	22.2	24.4	26.9	26.9	28.5	32.1	29.6
Holdings of government securities	2.5	3.6	3.4	4.5	5.6	5.1	4.5	6.1	5.3	...
Holdings of nongovernment securities	3.0	2.1	1.3	1.1	1.1	1.6	3.5	2.4	2.9	...
Foreign assets	7.3	7.4	8.1	8.8	8.6	10.3	8.5	8.8	9.1	7.3
Foreign liabilities	13.9	9.6	9.4	9.4	9.6	12.1	10.6	13.1	15.1	13.8
Sri Lanka										
Assets of commercial banks	39.1	37.0	39.1	43.2	42.2	41.1	41.7	43.6	48.9	50.3
Loans	24.2	23.0	24.9	26.0	26.5	25.4	25.3	26.6	25.1	24.8
Nongovernment deposits	23.9	21.8	22.5	22.1	22.0	21.1	23.1	24.2	25.7	26.0
Holdings of government securities	1.2	1.2	2.4	2.5	2.7	3.8	2.9	2.8	3.0	2.9
Holdings of nongovernment securities	1.3	1.7	0.6	0.6	0.5	0.3	0.3	0.4	0.9	1.6
Foreign assets[3]	2.2	2.5	3.2	3.5	3.0	3.8	3.7	4.3	4.1	4.2
Foreign liabilities[3]	2.4	2.7	3.4	3.4	4.0	3.8	4.8	5.0	5.4	5.5
Taiwan Province of China										
Assets of deposit money banks	110.0	115.2	127.9	140.5	156.3	157.6	168.9	182.8	192.8	204.7
Loans to private sector	59.2	57.5	64.1	84.0	93.0	96.0	106.1	124.0	130.8	140.9
Nongovernment deposits	75.9	80.1	87.8	100.1	108.9	111.8	119.8	127.4	138.3	145.6
Holdings of government securities	1.5	1.5	1.9	2.9	2.3	1.9	3.1	4.6	5.5	5.3
Holdings of nongovernment securities	13.0	22.2	33.3	21.9	19.0	14.8	17.8	13.6	16.0	15.4
Foreign assets	14.8	8.6	4.6	5.5	6.6	8.4	7.8	6.3	6.4	6.8
Foreign liabilities	5.4	9.9	13.3	10.4	8.2	7.1	8.2	7.4	7.8	8.2

Table I.11 (*concluded*)

	1985	1986	1987	1988	1989	1990	1991	1992	1993	1994[1]
Thailand										
Assets of commercial banks	67.5	68.5	72.6	73.4	76.8	82.5	86.6	91.0	102.4	109.8
Loans to nonfinancial private sector	45.5	44.2	47.3	51.0	56.3	64.3	67.7	72.8	79.1	89.3
Nongovernment deposits	50.0	52.9	55.4	54.9	58.5	63.4	67.1	68.9	73.2	70.0
Holdings of government securities	7.3	9.2	8.8	7.9	6.5	5.0	3.2	2.4	1.5	1.1
Holdings of nongovernment securities	0.8	1.0	1.0	1.1	1.2	1.2	2.5	2.9	3.6	4.9
Foreign assets	3.2	3.7	3.0	2.9	3.8	2.6	2.9	2.8	5.0	4.7
Foreign liabilities	4.3	2.8	2.9	4.0	4.6	5.0	4.9	6.0	11.3	19.9
Turkey										
Assets of deposit money banks	...	46.2	52.6	49.9	43.0	39.2	41.8	45.6	49.9	39.5
Loans to private sector	...	16.6	17.5	14.3	13.5	14.0	13.8	15.4	16.3	9.6
Nongovernment deposits	...	22.8	24.0	23.2	22.1	19.2	22.9	23.6	22.2	23.3
Holdings of government securities	...	4.2	5.2	5.1	4.8	4.0	4.8	4.8	4.8	4.0
Holdings of nongovernment securities	...	0.8	0.7	0.3	0.2	0.2	0.1	0.2	0.1	0.1
Foreign assets	...	4.0	4.2	6.9	4.3	3.7	4.4	6.7	8.1	7.8
Foreign liabilities	...	2.3	2.6	2.4	2.0	2.8	3.0	5.0	7.1	3.7

Sources: Bangko Sentral ng Pilipinas; Bank Indonesia; Bank Negara Malaysia; Bank of Korea; Bank of Thailand; Central Bank of China (Taiwan Province of China); Central Bank of Sri Lanka; Central Bank of Turkey; Comision Nacional Bancaria (Mexico); Superintendencia de Bancos e Instituciones Financieras Chile; and IMF staff estimates.

[1] Data as of September for Turkey, October for Malaysia, and November for Korea, Sri Lanka, and Thailand.

[2] Including foreign currency denominated loans.

[3] Foreign assets/liabilities plus foreign currency denominated assets/liabilities.

[4] Operating securities portfolio not including government securities.

[5] Including operations of foreign branches.

the central bank, which pays the interbank interest rate on such deposits.[117] Loans to other banks in Malaysia rose from 8 percent of total assets in 1991 to a high of 22 percent in 1993. Loan demand was also moderated by a slowdown in economic growth and because banks were cautious about using short-term foreign liabilities to extend domestic credit. In addition, corporations with direct access to foreign borrowing often used these borrowed funds to pay off relatively high-cost domestic loans. An expansion of lending also accompanied high capital inflows in Mexico, where the total loan portfolio in the banking system expanded from 27 percent of GDP in 1991 to 47 percent in 1994.

Lower capital inflows are associated with lower increases in lending. While an expansion in lending is generally beneficial, a very rapid expansion in lending can result in a loosening of credit conditions. Under these circumstances of extreme liquidity due to rapid capital inflows, the search for investments may lead banks to extend credit to less profitable ventures or to less creditworthy borrowers. The history of banking crises in industrial and developing countries alike has shown that certain types of lending—particularly

real estate finance, lending backed by shares, consumer credit, and loans to bank insiders or related parties—have been more important sources of risk than others.[118]

The Indonesian and Malaysian authorities have recently expressed concern over the volume of lending to the property sector and to equity market participants. In Malaysia, loans to the property sector, loans for the purchase of shares, and consumer loans amounted to 35 percent of total commercial bank loans at the end of September 1994. However, loans for the purchase of shares had doubled as a proportion of total loans, from 2.6 percent at the end of 1993, to 5.1 percent in September 1994; these loans accounted for 71 percent of new loans contracted in the first seven months of 1994. In Mexico, the fastest rising components of total loans have been real estate loans, which grew from 12 percent of the portfolio in 1991 to 18 percent in 1994, and foreign currency loans whose share rose from 7 percent to 12 percent. Personal consumption loans rose sharply in 1992, but actually declined over 1993–94.

Where banks have expanded their balance sheets the most has resulted in an increase in securities investments, particularly from nongovernment issuers. In Malaysia, Mexico, and Thailand, in particular, banks reduced their holdings of government securities and increased their holdings of private sector securities. Although banks' holdings of all securities as a share of assets or GDP did not rise significantly

---

[117] At the end of 1991, the commercial banks had a net credit due to the central bank of RM 3,971 million (International Monetary Fund (1994b), Table 40). In 1992, as commercial bank deposits with the central bank increased, they became net lenders to the central bank. By the end of 1992, they had a net credit from the central bank of RM 12,943 million. This increased to RM 52,064 million at the end of March 1994.

[118] See International Monetary Fund (1993) and (1994a).

114

in Malaysia, and actually fell in Thailand, in both countries bank investment in private securities more than doubled as a proportion of assets or GDP, or both between 1989 and 1993. Total securities investment by the banking industry in Mexico has changed little since 1991. However, investment in government securities fell from 50 percent of total assets in 1991 to 2 percent in 1994, holdings of domestic fixed income securities tripled to 27 percent of the total, and foreign securities holdings rose 3 percent of the total.

In summary, in countries that have received the most capital inflows, banks have tended to play an important role as direct importers of capital, as suggested by the increase in net foreign liabilities of the banking system. Even in countries that initially attempted to sterilize the expansion in liquidity that capital inflows created, the result has generally been a rapid expansion in domestic lending or securities investments, or both. Such a rapid expansion in bank balance sheets implies at least the possibility that credit risk exposures and market risk exposures have increased sharply.

The effects of capital controls are also discernible in the balance sheet data. In Chile, taxes on short-term capital inflows introduced in 1991 have constrained the growth of commercial bank foreign liabilities even while total foreign capital inflows have increased. Hence, the expansion in bank balance sheets has been more modest. The situation changed markedly in 1994, however, as foreign liabilities and assets both increased sharply, fueling a significant increase in bank assets. In Malaysia, the imposition of capital controls in February 1994 scaled back capital inflows into the banking system and led to a sharp decline in the size of the banking sector.

Impact on Securities Markets

An important feature of recent capital flows to developing countries is the relative size of portfolio flows, particularly equity investment.[119] Developing country equity markets provide foreign investors with opportunities to diversify their portfolios and to exploit risk-return profiles unavailable in their own markets. Foreign equity investment also provides developing countries with access to a broader investor base, new sources of capital at potentially lower cost, and greater market depth and liquidity.[120] Thus far, however, preferences for liquidity have limited foreign participation in emerging bond markets; corporate bond markets are underdeveloped in most developing countries, and in most cases foreign investors

can satisfy their demand for sovereign risk in international bond markets.[121]

Foreign investment in domestic equity markets is important for at least two reasons. First, such investment may affect the way in which some financial assets are priced. At one extreme, for example, is the possibility that foreign capital inflows may initiate a speculative bubble in asset prices. More generally, foreign inflows and outflows can introduce extraneous sources of price fluctuation, resulting in less efficient asset pricing and, therefore, less efficient resource allocation. Second, securities are important assets of banks and other types of financial institutions; in some countries, the definition of regulatory capital includes unrealized gains on securities holdings. Fluctuations in securities prices, therefore, can lead to fluctuations in bank earnings and capital. Regulations in many developing countries allow banks to deal in securities, either directly or through subsidiaries; this provides another mechanism through which developments in securities markets can affect bank income. Consequently, sharp declines in securities prices can, through their effects on the banking system, have important systemic consequences.

Market Efficiency

Information efficiency allows capital markets to perform their allocative function because securities prices reflect all available information.[122] Mispricing can lead to a misallocation of resources to relatively unproductive enterprises and industries, and ultimately raise the cost of capital for efficient enterprises. The presence of international investors might have a number of, possibly conflicting, effects on pricing efficiency. Foreign investment decisions often are influenced by events in other markets (e.g., low returns in industrial country markets) and do not always reflect the "fundamentals" in domestic markets. Foreign investors may also have less information about domestic companies, or may place much greater importance on liquidity, which may lead them to exclude many firms from consideration in their portfolio. Hence, relative prices may be distorted by the presence of foreign investors, particularly in those markets, such as Indonesia and Mexico, where foreign investors account for a large proportion of total turnover. Alternatively, foreign investors often are equipped with better valuation techniques and more advanced computer and information processing technology than local investors, and can speed

---

[119]See also Folkerts-Landau and others (1995).

[120]See Feldman and Kumar (1994) for a discussion of the costs and benefits to developing countries of equity markets.

[121]Mexico has been an important exception to this generalization, attracting significant amounts of foreign investment in Tesobonos.

[122]A market is said to be efficient if all available information is fully reflected in current market prices.

up the adjustment of prices to changes in fundamental economic factors. However, foreign investment often includes a significant amount of "round tripping" in which local investors invest through offshore accounts, in which case foreign investment flows may not be based on less information than flows from domestic investors.

Market efficiency can be tested by examining the ability of local stock returns to predict future returns and the extent to which stock returns in industrial country markets (the U.S. equity market, for example) affect future equity returns in emerging markets.[123] Predictability of future returns implies unexploited profit opportunities and hence, weak-form information inefficiency.[124] For Hong Kong and Korea, initial periods of low and relatively stable inflows were followed by a period of higher average inflows (Table I.12).[125] In both countries, the most recent period has been characterized by significantly higher volatility in flows. In Thailand, investment flows were highly volatile after the opening up of the market in late 1988. By mid-1991 this volatility had subsided, as had the average level of flows, but since late 1992 investment flows have been much more volatile. In Mexico, the initial period of low-level flows was followed by a period of high and volatile investment flows that subsided in 1993.

The first column of Table I.12 reports the proportion of variability in daily stock index returns that is explainable from past local market returns alone.[126] For Hong Kong and Mexico, an increase in the rate of inflows is associated with a slight decline in predictability (i.e., greater efficiency), while for Korea there seems to have been no change. For both Hong Kong and Thailand, an increase in the volatility of flows is associated with a decrease in efficiency.

When past returns from the U.S. stock market alone are used to explain variability in local market returns, predictability is found to be greater when portfolio flows are larger, especially when such flows are volatile (Column 2). Using both past local market returns and the returns from the U.S. stock market (Column 3), predictability seems to be higher when

flows have been volatile, suggesting that for all countries examined except Thailand, there was some loss of efficiency. Moreover, regardless of the nature of investment flows, combining past local and U.S. equity price returns increases the predictability of the regressions.

Market Volatility

The presence of foreign investors can also increase stock price volatility by magnifying price fluctuations in the local market.[127] For example, a decline in an emerging market's stock price index may lead foreign investors to redeem their shares in country funds invested in that market. Fund managers may then be obliged to sell shares in the local market, unless they have adequate cash funds, which further reduces prices. In this way, the participation of large mutual funds—which in some countries is the only way for nonresidents to invest—might have a destabilizing impact on the local market. In December 1993, for example, U.S. investors purchased $674 million worth of Hong Kong shares, on a net basis; however, in the following month, U.S. investors sold, on a net basis, $708 million of Hong Kong shares, and set the stage for the rapid decline in share prices in the coming months. A similar reversal of capital flows occurred in Mexico. In February 1994, there was a net equity inflow of $280 million from the United States; however, in the following month, U.S. investors sold a net $170 million of Mexican shares. This rapid change in capital flows was accompanied by a rapid stock price decline in Mexico. This points to the possibility that volatile equity flows can have an adverse effect on the variability of stock prices in even relatively large emerging stock markets.

In this context, three related questions arise: Has stock-return volatility increased in absolute terms in the emerging markets? Has this volatility increased in emerging stock markets relative to, for example, return volatility in the United States? And has the probability of large declines in stock prices increased? The results in Table I.13 show that the absolute volatility of stock returns has shown little evidence of increasing during periods of increased portfolio flows, the exception being Hong Kong in

---

[123]Other forms of pricing inefficiency include anomalies such as seasonality, day-of-the-week effects, and month effects. Weak-form efficiency can also be tested by looking for serial correlation in returns—another form of evidence of predictability. Claessens, Dasgupta, and Glen (1993) find significant month effects for 16 of the 20 emerging markets tracked by the International Finance Corporation. They also find significant autocorrelation for seven emerging markets.

[124]Weak-form efficiency holds when current or past market prices cannot predict future prices.

[125]For want of a more complete data set, only data on U.S. equity investment flows are used to identify periods of high inflows or periods of volatile flows.

[126]Predictability is measured by the regression R-squared from regressing daily index returns on returns from the previous ten days.

[127]Kim and Singal (1993) find evidence that the volatility of equity price returns increases when the market is opened to foreign investment. They conclude, however, that this is due not to the transmission of shocks from foreign markets, but from the effect of other domestic liberalization measures. Domowitz, Glen, and Madhavan (1994) explore another mechanism through which foreign equity investment affects volatility in the local market. They find that shares listed on the Mexican stock exchange that are open to foreign investment become more volatile, despite a narrowing of bid-ask spreads, when the company issues depository receipts in the United States. Although pricing margins narrow in Mexico, trading by foreign investors is diverted away from the local stock exchange, resulting in lower turnover and greater variability.

Table I.12. Market Efficiency Tests

	Predictability of Local Stock Market Return		
	Using past local returns	Using past Dow Jones Industrial Average (DJIA) returns	Using past local and DJIA returns
Hong Kong			
Low-inflow period (Jan. 1988–Aug. 1991)	6.5	6.4	13.2
High-inflow period (Sept. 1991–Oct. 1993)	4.3	4.1	8.0
Volatile-flow period (Nov. 1993–July 1994)	7.9	16.8	22.1
Korea			
Low-inflow period (Jan. 1988–Dec. 1991)	3.5	1.8	5.1
High-inflow period (Jan. 1992–June 1993)	3.9	3.1	7.1
Volatile-flow period (July 1993–July 1994)	5.3	3.0	8.0
Thailand			
Volatile-flow period (Jan. 1988–Apr. 1991)	3.6	14.2	15.7
Moderate-inflow period (May 1991–Oct. 1992)	7.4	4.5	12.2
High-flow-volatility period (Nov. 1992–July 1994)	5.5	4.8	9.9
Mexico			
Low-inflow period (Jan. 1988–Apr. 1990)	8.7	2.3	12.2
Volatile-flow period (May 1990–Jan. 1993)	6.2	17.2	20.7
More-steady-inflow period (Feb. 1993–July 1994)	4.4	10.2	14.0

Source: IMF staff calculations based on data from The WEFA Group.

Note: Predictability is measured by the regression R-squared from regressing daily local market return on returns from the past ten days. It represents the percentage of the variation in the daily local market return explained by returns from the past ten days. The separation of the overall sample into different subsample periods with different portfolio flow characteristics is performed by inspecting the monthly portfolio flow data from the United States to these emerging markets and the data on the changes in monthly flows. The separation is also jointly determined by the use of common structural-break test statistics including the CUSUM test statistics and the CUSUMSQ test statistics. The return data are the continuously compounded daily return from the Hang Seng Index for Hong Kong, the Korea Composite Index for Korea, the Bangkok SET Index for Thailand, and the Morgan Stanley Capital International Index for Mexico.

the period when portfolio flows were very volatile. The increased volatility in Hong Kong might have been related to sudden reversals of investor sentiment about the prospects for investment in China and about the impending transfer of sovereignty over Hong Kong to China. In Mexico and Korea, absolute price volatility actually declined.[128] The estimated declines in both absolute volatility and the probability of sharp price declines in Mexico and Korea do not support the view that increased portfolio flows will necessarily cause excessive speculative trading and price fluctuations. The decline in volatility might be due in part to an increase in liquidity associated with the inflow of capital.

The relatively minor change in price volatility in the emerging markets generally reflects a similar pattern in the more developed equity markets through-

out the world. For example, volatility in stock market returns in the United States declined during the period 1988–94.[129] Despite this similarity, in all of the emerging markets studied there is strong evidence that stock-returns volatility has increased relative to stock-returns volatility in the United States, especially in the period when portfolio flows were very volatile. The most extreme case is Hong Kong, where the ratio of the standard deviation of stock returns in the volatile-portfolio-flow period is more than twice that in the low-portfolio-flow period. This increase in relative volatility in the emerging markets is consistent with the view that volatile portfolio flows can magnify

---

[128]This is also true for Chile, another country that has been experiencing a surge in capital flows and a stock market boom; see Reinhart and Reinhart (1994).

[129]The standard deviation of returns on the Dow Jones Industrial Average declined with each successive time period described for each country in Table I.13. For example, using the three time periods identified for Hong Kong, the standard deviations of Dow Jones returns were 1.06 percent, 0.67 percent, and 0.63 percent. For the time period defined for some other countries, the decline in volatility is more pronounced.

Table I.13. Daily Market Index Return Volatility and Extreme Price Movement Analysis

	Absolute Volatility[1]	Relative Volatility[2]	Probability of Extreme Price Decline[3]
			(In percent)
Hong Kong			
Low-inflow period (Jan. 1988–Aug. 1991)	1.61	1.52	2.06
High-inflow period (Sept. 1991–Oct. 1993)	1.31	1.98	1.74
Volatile-flow period (Nov. 1993–July 1994)	2.33	3.68	9.94
Korea			
Low-inflow period (Jan. 1988–Dec. 1991)	1.51	1.42	3.22
High-inflow period (Jan. 1992–June 1993)	1.18	2.55	3.40
Volatile-flow period (July 1993–July 1994)	1.14	2.31	2.01
Thailand			
Volatile-flow period (Jan. 1988–Apr. 1991)	1.19	1.74	5.51
Moderate-inflow period (May 1991–Oct. 1992)	1.69	2.14	3.97
High-flow-volatility period (Nov. 1992–July 1994)	1.17	2.66	3.75
Mexico			
Low-inflow period (Jan. 1988–Apr. 1990)	1.99	1.88	5.11
Volatile-flow period (May 1990–Jan. 1993)	1.57	1.76	4.59
More-steady-inflow period (Feb. 1993–July 1994)	1.61	2.57	3.72

Source: IMF staff calculations based on data from The WEFA Group.
Note: The separation of the overall sample into different subsample periods with different portfolio flow characteristics is performed by inspecting the monthly portfolio flow data from the United States to these emerging markets and the data on the changes in monthly flows. The separation is also jointly determined by the use of common structural-break test statistics including the CUSUM test statistics and the CUSUMSQ test statistics. The returns data are the continuously compounded daily returns from the Hang Seng Index for Hong Kong, the Korea Composite Index for Korea, the Bangkok SET Index for Thailand, and the Morgan Stanley Capital International Index for Mexico.
[1]Standard deviation of the daily return.
[2]Standard deviation relative to standard deviation of the daily return of the Dow Jones Industrial Average.
[3]Probability of a larger than 3 percent daily drop.

the sensitivity of stock returns in emerging stock markets to fluctuations in stock returns in the larger developed equity markets, such as in the United States.

With regard to the probability of sharp stock price declines, the most striking example is Hong Kong, where the probability of a price decline larger than 3 percent is about 10 percent in the volatile-flow period and about 2 percent in the low-flow period. In Korea, the probability of a decline larger than 3 percent turns out to be lower in the volatile-flow period than in the other periods. For Thailand, the volatile-flow period has the highest probability of an extreme price drop. In Mexico, the probability of a sharp decline in the volatile-flow period is lower than in the low-flow period but higher than in the more-steady-flow period. It is such sudden and sharp changes in prices and, the risk of a sudden loss of liquidity—as is discussed below—that can significantly increase systemic risk.

Market Linkages and Spillovers

The increased participation of foreign investors in emerging markets can potentially strengthen the linkage between local and foreign markets. Even though foreign investment might not affect the relationship between market fundamentals in industrial and emerging stock markets, it can magnify the effect of industrial country market turbulence on the emerging equity markets.[130] Disturbances to foreign stock markets affect the relative returns on investments in developing country markets, which may cause foreign investors to adjust their positions. In

---

[130]Ng, Chang, and Chou (1991) find that active participation of foreign investors on local stock markets is necessary for there to be spillovers. Simply receiving information about developments in other markets, or having correlated economic fundamentals—as one might expect between close trading partners, for example—is not sufficient.

Table I.14. Volatility Spillover Analysis

	Correlation Measure of Volatility Spillover[1]
Hong Kong	
Low-inflow period	
(Jan. 1988–Aug. 1991)	0.068 **
High-inflow period	
(Sept. 1991–Oct. 1993)	0.023
Volatile-flow period	
(Nov. 1993–July 1994)	0.150 *+
Korea	
Low-inflow period	
(Jan. 1988–Dec. 1991)	0.055 *
High-inflow period	
(Jan. 1992–June 1993)	0.029
Volatile-flow period	
(July 1993–July 1994)	0.120 *
Thailand	
Volatile-flow period	
(Jan. 1988–Apr. 1991)	0.296 ***
Moderate-inflow period	
(May 1991–Oct. 1992)	0.115 **+++
High-flow-volatility period	
(Nov. 1992–July 1994)	0.103 **
Mexico	
Low-inflow period	
(Jan. 1988–Apr. 1990)	0.048
Volatile-flow period	
(May 1990–Jan. 1993)	0.324 ***+++
More-steady-inflow period	
(Feb. 1993–July 1994)	0.003 +++

Source: IMF staff calculations based on data from The WEFA Group.

Note: The separation of the overall sample into different sub-sample periods with different portfolio flow characteristics is performed by inspecting the monthly portfolio flow data from the United States to these emerging markets and the data on the changes in monthly flows. The separation is also jointly determined by the use of common structural-break test statistics, including the CUSUM test statistics and the CUSUMSQ test statistics. The return data are the continuously compounded daily return from the Hang Seng Index for Hong Kong, the Korea Composite Index for Korea, the Bangkok SET Index for Thailand, and the Morgan Stanley Capital International Index for Mexico.

[1]Correlation between squared daily local return and lagged squared daily return of the Dow Jones Industrial Average; ***, **, and * indicate significance at the 1 percent, 5 percent, and 10 percent levels, respectively. In addition, +++ and + indicate a significant change in the correlation measure from the previous period at the 1 percent and 10 percent levels, respectively.

some cases, foreign investors own such a large proportion of the tradable stock that their transactions have a large impact on prices. For example, in Indonesia, foreign investors own about 30 percent of listed equity, but because so much of the locally owned stock is closely held and not traded, foreign investors' transactions account for more than 70 percent of turnover on the Jakarta Stock Exchange.

Spillovers may arise when the behavior of non-resident investors leads to a defensive investment strategy by resident investors. Because local investors generally have no information about whether foreign investors are changing their portfolios because of liquidity constraints, a desire to rediversify, or special information about economic fundamentals in the local market, local investors will tend to react to such moves. Such reactions will magnify the effect of foreign turbulence on the local market.

Table I.14 reports correlations between stock price volatility—estimated by the squared daily stock market return—in the United States on one-day and stock price volatility in selected emerging stock markets on the following day. The data suggest that there have been volatility spillovers from the U.S. stock market to these emerging stock markets, and that these spillovers have been strongest when portfolio flows have been most volatile.[131] The correlation measures of volatility spillovers are highest during the volatile-flow periods in all countries examined except Thailand. For both Hong Kong and Korea, the correlation measure of volatility spillovers in the volatile-flow period are more than twice as large as in the low-inflow period. For Mexico, the correlation measure of volatility spillovers in the volatile-flow period (which occurs in a different time period than those of Hong Kong and Korea) is more than seven times the correlation measure for the low-inflow period.

---

[131]The increase in volatility spillover in Mexico, when portfolio flows became volatile, is statistically significant at the 1 percent level. The subsequent drop in spillover, when portfolio flows became less volatile, is also highly significant. In Thailand, there is a significant drop in volatility spillover when portfolio flows became less volatile.

VII

Financial Sector Constraints on Crisis Management

Financial markets and institutions play important roles in intermediating both capital inflows and outflows. At the same time, in times of financial market turbulence, for example, when there is a massive surge in capital outflows, the financial system is profoundly affected. Financial structure, and in particular the health of the banking system, can have an important impact on both the severity of the crisis and the ability to respond to a crisis. One implication of these complex relationships is that it may be difficult to operate a currency board in countries with relatively weak banking systems. The automatic adjustment mechanism of a currency board operates directly on the balance sheet of the banking system and can lead to instability if banks are not well capitalized.

Financial Markets During Periods of Capital Outflow

The domestic banking system provides the main channel for capital outflows by providing essential payment and currency conversion services. When investors take speculative positions against a currency, the banking system also provides the credit necessary to finance these positions. Illiquid money and securities markets, and constraints on the ability of banks to extend credit, may limit the speed with which capital outflows can occur.

Mechanics of Capital Outflows and Speculative Attacks

When investors, domestic or foreign, want to invest abroad they first must sell their local currency securities. In return they will obtain, in the first instance, a local currency deposit in a domestic bank. This deposit will then be converted to foreign exchange, and then transferred out of the country. The exchange of local currency for foreign currency in the spot market results in a decline in the central bank's foreign exchange reserves or puts pressure on the exchange rate depending upon the nature of the exchange rate regime, or both.

During a speculative attack, the domestic banking system takes on a somewhat different role that, in effect, increases its credit risk. The mechanisms are as follows. Ultimately, speculators must be able to draw on credit in the country whose currency is being attacked.[132] While an investor may be able to borrow Mexican pesos in New York, for example, the creditor bank would ultimately have to obtain pesos from the Mexican banking system. Speculators try to profit from currency movements by acquiring a short position in a currency that they expect to be devalued, usually by entering into forward contracts to deliver the currency. Some margin is required by the banks, but this can be leveraged up by a factor of ten or more by the speculator. As standard practice, banks will generally respond to the sale of a forward contract by entering into offsetting spot and swap transactions to eliminate the currency and maturity mismatches. Thus, for example, a bank's forward commitment to acquire domestic currency is balanced by selling domestic currency for foreign exchange in the spot market, and then entering into a swap contract to deliver foreign exchange for spot delivery and receive foreign exchange when the forward contract matures.[133]

Thus, a forward sale of domestic currency by a speculator immediately results in a spot sale by the bank, and although the bank hedges its currency and maturity risk, it takes on credit risk vis-à-vis both the speculator and the swap counterparty. Moreover, the hedging transactions require either a counterparty from outside the banking system or the central bank to buy the local currency on the forward market (the forward leg of the swap). The latter is often the only willing counterparty. In effect, the central bank finances both balancing operations: it eases pressure on the exchange rate arising from the spot sales by buying the domestic currency on the spot market; and it ultimately provides the credit to finance the forward leg of the swap transactions between banks. Lenders of domestic currency in the swap market finance this credit by borrowing through the discount window or other central bank financing devices. In this way, the central bank essentially finances the speculative attack against itself.

---

[132] While an investor may be able to borrow deutsche mark in London, for example, the creditor bank would ultimately have to obtain the deutsche mark from the German banking system.

[133] See International Monetary Fund (1993) for an illustration of these balancing operations.

When they agree to a forward transaction, banks take on credit risk. They will limit this risk by imposing credit limits on their counterparties. These credit limits constrain the volume of forward contracts that can be issued. Another prudential constraint on the extent of speculation is the foreign exchange exposure limits many banks are required to observe, or choose to impose on their own operations. Because they are also acquiring credit risk, speculators may be reluctant to enter into a large volume of forward foreign exchange contracts with a particular bank out of concern that the bank may be unable to honor the contract in the event of a sharp depreciation.

Constraints Posed by Illiquidity in Financial Markets

There are some obvious constraints on the process just described. In the case of a simple sale of domestic securities to finance the capital outflow, the less liquid are domestic securities markets (as measured by the bid-ask spread) the more costly it is for investors to sell securities. Consequently, the expected exchange rate depreciation would have to be larger to make it worth incurring these costs. In addition, the attempt to sell a large amount of securities in an illiquid market may significantly lower their market price.[134] Hence, illiquidity effectively increases transactions costs, which inhibits inflows and outflows. In Indonesia, for example, foreign investors own approximately 30 percent of listed equity, but historically have accounted for more than 70 percent of turnover. In the event of a loss of confidence in the currency, illiquidity might make it difficult to find buyers: the dominant traders—foreign investors—would be lined up on one side of the market. At the best of times on the Jakarta Stock Exchange, bid-ask spreads are wide and average transaction sizes are small; it can take some time to sell large shareholdings. There were similar conditions in Mexico in late 1994 and early 1995—foreign investors accounted for a greater proportion of turnover than their ownership stakes would imply.[135]

Similarly, illiquidity in money markets can also increase the cost of foreign investment. Holders of money market instruments in illiquid markets face wide bid-ask spreads that discourage selling, except when large depreciations are expected. In addition, illiquidity in money markets (especially the interbank credit markets) increases the cost of credit. This will make it more expensive for banks to finance their forward purchases of domestic currency.

Although it might appear that illiquid markets are less prone to experiencing a speculative attack, there are alternative mechanisms for speculators to attack currency. A simple alternative would be to take out a local currency loan, purchase foreign currency, and hold it until the loan matures. If the exchange rate depreciates by the time the loan matures, speculators will have profited by the difference. The scope of such operations is limited, however, by the prudential limits banks have on loans to single counterparties. Moreover, during a crisis, interest rates may rise more than the expected rate of depreciation, which increases the cost of this strategy.

Illiquid securities markets and tight credit markets clearly limit the speed at which sizable positions against a currency can be taken. However, the benefits to a country during brief episodes of market pressure and turbulence must be considered against the ongoing costs of illiquid markets. While wide bid-ask spreads may limit selling pressure, they may also deter investment in the first place. Illiquid domestic markets, in effect, inhibit both inflows and outflows. Liquid markets have important benefits, including lower capital costs, more efficient resource allocation and price discovery, and constant market feedback for policymakers. In addition, liquid money markets provide an important channel through which domestic financial institutions can manage their day-to-day risk exposures. Likewise, liquid forward exchange markets allow financial and nonfinancial firms the opportunity to hedge their foreign exchange risks.

Crisis Management

Foreign Exchange Market Intervention

The first line of defense against a weakening exchange rate is simply to support the currency by purchasing it in the foreign exchange market. In employing this defense, the central bank increases demand for the domestic currency by depleting its reserves. The ability to defend the exchange rate through spot intervention is clearly limited by the amount of available reserves, including borrowed reserves. While these are often large amounts, one lesson from the ERM crisis in the fall of 1992 was that market participants together, through leveraging, can mobilize much larger positions in foreign currencies than can be countered, because of either quantitative or political constraints on the authorities.

Central banks can increase their resources by borrowing foreign exchange on the international syndicated loan market or from other central banks. However, even central banks are limited in the amounts they can borrow. When borrowing from the domestic banking system, central bank borrowing is constrained by the prudential limits on credit and foreign

---

[134]Symmetrically, an attempt to purchase a large volume may sharply increase the market price.

[135]In Mexico, as of October 1994, foreign investors held approximately 26 percent of the stock market capitalization.

exchange exposures that domestic banks are obliged to meet. Although banks may have larger, even unlimited, credit limits on loans to the central bank as compared with loans to other counterparties, the main constraint on lending to the central bank is likely to be the interbank credit limits. When the central bank borrows large amounts of foreign currency from domestic banks, the loaned amounts must be acquired in the interbank market. The size of these amounts is constrained by both foreign exchange exposure limits and by large exposure (single counterparty) lending limits on interbank borrowing imposed by the counterparty banks that provide the foreign currency.

Because the scope for borrowing from the domestic banking system is limited, central banks often turn to official sources of credit, for example, official swap facilities between central banks such as the very short-term financing facility in the ERM. Two factors limit such borrowing. The main constraint is actually from the creditor institutions. The provision of large amounts of credit between central banks can introduce a conflict in the creditor central bank between the defense of the exchange rate and its own domestic monetary policy objectives. Unless the creditor central bank wants to expand the domestic money supply in its own country, it will sterilize the expansion in credit implied by the use of the inter-central bank swap facility. Sterilization in this case means selling other assets, for example, government securities. Sterilization, however, can be costly. In the 1992 ERM crisis for example, the Bundesbank was undertaking currency swaps with German banks in non-ERM currencies at rising deutsche mark interest rates. Moreover, central banks can exhaust their supply of securities to sell to the market, and may be limited in their ability to, for example, issue securities of their own. Consequently, the creditor central bank may be soon confronted with the need to abandon domestic monetary policy objectives or to stop lending to the central bank whose currency is being attacked.

Second, the more a central bank borrows to defend its currency, the greater are its potential losses if the defense is unsuccessful. Given the limited resources available to a central bank, if there is a high probability that the defense will not succeed, for example, because of a declining willingness of creditor central banks to lend, then the central bank will have to consider other strategies for using its limited resources in defense of the currency.

Interest Rate Defense

Because spot intervention is constrained by the amount of reserves that can be mobilized, the central bank may have to consider other policy options. In response to gradual capital outflows, one option is to make local assets more attractive, by increasing interest rates relative to those in industrial countries.[136] During periods of great stress, this policy would be most effective if interest rates are increased on the most liquid assets, interbank deposits and government bonds. During a speculative attack, central banks often use sharp increases in interest rates to inhibit speculation by making it more costly for speculators to finance or settle their forward positions, or for banks to finance their own positions (for example, if one-month forwards are financed in overnight loan markets). A sharp increase in interest rates penalizes those who are short of local currency, thus making it more costly to speculate; it also increases the returns to holding local currency assets. This is the classic interest rate defense of a fixed exchange rate.[137]

In a currency board regime these defensive interest rate increases are automatic.[138] Under the rules of a currency board, foreign exchange can only be acquired by surrendering an equal amount of local currency assets. Thus, capital outflows reduce the monetary base. This leads to a contraction in monetary aggregates (via the monetary multiplier) and to an increase in interest rates, which encourages investors to hold domestic assets.

To be effective, the central bank must have credibility. Experience suggests that central banks obtain this credibility by taking actions that convince the market that it is prepared to take whatever action is necessary, including enduring high interest rates for a protracted period, to defend the exchange rate.

Nevertheless, there are important reasons why the interest rate defense might not be employed. In particular, there may be certain characteristics of the domestic financial system that make the interest rate defense less effective, or too costly.[139] The initial problem with the interest rate defense is that higher interest rates may not affect the behavior of speculators if they have previously arranged medium-term financing for their positions. The higher interest rates might, however, affect the financial condition

---

[136]Empirical studies of the determinants of capital inflows to developing countries have identified interest rate differentials between industrial and developing countries as being perhaps the most important.

[137]Garber and Spencer (1994) discuss how the widespread use of dynamic hedging operations can actually reverse the effects of the interest rate increase.

[138]See below for a discussion of the adjustment mechanism in a currency board.

[139]There are other important constraints on the use of interest rate increases to defend the currency, including the impact on debt-financing costs for the government. This was apparently an important reason why the increase in the discount rate by the Banca d'Italia in August 1994 was not effective. Since a large proportion of Italian government debt is in the form of domestic floating rate or very short-term securities, investors questioned the sustainability of high interest rates.

of banks that financed the speculation.[140] For example, if banks had provided one-month credit to speculators and funded the credit through short-term (e.g., overnight) interbank loans, then an increase in interbank interest rates would increase the cost of funding the speculators. All banks, however, including those who had no part in the speculative attack, would incur higher costs.

In many countries, including Argentina, Indonesia, and Mexico, some of the smaller banks fund themselves to a significant extent through interbank borrowing. When the central bank increases its intervention rate, interbank interest rates are the first rates to rise. The deliberate increase in interest rates therefore creates losses for the entire banking system. For well-capitalized banks with healthy balance sheets, these losses can be incurred without threatening the soundness of these institutions or the stability of the financial system. The HKMA responded to a speculative attack in January 1995 by tightening liquidity and forcing overnight interbank interest rates to rise sharply from 5.38 percent at the end of January 12 to 12 percent in early trading on January 13. This swift policy response imposed much higher funding costs on the banking industry in Hong Kong, which relies on borrowing from the HKMA on the interbank market for liquidity management purposes. The HKMA, however, was confident that a brief increase in interest rates and the associated losses could easily be borne by the banking system, in part because the average bank capital/risk-weighted assets ratio was in the neighborhood of 15–20 percent.

In contrast, in countries where the banking sector is weak, the use of an aggressive interest rate policy is constrained by concerns about the ability of the banking sector to survive the shock. If the banking sector is characterized by low capital ratios and weak balance sheets, the losses resulting from the high interest rates associated with the interest rate defense could raise concerns about the solvency of the banking system. The interest rate defense could potentially result in bank failures or the use of official funds to provide emergency liquidity assistance, capital to the banking industry, or to pay out deposit insurance benefits.

The interest rate defense can also affect bank capital through its impact on the quality of bank assets. If the capital outflows are driven by fundamental concerns about the economy rather than by a brief period of purely speculative activity, it may be necessary to keep interest rates high for a protracted period of time. Persistently high interbank interest rates will eventually affect the whole interest rate structure as banks will pass these increases on to their customers

through higher loan rates.[141] In this way, a sustained increase in interest rates designed to prevent capital outflows runs the risk of affecting the quality of banks' loan portfolios. Whenever the banking sector already has a large number of nonperforming loans, a sharp increase in interest rates can reduce cash flows from loans and create severe liquidity problems.

In a country that has had a fixed exchange rate for a substantial period of time, capital outflows pose a particular dilemma. If the exchange rate was fixed as part of a stabilization program, domestic banks and nonbanks might have had an incentive to acquire foreign currency liabilities. At least initially, foreign interest rates probably would have been lower (lingering inflation expectations would have kept domestic real rates relatively high) and currency risk might have been perceived to have declined. In such a situation, foreign currency loans might have been much more attractive than loans denominated in domestic currency. In Mexico, for example, a substantial portion of the domestic foreign currency loans was apparently made to firms with no obvious foreign currency income. The dilemma facing the authorities is that, if bank balance sheets are already weak, an increase in interest rates to defend the exchange rate raises borrowing costs to all, resulting in rising loan defaults and declining bank income. The alternative, however, of allowing the exchange rate to depreciate, is also a problem because it raises the cost of foreign currency loans and results in higher default rates.

The crucial factor is the speed with which interest rate increases are passed on to borrowers. In the United Kingdom during the ERM crisis, for example, an important constraint on the interest rate defense was the fact that most mortgages carried floating interest rates tied to the bank rate. Consequently, there was a direct and rapid pass-through from the central bank's interest rate policy to an important interest rate for consumers. This transmission mechanism was widely seen as imposing large costs on consumers and businesses. In Mexico and Indonesia, the majority of loans have floating interest rates. In these countries, most loans would have their interest rates adjusted within three months.

Currency Boards: Automatic Adjustment Mechanism at Work

A currency board is an institutional arrangement in which the board is committed to exchanging, on

---

[140]Higher rates would also squeeze the funding of securities and banking operations, which typically finance their positions through short-term rollover credit.

[141]Unless of course, the higher interest rates can be applied selectively to banks that are funding speculators, or even to particular liquidity demands. In France, for example, during the ERM crisis in September 1992, the central bank discriminated between requests for funds through the discount window to finance commercial activity rather than speculation, and offered discounts to the former at much lower rates.

demand and without limit, foreign currency and local currency—and in some cases bank reserves—at a preannounced exchange rate.[142] The credibility of the currency board stems from the complete backing of the currency with foreign assets, usually invested in interest-bearing government securities denominated in the reserve currency.[143] Currency boards are viewed as implying a stronger commitment than a simple pegged exchange rate rule because there are legal constraints to reneging on the commitment to fixed exchange rates. For instance, in Argentina, the abandonment of the convertibility law requires a change in legislation. In addition, under a pure currency board arrangement, the monetary authority is not allowed to lend to the government, to act as a lender of last resort to the banking system, or to engage in open market operations.[144]

Under a currency board arrangement, capital outflows directly affect the supply of liquidity in local currency money markets. In the simplest currency board regime—in which the currency board exchanges foreign currency for domestic currency only—when a local currency deposit is converted to a foreign currency deposit, it must first be exchanged for local currency and then be presented to the currency board for conversion to foreign currency. Initially, deposit withdrawals from the banking system will be accommodated by a reduction in the banks' cash reserves. As the volume of capital outflows increases, commercial banks will exhaust their supply of local currency cash reserves and be forced either to liquidate domestic assets (including ultimately part of their domestic currency loan portfolio) for cash or to acquire domestic currency from the currency board by selling foreign assets.[145] This process leads to a decrease in total credit and

in the money supply, and to an increase in interest rates. As interest rates rise, the relative return to domestic investment increases, and the incentive for capital to flow out declines. Hence, under the currency board, or indeed any fixed exchange rate regime, capital outflows affect the domestic financial system through an expansion or contraction of bank balance sheets. In this simple currency board regime, capital outflows will eventually cease when the banking system runs out of foreign assets to sell to the currency board.[146] All cash and commercial bank foreign assets would have been converted to foreign currency, but there will remain a stock of local currency denominated deposits and loans.

In the Argentine, Estonian, and Hong Kong currency boards, capital outflows will quickly lead to pressure on the interbank interest rate. In these regimes, the currency board will convert banks' deposits at the central bank into foreign currency.[147] Hence, banks will initially turn to the interbank market to acquire reserves.[148]

If capital outflows are sufficiently large, a currency board could collapse because of a shortage of foreign assets. If it did not initially provide complete cover for the domestic currency, the currency board might deplete its foreign currency reserves before the entire domestic currency stock had been converted. If it did have full backing, massive capital outflows might lead to the elimination of domestic currency from circulation and its replacement by the foreign reserve currency. The currency board would still exist—albeit with a greatly reduced balance sheet—and it would still be prepared to exchange foreign assets for domestic currency at the original exchange rate. However, once the domestic currency supply has been completely converted, and until demand for local currency returned, there would be no transactions, the currency board would no longer provide seigniorage, and it would be largely irrelevant.[149]

Even assuming the currency board had sufficient reserves to stave off a collapse, large-scale capital outflows would still have serious adverse consequences for the financial system. As demand for foreign currency increases, interest rates would increase sharply.[150] Indeed, this is the intended

---

[142]Currency boards are operating in several countries, including Argentina (since 1991), Estonia (1992), Hong Kong (1983), and Lithuania (1994).

[143]In a pure currency board regime, foreign reserves are held to back currency in the hands of the public and in bank vaults only. In practice, currency boards differ on the definition of the monetary aggregate that is backed by the foreign reserves, and the extent of coverage of these reserves. For example, in Hong Kong, the Exchange Fund is committed to 100 percent foreign currency backing for Hong Kong dollar bank notes. In Argentina and Estonia, the currency board backs both currency and commercial banks' reserves, but these liabilities are backed in part by domestic government debt denominated in foreign currency. See Bennett (1994) for a discussion of these issues.

[144]This is not true, however, in Hong Kong where the HKMA has an explicit mandate to act as an official lender of last resort and has been involved in open market operations since 1990.

[145]The currency board mechanism effectively adds a step in the process of converting domestic currency deposits into foreign currency: the holder of the deposit demands a withdrawal, which the bank satisfies by selling foreign assets to the currency board, which then sells an equivalent amount of foreign currency to the deposit holder.

[146]Banks will likely be unwilling or unable to borrow foreign exchange from abroad since the potential losses from a devaluation, which at this point most investors would anticipate, would be significant.

[147]This is true in Hong Kong for the note-issuing banks only.

[148]Alternatively, banks could liquidate other assets and convert them to interbank deposits to acquire reserve assets.

[149]Some residual demand for local currency might remain, for example, to pay taxes and other such obligations to the government.

[150]In fact, interest rates rise as demand for the domestic currency needed for presentation to the currency board for conversion to foreign currency rises.

effect—the classic fixed exchange rate adjustment mechanism. Rather than increasing as a matter of policy (as in the interest rate defense described earlier) under a currency board arrangement, interest rates increase automatically as demand for foreign currency increases.

Sharp increases in interest rates likely worsen asset quality and liquidity, at precisely the time that liquidity is most needed. Consequently, rigid adherence to a currency board in the face of large-scale capital outflows can carry the cost of instability in the banking sector. The quality and solvency of the banking system would determine the resilience of the system to the interest rate defense.[151]

Recent Developments in the Mexican Banking System

The devaluation of the Mexican peso has affected, and is likely to continue to affect, Mexican banks. The immediate impact of the devaluation fell on foreign currency and money market positions, the peso value of net foreign currency assets and liabilities, and the valuation of their fixed income and equity holdings. Another, and potentially more important, impact is on the quality of loan portfolios, capitalization levels, and the condition of the banking system as a whole.

Impact of Devaluation on the Mexican Banking System

The immediate effect of the peso devaluation on Mexican commercial banks does not appear to have been severe. The net foreign exchange position of Mexican banks is limited by regulation to 15 percent of net capital, and foreign currency liabilities are limited to 10 percent of total peso and foreign currency liabilities. It has been reported that the banking system had a small net asset position at the time of the devaluation. This implies that banks realized a gain, on average, on their net foreign currency position.[152] By contrast, the marked-to-market value of the fixed income portfolios of commercial banks is estimated to have declined by MexN$660 million after the devaluation. Moreover, although it is difficult to estimate the impact of the subsequent decline in the Mexican stock market on the value of bank equity holdings, it is likely to have been significant.[153]

After the devaluation and the resulting loss of confidence, some Mexican banks experienced pressures on their liquidity positions because of the difficulties they encountered in refinancing their maturing dollar-denominated certificates of deposit, estimated at $7 billion.[154] At least part of the problem was that Mexican banks offered Tesobonos as collateral for their foreign borrowing. In the first few weeks after the devaluation, foreign investors preferred not to acquire Tesobonos; as a result, banks could not sell Tesobonos to repay dollar loans, even as interest rates on these loans rose sharply. The resulting tight liquidity conditions in the domestic market most affected the smaller and weaker banks that lost their domestic and foreign currency interbank credit lines at the same time that they lost deposits—mostly demand deposits in the case of the small wholesale banks.

The more fundamental impact of the peso devaluation has fallen on the asset quality of the banking system. Even before the devaluation, Mexican commercial banks had experienced a decline in asset quality. Past-due loans increased from 3.5 percent of total loans at the end of 1991 to 8.5 percent in March 1994; and by the end of 1994 they had declined modestly to 7.9 percent.[155] More significantly, past-due loans increased sharply from 35.1 percent of total capital at the end of 1991 to 97.5 percent at the end of 1994.

The devaluation adversely affected foreign currency loans, which, as of December 1994, represented almost a third of total loans by Mexican banks. As much as 25 percent of these dollar loans may have been extended to firms without an obvious source of foreign currency income.[156] These firms have encountered difficulties in servicing their loans at the new rates, and the difficulties mean higher default rates and greater strains on the banking system.

The sharp rise in interest rates also affected the domestic currency loan portfolio. Since most loans in Mexico are made at variable interest rates tied to the one-month Cetes rate or the TIIP (*tasa interbancaria promedia*) rate, as these rates increased steadily in early 1995, peaking at over 90 percent in early March, payments ceased on a large proportion of loans of all types. Banks generally chose to restructure these loans, or simply to suspend interest payments, rather than be forced to recognize them as high-risk assets and to make provisions by writing off a certain amount of their already declining capital. Moreover, in Mexico, once a loan is designated

---

[151]The high volatility in interest rates led the HKMA to develop institutional arrangements to allow it to conduct open market operations in order to smooth short-run fluctuations in liquidity.

[152]At the end of September 1994, commercial banks had net foreign currency assets of MexN$53 billion. However, the Mexican banking system—commercial banks and development banks combined—had a net foreign liability of MexN$11 billion. By the end of December this net liability had increased to MexN$23 billion.

[153]At the end of 1994, banks' domestic equity holdings amounted to MexN$13.4 billion, or 1.6 percent of their total assets.

[154]García-Cantera and Pearl (1995).

[155]Because the exchange rate depreciation and interest rate increase occurred in the last ten days of 1994, and since loans are declared past due when payments are fifteen days late, the effects of these price changes are not reflected in end-year data.

[156]Moody's Investors Service (1995).

as nonperforming, the penalty interest rate applied to the loan is 150 percent of the contracted rate. Because interest rates more than doubled, borrowers would actually have an incentive not to service the loan.

A number of factors led to a decline in the risk-weighted capital ratios of several Mexican banks, below the 8 percent minimum. First, the depreciation of the peso resulted in a significant decline in banks' capital ratios: the value of foreign currency assets increased in local currency terms, but they had no foreign currency denominated capital. Second, capital declined as banks increased their provisions against nonperforming assets.

Measures to Strengthen the Banking System

The National Banking Commission (CNB) took several measures in early 1995 to strengthen the Mexican banking system. The first measure requires that banks maintain a minimum level of loan-loss reserves equal to the greater of 60 percent of their nonperforming loan portfolio or 4 percent of their total loan portfolio. This measure sought to ensure that bank reserves were increased sufficiently to withstand the anticipated decline in asset quality.

The second measure adopted by the CNB was the creation of the temporary capitalization program (programa de capitalización temporal (PROCAPTE)), administered by the deposit guarantee fund (Fondo Bancario de Protección al Alhorro (FOBAPROA)), to recapitalize banks which fall under the 8 percent required capitalization ratio. Under PROCAPTE, banks may borrow from FOBAPROA to increase their capital, by issuing five-year convertible subordinated debt. The funds raised from FOBAPROA are placed in a blocked account with the central bank so that they will not result in an expansion of the monetary base. FOBAPROA, in turn, borrows the funds from Banco de México at the same interest rate as that paid by Banco de México to the commercial banks.[157] As long as a bank participates in PROCAPTE, it will have to restrict its loan growth and maintain a 9 percent capital adequacy ratio instead of the official 8 percent. In the event that a bank cannot repay its debt by the end of the five-year period, or if its net capital excluding the subordinated debt issued under the program falls under 2 percent or significantly below that of the other banks participating in PROCAPTE, FOBAPROA will convert the subordinated debt into stock and sell it. As of the end of March 1995, six banks had obtained assistance totaling MexN$6.49 billion (equal to 14.5 percent of the net worth of all Mexican commercial banks at the end of 1994) from FOBAPROA under the PROCAPTE program.

The Mexican authorities announced in March 1995 three additional facilities for restructuring loans, with additional funding totaling MexN$148 billion. The first program targets small and medium-sized companies. Under the plan, banks will transfer about MexN$76 billion of nonperforming loans—equal to 13 percent of the value of all peso loans, or 150 percent of past due loans, at the end of December 1994—from their balance sheet to off-balance-sheet special purpose vehicles or trusts. At that time, the banks will also transfer a 15 percent reserve to the trust. The banks would each receive an amount of government zero-coupon bonds, accruing interest at the 28-day Cetes rate, equal to the amount of loans, net of provisions, that they transferred to their trust. Each bank will be allowed to restructure not more than 20 percent of its loan portfolio.

The nonperforming loans will be restructured into new instruments based on units of investments (UDIs), which would increase in line with the inflation rate.[158] As UDIs, the loan principal would be indexed to inflation and carry a real interest rate of up to 12 percent.[159] That is, the new restructured loans will have nominal interest rates significantly below those of the original contracts as the depreciation of the real value of the principal is eliminated. This approach automatically capitalizes inflation premiums into the loans; it is a way of rolling over debt service due from borrowers, of lessening their current debt burdens, and of pushing the problem into the future. The restructuring will extend the original maturities to between 5 and 12 years, with up to a 7-year grace period.

The trusts, which will be administered by the banks, will raise funds by issuing 5- to 12-year UDI-indexed bonds, carrying an interest rate equal to the UDI rate plus 4 percent, that will be purchased by the federal government.

The authorities have also agreed to implement restructuring programs, following the UDI model, for mortgages and dollar-denominated loans. The program for mortgages will apply to MexN$33 billion in mortgages (31.6 percent of the current housing loan portfolio). The loans will be transferred to an off-balance-sheet trust along with a 15 percent reserve (which will be invested at the central bank to earn UDI + 2 percent), and restructured with a maximum interest rate of UDI + 6 percent. The trust will be financed by subordinated debt issued at UDI + 2 percent and with maturities of 15 to 25 years. The management of the loans, and the credit risk, will remain with the banks.

---

[157]The subordinated bonds and the banks' blocked accounts with the central bank will both pay a zero real rate of interest.

[158]On April 1, the conversion rate between pesos and UDIs was set at 1.0. By April 25, the conversion rate was UDI 1 = MexN$1.046896.

[159]This inflation indexing restructuring mechanism is similar to that employed in Chile.

The program applying to foreign currency loans will cover $6 billion in loans (about 27 percent of foreign currency loans at the end of 1994) that will be distributed among the banks in proportion to their share in the total volume of such loans. Loans will be transferred along with an 8 percent reserve to a trust. The loans will be converted to pesos to eliminate the currency risk and the maturity will be increased to between 5 and 12 years. The loans would be restructured into UDIs plus an intermediation margin, and the trusts would be funded at UDI + 4 percent by liabilities with maturities also between 5 and 12 years with a 7-year grace period. The government would acquire these liabilities with funds received from the banking system in exchange for Tesobonos with the same maturity and interest rates equal to the average cost of dollar funding. Interest payments will be capitalized.

Bibliography

Agenor, Pierre-Richard, and Robert Flood, "Speculative Attacks and Balance of Payments Crises," in *The Handbook of International Macroeconomics*, ed. by Fredrick van der Ploeg (Cambridge, Massachusetts: Basil Blackwell, 1994).

Alfiler, F. Enrico, "Monetary and Exchange Rate Policy Responses to Surges in Capital Flows: The Case of the Philippines" paper prepared for the Eleventh Pacific Basin Central Bank Conference held in Hong Kong, October 31–November 2, 1994.

Aziz, Zeti Akhtar, "Capital Flows and Monetary Management: The Malaysian Experience" paper prepared for the Eleventh Pacific Basin Central Bank Conference held in Hong Kong, October 31–November 2, 1994.

Bacchetta, Philippe, and Eric Van Wincoop, "Net Capital Flows Under Exchange Rate and Price Volatility," Studienzentrum Gerzensee Working Paper No. 94/03 (1994).

Banco Central de Chile, *Memoria Anual*, various issues.

———, *Boletín mensual*, various issues.

———, *Evolución de la Economía*, various issues.

Banco de la República, Colombia, *Annual Report*, various issues.

Banco de México, *Informe Anual* (1992).

Bank Indonesia, *Annual Report*, various issues.

———, *Indonesian Financial Statistics*, various issues.

Bank Negara Malaysia, *Annual Report*, various issues.

———, *Quarterly Economic Bulletin*, various issues.

Bank of Korea, *Monthly Bulletin*, various issues.

Bank of Thailand, *Quarterly Bulletin*, various issues.

Bangko Sentral ng Pilipinas, *Annual Report*, various issues.

Bartolini, Leonardo, and Allan Drazen, "Capital Account Liberalization as a Signal" (mimeograph, University of Maryland, November 1994).

Bennett, Adam, "Currency Boards: Issues and Experiences," Papers on Policy Analysis and Assessment, PPAA/94/18 (Washington: International Monetary Fund, September 1994).

Bercuson, Kenneth B., and Linda M. Koenig, *The Recent Surge in Capital Inflows to Three Asian Countries: Causes and Macroeconomic Impact*, Occasional Paper, No. 15 (Kuala Lumpur, Malaysia: South East Asian Central Banks, 1993).

Blanco, Herminio, and Peter Garber, "Recurrent Devaluation and Speculative Attacks on the Mexican Peso," *Journal of Political Economy*, Vol. 94 (February 1986), pp. 148–66.

Budnevich, Carlos, and Rodrigo Cifuentes, "Manejo Macroeconómico de los Flujos de Capitales: La Contrastante Experiencia de Chile," paper presented at the CIEPLAN conference on capital flows held in Cartagena, Colombia, July 29–30, 1993.

Calvo, Guillermo, "The Perils of Sterilization," *Staff Papers*, International Monetary Fund, Vol. 38 (December 1991), pp. 921–26.

———, Leonardo Leiderman, and Carmen M. Reinhart, "Capital Inflows and Real Exchange Rate Appreciation in Latin America: The Role of External Factors," *Staff Papers*, International Monetary Fund, Vol. 40 (March 1993), pp. 108–51.

———, "The Capital Inflows Problem: Concepts and Issues," *Contemporary Economic Policy*, Vol. 12 (July 1994), pp. 54–66.

Carrasquilla, Alberto, "Exchange Rate Bands and Shifts in the Stabilization Policy Regime: Issues Suggested by the Experience of Colombia," IMF Working Paper, WP/95/42 (Washington: International Monetary Fund, April 1995).

Central Bank of China, Taiwan Province of China, *Balance of Payments*, various issues.

———, *Financial Statistics Monthly*, various issues.

Central Bank of the Republic of Turkey, *Quarterly Bulletin*, various issues.

Central Bank of Sri Lanka, *Bulletin*, various issues.

Claessens, Stijn, Susmita Dasgupta, and Jack Glen, "Stock Price Behavior in Emerging Markets," in *Portfolio Investment in Developing Countries*, ed. by Stijn Claessens and Sudarshan Gooptu, World Bank Discussion Paper, No. 228 (Washington: The World Bank, 1993), pp. 323–31.

Claessens, Stijn, Michael P. Dooley, and Andrew Warner, "Portfolio Capital Flows: Hot or Cool?" in *Portfolio Investment in Developing Countries*, ed. by Stijn Claessens and Sudarshan Gooptu, World Bank Discussion Paper No. 228 (Washington: The World Bank, 1993), pp. 18–27.

Comisión Nacional Bancaria, México, *Boletín Estadístico de Banca Multiple*, various issues.

Conselho Monétario Nacional, "Medidas na Area Cambial" (mimeograph, Brazilia: Conselho Monétario Nacional, October 1994).

————, "Medidas na Area Cambial" (mimeograph, Brazilia: Conselho Monétario Nacional, March 1995).

Coorey, Sharmini, and Claudio Loser, eds., "Financial Liberalization and Reform in Mexico," in *Mexico: The Strategy to Achieve Sustained Economic Growth*, IMF Occasional Paper, No. 99 (Washington: International Monetary Fund, 1992).

Dellas, Harris, and Alan Stockman, "Self-Fulfilling Expectations, Speculative Attack, and Capital Controls," *Journal of Money, Credit and Banking*, Vol. 25 (November 1993), pp. 721–30.

Dominguez, Kathryn M., and Jeffrey A. Frankel, "Does Foreign Exchange Intervention Matter? The Portfolio Effect," *American Economic Review* (forthcoming).

Domowitz, Ian, Jack Glen, and Ananth Madhavan, "International Cross-Listing, Market Quality, and Ownership Rights: An Analysis of the Mexican Stock Market" (mimeograph, Washington: International Finance Corporation, July 1994).

Dooley, Michael P., "Capital Flight: A Response to Differences in Financial Risks," *Staff Papers*, International Monetary Fund, Vol. 35 (September 1988), pp. 422–36.

Edwards, Sebastian, "The Order of Liberalization of the External Sector in Developing Countries," Essays in International Finance 156 (Princeton: Princeton University, December 1984).

————, "Capital Flows, Foreign Direct Investment, and Debt-Equity Swaps in Developing Countries," in *Capital Flows in the World Economy*, ed. by Horst Siebert (Tübingen: Mohr, 1991), pp. 255–81.

Eichengreen, Barry, and Charles Wyplosz, "The Unstable EMS," *Brookings Papers on Economic Activity: 1* (May 1993), pp. 51–143.

————, James Tobin, and Charles Wyplosz, "Two Cases for Sand in the Wheels of International Finance," *Economic Journal*, Vol. 105 (January 1995), pp. 162–72.

————, "Trends and Cycles in Foreign Lending," in *Capital Flows in the World Economy*, ed. by Horst Siebert (Tübingen: Mohr, 1991), pp. 3–28.

Fanelli, José M., and Mario Damill, "Los Capitales Extranjeros en las Economías Latinoamericanas: Argentina," Documento CEDES/84 (Buenos Aires: CEDES, 1993).

Feldman, Robert A., and Manmohan S. Kumar, "Emerging Equity Markets: Growth, Benefits, and Policy Concerns," Papers on Policy Analysis and Assessment, PPAA/94/7 (Washington: International Monetary Fund, March 1994).

Fieleke, Norman S., "International Capital Transactions: Should They Be Restricted?" *New England Economic Review* (March/April 1994), pp. 27–39.

Flood, Robert, and Peter Garber, "Collapsing Exchange-Rate Regimes: Some Linear Examples," *Journal of International Economics*, Vol. 17 (August 1984), pp. 1–13.

Folkerts-Landau, David, and others, "Effect of Capital Flows on Domestic Financial Sectors in APEC Developing Countries," in *Capital Flows in the APEC Region*, ed. by Mohsin S. Khan and Carmen M. Reinhart, IMF Occasional Paper, No. 122 (Washington: International Monetary Fund, March 1995).

Frankel, Jeffrey A. (1994a), "Have Latin American and Asian Countries So Liberalized Portfolio Capital Inflows That Sterilization Is Now Impossible?" (mimeograph, Washington: Institute for International Economics, 1994).

———— (1994b), "Sterilization of Money Inflows: Difficult (Calvo), or Easy (Reisen)?" IMF Working Paper, WP/94/159 (Washington: International Monetary Fund, 1994).

Galbis, Vicente, "Sequencing of Financial Sector Reforms: A Review," IMF Working Paper, WP/94/101 (Washington: International Monetary Fund, September 1994).

Garber, Peter, and Mark P. Taylor, "Sand in the Wheels of Foreign Exchange Markets: A Skeptical Note," *The Economic Journal*, Vol. 105 (1995), pp. 173–80.

Garber, Peter M., and Michael G. Spencer, "Foreign Exchange Hedging with Synthetic Options and the Interest Rate Defense of a Fixed Exchange Rate Regime," IMF Working Paper, WP/94/151 (Washington: International Monetary Fund, December 1994).

García-Cantera, José, and Brian R. Pearl, "Mexican Banking System: A Major Crisis Is Improbable" (New York: Salomon Brothers, January 17, 1995).

————, "Mexican Banking System: Interest Rates and Regulatory Changes Hit Banks When They Are Down" (New York: Salomon Brothers, March 1, 1995).

Greenaway, David, "Policy Forum: Sand in the Wheels of International Finance," *The Economic Journal*, Vol. 105 (1995), pp. 160–61.

Grilli, Vittorio, and Gian Maria Milesi-Ferretti, "Structural Determinants and Economic Impact of Capital Controls," *Staff Papers*, International Monetary Fund (forthcoming).

Grobar, Lisa M., "The Effect of Real Exchange Rate Uncertainty on LDC Manufactured Exports," *Journal of Development Economics*, Vol. 41 (1993), pp. 367–76.

Gurria, José Angel, "Capital Flows: The Mexican Case," paper for the ECLAC-IDRC workshop, "New Private Flows into Latin America" held in Santiago, Chile, December 6–7, 1993.

Hanke, Steve H., and Kurt Schuler, *Currency Boards for Developing Countries: A Handbook* (San Francisco: International Center for Economic Growth, 1994).

Harinowo, C., and William C. Belchere, "Monetary and Exchange Rate Management with International Capital Mobility: The Indonesian Experience" paper prepared for the Eleventh Pacific Basin Central Bank Conference held in Hong Kong, October 31–November 2, 1994.

Helpman, Elhanan, Leonardo Leiderman, and Gil Bufman, "A New Breed of Exchange Rate Bands: Chile, Israel, and Mexico," *Economic Policy: A European Forum*, Vol. 9 (1995), pp. 260–306.

Hettiarachchi, W., and U. Herat, "Coping with Capital Inflows—the Case of Sri Lanka" paper prepared for the Eleventh Pacific Basin Central Bank Conference held in Hong Kong, October 31–November 2, 1994.

International Monetary Fund, *International Capital Markets: Part I. Exchange Rate Management and International Capital Flows*, World Economic and Financial Surveys (Washington: International Monetary Fund, April 1993).

——— (1994a), *International Capital Markets: Part II. Developments, Prospects, and Policy Issues*, World Economic and Financial Surveys (Washington: International Monetary Fund, September 1994).

——— (1994b), *Malaysia* IMF Staff Country Report No. 4 (Washington: International Monetary Fund, 1994).

———, "Factors Behind the Financial Crisis in Mexico," Annex I, in *World Economic Outlook, May 1995*, World Economic and Financial Surveys (Washington: International Monetary Fund, May 1995).

Kang, Joong-Hong, "Monetary Policy Implementation Under Financial Liberalization: The Case of Korea," in *Financial Opening: Policy Issues and Country Experiences in Developing Countries*, ed. by H. Reisen and B. Fischer (Paris: Organization for Economic Cooperation and Development, 1992), pp. 201–25.

———, "Monetary and Exchange Rate Policies in a Newly Industrializing Economy: The Korean Experience," paper prepared for the Eleventh Pacific Basin Central Bank Conference held in Hong Kong, October 31–November 2, 1994.

Kenen, Peter B., "Capital Controls, The EMS and EMU," *The Economic Journal*, Vol. 105 (1995), pp. 181–92.

Kiguel, Miguel, and Leonardo Leiderman, "On the Consequences of Sterilized Intervention in Latin America: The Case of Colombia and Chile" (mimeograph, Tel Aviv: Tel Aviv University, 1994).

Kim, E. Han, and Vijay Singal, "Opening Up of Stock Markets by Emerging Economies: Effect on Portfolio Flows and Volatility of Stock Prices," in *Portfolio Investment in Developing Countries*, ed. by Stijn Claessens and Sudarshan Gooptu, World Bank Discussion Paper 228 (Washington: The World Bank, 1993), pp. 383–403.

Krugman, Paul, "A Model of Balance of Payments Crises," *Journal of Money, Credit and Banking*, Vol. 11 (August 1979), pp. 311–25.

———, "The Narrow Moving Band, the Dutch Disease, and the Competitive Consequences of Mrs. Thatcher: Notes on Trade in the Presence of Scale Economies," *Journal of Development Economics*, Vol. 27 (1987), pp. 41–55.

Labán, Raúl, and Felipe Larraín, "Can a Liberalization of Capital Outflows Increase Net Capital Inflows?" Pontificia Universidad Católica de Chile (mimeograph, Santiago, Chile, January 1994).

Mathieson, Donald J., and Liliana Rojas-Suárez, *Liberalization of the Capital Account, Experiences and Issues*, IMF Occasional Paper, No. 103 (Washington: International Monetary Fund, 1993).

Moody's Investors Service, "Asset Quality Looms as Major Problem for Mexican Banks," January 1995.

McKinnon, Ronald I., *The Order of Economic Liberalization* (Baltimore: Johns Hopkins University Press, 1991).

Mussa, Michael L., "The Role of Intervention," Occasional Paper, No. 6 (New York: Group of Thirty, 1981).

Ng, Victor K., Rosita P. Chang, and Ray Y. Chou, "An Examination of the Behavior of Pacific-Basin Stock Market Volatility," in *Pacific Basin Capital Markets Research*, ed. by S.G. Rhee and R. P. Chang (New York: Elsevier Science Publishers, 1991), pp. 245–60.

Nijathaworn, Bandid, and Thanisorn Dejthamrong, "Thailand: Monetary and Exchange Rate Management with International Capital Mobility" paper prepared for the Eleventh Pacific Basin Central Bank Conference held in Hong Kong, October 31–November 2, 1994.

Obstfeld, Maurice, "The Effectiveness of Foreign Exchange Intervention: Recent Experience," in *International Policy Coordination and Exchange Rate Determination*, ed. by W. Branson, J. Frenkel, and M. Goldstein (Chicago: University of Chicago Press, 1990).

Porter, Michael G., "Capital Inflows as an Offset to Monetary Policy: The German Experience," *Staff Papers*, International Monetary Fund, Vol. 19 (1972), pp. 395–419.

Reinhart, Carmen M., and Vincent Reinhart, "The Role of Capital Markets in Emerging Markets" (mimeograph, Washington: International Monetary Fund, 1994).

Reinhart, Vincent, "The Tobin Tax, Asset Accumulation, and the Real Exchange Rate," *Journal of International Money and Finance*, Vol. 10 (1991), pp. 420–31.

Reisen, Helmut, "The 'Impossible Trinity' in Southeast Asia," *International Economic Insights*, Vol. 4 (March/April 1993).

Rodríguez, Carlos A., "Situación Monetaria y Cambiaria en Colombia" (mimeograph, Buenos Aires: CEMA, November 1991).

Salant, Stephen, and Dale Henderson, "Market Anticipations of Government Policies and the Price of Gold," *Journal of Political Economy*, Vol. 91 (August 1978), pp. 627–48.

Saporan Mingguan Weekly Report, various issues.

Schadler, Susan, and others, *Recent Experiences with Surges in Capital Inflows*, IMF Occasional Paper, No. 108 (Washington: International Monetary Fund, 1993).

"Shakeout in Argentina Benefits Biggest Banks," *International Banking Report* (January 1995), pp. 1–2.

Spahn, Paul Bernd, "International Financial Flows and Transactions Taxes: Survey and Options," IMF Working Paper (Washington: International Monetary Fund, forthcoming).

Summers, Lawrence H., "Tax Policy and International Competitiveness," in *International Aspects of Fiscal Policies*, ed. by Jacob A. Frenkel (Chicago: University of Chicago Press, 1988).

———, and Victoria P. Summers, "The Case for a Securities Transactions Excise Tax," *Tax Notes* (August 13, 1990), pp. 879–84.

Superintendencia de Bancos e Instituciones Financieras, Chile, *Informacion Financiera: Estados Financieros Anuales*, various issues.

Taylor, Mark P., "The Economics of Exchange Rates," *Journal of Economic Literature*, Vol. 33 (1995), pp. 13–47.

"Tequila Slammers," *International Financing Review*, No. 1064 (January 14, 1995), pp. 74–80.

Tobin, James, "A Proposal for International Monetary Reform," *Eastern Economic Journal*, Vol. 4 (1978), pp. 153–59.

———, "International Currency Regimes, Capital Mobility, and Macroeconomic Policy," Cowles Foundation Discussion Paper, No. 993 (1991).

II. Background Papers

Financial Supervisory and Regulatory Issues

I

Capital Adequacy and Internal Risk Management

Banks now actively participate in derivative markets, especially in the largely unregulated over-the-counter (OTC) derivative markets. They also now operate in a global financial environment in which new products, new pricing techniques, and new risk-management techniques are being introduced continuously and at breakneck speed. During the last few years, regulators and leaders in the financial industry have been engaged in a process of designing a new, more relevant set of regulatory capital requirements for banks that operate in this high-risk and fast-changing environment. In effect, structural changes in financial markets led regulators to reconsider the traditional approaches to supervision and regulation and to develop new more flexible approaches to bank regulation. Through this process, regulators have come to recognize private internal risk management as the foundation for ensuring the safety and soundness of individual financial institutions, and in reducing systemic risk.

Although this process is likely to continue, bank regulators are now considering revolutionary changes in the way banks are supervised and regulated. On April 12, 1995, the Basle Committee on Banking Supervision issued for comment a new set of capital requirements that allows banks to use their own internal risk-management models to estimate an important component for determining regulatory capital requirements—value-at-risk. The proposal moves bank regulation in a new direction in that it allows banks to actively participate in the design of the framework for establishing capital requirements. The Basle Committee expects comments by July 1995. The plan is to adopt the new requirements by the end of the year and have them implemented by the end of 1997.

A review of the developments that led regulators to take this new direction is followed by an examination of the new Basle approach for calculating capital requirements. This is followed by a discussion of current efforts to improve internal risk management by banks, which is likely to become an integral part of the internal model-based approach to market risk-based capital requirements.

Background

Growth and Impact of Derivatives

Between the end of 1986 and the end of 1994, the total notional principal of outstanding exchange-traded derivative contracts—including interest rate futures and options, currency futures and options, and stock-market index futures and options—has grown at an annual average rate of 140 percent, from $0.6 trillion to $8.8 trillion (Table II.1). In the same period, annual turnover has grown about four times, from 315 million contracts to 1,140 million contracts a year (Table II.2).

Meanwhile, OTC derivative markets have expanded at a similar pace. The notional principal of outstanding interest rate and currency swaps increased from $1.0 trillion at the end of 1987 to almost $8.0 trillion at the end of 1993 (Table II.3). In the second half of 1993 alone, close to $2.4 trillion new interest rate swaps and currency swaps were transacted (Table II.4). In addition, the total notional principal of more complex swap-related OTC derivative products—caps, collars, floors, and swaptions—has increased from $0.6 trillion at the end of 1990 to $1.4 trillion at the end of 1993. Underlying this rapid growth in OTC derivative markets has been the increased globalization of derivative activities. At the end of 1987, non-U.S. dollar-denominated interest rate swaps represented about 21 percent of all interest rate swaps; by the end of 1992, this share had expanded to more than 60 percent (Table II.5).

Accompanying this overall expansion in derivative markets has been a gradual, but now very noticeable, change in the nature of banking, in which the activity of banks has shifted from traditional lending to derivative markets activities. Although these changes have occurred across a wide range of countries, they are seen most clearly in the activities of large U.S. banks. Among the seven major U.S. money center banks, interest income has declined, on average, from 70 percent of total revenue at the end of 1987 to less than 50 percent at the end of 1993. By contrast, trading income has more than doubled from $5\frac{2}{3}$ percent of total revenue to more than $13\frac{1}{2}$ percent and fee income revenue has increased from about $12\frac{1}{2}$ percent

Table II.1. Markets for Selected Derivative Financial Instruments: Notional Principal Amounts Outstanding

(In billions of U.S. dollars, end-year data)

	1986	1987	1988	1989	1990	1991	1992	1993	1994
Interest rate futures	370.0	487.7	895.4	1,200.8	1,454.5	2,156.7	2,913.0	4,942.6	5,757.4
Futures on short-term interest rate instruments	274.3	338.9	721.7	1,002.6	1,271.1	1,906.3	2,663.7	4,616.7	5,401.8
Three-month Eurodollar[1]	229.5	307.8	588.8	671.9	662.6	1,100.5	1,389.6	2,178.7	2,468.6
Three-month Euro-yen[2]	—	—	—	109.5	243.5	254.5	431.8	1,080.1	1,467.4
Three-month Euro-deutsche mark[3]	—	—	—	14.4	47.7	110.0	229.2	421.9	425.7
Futures on long-term interest rate instruments	95.7	148.8	173.7	198.2	183.4	250.4	249.3	325.9	355.6
U.S. Treasury bond[4]	23.0	26.5	39.9	33.2	23.0	29.8	31.3	32.6	36.1
Notional French Government bond[5]	2.1	7.6	7.0	6.1	7.0	11.4	21.0	12.6	12.7
Ten-year Japanese Government bond[6]	63.5	104.8	106.7	129.5	112.9	122.1	106.1	135.9	164.3
German Government bond[7]	—	—	1.4	4.2	13.7	20.2	27.8	33.3	41.7
Interest rate options[8]	146.5	122.6	279.2	387.9	599.5	1,072.6	1,385.4	2,362.5	2,622.7
Currency futures	10.2	14.6	12.1	15.9	16.9	17.9	24.9	32.2	33.0
Currency options[8]	39.2	59.5	48.0	50.2	56.5	62.8	70.9	75.4	54.5
Stock market index futures	14.5	17.8	27.1	41.3	69.1	76.0	79.7	109.9	127.7
Stock market index options[8]	37.8	27.7	42.9	70.6	93.7	132.8	158.6	238.3	242.4
Total	618.3	729.9	1,304.8	1,766.6	2,290.2	3,518.8	4,632.5	7,760.8	8,837.8
In the United States	517.9	577.7	950.3	1,152.3	1,263.0	2,132.1	2,675.5	4,324.9	4,754.9
In Europe	13.1	13.3	177.7	250.8	461.2	710.1	1,114.3	1,777.9	1,832.0
In Japan	63.5	107.7	106.6	260.9	424.2	441.2	576.1	1,193.5	1,498.2
In other countries	23.7	31.2	70.2	102.6	141.8	235.4	266.6	464.5	752.8

Source: Bank for International Settlements.

[1]Traded on the Chicago Mercantile Exchange-International Monetary Market (CME-IMM), Singapore Mercantile Exchange (SIMEX), London International Financial Futures Exchange (LIFFE), Tokyo International Financial Futures Exchange (TIFFE), and Sydney Futures Exchange (SFE).

[2]Traded on the TIFFE and SIMEX.

[3]Traded on the Marché à Terme International de France (MATIF) and LIFFE.

[4]Traded on the Chicago Board of Trade (CBOT), LIFFE, Mid-America Commodity Exchange (MIDAM), New York Futures Exchange (NYFE), and Tokyo Stock Exchange (TSE).

[5]Traded on the MATIF.

[6]Traded on the TSE, LIFFE, and CBOT.

[7]Traded on the LIFFE and the Deutsche Terminbörse (DTB).

[8]Calls plus puts.

to about $17^3/4$ percent. By the end of 1992, the notional principal of interest rate swaps held off-balance sheet by the seven largest U.S. money center banks ($1.7 trillion) was almost twice as large as their total balance sheet assets ($854 billion), reflecting the increasing concentration of bank activities in the OTC derivative transactions.

Advances in technology, the rapid growth of the OTC derivative markets, the globalization and liberalization of financial markets, and the change in bank activities have the following important implications: (1) market and operational risk have become more important for banks;[1] (2) new and more complicated products are being introduced continuously; (3) linkages between financial markets and institutions have

strengthened significantly; (4) banks now have the ability to change their portfolios and risk exposures very quickly; and (5) financial market conditions and the value of bank portfolios can change very rapidly. These structural changes in the financial services industry have forced bank supervisors and regulators and other financial market regulators to re-examine the current regulatory regime.

Earlier Proposals for Revising Capital Adequacy Standards

Until recently, the most important tools of bank supervisors and regulators have been capital requirements, on-site examinations, and regular reporting requirements. As discussed in previous capital markets reports, shortly after the 1988 Basle Accord was agreed, both supervisors and bankers came to see that the minimum capital adequacy standards defined in the Accord were inadequate, in part because of changes in the nature of banking and, more generally, in the financial services industry.[2] It was

---

[1]Banks in general face the following risk elements: credit risk—that a counterparty might default on its position; market risk—a loss due to unexpected general market price and interest rate changes; operation risk—a loss due to human error, fraud, or the lack of internal controls; legal risk—related to the legal status of a contract; liquidity risk—that a position cannot be sold very quickly without a huge price concession; settlement risk—the market and credit risk exposure during the settlement period; and specific risk—a decline in value of a particular position that is not the result of a general market movement.

[2]The 1988 Basle Accord establishes a capital requirement as a percentage of the credit risk exposure of a bank. Under this

Table II.2. Annual Turnover in Derivative Financial Instruments Traded on Organized Exchanges Worldwide[1]

(In millions of contracts traded)

	1986	1987	1988	1989	1990	1991	1992	1993	1994
Interest rate futures	91.0	145.7	156.3	201.0	219.1	230.9	330.1	427.1	627.8
Futures on short-term interest rate instruments	16.4	29.4	33.7	70.2	76.0	84.8	130.8	161.0	252.9
Three-month Eurodollar[1]	12.4	23.7	25.2	46.8	39.4	41.7	66.9	70.2	113.6
Three-month Euro-yen[2]	—	—	—	4.7	15.2	16.2	17.4	26.9	44.2
Three-month Euro-deutsche mark[3]	—	—	—	1.6	3.1	4.8	12.2	21.4	29.5
Futures on long-term interest rate instruments	74.6	116.3	122.6	130.8	143.1	146.1	199.3	266.1	374.9
U.S. Treasury bond[4]	54.6	69.4	73.8	72.8	78.2	69.9	71.7	80.7	101.5
Notional French Government bond[5]	1.1	11.9	12.4	15.0	16.0	21.1	31.1	36.8	50.2
Ten-year Japanese Government bond[6]	9.4	18.4	18.9	19.1	16.4	12.9	12.1	15.6	14.1
German Government bond[7]	—	—	0.3	5.3	9.6	12.4	18.9	27.7	51.5
Interest rate options[8]	22.3	29.3	30.5	39.5	52.0	50.8	64.8	82.9	114.5
Currency futures	19.9	21.2	22.5	28.2	29.7	30.0	31.3	39.0	69.7
Currency options[8]	13.0	18.3	18.2	20.7	18.9	22.9	23.4	23.8	21.3
Stock market index futures	28.4	36.1	29.6	30.1	39.4	54.6	52.0	71.2	109.0
Stock market index options[8]	140.4	139.1	79.1	101.7	119.1	121.4	133.9	144.1	197.9
Total	315.0	389.6	336.2	421.2	478.3	510.5	635.6	788.0	1,140.2
In the United States	288.4	317.6	251.4	287.0	310.9	301.5	340.1	380.3	509.5
In Europe	10.3	35.9	40.7	64.4	83.0	110.5	185.0	263.5	398.5
In Japan	9.4	18.5	23.1	45.7	60.6	66.2	51.7	57.8	70.5
In other countries	6.9	17.7	21.0	24.1	23.8	32.4	58.8	86.4	161.7

Source: Bank for International Settlements.

[1]Traded on the Chicago Mercantile Exchange-International Monetary Market (CME-IMM), Singapore Mercantile Exchange (SIMEX), London International Financial Futures Exchange (LIFFE), Tokyo International Financial Futures Exchange (TIFFE), and Sydney Futures Exchange (SFE).

[2]Traded on the TIFFE and SIMEX.

[3]Traded on the Marché à Terme International de France (MATIF) and LIFFE.

[4]Traded on the Chicago Board of Trade (CBOT), LIFFE, Mid-America Commodity Exchange (MIDAM), New York Futures Exchange (NYFE), and Tokyo Stock Exchange (TSE).

[5]Traded on the MATIF.

[6]Traded on the TSE, LIFFE, and CBOT.

[7]Traded on the LIFFE and the Deutsche Terminbörse (DTB).

[8]Calls plus puts.

recognized that the Basle Accord ignored market risk, by focusing primarily on credit risk, and did not cover adequately many new and complex OTC derivative products. The Accord was drafted at a time when most of these products did not exist, when banks were concentrating on traditional banking functions, and when credit risk was the single most important risk factor.[3]

---

approach, each on-balance-sheet item is assigned a risk weight reflecting the credit quality of the counterparty involved, which is determined by such factors as whether the counterparty is a government or a private institution, and whether the counterparty is from an OECD country or not. Off-balance-sheet interest rate and exchange rate contracts are first converted to a so-called credit-equivalent amount under one of two permitted conversion methods. The risk weights are then applied to these credit equivalent amounts as if they are on-balance-sheet positions. The two conversion methods are (1) the so-called current exposure method, under which the credit equivalent is calculated as the current replacement cost of the position plus an add-on factor equal to a percentage of the notional principal; (2) the so-called original exposure method, under which the credit equivalent is calculated by multiplying the notional principal by a conversion factor.

[3]A detailed discussion of the Basle Proposal and the CAD is provided in International Monetary Fund (1994).

Despite these weaknesses, the minimum capital adequacy standard defined in the Accord (slightly modified in July 1994 to accommodate more general recognition of bilateral netting arrangements) is still the current international standard for bank capital requirements.[4] As a result of these perceived weaknesses, the European Union (EU) released in March 1993 a new Capital Adequacy Directive (CAD) for implementation starting January 1996.[5] Similarly, the Basle Committee on Banking Supervision issued for comment, in April 1993, a proposal on a capital standard based on market risk.[6] Under both the EU and

---

[4]See Basle Committee on Banking Supervision (1988) and (1994a). The collapse of Barings suggests that market risk, operational risk, and internal management controls are very important elements of risk management. At the end of 1993, Barings had a total capital ratio well in excess of the 8 percent requirement, and in January 1995, it was still considered to be a safe bank. By the end of March 1995, however, Barings was in administration. The failure of a well-capitalized institution raises important questions about the adequacy of current regulatory capital requirements and the role they play in safeguarding individual financial institutions from financial distress.

[5]See European Community (1993).

[6]See Basle Committee on Banking Supervision (1993a–d).

Table II.3. Notional Principal Value of Outstanding Interest Rate and Currency Swaps[1]

(In billions of U.S. dollars)

	1987	1988	1989	1990	1991	1992	1993
Interest rate swaps							
All counterparties	682.9	1,010.2	1,502.6	2,311.5	3,065.1	3,850.8	6,177.3
Interbank (ISDA member)	206.6	341.3	547.1	909.5	1,342.3	1,880.8	2,967.9
Other (end-user and brokered)	476.2	668.9	955.5	1,402.0	1,722.8	1,970.1	3,209.4
End-user	476.2	668.9	955.5	1,402.0	1,722.8	1,970.1	3,209.4
Financial institutions	300.0	421.3	579.2	817.1	985.7	1,061.1	1,715.7
Governments[2]	47.6	63.2	76.2	136.9	165.5	242.8	327.1
Corporations[3]	128.6	168.9	295.2	447.9	571.7	666.2	1,166.6
Unallocated	...	15.5	4.9	—	—	—	—
Brokered	—	—	—	—	—	—	—
Currency swaps							
All counterparties	365.6	639.1	898.2	1,155.1	1,614.3	1,720.8	1,799.2
(Adjusted for reporting of both sides)	(182.8)	(319.6)	(449.1)	(577.5)	(807.2)	(860.4)	(899.6)
Interbank (ISDA member)	71.0	165.2	230.1	310.1	449.8	477.7	437.0
Other (end-user and brokered)	294.6	473.9	668.1	844.9	1,164.6	1,243.1	1,362.2
End-user[4]	147.3	237.0	334.1	422.5	582.3	621.5	681.1
Financial institutions	61.9	102.7	141.7	148.2	246.7	228.7	221.9
Governments[2]	33.9	54.0	65.6	83.2	96.9	110.6	135.8
Corporations[3]	51.6	76.5	116.5	191.1	238.7	282.2	323.4
Unallocated	...	3.8	10.3	—	—	—	—
Brokered	—	—	—	—	—	—	—
Total (interest rate and currency swaps for all counterparties)	1,048.5	1,649.3	2,400.8	3,466.6	4,679.4	5,571.6	7,976.5

Sources: Bank for International Settlements, *International Banking and Financial Market Developments*, various issues; and International Swaps and Derivatives Association, Inc. (ISDA).

[1] As of end of December.
[2] Including international institutions.
[3] Including others.
[4] Adjusted for double-counting as each currency swap involves two currencies.

Basle initiatives, a bank's assets and liabilities would be separated into a banking book, which includes traditional bank loans and deposits, and a trading book, which includes short-term trading and hedging positions. Capital charges for positions in the banking book would continue to be determined according to the 1988 Basle Accord. However, the capital charges for positions in the trading book would be determined by a new set of market-risk-based capital standards that utilize a product-based approach. There are separate rules for three major classes of products—equity, interest rate, and exchange rate products. A building block approach, by which market risk and specific risk would be considered separately, would be used to compute capital charges for each product type, which would then be summed to generate capital requirement for the trading book.

Weaknesses of the 1993 Basle Proposal and the CAD

The Basle and EU proposals have stimulated intense discussions among regulators and market participants on the appropriate approach for determining market-risk-based capital requirements. Market participants have suggested that both proposals are too complex for small banks and for the public to understand and too crude for banks active in the derivative markets. It also has been suggested that the proposals, if adopted, are likely to create inefficiencies because banks would have to maintain two risk-measurement systems: one for calculating regulatory capital requirements, and one for daily risk management and trading. The proposals would also reduce banks' incentives to improve their own risk-management system.

The Basle proposal has also been challenged on the grounds that it cannot yield accurate capital requirements, not because it lacks rigor or complexity but because it employs ad hoc disallowances to account for spread risks and gap risks;[7] it uses crude maturity bands and sensitivity factors to account for interest rate risk; and it ignores correlations and offsets between risk factors by simply adding the capital

---

[7] Spread risk is the risk that the relationship between the prices or yields of two similar, but not identical, assets of the same maturity will change. Gap risk is the risk that the relationship between the prices or yields of two instruments of the same type, but of different maturities, will change.

Table II.4. New Interest Rate and Currency Swaps[1]

(In billions of U.S. dollars)

	1987 First half	1987 Second half	1988 First half	1988 Second half	1989 First half	1989 Second half	1990 First half	1990 Second half	1991 First half	1991 Second half	1992 First half	1992 Second half	1993 First half	1993 Second half
Interest rate swaps														
All counterparties	181.5	206.3	250.5	317.6	389.2	444.4	561.5	702.8	762.1	859.7	1,318.3	1,504.3	1,938.5	2,166.3
Interbank (ISDA member)	58.9	67.0	86.6	106.5	140.4	177.6	223.2	261.3	335.4	426.4	617.7	718.7	959.2	1,044.8
Other (end-user and brokered)	122.6	139.3	163.9	211.1	248.7	266.8	338.2	441.5	426.8	433.3	700.6	785.6	979.3	1,121.5
End-user	121.0	136.0	162.3	209.1	242.8	260.6	334.5	370.8	419.2	425.5	681.0	755.7	922.9	1,077.7
Financial institutions	82.3	86.4	102.8	135.3	152.9	165.0	200.2	219.9	229.3	263.1	404.6	449.3	518.1	597.7
Governments[2]	10.9	10.8	15.7	17.2	23.0	16.6	33.7	41.0	43.4	35.5	64.9	84.0	107.7	90.8
Corporations[3]	27.8	34.8	43.9	54.3	60.5	79.0	100.6	110.0	146.4	126.9	211.5	222.4	288.8	389.2
Unallocated	...	4.1	—	2.3	6.5	—	—	—	—	—	—	—	8.3	—
Brokered	1.6	3.3	1.6	1.9	5.9	6.2	3.7	70.7	7.6	7.7	19.6	29.9	56.5	43.8
Currency swaps														
All counterparties	87.1	85.7	122.3	126.2	166.7	189.6	189.3	236.2	322.6	334.1	312.1	291.6	313.6	276.7
(Adjusted for reporting of both sides)	(43.5)	(42.8)	(61.1)	(63.1)	(83.4)	(94.8)	(94.6)	(118.1)	(161.3)	(167.1)	(156.1)	(145.8)	(156.8)	(138.4)
Interbank (ISDA member)	17.5	18.3	25.4	33.3	50.8	50.5	53.0	69.6	105.9	102.0	68.3	64.2	61.3	49.6
Other (end-user and brokered)	69.5	67.4	96.9	92.9	115.9	139.1	136.3	166.6	216.7	232.1	243.9	227.4	252.3	227.2
End-user[4]	34.3	33.5	47.5	46.4	57.5	69.6	67.7	83.0	103.1	116.0	121.6	113.1	126.0	112.9
Financial institutions	18.9	13.0	23.3	20.2	22.4	29.8	22.8	28.6	41.1	57.4	40.9	38.0	39.3	37.9
Governments[2]	7.6	6.3	10.6	8.7	13.2	9.8	12.5	10.9	13.7	17.1	23.6	18.5	30.8	21.8
Corporations[3]	7.9	13.6	12.9	16.2	18.5	27.7	32.4	43.5	48.2	41.5	57.1	56.6	55.9	53.1
Unallocated	...	0.6	0.7	1.3	3.5	2.2	—	—	—	—	—	—	—	0.1
Brokered	0.9	0.3	1.9	0.2	1.0	—	0.9	0.7	10.7	0.1	0.7	1.2	0.3	1.3
Total (interest rate and currency swaps for all counterparties)	268.6	292.0	372.8	443.8	555.9	633.9	750.8	939.0	1,084.7	1,193.8	1,630.4	1,795.9	2,252.1	2,443.0

Sources: Bank for International Settlements, *International Banking and Financial Market Developments*, various issues; and International Swaps and Derivatives Association, Inc. (ISDA).

[1] During the respective half of the year.
[2] Including international institutions.
[3] Including others.
[4] Adjusted for double-counting as each currency swap involves two currencies.

Table II.5. Currency Composition of Notional Principal Value of Outstanding Interest Rate and Currency Swaps

(In billions of U.S. dollars)

	1987	1988	1989	1990	1991	1992	1993
Interest rate swaps							
All counterparties	682.9	1,010.2	1,502.6	2,311.5	3,065.1	3,850.8	6,177.3
U.S. dollar	541.5	728.2	993.7	1,272.7	1,506.0	1,760.2	2,457.0
Japanese yen	40.5	78.5	128.0	231.9	478.9	706.0	1,247.4
Deutsche mark	31.6	56.5	84.6	193.4	263.4	344.4	629.7
Pound sterling	29.7	52.3	100.4	242.1	253.5	294.8	437.1
Other	39.5	94.8	195.8	371.5	563.3	745.3	1,406.1
Interbank (ISDA member)	206.6	341.3	547.1	909.5	1,342.3	1,880.8	2,967.9
U.S. dollar	161.6	243.9	371.1	492.8	675.0	853.9	1,008.4
Japanese yen	19.5	43.0	61.1	126.1	264.9	441.3	820.8
Deutsche mark	7.9	17.2	32.6	78.4	111.2	175.6	356.1
Pound sterling	10.4	17.6	40.0	100.1	106.3	137.2	215.2
Other	7.1	19.6	42.2	112.1	184.9	272.7	567.4
End-user	476.2	668.9	955.5	1,402.0	1,722.8	1,970.1	2,209.4
U.S. dollar	379.9	484.3	622.6	779.9	831.0	906.3	1,448.6
Japanese yen	21.0	35.5	66.9	105.8	214.0	264.7	426.7
Deutsche mark	23.7	39.3	52.0	115.0	152.2	168.8	273.7
Pound sterling	19.3	34.7	60.4	142.0	147.3	157.6	222.0
Other	32.4	75.2	153.6	259.4	378.3	472.7	838.4
Currency swaps[1]							
All counterparties	182.8	319.6	449.1	577.5	807.2	860.4	899.6
U.S. dollar	81.3	134.7	177.1	214.2	292.1	309.0	320.0
Japanese yen	29.9	65.5	100.6	122.4	180.1	154.3	158.8
Deutsche mark	10.7	17.0	26.9	36.2	47.6	53.3	69.7
Pound sterling	5.3	8.9	16.7	24.5	37.4	40.1	44.2
Other	55.7	93.5	127.8	180.3	250.0	303.6	306.9
Interbank (ISDA member)	35.5	82.6	115.1	155.1	224.9	238.9	218.5
U.S. dollar	16.7	34.1	48.2	59.7	86.8	90.9	82.3
Japanese yen	7.2	18.6	28.3	37.4	60.9	53.9	53.2
Deutsche mark	1.6	3.0	5.4	7.6	9.4	12.6	12.9
Pound sterling	1.1	1.6	4.3	6.2	8.4	10.4	7.1
Other	9.0	25.4	28.8	44.1	59.5	71.1	63.0
End-user	147.3	237.0	334.1	422.5	582.3	621.5	681.1
U.S. dollar	64.6	100.7	128.9	154.5	205.3	218.1	237.7
Japanese yen	22.7	47.0	72.2	85.0	119.2	100.4	105.6
Deutsche mark	9.1	14.0	21.5	28.5	38.2	40.7	56.8
Pound sterling	4.2	7.3	12.4	18.3	29.0	29.7	37.0
Other	46.7	68.1	99.0	136.2	190.6	232.6	244.0

Sources: Bank for International Settlements, *International Banking and Financial Market Developments*, various issues; and International Swaps and Derivatives Association, Inc. (ISDA).

[1] Adjusted for double-counting as each currency swap involves two currencies.

charges for different classes of products together to give the aggregate capital requirement. This last feature represents a conservative approach because it is justified only if all product classes are perfectly correlated. Some have argued that this approach might not reduce risk in the long run; while a bank still has the flexibility to increase its capital reserves when its capital requirement is too low, it cannot reduce its capital requirement when it is too high. Excessive capital requirements can reduce the competitiveness of banks relative to nonbanks and, in the long run, affect the banking system.

Another concern often expressed about the two initiatives is that uneven capital charges might distort bank activities. For example, because both proposals ignore correlations among product classes, hedging and diversification will be discouraged because neither will lead to lower capital requirements. In addition, the Basle Accord, the Basle proposal, and the CAD ignore the risk of a change in the sensitivity of derivative prices to the price of the underlying primary asset (gamma risk) and the risk of a change in the volatility of the underlying asset (vega risk). The proposed capital standards would, therefore, encourage options strategies, such as straddles (bets on changes in volatility).[8]

Basle's product-based approach for determining capital charges has been criticized as being unduly rigid. Given demand pressures and the rapid pace of advances in technology, new hybrid products are being introduced continuously. The Basle proposal does not have the flexibility to cover these new products. Others are also uncomfortable with applying market-risk-based capital requirements to the trading book and credit-risk-based capital requirements to the banking book, because items in the banking book entail market risk. Furthermore, market risk and credit risk are not unrelated. A default on a derivative contract can occur because of a major market movement. In addition, by classifying items into banking and trading books according to the length of the intended holding period, significant distortions in banking activities might be created. In effect, it has been argued that it might be more appropriate to apply the same standard on the entire portfolio of a bank. Finally, capital requirements are based on a snapshot of risk exposures. When dynamic trading strategies are employed, however, the EU and Basle approaches will not accurately measure the risk inherent in these strategies.[9]

The intense discussions surrounding the Basle and EU initiatives have clarified that from the perspective of the financial industry, an "ideal" capital standard would have the following characteristics: (1) simple enough to be understood and implemented by even the less sophisticated banks; (2) as close as possible to a bank's internal risk-management system; (3) comprehensive enough to avoid distorting bank activities; (4) built on a full portfolio approach, taking into account correlations and offsets; (5) easily extendable to cover new products and new markets; (6) applicable to all banks regardless of their size and primary activities; and (7) structured in a way such that improvements in internal risk-management systems are encouraged.

An important question is whether it is possible for regulators to establish a set of capital adequacy standards with these characteristics. The intense discussions among regulators and market participants, following the Basle proposal and the CAD, have led to the conclusion that the traditional approach established in the 1988 Basle Accord—and extended by the Basle proposals and the CAD—might not work very well in a dynamic environment where product innovations can render obsolete any rigidly defined minimum capital adequacy standard.

Basle Committee's New Approach: Using Internal Risk-Management Models

In light of the difficulties encountered in producing a new set of comprehensive capital adequacy requirements, the Group of Ten regulators have apparently taken a new direction toward the calculation of capital adequacy requirements. On April 12, 1995, the Basle Committee on Banking Supervision issued a proposal that recommends a new approach toward the calculation of bank capital requirements. The new approach would allow banks, for the first time, to use their internal risk-management models to determine regulatory capital requirements. Instead of adhering to a detailed framework for computing risk exposures (for reporting purposes) and capital requirements, banks would be able, under certain conditions, to use their own models—the ones they use for day-to-day trading and risk management—to determine an important component of their regulatory capital requirements.

Value-at-Risk: Key to Risk Measurement

Although Basle's new approach for establishing capital adequacy requirements does not, as proposed, restrict a bank from using one or another risk-measurement model or estimation method, it does require that banks use a common measure of risk. Specifically, the Basle Committee advocates "value-at-risk" as the standard measure for risk exposures.[10] Value-at-risk is an estimate of the "maximum" loss in the value of a portfolio or financial position over a given time period with a certain level of confidence. This level of confidence is represented by the probability that the actual loss will not exceed a prespecified "maximum." The probability is usually referred to as the confidence interval. The new approach requires the use of a value-at-risk corresponding to a ten-day holding period and a 99 percent confidence interval. Under these standards, a $100 million value-at-risk means that there is a 99 percent chance that the loss in the portfolio value over a ten-day period will be less than $100 million. Specifying value-at-risk as the standard risk measure is not more than specifying a common unit of measurement.

---

[8]Barings, which collapsed following a loss of about $1 billion from derivatives trading, was believed to have entered initially into a short-straddle position, before the Kobe earthquake, that took a bet on low volatility in the Japanese stock market.

[9]A dynamic trading strategy is one in which the portfolio of assets is changed continuously according to a certain rule so as to achieve a risk-exposure target.

---

[10]The Group of Thirty, in its report on derivatives released in July 1993, has highly recommended value-at-risk as a useful way to describe market risk exposure. The Fisher report, issued by the Bank for International Settlements (BIS) in September 1994, has also recommended banks to disclose their value-at-risk.

Value-at-risk can be, and currently is, estimated by using various techniques. The so-called asset-normal approach is commonly used and assumes that asset returns are jointly normally distributed.[11] Under this assumption, the probability distribution of the rate of return of a portfolio can be estimated easily and quickly, which makes the calculation of value-at-risk relatively easy. The main disadvantage of this approach is that the value-at-risk calculation might not be accurate if the normal distribution does not offer a good description of the underlying price data. Some have argued that the *t*-distribution, which allows extreme price changes to occur more often, offers a better description of the statistical properties of asset returns. Furthermore, the asset-normal approach cannot easily deal with option risk.[12]

An approach that can be used to compute the value-at-risk of a portfolio with options and other derivative instruments is the so-called delta normal method. This approach, which is used in Basle's 1993 proposal and the CAD, treats an option as a position equal to the market value of the underlying asset multiplied by the delta[13] of the option.[14] This approach is conceptually and computationally easy, but it ignores the effect of a change in the delta of an option (the gamma risk).[15] More importantly, since the linear approximation only works for small changes in the process of the underlying asset prices, the approach can produce a significantly biased estimate of value-at-risk when large price changes are being considered.

The "delta gamma" approach is an extension of the delta normal approach. It incorporates both the delta and the gamma of an option to construct an approximation of the option position.[16] While this approach can yield more accurate results, it is also computationally more intensive. In the spirit of this approach, Basle's new approach also contains a provision for gamma and vega risk under the heading of a "delta-plus" method for banks that do not want to follow the internal model-based approach for calculating their regulatory capital requirements.[17]

An approach that has become very popular among the sophisticated derivative houses is the so-called model-simulation or Monte Carlo approach. This approach directly assesses the value of a derivative asset by evaluating its price for a large number of simulated price paths for the underlying asset, which are generated according to a particular dynamic model. An advantage of this approach is that it can be used for any kind of derivative contract. Furthermore, provided that the assumed price dynamics are correct, this method would produce more accurate estimates of value-at-risk because it does not rely on approximations of any kind. This method, however, introduces model risk into the calculation—the risk that the underlying model of price dynamics might not be correct. Moreover, because banks make different assumptions about price behavior, the same Monte Carlo approach can produce very different estimates of value-at-risk.

There are also many other alternative approaches that can be used to estimate value-at-risk: the historical distribution method, which utilizes the past distribution of asset returns;[18] the so-called factor-push approach, which computes value-at-risk by considering hypothetical changes in the value of the underlying risk factors;[19] and the maximum loss approach, which computes value-at-risk by locating the combination of asset prices that can yield the biggest loss for a given probability.[20]

---

[11]The asset normal approach is the method employed by J.P. Morgan's highly publicized RiskMetrics, risk-management system. Under this distributional assumption, the standard deviation of portfolio return can be computed from the standard deviations of the asset returns, their correlations, and the individual weights of the assets in the portfolio using a standard statistical formula. The value-at-risk under a 99 percent confidence interval is simply the level of loss corresponding to a 2.32 standard deviation drop in the value of the portfolio.

[12]Because the value of an option relates to the price of the underlying asset in a nonlinear fashion, even if the underlying asset return is normally distributed, the return on an option position will not be normally distributed.

[13]The delta of an option is the sensitivity of the option price with respect to changes in the value of the underlying asset.

[14]The idea is to apply a first-order Taylor approximation to the nonlinear option payoff.

[15]The gamma of an option is the sensitivity of the option's delta to a change in the price of the underlying asset. The gamma risk is therefore the risk that the delta of an option might change.

[16]The approach utilizes a second-order approximation instead of a first-order approximation.

[17]Vega risk is the risk of a change in the value of an option due to a change in the volatility of the underlying asset.

[18]The historical (bootstrapping) approach does not rely on any assumption about the statistical distribution of asset returns. Basically, it uses past data to construct a histogram that is then used as the distribution of asset return. Hypothetical price changes are drawn randomly and repeatedly from this probability distribution to obtain an estimate of the value-at-risk. An obvious advantage is that the results are not dependent on assumptions regarding the probability distribution of asset returns. A disadvantage is that the histogram from past data might not be a very accurate description of the asset return distribution in the future. Furthermore, the method is computationally very intensive and is therefore not very practical for a large portfolio.

[19]The factor-push approach is quite different from the other approaches in that the focus is on the risk factors themselves. The idea is that each factor will be pushed toward a direction that reduces the value of the portfolio. A large loss value produced by large changes in the factors is taken to be the value-at-risk. This approach ignores the combined effects of the factors and the correlations among the factors.

[20]The maximum loss approach computes the maximum portfolio loss under the constraint that the probability of the combination of price moves is not bigger than, say, 5 percent of the time. That is, this approach locates the worst scenario while making certain distributional assumptions. The approach is computationally very intensive.

To summarize, the new 1995 Basle proposal does not impose restrictions on the choice of models or the estimation method a bank can use to calculate value-at-risk. Even for the simplest asset-normal approach, there are various ways to estimate the asset return standard deviations and correlations. One can employ standard statistical formulas for these statistics. Alternatively, some have suggested that older observations can be assigned a smaller weight in the estimation;[21] others have suggested that such weights should be estimated simultaneously with the statistics. These differences in estimation methods can lead to differences in estimates of value-at-risk for the same portfolio (Box II.2).[22]

Capital Requirements for Banks Using Internal Models

Under Basle's new approach, a bank's capital requirement on a particular day would be the higher of either the previous day's value-at-risk or the average of value-at-risk on each of the preceding sixty business days, multiplied by a safety factor that is greater than or equal to three. The safety factor creates a buffer to safeguard against the underestimation of a bank's capital requirement. The exact value of the safety factor would be related to the ex post performance of the bank's internal model; that is, a bank with a model that produces estimates of value-at-risk that are regularly inaccurate would be obliged to use a higher safety factor. The proposal does not explicitly specify how this safety factor should be determined in cases when it would exceed three, however. In addition to the capital charges related to value-at-risk, a bank that uses its internal model would be subject to a separate capital charge that covers the specific risk of traded debt and equity securities if such risk has not been incorporated into the model.

Quantitative and Qualitative Standards

In addition to requiring the use of a ten-day value-at-risk corresponding to a 99 percent confidence interval, the 1995 Basle proposal also contains a number of other requirements on the computation of the value-at-risk. For instance, the sample period for estimating the value-at-risk is required to cover at least a one-year period. The data set is also required to be updated at least once every three months. Furthermore, estimates of value-at-risk from different risk categories must be aggregated by simple summing, although the use of correlations between assets in the same risk category is allowed in the estimation of value-at-risk for a particular risk category.

The new approach also contains special requirements on the measurement of option risk. First, a minimum ten-day holding period is to be applied to option positions. Second, because option risk is nonlinear, banks are not allowed to estimate the ten-day value-at-risk by scaling up the estimate of daily value-at-risk by the square root of time. Third, banks are required to measure the volatilities of option positions according to their maturities.

In addition to quantitative standards, banks that choose to use their internal models to determine market-risk-based capital requirements are required to meet several qualitative standards. These standards specify minimum requirements on a bank's internal control and risk-management process. First, the bank is required to maintain an independent risk-control unit that reports directly to senior management. Second, the unit must conduct ex post performance analysis regularly to check the accuracy of the bank's model. Third, the bank is required to have its senior management actively involved in the risk-control process. Fourth, the bank's risk-measurement model is required to be fully integrated into the day-to-day risk-management process. Fifth, trading and exposure limits should be used in conjunction with the risk-measurement system. Sixth, the bank is required to have in place a routine program of stress testing. Seventh, the bank should have its internal policies, control procedures, and risk-management systems well documented. Finally, the bank should have an internal auditing process that regularly reviews its risk-measurement system and its risk-control unit.

Capital Requirements for Smaller Banks

Under Basle's new approach, smaller banks that prefer not to use an internal model are required to follow a revised version of the standards proposed in April 1993. The modifications address many of the earlier criticisms on the 1993 Basle proposal. For instance, the heavily criticized vertical disallowance in the computation of interest rate risk is significantly reduced.[23]

The new standards cover the market risk of commodities, which is ignored in the 1993 proposal.

---

[21]In J.P. Morgan's RiskMetrics system, an exponentially declining weight approach, which assigns a smaller weight to an older observation, is used in the estimation of variances and covariances.

[22]Box II.1 gives examples of value-at-risk calculations for a portfolio using different methods.

[23]In the April 1993 Basle Proposal, vertical disallowance is an adjustment made to the capital charge for offsetting long- and short-debt securities positions in the same time band. The proposal slots debt securities into 13 time bands according to their maturities in the process of calculating the capital charges. The vertical disallowance is for covering the gap risk related to long and short positions in the same time band that are similar but not identical securities and hence are not perfect hedges for one another.

Box II.1. Estimates of Value-at-Risk for a Hypothetical Derivatives Portfolio

The portfolio consists of various over-the-counter and exchange-traded derivatives from three main product classes: interest rate, currency, and equity products. The products considered include interest rate swaps, Eurodollar futures and futures options, yen futures and futures options, and S&P 500 index futures and futures options. The analysis is based on actual prices and rates obtained from Bloomberg Business News on April 26, 1995. The notional principal of the portfolio is about $340 million. The replacement value of the portfolio, given the prices and rates on April 26, 1995, is $1.27 million.

For swaps, the estimation of value-at-risk involves examining extreme movements in the swap-rate curve. Two possibilities are considered: (1) parallel shifts in the swap-rate curve governed by the 90-day Eurodollar interest rate, and (2) nonparallel shifts, where movements in swap rates corresponding to different maturities are given by the differences in their sensitivities to changes in the 90-day Eurodollar rate. These sensitivities are estimated using daily data over the six-month period ending on April 26, 1995.[1] Changes in the replacement value of swap positions are computed using the bootstrap method. This method infers the implied (zero-coupon) spot rates from the swap curve (that provides coupon rates for each maturity) by solving recursively for the discount rate corresponding to the last cash flow of a hypothetical par-value bond that pays a coupon rate equal to the swap rate for the maturity considered.[2] Given the implied spot rates, a set of implied forward rates can be computed. The expected future payments on the floating rate side of the swap can be computed by multiplying the implied forward rates by the notional principal. The value of the swap is obtained by discounting the stream of differences between the fixed and floating payments using discount rates derived from the implied spot rates.

For futures options, three methods are considered for calculating value-at-risk: an analytic approach, which uses no approximation to the nonlinear relationship between the value of an option and the underlying asset; a delta-normal approach, which uses a first-order Taylor approximation; and a delta-gamma approach, which uses a second-order Taylor approximation. The analytic approach calculates the effect of an extreme movement in the price or rate of the underlying asset on the value

of an option position by computing the theoretical difference in the option value using the exact option pricing formula. The delta-normal approach calculates the change in option value by multiplying the delta of the option by the extreme price change of the underlying asset. The delta-gamma approach is the same as the delta-normal approach except that a term (the gamma) that captures the effect of a change in the delta is added to yield a better approximation. For futures, the value-at-risk is simply computed as the change in the value of the futures position following a hypothetical extreme movement in the futures price.[3]

The key parameters used in the calculations are the volatilities of the various underlying assets. Various volatility estimates are used. These include historical volatility estimates based on samples of historical data of different period lengths (30 and 100 days) and implied volatility estimates that are inferred from actual call option prices on April 26, 1995.[4] The various combinations of methods and parameters produce 18 different ways of estimating value-at-risk for all of the positions in the portfolio.

In the April 1995 Basle proposal, estimates of value-at-risk for different product classes are to be added together to produce the overall value-at-risk. This method of aggregation is equivalent to assuming that products from different classes are perfectly correlated. The Basle proposal allows correlations among products in the same class to be used in the computation of the value-at-risk for a particular class. Here, for each of the 18 ways of estimating individual position value-at-risk, the portfolio value-at-risk is computed using the Basle aggregation method. For comparison, estimates of value-at-risk for the individual positions also are aggregated using three alternative assumptions: (1) asset returns are perfectly correlated such that the portfolio value-at-risk is the simple sum of the individual

[1]Essentially, a so-called one-factor model is used for the swap curve and two sets of factor sensitivities are considered in the value-at-risk analysis. The one-factor model, given its simplicity, is a popular approach for modeling the dynamics of the yield curve. Other approaches that market participants have used include a two-factor model, for which a long rate factor is added, and a two-factor model, for which a second volatility factor is included.

[2]A par-value bond is a bond whose current market value is the same as its principal amount.

[3]An extreme price movement is computed as a price movement corresponding to a rate of return that is 2.32 times the ten-day standard deviation below the mean. This corresponds to a one-tail 1 percent critical value under a normal distribution.

[4]The use of relatively short samples in the estimation of the underlying futures price volatility is more or less driven by the availability of data. Many short-term futures contracts are only actively traded in the two-to-three month period prior to contract expiration. For instance, on April 28, 1995, a total of 52,921 contracts of the June 1995 S&P 500 futures was traded, compared with 55 contracts of the same contract on April 29, 1994. The use of a longer sample for futures contracts, while feasible, would require contract switching, which can further complicate the estimation of futures-price volatility. The implied volatility method treats the actual option price as an input. The option pricing formula is then inverted to yield the volatility that corresponds to such an option price. When multiple options of different exercise prices are used, the implied volatility is usually found by minimizing the sum of squared discrepancies between the observed option prices and their corresponding theoretical values.

Banks that do not use an internal model for commodity risk will have to follow either a standard approach or a simplified approach. Under the standard approach, the net position in each commodity

is converted at the current spot rate into the national currency. A maturity ladder approach, similar to the one used for debt instruments, is then used to determine the capital charge. Under the simpli-

Value-at-Risk for a Hypothetical Portfolio[1]

(In thousands of U.S. dollars)

Summary Statistics[2]	Basle Internal Model-Based Approach	Assuming Perfect Correlation	Assuming Zero Correlation	Using Historical Correlation
Mean	9,705	9,796	8,025	8,304
Maximum	17,975	18,131	16,228	16,568
Minimum	3,953	4,009	2,503	2,680
Maximum/Minimum	4.5	4.5	6.5	6.2
Replacement value of the portfolio[3]	1,270			

Source: IMF staff calculations.

[1]The portfolio is made up of the following positions: (1) a $20 million (notional) three-year interest rate swap receiving a fixed rate of 7.07 percent and paying LIBOR semiannually; (2) a $10 million (notional) four-year interest rate swap receiving a fixed rate of 7.47 percent and paying LIBOR semiannually; (3) a long position in 100 contracts of the September 1995 Eurodollar futures (the size of each contract is $1 million); (4) a long position in 150 contracts of the September 1995 Eurodollar futures call option (the settlement amount for a contract is $2,500 times the call option price) and a long position in 40 contracts of the September 1995 yen futures (the size of each contract is ¥ 12.5 million); (5) a long position in 60 contracts of the September 1995 yen futures call option with a strike price of 119 (i.e., 1.19 cents for a yen); (6) a long position in 40 contracts of the June 1995 Standard & Poor's (S&P) 500 futures (the contract size is 500 times the S&P 500 Index); and (7) a long position in 60 contracts of the June 1995 S&P 500 futures call option (the contract value is 500 times the call option price).

[2]For each aggregation method (column) the statistics are computed from the 18 estimates of value-at-risk.

[3]Replacement value of the portfolio is the amount of money that would have to be paid to a third party to induce it to enter into a transaction to replace an existing deal. For a portfolio, the replacement value is equal to the present value of all profitable outstanding contracts.

value-at-risk of all positions; (2) asset returns are not correlated across product class, for which the portfolio value-at-risk is the square root of the sum of the squared individual value-at-risk; and (3) asset returns obey historical correlations.

The table above presents summary statistics of the 72 estimates of value-at-risk that result from the 18 combinations of estimation methods and parameters and the 4 aggregation methods. Under the Basle aggregation approach, the highest value-at-risk obtained is as much as 4.5 times the lowest value-at-risk estimated. For the aggregation method utilizing actual historical correlations, the highest portfolio value-at-risk estimate

Value-at-Risk from Alternative Aggregation Approaches

(As a ratio of value-at-risk using the Basle aggregation approach)

Summary Statistics	Assuming Perfect Correlation	Assuming Zero Correlation	Using Historical Correlation
Mean	1.01	0.76	0.80
Maximum	1.02	0.90	0.93
Minimum	1.00	0.61	0.66

Source: IMF staff calculations.

($16.6 million) is 6.2 times that of the lowest portfolio value-at-risk estimate ($2.7 million).

To highlight the differences across aggregation methods, The table on the left presents summary statistics of 54 ratios that, for each of the 18 combinations of estimation methods and parameters, compare estimates of value-at-risk using the last three aggregation methods (numerators) to the Basle aggregation method (the denominator). The portfolio value-at-risk utilizing historical correlations was as low as 66 percent of the value-at-risk computed under the Basle approach. On average, the ratio is 80 percent for the historical correlation method and 76 percent for a method assuming zero correlations among all assets. The portfolio value-at-risk assuming perfect correlations is close to the Basle approach because, for the portfolio considered, there is little gain from accounting for within-product-class correlations, as products in the same class are either dependent on the same underlying asset or highly correlated. This might not be the case for a more general portfolio.

Several observations can be made. First, there is variation in estimates of value-at-risk across different estimation methods and parameter inputs. Second, there is significant variation in value-at-risk estimates across aggregation methods. Third, the portfolio value-at-risk can be very large relative to the current replacement value of the portfolio. The highest value-at-risk found is more than 14 times the actual replacement value of the portfolio.

fied approach, a capital charge equal to the sum of a 15 percent charge on the net position and a 3 percent charge on the gross position of a commodity is imposed.

In addition, more refined approaches are included for option risk. Specifically, gamma and vega risks are explicitly incorporated. Under the so-called delta-plus approach, a bank is required to calculate the gamma and vega for each of its option positions. For interest rate derivatives, the gammas and vegas are slotted into separate maturity ladders by currency. The capital charge for gamma risk for each time band is computed by multiplying the net negative gammas by a given risk weight and then by the square of the market value of the underlying asset. The positive gammas are ignored, because they are related to an increase in the sensitivity of the value of the derivative position to the underlying asset value when it is moving in a direction that will increase the value of the derivative asset. Hence, strictly speaking, a positive gamma does not represent risk. The capital charge for vega risk for each time band is computed by multiplying the vega by a proportional shift in volatility of ±25 percent.

Challenges for the Own-Models Approach

The new Basle proposal has several advantages. First, it eliminates the need for banks to maintain two parallel systems, one for regulatory purposes and another for trading and portfolio allocation. This will reduce costs and promote efficiency. Second, it eliminates the distortionary effects of incomplete and rigid capital rules on bank activities. Third, it promotes efficient updating of capital requirements to cover new products. Finally, it provides banks with additional incentives to improve their risk-management systems.

There are many challenges in implementing this new approach. There is very little agreement in the banking industry about how to model and measure risk; different banks employ different models, estimation procedures, and model parameters. A potential problem with the new internal-model-based approach is that two banks holding the same portfolio will most likely come up with different estimates of value-at-risk. This will imply different capital requirements for banks that incur the same risks and violates one of the major objectives of international capital requirements, namely, the achievement of a level playing field.

This problem was discovered in the second half of 1994 during an experiment conducted by the Basle Committee on Banking Supervision; the Committee asked an internationally diversified group of major banks dealing in the OTC derivative markets to estimate the value-at-risk associated with four hypothetical portfolios with and without options. Very different estimates were reported by the group of banks even though they were asked to use the same confidence interval and the same holding period. The problem with this divergence of estimates is that it can lead to issues regarding bank competitive equity and, more important, questions about model quality. For example, a bank might choose to use a model that produces a lower capital requirement rather than one

that produces more accurate estimates of value-at-risk.

Supervisors in the Group of Ten countries have more or less concluded that a full-fledged, model-validation approach to bank supervision is not a practical way of dealing with these modeling issues. There is little agreement about what constitutes a good model for measuring risk, and supervisors generally lack the experience and technical knowledge required to validate the models currently in use by the more sophisticated banks. Instead, the new approach attempts to combine minimum standards, regular external auditing, a safety factor, and performance criteria in determining regulatory capital requirements for individual banks. Assessing performance might involve comparing the profit-and-loss performance of a bank to verify that its portfolio return is consistent with the ex ante value-at-risk estimates produced by the bank's model. If a bank experiences losses in excess of its ex ante estimates of value-at-risk more often than what is implied by the underlying confidence interval used in estimating value-at-risk, then the bank's internal model might fall short of acceptable quality. In such cases, capital requirements greater than "value-at-risk times three" would be imposed. This would be achieved by setting the safety factor above the minimum of three.

A strength of this performance-based approach appears to be that the need to examine and validate a bank's model would, to a certain extent, decrease. A weakness of this approach is that ex post performance analysis is usually not very powerful statistically because it requires a long history of stable market behavior to judge the performance of a model. Moreover, past performance might not reflect future model performance because banks continuously change their models to accommodate changes in the market environment, the introduction of new products, and the introduction of new pricing and risk management techniques.

Although Basle's draft proposal suggests that the size of a bank's safety factor will be related directly to the ex post performance of the bank's model, it does not provide details about how the safety factor is to be determined. Setting the right criteria for assessing model performance is key to providing banks with incentives to improve model accuracy. In short, the effectiveness of Basle's model-based approach depends crucially on whether this incentive structure encourages banks to choose model accuracy over lower capital requirements. It is likely that the Basle Committee will have to establish a framework in which capital requirements can be related directly to performance before the new model-based approach can be fully implemented.

An alternative approach to performance evaluation, the so-called precommitment approach, requires that each bank commits to a ceiling level of capital losses that will not be exceeded.[24] Should this ceiling be breached, a severe penalty would be imposed on the bank. This alternative would provide the incentive for banks to dynamically control their risk exposures by accounting for changes in future portfolios and strategies. Model validation is not necessary under this alternative approach.

A potential difficulty in implementing the precommitment approach is that it may be as difficult to establish rules for assessing penalties—a penalty function—as it has been to establish simple capital adequacy standards. For example, in principle, the penalties should reflect the cost to taxpayers of a bank failure or the indirect costs of an increase in future funding costs should a bank violate its capital precommitment or both; each is difficult to measure. Furthermore, given that the market environment is changing all the time, it also would be difficult to establish a robust penalty function. Another potential problem involves credibility. A bank would violate its capital commitment only because it has suffered a big loss. In such cases, regulators would be unable to credibly impose a sizable penalty on a bank that is at risk of failing. In fact, a huge penalty might force a bank to adopt a go-for-broke strategy after losing a significant amount of its capital. Flexibility in applying penalties is another issue. A bank might violate its capital commitment because of bad luck or because of a systemic event. In such cases it would not be appropriate to penalize an otherwise safe and sound bank. But if application of the penalty function is flexible, then a measure of the quality of the bank's risk-management model is necessary and supervisors will then have to validate the bank's model.

There are also open questions about implementation of the new Basle approach. The emphasis on quantitative measures, like value-at-risk, might lead banks to miss major market events that are not easily quantifiable. A recent example of such an event is the Mexican financial crisis. Many market participants and regulators have serious doubts about whether a statistical-mathematical model could have detected the increase in risk associated with this crisis. While Basle's new approach would require stress testing, there is no consensus about how the results of stress tests should be incorporated into the estimation and analysis of value-at-risk.

Another issue is that the new Basle approach does not deal with legal risk and operational risk. The collapse of Barings and the legal problems encountered by Bankers Trust have revealed that such risks can be important. Furthermore, even though the Basle approach incorporates liquidity risk—a ten-day holding period in the computation of the value-at-risk—

a uniform treatment might not be appropriate because changes in liquidity depend on the instrument in question, the size of the position, and the market conditions. By treating each position identically, bank portfolio decisions might well be distorted; the risk of holding a very large concentrated position, which is often difficult to liquidate, might be underestimated.

International and Bank-Nonbank Coordination Issues

The Basle Committee is planning to adopt the new approach by the end of the year and to implement it by the end of 1997.[25] Meanwhile, the CAD, which does not allow the use of internal models for determining capital requirements, is required to be implemented by EU countries by January 1, 1996. The EU has tried to accommodate the new internal model-based approach proposed by the Basle Committee by agreeing to allow top European banks to follow the Basle approach to some extent. In April 1995, the commission's directorate-general has agreed that daily value-at-risk models can be used in conjunction with the CAD provided that the capital requirement according to the firm's estimate of value-at-risk is not less than the capital requirement according to the CAD. In any event, should the Basle proposal be adopted, the EU has to amend its CAD sometime after its implementation. Without careful harmonization, some EU banks might have to adjust their risk-management system twice; once to meet the CAD deadline, and once to adopt Basle's new approach in 1997.

Also at issue is whether there will be a level playing field in areas where both banks and securities houses compete. This issue is more serious for U.S. banks than for European banks, which are universal banks. It is unclear whether, and to what extent, securities house regulators will allow securities houses to use internal models to determine capital requirements.

The Basle Committee and the International Organization of Securities Commissions (IOSCO) have tried to coordinate efforts on capital requirement issues but have not had much success. A major difficulty is the difference in the regulatory focus of bank and securities regulators. Bank regulators tend to focus on systemic risk issues as banks are relatively more vulnerable to contagious collapses; securities regulators tend to pay more attention to investor protection issues. As a result, securities regulators concentrate primarily on liquid capital that measures the ability of a securities firm to meet its obligations to investors and creditors.

---

[24]See Kupiec and O'Brien (1995).

[25]See background paper "Mechanisms for International Cooperation in Regulation," pp. 158–61, for a discussion of the mechanisms that currently exist for international coordination of financial regulation and supervision.

The Focus on Process of Internal Risk Management

Initiatives to Improve Risk Management

Regulators have come to recognize that maintaining a minimum capital requirement is just one part of the overall risk-management system of a bank. In a report on derivatives released in May 1994, the U.S. General Accounting Office recommended that regulators should assess the quality of the major OTC derivatives dealers' risk-management systems.[26] Some market participants have argued that having a top-rated, risk-measurement model but a poor risk-management and -control process could be worse than having a poor internal model but a good risk-control process.[27]

A recent survey by the Group of Thirty has shown that, in general, dealers do not follow uniformly the recommendations on sound risk-management practice of the Group of Thirty report issued in July 1993.[28] The earlier report contained recommendations in five major areas: (1) general policies; (2) valuation and market risk management; (3) credit risk measurement and management; (4) enforceability, systems, operations, and controls; and (5) accounting and disclosure.

The survey examines to what extent the recommendations in the July 1993 Report are followed by market participants. On the measurement and management of market risk, only 21 percent of dealers measure and compare market-risk exposure against established limits on an intraday basis. Regarding the use of value-at-risk for measuring market risk, only 43 percent of the dealers surveyed employed this approach, and fewer than half of those who employed the value-at-risk approach used a consistent confidence interval and time horizon for different derivative portfolios. Furthermore, only 54 percent of the dealers performed stress tests and simulations to measure how their portfolios would perform under abnormal changes in market conditions. In addition, in conducting stress tests, only 27 percent of the dealers account for decreases in liquidity and only 28 percent account for failures of a significant counterparty.

On the operation of an independent market-risk function, the survey revealed that only 29 percent of the dealers monitor the variance between a portfolio's actual and predicted volatility. Furthermore, more than 20 percent of the dealers do not establish counterparty credit limits by current and potential exposure.

To further promote the importance of having a high-quality risk-management system and to establish a benchmark for good risk management, the Basle Committee on Banking Supervision and IOSCO issued under the same cover, in July 1994, two separate reports on risk management regarding derivatives.[29] Although styles differ significantly, due to traditional differences in the supervision of banks and nonbanks, there are only minor differences in the substance of the recommendations.

The reports identified many important elements of sound risk management. First, senior management must be involved in setting the overall policy of the firm regarding the use of derivatives including the level of risk tolerance and the range of products allowed. Second, a line of authority and responsibility for managing risk and conducting derivative activities should be clearly established. Third, before a new derivative activity is undertaken, a detailed proposal describing the product, market, and strategy should be prepared. A bank should not get involved significantly in a new product until it has been fully integrated into the bank's risk-measurement system. Fourth, compensation policies should be set up in a way to avoid excessive risk taking. Fifth, banks should have their internal auditors to evaluate compliance with risk limits. If limits are exceeded, the system should automatically notify senior management.

Sixth, the internal auditors should check for adequate separation of duties and oversight. Seventh, the reliability and timeliness of information reported to the bank's senior management and the board of directors should be emphasized. In particular, the measured risk for derivative activities should be translated from a technical and quantitative format to one that can be easily understood by senior management who might not have the technical background. Eighth, risk should be measured and aggregated on an institution-wide basis including both trading and nontrading activities. That is, it is not sufficient to concentrate on the trading book. Ninth, stress tests should be conducted. Stress analysis should include the identification of possible adverse events, an evaluation of the likelihood of adverse events, the analysis of worst-case scenarios, and an evaluation of the bank's ability to withstand the worst events. Stress tests should also include qualitative analysis of hard-to-quantify events and the actions management can take under those scenarios. Tenth, the institution should regularly review the underlying methodologies and assumptions of its models.

---

[26]United States (1994).

[27]The collapse of Barings serves as an example of the importance of internal controls.

[28]See Group of Thirty (1993) and (1994b).

[29]See Basle Committee on Banking Supervision (1994b) and Technical Committee of the International Organization of Securities Commissions (1994).

Difficulties in Supervising Internal Risk-Management Systems

Supervisors face many challenges in examining the internal risk-management systems of banks. First, supervising a bank's risk-management system is significantly more complicated than determining a bank's regulatory capital requirements. Second, the quality of different aspects of a risk-management system is difficult to quantify and to aggregate to obtain an overall measure of the quality of the risk-management system of a bank. For instance, while it might be easy to tell whether a bank has performed stress testing or not, it is very difficult to judge the quality of the stress-testing exercise. Even banks might not agree among themselves on what is a reasonable set of stress scenarios. Assumptions on the holding period and liquidity can also significantly affect the stress test results. In addition, stress testing of derivatives-like options is difficult, because the pricing of options is generally based on certain distributional assumptions. Large jumps in prices might not be consistent with these assumptions. Third, there might not be one optimal risk-management system for banks of all size and business emphasis. The system that is optimal for a large bank that does significant trading in the OTC derivative markets is probably not optimal for a smaller bank that concentrates on more traditional banking business. It would be difficult for the regulators to design specialized risk-management benchmarks for different banks.

II

Initiatives Relating to Derivatives

The sudden collapse of Barings has heightened concerns about whether existing transparency and disclosure requirements for the derivative activities of individual financial institutions are adequate for judging the safety and soundness of individual financial institutions and for safeguarding financial systems against systemic problems. It is possible that had there been greater information about the derivative positions taken by Barings, the investment bank might have been prevented from accumulating positions risky enough to put at risk the entire capital of the firm.[30] The lack of transparency also can lead, during periods of market distress, to overreactions by market participants and prevent policymakers from making timely decisions about how to contain the effects of extreme events when they occur.

The misfortunes of various end-users also have raised concerns about the adequacy of investor protection in the unregulated OTC derivatives markets.[31] In several cases, end-users have accused dealers of selling high-risk derivative instruments that were not suitable for their purposes and for withholding information about the riskiness of the derivative instruments. Many end-users, especially those lacking expertise, also are concerned about their current exposures, which they fear to be unsuitable for their purposes and the result of aggressive marketing by dealers.

Motivation for Industry and Regulatory Initiatives

Derivative markets have grown rapidly in recent years. In addition to this rapid growth, many sectors of the economy have made extensive use of derivative instruments; even firms engaged in nonfinancial activities are now using derivatives, especially OTC derivatives. Derivative instruments obtain their value from the value of the underlying securities, interest rates, or price indices, and the reasons for their popularity are clear. If used properly, derivative instruments are useful and convenient for hedging against

many kinds of risk, including fluctuations in interest rates, exchange rates, and commodity prices, for example oil prices, and for unbundling risk so that risks can be distributed to those willing to incur them. OTC derivative contracts are especially popular because they are privately negotiated contracts between two parties and often are custom designed to suit the specific needs of counterparties. Thus, OTC derivative contracts can be used to achieve highly specialized funding and risk-bundling objectives.

For a number of important reasons, a financial institution's active participation in OTC derivative markets might reduce the transparency of the institution's financial condition and risk exposures. First, OTC derivative positions are held as off-balance-sheet items. As a result, very limited information is available about a firm's derivative activities, making it difficult to judge what part of a firm's profitability and risk exposure is attributable to these activities. Second, most accounting standards were established before the introduction of many OTC derivative instruments and were not designed to account for the risk exposures and income flows associated with these instruments. Third, the risk exposure of a derivative position cannot be assessed without knowing all related positions and the exact nature of the dynamic trading strategy employed. Fourth, the value of derivatives can be sensitive to changes in the prices of the underlying securities, and the value of an institution's derivative portfolio can change dramatically and rapidly.[32] The speed with which a firm's financial condition and risk exposure can change has significantly reduced the value of annual or semiannual reporting of income statements and balance sheets. Finally, OTC derivatives are privately negotiated, custom-designed products, which may involve many counterparties in different countries; these features make it very difficult to gather and maintain market-wide information.

It is generally recognized by regulators and market participants that without transparency it is difficult to assess the safety and soundness of financial institutions and, therefore, to limit systemic risk. Although regulatory capital requirements and internal

---

[30]See the background paper "Regulatory Implications of the Barings Failure," pp. 162–64.

[31]End-users that have suffered big losses in derivatives or highly leveraged structured instruments include Orange County, Metallgesellschaft, Proctor & Gamble, and Gibson Greetings.

[32]For instance, Barings lost close to $1 billion in less than two months on Nikkei index derivatives following the Kobe earthquake.

risk management are necessary for safeguarding the soundness of financial institutions, they are by themselves insufficient for eliminating systemic risk. For example, a sound financial condition alone cannot prevent a massive withdrawal of funds from an institution at a time of market distress unless depositors and creditors are fully informed. As in the case of a bank run, a massive withdrawal of credits can render an otherwise solvent and sound bank insolvent if it has to liquidate its assets quickly, at highly discounted values, to satisfy its need for liquidity.

There are other advantages to greater transparency. Institutions known to have a good risk-management system might face lower funding costs (including higher stock prices), receive greater credit lines, and attract more business. Thus, transparency can provide incentives for financial institutions to improve their risk-management systems. Greater disclosure also would allow market participants to obtain better information and to better assess the risk exposures of its counterparties. Good information is essential for making trading and risk-management decisions, such as counterparty position limits, and also allows investors to make better investment decisions. Thus, greater transparency and disclosure can improve the allocative efficiency of financial markets.

Not all market participants agree, however, that more transparency is beneficial. An important impediment to greater transparency and disclosure has been the reluctance on the part of some market participants to disclose too much information about their financial positions, risk exposures, pricing models, and risk-management systems, This proprietary information is viewed as the source of revenue and market shares and, therefore, should not be disclosed. This is particularly true for large, sophisticated, and successful market participants who utilize leading edge pricing and risk-management technologies and who have large exposures in a wide variety of markets. Another impediment to greater transparency and disclosure is that there is no consensus about what information to disclose, when to disclose it, and to whom to disclose it.

Initiatives to Deal with Transparency

Initiatives have been taken in the past year by some of the major industry and regulatory bodies in the financial industry to improve transparency and disclosure. These initiatives included the Institute of International Finance (IIF) proposal, issued in August 1994, for a framework for public disclosure of derivatives activities and related credit exposures;[33] the Bank for International Settlements (BIS) report, issued in September 1994, on the public disclosure of

market and credit risk by financial intermediaries (the Fisher report);[34] and the U.S. Financial Accounting Standards Board (FASB) statement (Statement of Financial Accounting Standards No. 119), published in October 1994, on the disclosure of derivative positions. After reviewing these initiatives, many of the unresolved issues involving the disclosure of information by individual institutions are examined.

Institute of International Finance Report

The IIF proposal focuses on the disclosure of credit risk in annual reports and develops an international standard for public disclosure of derivatives-related credit exposures. The report emphasizes the importance of disaggregated data on credit risk exposures and activity levels, and specifically recommends that replacement value (or net replacement value if netting arrangements are enforceable) be disclosed by categories of counterparty credit quality based on credit ratings by rating agencies, internal credit ratings, or the 1988 Basle Accord classification based on the OECD membership.[35] For example, replacement value would be reported according to the private credit ratings AAA, AA, A, B, and non-investment grade. When internal credit ratings are used, information would be required to be reported on the institution's credit-scoring system.

The report also calls on financial institutions to provide more detailed information about their derivative activities, including notional values by product types—such as interest rate contracts, foreign exchange contracts, and equity contracts—and their maturities. Under the category of interest rate contracts, for example, an institution should report its exposures in swaps, options, futures, forwards, and other derivative products, and according to whether they are OTC or exchange-traded products. The total market value for each product type—the sum of positive mark-to-market values—also would be disclosed. The report does not recommend adjustments for netting and collateral arrangements in the calculation of market value, however, because they are difficult to quantify.

Some market participants have criticized the approach recommended by IIF because it uses notional value rather than replacement value as a measure

---

[33]See Institute of International Finance (1994).

[34]See Bank for International Settlements (1994).

[35]See Basle Committee on Banking Supervision (1988). Replacement value is the amount of money that would have to be paid to a third party to induce it to enter into a transaction to replace an existing position. Net replacement value of a portfolio is the replacement value of the portfolio after allowing long and short positions with the same counterparty to offset each other. An enforceable netting arrangement is an arrangement by which the offsetting of long and short positions with a counterparty is legally enforceable at the time of bankruptcy.

of market size. The relationship between these measures can vary significantly from institution to institution. For example, at the end of 1993, the ratio of gross replacement value to notional value was 3.4 percent for one firm and 0.5 percent for another.[36] In addition, the notional value of interest rate swaps and currency swaps cannot be compared because the notional principals are exchanged at maturity for currency swaps but not for interest rate swaps. The report has been criticized for other reasons as well: the usefulness of annual reporting is limited for volatile derivative contract, and credit-risk exposures cannot be accurately represented by the total current replacement values for all derivative contracts because they ignore potential future exposure. OTC contracts are marked-to-model, which cannot be verified by outsiders; most OTC derivative products are custom designed and cannot be traded in liquid markets, which makes it difficult to value them.

The Fisher Report

The Fisher report addresses the disclosure of both market and credit risk and emphasizes the reporting of market risk and the performance of risk-management systems. Its recommendations on credit risk are in line with those of the IIF report. The Fisher report also recommends the reporting of potential future credit exposures, but it does not provide guidelines on how to compute and report potential credit exposure.

Among the important features of the report is its endorsement of value-at-risk as a measure of market-risk exposure. It makes specific recommendations about how value-at-risk should be disclosed to reveal the risk appetite and risk exposure of an institution, such as providing high, low, and average measures of value-at-risk for different holding periods (say one day and two weeks) during the reporting period; confidence interval at which value-at-risk is computed; a comparison of the average value-at-risk for a holding period of one day and the average change in portfolio value; and measures of the volatility of the change in portfolio value. The report also recommends comparisons of ex ante value-at-risk estimates to actual losses incurred by the institution to observe the frequency with which actual performance is worse than predicted by the firm's risk-management system.

A key issue not addressed by the report is the comparability across financial institutions of their estimates of value-at-risk. As discussed earlier, there are many ways to compute value-at-risk and estimates depend on the holding period, the confidence interval, the derivatives-pricing models, and the parameter inputs chosen. As such, two firms with the same

portfolio might produce very different estimates of value-at-risk. Another issue is that value-at-risk is a snapshot of a firm's risk exposure and cannot reflect the effects of any dynamic hedging strategies that the institution might be using.

Statement of Financial Accounting Standards

In October 1994, a new accounting rule for derivatives, SFAS No. 119, was issued by the U.S. Financial Accounting Standards Board.[37] Inappropriate accounting rules for derivatives often have been cited as a major impediment to better disclosure in OTC derivative markets. Previous rules related to derivatives were deemed insufficient for many complex OTC derivative instruments.[38] A problem with traditional accounting standards is that they were designed using an instrument-specific approach that is not appropriate for OTC derivatives, which often cut across different product classes. In addition, many accounting standards were drafted before the introduction of many OTC derivative products. Moreover, many standards require differential treatment of derivative positions for hedging purposes and for other purposes. Under the so-called hedge accounting approach, positions for hedging are reported together with the position being hedged and no marking-to-market is required. But a derivative position can also be used to partially hedge a portfolio, which introduces ambiguity about whether a position should be identified as a hedge for accounting purposes.

The new accounting standard, SFAS 119, applies to all U.S. business enterprises and nonprofit organizations and covers derivative instruments including futures, forwards, swaps, and options and similar contracts. It does not include on-balance-sheet instruments like structured notes. The standard applies differential treatment for derivatives used for trading and derivatives used for other purposes.

For derivative positions for trading purposes, SFAS 119 requires (1) disclosure of the average fair value of the position during the reporting period and at the end of the period, (2) distinction between positive and negative values to prevent institutions from netting winning and losing positions unless they are with the same counterparty, and (3) disclosure of net gains and losses disaggregated by product types and

---

[36]"Books of Revelations" (1994).

[37]See Financial Accounting Standards Board (1994).
[38]These rules include FAS No. 52, which applies only to foreign exchange transactions, not to currency options; FAS No. 80, which applies to futures but not forwards; FAS 105, which only requires the notional amount of OTC derivative positions be reported with their nature and terms; FAS No. 107, which requires the disclosure of fair value of related on- and off-balance-sheet derivatives; and, FASB Interpretation No. 39, which only allows netting of positions with a counterparty under a master netting arrangement.

risk classes. For other derivatives, the standard requires (1) disclosure of the objective for holding the positions, (2) an explanation of the strategies used to achieve the objective, and (3) a description of the reporting methodology. For those derivatives receiving hedge-accounting treatment, the end-user must also provide a description of the underlying positions being hedged and the amount of deferred gains and losses.

In contrast with the recommendations of the IIF and the Fisher reports, SFAS 119 focuses on the disclosure of qualitative information. In particular, it does not require disclosure of value-at-risk, stress analysis, durations, and details on current positions. The FASB took the position that a quantitative measure of risk should not be required unless there is general agreement on the most appropriate measure of risk and the best way to calculate it. Many market participants feel this approach is conservative, however, and think that imperfect quantitative disclosure is better than none at all.

Challenges for Improving Disclosure

The above-mentioned reports have made significant progress in raising important issues involving the disclosure of credit and market risk. There are still a significant number of challenges, of a more general nature, that the industry and regulators are likely to face in the period ahead. All of these challenges point out the difficulties involved in defining a single measure of risk that captures comprehensively all of the risks inherent in the financial activities of a single financial institution. These difficulties pose major challenges for internal risk management, for supervisors in assessing safety and soundness, and for assessing the potential for systemic risk.

Risk Aggregation

Quantitative disclosure requirements have focused mainly on the trading book of an institution. A case has been made by some market participants for not treating the trading book separately, however. One reason is that a more comprehensive picture of the risks that a financial institution is incurring is necessary to properly assess the safety and soundness of the institution. An additional problem is that because credit and market risk are not independent, they cannot be measured separately and then simply added together. In general, how to aggregate market and credit risk in order to obtain a comprehensive picture of a firm's risk exposure is a question that still needs to be answered.

Nonquantifiable Risks

In addition to market and credit risk, there are liquidity, legal, and operational risks; all of them can be significant. The failure of Barings can be attributed to operational risk, the risk of losses due to mismanagement, human error, and lack of control. Legal risk, uncertainty about the validity and enforceability of contracts, has also become important. For example, there is considerable uncertainty about whether some netting arrangements are enforceable, especially when they involve institutions from more than one country, and there is also uncertainty about the validity of the transaction itself. After suffering major losses from derivatives trading, various end-users have sued or accused dealers of unauthorized trading, misrepresentations of risks inherent in instruments, and not disclosing valuable information on pricing and risk.[39] Liquidity risk, uncertainty about whether a position can be liquidated rapidly at current prices, has also increased in importance. Although there are indicators of market liquidity, such as bid-ask spreads and market-trading volume, they tend not to be accurate measures of risk in times of market distress. Moreover, it is difficult to estimate how quickly liquidity can change under extreme market conditions.

Because of the dearth of good measures of these kinds of risk, it is difficult for financial institutions to provide senior management, shareholders, and counterparties with accurate assessments of the riskiness of their portfolios. In addition, these nonquantifiable risks are not independent of market and credit risk. When there have been legal disputes, the party has sued after a significant increase in market risk or market event. Moreover, an increase in credit risk may be associated with an increase in liquidity risk. When the market has information (or hears a rumor) that a major counterparty might default on its obligations, the counterparty may lose its access to existing credit lines and credit markets in general.

Quantitative Versus Qualitative Disclosure

There is some disagreement about the relative importance of quantitative and qualitative disclosure. Numerical estimates of risk exposure are crucial for judging the financial condition of a financial institution. Some market participants caution, however, that a single number might be misleading especially since there are important measurement and aggregation problems. In addition, focusing on one aspect of risk that is quantifiable might detract attention from the other, and in some cases more important, less-quantifiable risks. Qualitative information, such as detailed consultations with management and analyses of accounting, risk management, netting, trading, limit setting, collateral, and how derivatives activities

---

[39]The most publicized cases have been Proctor & Gamble and Gibson Greetings against Bankers Trust.

fit into the firm's business, can be more useful than reporting a single measure like, for example, value-at-risk.[40]

Uniformity and Flexibility

There is a trade-off between uniformity (or comparability) and flexibility in disclosing information. Incomparability makes it difficult for market participants to distinguish sound from less sound institutions. In times of market distress, this inability to accurately distinguish the riskiness of one institution from another can lead to a massive and uniform withdrawal from all institutions at the same time, and create systemic problems. Incomparability might also lead to higher funding costs—through risk premiums—for all institutions, thus reducing allocative efficiency. Incomparable disclosure would also limit the government's ability to implement appropriate policies.

Market participants might not always face the kinds of incentive structures that encourage them to disclose comparable information. For example, according to market analysts, institutions may deliberately confuse their competition by disclosing noncomparable data. This might be why one bank discloses gross replacement value as a measure of credit risk exposure, another discloses net replacement value, and still another discloses net replacement value net of collateral for credit risk disclosure.

There is also disagreement about whether rigid standards are appropriate. Some market participants have noted that rigid standards cannot accommodate changes in market structure, such as the introduction of new products, and there is still considerable disagreement about the best method for measuring risk. There is also the concern that the development of a comparable risk measure might imply the choice of an industry standard that is not necessarily the most accurate risk measure. For example, it is generally agreed that net replacement value is more accurate than gross replacement value as a measure of credit risk; however, the net measure is less comparable than the gross measure because some institutions might have more netting agreements and there might be differences in legal judgment on the enforceability of some netting agreements. In addition, net replacement value cannot be easily broken down by

maturity, product type, and currency. Finally, different countries have different accounting and reporting standards. It might not be fair or feasible to impose the same standard on market participants from different countries.

Disclosure of Risk-Management System

Many market participants and regulators have found it useful to have information on the quality of the risk-management system of an institution, as risk exposures can change significantly and rapidly. The Fisher report recommends using a comparison between ex ante risk estimates and ex post losses as a way to test the performance of a firm's risk-management system. This approach requires a long history of past performance in similar market environments and might not produce a good indicator of future performance in different market environments. Moreover, this approach might not provide very precise information. Given that institutions are likely to use different risk-management systems and different derivative-pricing models, an important challenge is to determine what to disclose about risk management. An equally important and difficult challenge is to design a common framework for the reporting of risk-management systems and processes.

How Much Disclosure Is Enough?

An important issue in disclosing information about risk-management systems is where to draw the line between adequate and excessive reporting. In the dispute between Bankers Trust and Proctor & Gamble, the latter had accused the former of not sharing its complex pricing model used in pricing the derivatives it had transacted. This raises the question, Should a dealer be required to disclose proprietary information, including its pricing model, to its customers? From the end-users' point of view there are no market prices for OTC derivative products and they should have access to information about how the dealer values these instruments. From the dealers' point of view, the proprietary model is a trade secret. In another dispute between Bankers Trust and Gibson Greetings, the latter accused the former of not disclosing information about the effects of volatility on the market values of its positions. This raises another question: How many stress tests are enough? Given that there are many ways to design stress tests and many scenarios, it would be difficult and costly for dealers to examine every possible case. On the other hand, end-users would want to know whether the dealer has selectively omitted stress tests in their reporting and misrepresented the risks involved in the transaction.

A related question is whether more disclosure is beneficial. Many end-users and investors have found

---

[40]The Group of Thirty report emphasized the importance of qualitative disclosure including (1) management's attitude to financial risk; (2) how instruments are used; (3) how risks are monitored and controlled; (4) accounting policies; (5) analysis of positions at the balance sheet date; and (6) analysis of credit risk inherent in those positions. See Group of Thirty (1993).

that a large amount of information can be overwhelming and distract them from focusing on key issues. In addition, there are obvious economies of scale on information collection and maintenance. Large institutions, active in OTC derivative markets, most likely have very sophisticated reporting systems in place. The cost of extensive reporting to these institutions is relatively low. However, the cost of the same level of reporting can be very high for a relatively small institution. Requiring the same amount of disclosure for all institutions might tilt the playing field against the less sophisticated players. What the optimal amount of information to disclose is and whether differential standards should be applied to different institutions are important questions to be answered.

Frequency of Reporting

Another important issue is the frequency of reporting. The consensus of market participants and the regulators is that low frequency reporting, like annual or semiannual reporting, is not as useful as in the past. The question then is, What is the optimal frequency of reporting? The answer is not independent of the amount of information to be disclosed or reported. The optimal trade-off between the two is an unresolved issue.

Who Should Report and to Whom?

Although many of the large, sophisticated banks obtain a large share of their revenues from derivative activities, many banks, large and small do not. A key question is, Should all banks be subject to the same reporting requirements for their derivative activity regardless of the scale of their activities? One reason why it might be beneficial to have differential requirements is the cost involved in maintaining accounting and auditing for these systems, and there may be economies of scale that cannot be obtained in these areas by banks not actively engaged in derivative markets. On the other hand, from the perspective of providing investor protection, it is difficult to justify this differential treatment for disclosure requirements.

There are three potential groups that would benefit from greater transparency and disclosure: regulators, counterparties, and the general public, including creditors, investors, and shareholders. A problem is that each of these groups might find useful different types of information. If investor protection is the key concern, then disclosure of derivative activities and risk exposures to counterparties and shareholders would be justified. To control systemic risk and to contain market reactions during periods of market distress, disclosure of all this information to the general public would be useful. However, there is a trade-off between disclosing a lot of sophisticated

information that overloads the average investor and not supplying enough to the sophisticated investor or counterparty. In addition, it is not agreed what the best channel is for distributing a large amount of information to the general public. While electronic networks can be very useful, most investors still do not have access to such facilities.

Currently, the U.S. Securities and Exchange Commission (SEC) is considering a two-tier reporting system. The idea is that more frequent and detailed information is reported first to the regulators on a confidential basis, and the regulators in turn then aggregate and simplify this information and provide it to the general public. What is undecided is just how regulators can transform this core data into an information base that is useful for the many different kinds of investors. Also undecided are how often regulators should receive this information and how the information ought to be provided to the general public.

Role of Credit-Rating Agencies

Credit ratings by private agencies are viewed by some market participants as providing the same benefits to the general public that greater information disclosure would. Given that funding costs are often dependent on credit ratings, financial institutions have sufficient incentives to provide information to the rating agencies, and to appropriately modify disclosure to the agencies to reflect changes in their business activities. Some market participants have suggested that private ratings are a more flexible and incentive-compatible way of satisfying disclosure requirements. One potential problem with this approach is that a single credit-rating agency might not require all of the information necessary to accurately measure the complex risk exposures of a firm. Furthermore, the rating itself might not reflect the financial condition of an institution during a period of market distress; for example, Orange County, California, went from a rating of AA to a rating of junk in one day.

There are also important issues that arise from the growing dependence of financial regulations on credit ratings. The 1993 Basle capital proposal, for example, imposes lower capital charges on instruments with investment grade ratings, and the U.S. SEC's net capital rule gives preferential treatment to some instruments with investment grade ratings by at least two nationally recognized rating agencies. The important role now played by rating agencies may be such that regulators would find it necessary to evaluate their performance and approve their activities. But, if regulators were able to "rate" the rating agencies, then why would they need to rely on the rating agencies in the first place?

Macro Disclosure

As important as institution-specific information can be for assessing the safety and soundness of an institution, the availability of market-wide information on derivatives—what is meant by "macro-disclosure"—is equally important for assessing the condition of derivative markets. Currently, there are no comprehensive data for these markets. How then can policymakers assess the extent to which a market disturbance would have the potential to create a systemic problem in the derivative markets and in other related markets? Equally important is the ability of regulators and market participants to properly assess risk and act on these assessments during a crisis situation.

An important impediment to collecting market-wide information on derivatives is that data across a broad range of financial institutions are not comparable. Noncomparability also makes it difficult to aggregate data across institutions, and across institutions from different countries, where there may also be differences in accounting practices and inconsistencies in report formats. In addition, differences in reporting cycles create aggregation problems and problems of interpretation of the resulting data.

The BIS released a report, in February 1995, on how to improve macro-disclosure (The Brockmeijer report).[41] The report emphasizes the importance of coordination by central banks in the collection of timely, global, aggregate data for derivative markets. The report called for an extension to derivative markets of the Triennial Survey of Foreign Exchange Markets, conducted by central banks and coordinated by the Bank for International Settlements. Data on notional size, geographical distribution, gross replacement value, and turnover would be collected across a wide range of countries. The report also recommended that the largest financial institutions in the derivatives markets, both banks and nonbanks, should be surveyed regularly on a consolidated basis. The information to be collected should include the concentration of activity and exposures, and market liquidity, which can be collected from turnover data and real-time monitoring of average transactions size and bid-offer spreads. The BIS launched in April 1995 a statistical survey on activity in the derivatives markets covering 26 countries as a part of the Triennial Foreign Exchange Survey.

Investor Protection and Suitability Issues

The rapid growth in the popularity of OTC derivative contracts has led to concerns about investor protection. Complex derivative products are created and priced by in-house technical experts at the major dealers, using sophisticated mathematical models, proprietary data, and high-powered computers. Were it not for these dealers, who reap substantial economies of scale, most end-users would be unable to afford to create these instruments. Because of the custom-design nature of many OTC derivative products, there generally is not a readily available secondary market for many of the OTC products. The dependence of end-users on dealers for both product design and for "market-making" makes them vulnerable to legal and operational risk and to fraud. In addition, there is the problem of adverse incentives; dealers earn higher fees by selling more complex and leveraged products to end-users. Moreover, the compensation of traders is related to the revenues they generate rather than to the risks that they take.

In part in reaction to these concerns, the Federal Reserve Bank of New York released a code of conduct, in January 1995, titled "Wholesale Transaction Code of Conduct."[42] The code proposes, but does not require, general rules of conduct for the relationship between derivative dealers and end-users. Participants are encouraged to evaluate counterparty capability, either internally or through independent professional advice, in order to understand and make independent decisions about the terms of its transactions. The code recommends that should a dealer determine that a counterparty does not have the capability to understand certain transactions, it should either enter into a written agreement stating that the end-user is relying on the advice of the dealer or simply not enter into the transaction. In addition, if a dealer decides that its counterparty does understand the transaction, but the nature or the riskiness of the proposed transaction seems to be inappropriate for the counterparty, it should then inform the counterparty of its views and document, in writing, its own analysis.

Some dealers have expressed concern that the voluntary code of conduct might ultimately become an enforceable code, which would imply higher operating costs. In addition, it is feared that adherence to the code, which can be judged on a subjective basis, might be used as court evidence when there is a dispute between a dealer and an end-user. The code is currently under review by the members of the International Swaps and Derivatives Association, Inc. (ISDA), the New York Clearinghouse Association, the Public Securities Association, the Securities Industry Association, the Foreign Exchange Committee of the Federal Reserve Bank of New York, and the Emerging Markets Traders Association.

In addition to this code of conduct, two other codes of conduct were released in March 1995. One

---

[41]See Bank for International Settlements (1995).

[42]See Federal Reserve Bank of New York (1995).

is by a Derivatives Products Group (DPG) formed by six major securities firms—Goldman Sachs, Salomon Brothers, Morgan Stanley, CS First Boston, Merrill Lynch, and Lehman Brothers. The other code was issued by the ISDA. The DPG has agreed with the U.S. SEC and the U.S. Commodity and Futures Trading Commission to disclose their derivative exposures and marketing approaches for derivatives. The DPG has also agreed to provide end-users written statements about the risk of derivatives. The ISDA code also emphasizes relationships with customers and the mechanics of derivative transactions.

III

Mechanisms for International Cooperation in Regulation

The increased international integration of financial markets and recent advances in communications technology mean that a financial crisis is unlikely to remain isolated to one institution and one national jurisdiction. The prevention and the containment of systemic problems now require the cooperation and coordination of supervisory and regulatory authorities across national boundaries.

Multilateral Banking Supervisory Organizations

Basle Committee on Banking Supervision

Among the several banking supervisory organizations, the Basle Committee on Banking Supervision is the most recognized.[43] The Basle Committee was established in 1974 by the central bank governors of the Group of Ten and now consists of representatives from the bank supervisory authorities and central banks of 12 countries.[44] The Bank of International Settlements facilitates meetings and provides secretariat support for the Committee.

The Basle Committee often establishes working groups to examine specific issues. Frequently the role of the working groups, headed by a chairman, is to produce discussion papers or policy reports for review by the Committee. Consensus decisions regarding the content of the reports are made within the working group, with the chairman providing clear direction. The Committee releases the report for comment, discusses the submitted comments, and, if it deems appropriate, reissues its recommendation as a guide to best supervisory practice. The Committee has no enforcement authority and implementation takes place through members' national regulatory structures. To assure widespread adoption of its recommendations, the Committee strives for consensus.

European Union

The European Union (EU) formally entered the banking supervisory arena in 1977 with the enactment

of the "First Banking Directive," setting the stage for regulatory coordination among EU members.[45] Of primary importance in the area of banking supervision are the European Commission (the Commission), the body that initiates legislative actions, the Council of Ministers (the Council), the body that ultimately approves or rejects proposals for directives, and the European Parliament, a consultative body in the area of bank supervision.[46]

The Banking Advisory Committee (BAC), established in the First Banking Directive, advises and assists the Commission in the area of banking.[47] An informal contact group of the EU Banking Supervisory Authorities (the Contact Group) meets and discusses a wide range of topics related to national supervisory developments. Descriptive papers on the discussed topics are presented to the Banking Advisory Committee. Banking supervisory issues are also discussed within the European Monetary Institute (EMI), the future central bank for the EU. The EMI has no executive responsibility for prudential supervision but is expected to examine issues of a macro-prudential nature and to be consulted on legislation that influences financial market stability. The Banking Supervisory Sub-Committee assists the Council of the EMI.

Unlike the recommendations of the Basle Committee, EU Directives are binding and oblige the member states to adapt their national law to the directives. The process by which a directive becomes EU law is as follows.[48] All legislation for the EU must be initiated by the Commission. The relevant committees, staff of the Commission, and other experts aid the Commission department in drafting proposals. The Commission votes on the draft proposal: passage occurs with a simple majority.[49] The Commission's proposal is then sent to the Council. The Council's

---

[43]Hayworth (1992).

[44]The Committee's members are from Belgium, Canada, France, Germany, Italy, Japan, Luxembourg, the Netherlands, Sweden, Switzerland, the United Kingdom, and the United States.

[45]Members of the EU are Austria, Belgium, Denmark, Finland, France, Germany, Greece, Ireland, Italy, Luxembourg, the Netherlands, Portugal, Spain, Sweden, and the United Kingdom.

[46]Noel (1993).

[47]A description of the roles and current developments of the EU committees involved in banking supervision along with the other multinational banking supervisors organizations are in Basle Committee on Banking Supervision (1994c).

[48]See Borchardt (1993) for more details.

[49]The weighting of votes in the Commission is two votes each for France, Germany, Italy, Spain, and the United Kingdom; one vote each for the remaining seven member countries.

"Economic and Finance" (ECOFIN) formation, composed of finance ministers, considers banking proposals, following the new "co-decision" procedure. First, the Council requests opinions from the Parliament and the Economic and Social Committee, an ancillary body that must be consulted on economic matters. Using their opinions, the Council then adopts a common position and transmits it to Parliament for a second reading. If Parliament approves the common position without amendment, it may be approved by the Council by a qualified majority[50] without being altered by the Commission. However, if Parliament rejects the common position or wishes to make amendments, the new co-decision procedure provides for a "Conciliation Committee," which attempts to negotiate a compromise between the Council and Parliament. If agreement is still not attained, Parliament has veto power; its rejection means the proposal is lost.

Compared with the consensus decision process of the Basle Committee, which consists of a working group report and the Committee's final recommendation, the EU Directive process requires a more structured interactive process of several bodies, including the Commission, the Council, the Parliament and their attendant committees. Because the EU enacts binding legislation, the checks and balances among its different institutions purposely provide for broad participation by the member states that will be required to enact national legislation.

The Basle Committee and the EU Directive processes are compared in Figure 1 for the issue of monitoring and controlling large exposures of credit institutions, a subject on which both organizations have issued guidelines. The formal process, starting from the adoption of the proposal by the Commission and ending at the final adoption of the proposal as a directive by the Council, took 1¾ years for the Directive on Monitoring and Control of Large Exposures.[51] The Basle Committee put forth their recommendations on the subject, Measuring and Controlling Large Credit Exposures, in October 1990. After taking account of various comments, the recommendation was reissued as a guide to best practice in January 1991.

Other Multilateral Banking Supervisory Organizations

In addition to the Basle Committee and the European Union, there are several other international

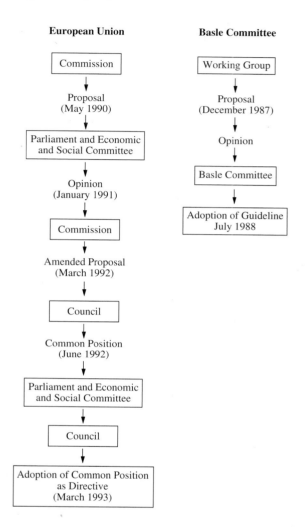

Figure II-1. Decision-Making Procedures for Capital Adequacy

---

[50]A qualified majority is 54 out of 76 votes. The weighting of votes in the Council is 10 votes each for France, Germany, Italy, and the United Kingdom; 8 votes for Spain; 5 votes each for Portugal, Greece, the Netherlands, and Belgium; 3 votes for Denmark and Ireland; and 2 votes for Luxembourg.

[51]Records of the amount of time the issue was discussed at the EU Committee level before reaching the Commission are not available.

banking supervisory organizations. They are the Offshore Group of Banking Supervisors; the Association of Banking Supervisory Authorities of Latin America and the Caribbean; SEANZA (Southeast Asia, New Zealand, Australia) Forum of Banking Supervisors; the GCC (Gulf Cooperation Council) Committee of Banking Supervisors; the Arab Committee on Banking Supervision; the Caribbean Group of Banking Supervisors; the Group of Banking Supervisors from Central and Eastern European Countries; the East and Southern Africa Banking Supervisors' Group; and the West and Central African Group of Banking Supervisors. Each organization has been formed to pay special attention to the needs of its members and therefore adopts an agenda reflecting these special requirements.

Multilateral Securities Firm Supervisory Organizations

There is only one primary multinational securities firm supervisory organization, the International Organization of Securities Commissions (IOSCO).[52] Perhaps one reason for this striking difference is the nascent development in many countries of organized securities markets. Further, in many countries self-regulatory organizations, instead of a government-sponsored regulatory agency or commission, assume formal oversight.

IOSCO, established in 1983, has 115 regular (voting), affiliate, and associate members, who are primarily securities regulators, self-regulatory organizations, and related international organizations.[53] The Technical Committee, composed of developed country members, and development committees, composed of members from countries with emerging markets, are the two principal committees through which policies or recommendations are proposed.[54] Each committee has several Working Parties or Groups.

Working Parties and Groups provide their oversight committee with consensus recommendations, taking the form of a paper, guideline, or general principle. If consensus is not reached the nature of the comments on the issue are transmitted to the oversight committee. Usually approval by the oversight committee and, subsequently, the Executive Committee are pro forma when consensus is reached within the Working Party or Group. Like other organizations, IOSCO has no binding authority on its members and implementation is subject to member countries' internal regulatory and legislative procedures.

An interesting feature of IOSCO, unlike the international banking supervisory organizations, is that it permits participation of self-regulatory organizations and other international organizations as associate and affiliate members.[55] Affiliate members provide constructive input as members of the Consultative Committee, whose working groups mirror those of the Technical Committee.

Accounting Organizations

Somewhere between the public sector supervisory organizations and purely private organizations are accountancy bodies. Though technically private professional groups, many accountancy bodies can impose their standards on public companies within their jurisdiction. The two bodies most recognized as influencing banking and securities firm supervision through their accounting standards and practices are the International Accounting Standards Committee (IASC) and the Financial Accounting Standards Board (FASB) of the United States.

Established in 1973, the mission of the IASC is to establish international accounting standards. Its members consist of professional accountancy bodies, such as the American Institute of Certified Public Accountants (AICPA).[56] To establish an accounting standard the IASC sets up a Task Force, which recommends a proposal to the Committee. The members vote on it (one vote per country) and it is then circulated for comment. Comments are examined by the Committee, revisions made, if necessary, and a vote is taken. If approved, the proposal becomes an accounting standard.

Not all proposals become standards, because sometimes a proposal is not acceptable to enough member countries. Thus, many IASC standards include "optional" accounting treatment of items to accommodate differences among member countries. The IASC has no binding authority, although some countries require use of IASC standards by corporations under their authority.

The United States is recognized as containing the most detailed accounting standards, and the standards of its accountancy body, the FASB, are often used as a model for IASC standards. One reason the FASB may be viewed as a leader in accounting standards is that, in the United States, the primary goal of accounting standards is to provide information to potential investors, whereas in other countries accounting standards are meant to satisfy legal or regulatory criteria, not a public disclosure requirement.

Multilateral Private Organizations

The Group of Thirty is a private, nonprofit organization aiming to "deepen understanding of international economic and financial issues, to explore the international repercussions of decisions taken in the public and private sectors, and to examine the choices available to market practitioners and to policymakers."[57] The Group sponsors symposiums and seminars and commissions monographs and reports on important topics from experts.

The Institute of International Finance (IIF) is a nonprofit, worldwide association of financial

---

[52]The EU also passes directives in the investment services area using the same procedures and a similar committee structure as described in the banking supervisory organization section above.

[53]IOSCO (1994).

[54]There are four regional committees that discuss specific problems of concern in their region. The regional groupings within IOSCO may be another reason why other regional securities firm supervisory organizations have not been formed.

[55]If there is no government regulatory agency, a self-regulatory organization can become a regular member with voting rights.

[56]When a country has multiple accountancy bodies, one is chosen to be its representative.

[57]Group of Thirty (1994a), p. 3.

institutions.[58] Members include commercial banks, investment banks, and other multinational firms and organizations. The Institute monitors global banking and financial services regulation and advances the consensus views of its members through an informal dialogue with central banks and regulatory and supervisory authorities. The Institute uses working groups and task forces to gather information and provide members with a forum for discussion of major regulatory developments.

The International Securities Market Association (ISMA) consists of member institutions from 43 countries and territories. The Association provides discussion of questions relating to international securities markets through educational seminars. It establishes uniform market practices and provides data bases and information to central monetary authorities and other institutions. ISMA uses various committees to examine issues and make recommendations on subjects of interest to its members.

Bilateral Methods of International Cooperation

Although multilateral supervisory organizations are more visible, the exchange of information among supervisors and regulators also occurs through bilateral channels. Most bilateral communication is informal, but formal bilateral agreements are well suited for some supervisory practices, poten-

tially enhancing supervision and reducing regulatory overlap.

One common type of formal agreement is a Memorandum of Understanding (MOU), an agreement between two institutions outlining their obligations to one another. In bank and securities firm regulations, the most common MOUs provide access to official documents and information in possession of other authorities for investigatory or enforcement reasons, such as cross-border fraud. In some cases, an MOU may require affirmative action by a regulator, requiring them to report to other regulators a firm that is experiencing financial difficulties. A second type of MOU, termed a Financial Information Sharing Agreement or FISMOU, usually specifies that the parties have access to general information. FISMOUs might specify that certain information about firms operating in two jurisdictions be routinely disclosed to the regulators of both jurisdictions, such as risk assessments of related firms.

Of course, informal communication among central banks and bank supervisors continues to be the predominant form of bilateral information sharing and formal MOUs are relatively rare. For securities supervision, however, formal bilateral agreements, such as MOUs and FISMOUs, are used much more routinely. Bank secrecy laws and the relative youth of supervised securities markets, compared with banking systems, may partly account for this difference. The importance of informal bilateral communication among all bank and securities firm supervisors, however, should not be underestimated as it is the most flexible and timely, making it invaluable during crisis management.

---

[58]The Institute of International Finance, Inc., informational pamphlet.

IV

Regulatory Implications of the Barings Failure

Barings plc, the oldest merchant banking group in the United Kingdom (established in 1762), was placed in "administration" by the Bank of England on February 27, 1995.[59] Barings is reported to have experienced losses exceeding the entire equity capital of the firm—estimated to be $860 million at the time—from very large accumulated unhedged positions in futures contracts on the Nikkei 225 index.[60] Barings' losses apparently resulted from a $27 billion exposure that mushroomed during the three-week period ending on Friday, February 24, and especially in the last three days of this period. Barings' position comprised relatively simple financial contracts and instruments: a $7 billion long position in exchange-traded futures contracts; a large short position in OTC Japanese government bond futures and three-month Euro-yen contracts; and significant short positions in put options and call options on the Nikkei 225 index.

While much is still not known about the Barings failure, there appears to have been a breakdown in Barings' internal risk-management system. Barings apparently pursued a risky trading strategy that was reported, at the time, to have been undetected by Barings' internal management control mechanisms until Friday, February 24, 1995 when it became clear that it would be unable to meet its margin requirements.[61] Barings' operations in Singapore then reported to the London operation that the bank's derivatives contracts exposed the bank to catastrophic losses. On Friday, February 24, the management of Barings informed the Bank of England about its situation.

The collapse of Barings provides several lessons about today's high-technology, fast-communications financial environment: (1) financial institutions can quickly become overexposed to financial risk; (2) large financial losses can result from financial positions in standard futures and options contracts, proving that it is still possible to lose money "the old-fashioned way"; (3) financial institutions need adequate management control mechanisms to assess and contain their risks; (4) financial institutions can be allowed to fail without bailouts using public funds—as an essential part of the mechanism of market discipline—at least for moderate-sized institutions when the condition of other institutions is not suspect; and (5) financial markets are truly global—actions by a single Singapore-based trader of a British merchant bank can have pronounced effects in markets around the globe.

The collapse of Barings has come at a time when regulators are considering a "new approach to regulatory capital requirements," which permits money center banks to rely on their internal risk-management models to determine how much capital to hold against OTC transactions. In addition, the systemic implications of Barings' failure were more easily contained partly because their positions on the exchanges had been marked-to-market daily. This experience demonstrates that risk management in futures exchanges is generally more reliable than risk management in the OTC derivative markets operated by international banks.

The Barings failure raises questions about how managers of financial institutions and regulators together can prevent similar events in the future. The crisis points to three important issues of concern: (1) the effectiveness of internal management-control systems and risk management; (2) the quality of risk management, surveillance, and coordination by financial exchanges; and (3) the important roles, and the coordination, of home and host country supervisors in detecting risks for individual institutions and in preventing systemic risks.

Internal Risk Management

Current information suggests that the Barings failure was brought on by the absence of adequate internal audit and management-control systems.

---

[59]"Administration" is a court-supervised reorganization. Barings plc is composed of Baring Brothers, the merchant banking operation, Baring Securities, the brokering and market-making operations, and Baring Asset Management, the fund-management operation; it also owns a 40 percent stake in Dillon Reed, the New York investment bank.

[60]The Bank of England immediately and clearly indicated that the collapse of Barings was an isolated incident—with no systemic implications—and that the failure resulted from the activities of a single "rogue" trader who, "concealed this [the positions and losses] from his senior management, the management in London, from the local regulator and of course through them from ourselves, through collusion with his settlement people." (See transcript of Governor George's interview on "Today," BBC Radio 4, February 27, 1995.)

[61]More recent reports have suggested that Barings operations in London had sanctioned the overall trading strategy, and supplied funds to, the operation in Singapore.

Because the losses occurred in exchange-traded markets, where positions are marked-to-market, variation margin payments to the various exchanges occurred daily. At least one person at Barings was responsible for making these daily payments, and it has been alleged that the same person who was placing the trades was also responsible, at least in part, for settling the daily margin payments. If a trader at Barings could make margin payments and enter trades into the computer systems without independent verification then there were opportunities to falsify or conceal positions. If this is what occurred, then Barings was lacking appropriate checks and balances that are normally secured by dividing responsibilities among different levels of management. The separation of the responsibility for payments and settlements from trading functions and independent trade verification are important elements of an effective risk-management system.

A broader implication is that operational risk (the risk due to mismanagement, trading errors, imprudent trading strategies, and so on) should receive greater attention in risk-management systems by all parties involved, including financial institutions, exchanges, and supervisors. Formal risk-management models constitute one part of a comprehensive risk-management process that includes independent risk control and management, extensive auditing and verification procedures, and formal position limits. Effective management and control requires that senior management understand the derivatives positions taken by the firm.

Assuming Barings utilized the latest risk-management technologies, what caused the Barings model, or its other internal controls, to fail to detect that the value-at-risk from positions taken potentially exceeded the capital of the firm? Why were these risky positions not detected by host or home country regulators? If a "rogue" trader can put at risk the entire capital of a merchant bank like Barings, then to what extent should banks be permitted to determine regulatory capital requirements on market risk based on their own internal model? In light of the Barings failure, should the Basle Committee on Banking Supervision rethink its current proposals to allow banks to use their internal risk-management models to calculate regulatory capital requirements?

Risk Management on Organized Exchanges

Because Barings' large unhedged position resulted from the accumulation of exchange-traded contracts, the quality of risk management at the exchanges comes into question. The exchanges involved are the Singapore International Monetary Exchange (SIMEX), the Osaka Securities Exchange (OSE), and the Tokyo International Financial Futures Exchange (TIFFE). The SIMEX continued

to collect margin deposits from Barings until Friday, February 24. On Monday, SIMEX doubled the requirements of both initial and variation margins on the Nikkei 225 futures contract. Some clearing members and customers expressed concern about the ability of SIMEX to continue to guarantee settlement of payments, and the Singapore Monetary Authority immediately issued a press release agreeing to stand behind the SIMEX clearinghouse. While the Monetary Authority's guarantee is important to quell concerns of market participants, the exchange's clearinghouse has procedures to ensure payment should a clearing member default. SIMEX, like most exchanges, has a "guarantee fund" or "compensation fund" providing a method for collecting monies from exchange members in case a defaulting clearing member's losses exceeds clearinghouse funds.

SIMEX has a large trader-reporting system whereby accounts with more than 100 Nikkei 225 futures contracts are reported to their surveillance authorities. House (the firm's proprietary account) and customer accounts are separated, so in principle, the exchange and other authorities can view the trades of the proprietary trading arm of the firm. It is possible that viewed from SIMEX, the trader was not taking abnormal positions. Apparently, the Barings' operation in Singapore frequently carried large positions, which were offset by the opposite positions in similar contracts on the Osaka and Tokyo exchanges, in an attempt to profit from the small differences between the prices of like contracts. This may have entitled Barings to a "hedge exemption" from speculative position limits, which typically is granted to nonspeculators holding "hedged" positions. If so, then SIMEX may not have noticed an abnormal pattern associated with the size of the position on the exchange.[62] The implication is that SIMEX may have observed Barings' large proprietary position in advance of the defaulted margin call, but it may not have viewed the position as a problem. Alternatively, there is some speculation that Barings "hid" large trades by creating fictitious customer accounts, none of which appeared to have excessively large positions. Assuming SIMEX was able to observe Barings' large positions and viewed them as hedged positions, better international coordination among exchange surveillance authorities or more frequent verification of the associated hedged positions might have detected a problem.

Another important issue with potential systemic implications is the efficiency and speed with which positions of an insolvent entity are unwound, and the distribution of losses, if any, among counterparties. If a customer of a firm in default cannot gain access

---

[62]To obtain an exemption from position limits, verification of a hedged position is required at periodic intervals and whenever there is a material change in the hedged position.

to its own funds, then that customer may not be able to make payments to its counterparties in other unrelated transactions. In principle, this could lead to the failure of otherwise solvent entities.

The contracts of an insolvent financial institution are more easily resolved, and expose the financial system to fewer systemic problems, if they are exchange traded. On Monday, February 27, all of Barings' accounts on the three exchanges were suspended; the accounts were quickly freed on Tuesday, February 28. Customer accounts with Barings were then transferred to another clearing firm, while Barings' proprietary accounts are being handled by the "administration" process. SIMEX separates clearing members' customer and proprietary accounts, making it relatively easy to transfer customer positions without customers incurring losses due to Barings' proprietary trading. There was, however, some temporary uncertainty over customers' access to their accounts due to reports that Barings had not maintained this strict separation of proprietary and customer accounting. In contrast, neither the OSE or TIFFE separated customer and proprietary trading accounts. As a result, the separation of Barings' proprietary trading from that of its own customers is taking some time to sort out. This could potentially pose difficulties for customers and their counterparties. On the whole, however, the relative ease with which Barings' default is being managed might be taken as evidence that the clearinghouse mechanism is useful for reducing systemic risk. In contrast, the resolution of positions taken by an insolvent entity, such as Barings, is less straightforward on over-the-counter contracts, and will take considerably more time to unwind. The identity of the over-the-counter counterparties, the size of their exposures, and how these contracts will be resolved under the process of U.K. "administration," is currently unknown.

Overall, the futures exchanges in Osaka and Singapore operated effectively and efficiently and have retained their capital and reputations. Daily marking-to-market of positions, combined with initial margins—keyed to statistical estimates of price volatility—provided a sufficient cushion to deal even with this extraordinary situation. Nevertheless, several improvements are possible. First, Barings had been able to borrow securities—unsecured—from Japanese financial institutions, in the informal Tokyo securities repurchase market, to meet margin calls at Osaka. These securities were liquidated by the Osaka exchange and lost to the original owners. One way to reduce risks in the future would be to formalize the securities repo market into a collateralized lending facility. Second, the legal claim to margin money under national bankruptcy laws will need to be clarified. Third, the loss-sharing rules of the futures exchanges, particularly SIMEX, will also need to be strengthened and made transparent.

V

Increasing Importance of Institutional Investors

One of the most significant recent developments in international financial markets is that individual investors have increasingly delegated the management of their portfolios to professional fund managers. The consequence of this is that the investor base in securities markets in industrial countries, and increasingly in developing countries, is dominated by a relatively small number of large institutional investors. In addition, the international diversification of institutional portfolios has developed in tandem with the institutionalization of savings and portfolio management. This trend toward the international diversification of institutional portfolios has increased the sensitivity of securities markets—especially the smaller, less liquid markets, notably in developing countries—to the behavior of a relatively small number of investors.

Size of Institutional Investors' Portfolios

The institutional investor community can be defined broadly to include public and private pension funds, life and other insurance companies, mutual (open-end) funds, closed end funds, hedge funds, trusts, foundations, endowments, and proprietary trading by investment banks, commercial banks, and securities companies. To illustrate the growing importance of these investors, total assets of the 300 largest U.S. institutional investors rose from 30 percent of GDP in 1975 ($535 billion) to more than 110 percent of GDP in 1993 ($7.2 trillion).[63] Similar changes in total assets under management are recorded for other industrial countries.

Pension funds, insurance companies, and mutual funds in five major industrial countries had close to $13 trillion in assets under management in 1993.[64] To put this number in perspective, the global equity market capitalization in the same year was $14.1 trillion, and the outstanding stock of government debt for the seven largest industrial countries was $9 trillion.[65] The importance of institutional

investors has increased markedly: since 1980, the assets managed by the institutional investors in five of the major industrial countries have increased by more than 400 percent and have more than doubled as a percent of GDP.

U.S. institutional investors control the largest pool of assets by a significant margin—U.S. pension funds, insurance companies, and mutual funds alone managed more than $8 trillion of assets in 1993 (Table II.6). U.S. pension funds have maintained their status as the largest institutional investor in the world. Insurance companies in all industrial countries control sizable asset pools, with Japanese life insurers being especially notable with $1.48 trillion of assets in 1993. Expressing managed assets as a percent of GDP, the United Kingdom takes the lead with professionally managed assets representing 165 percent of GDP in 1993. Institutional investors in the United States also control assets in excess of annual GDP.

Pension funds and insurance companies have traditionally been the most important institutional players in industrial country financial markets. Although pension funds and insurance companies still control sizable (and growing) portfolios of securities, an important factor in the institutionalization of savings has been the rapid growth of mutual funds and closed end investment companies. Mutual funds alone accounted for about $3 trillion in 1993 of private wealth. Although this sum is not as large (yet) as managed assets of insurance companies and pension funds, mutual fund assets have increased at a much faster pace than have the assets of other institutional investors. Some of the important factors underpinning this growth are the increased sophistication of individual investors, technological improvements in information transmission and clearance and settlement of securities, and increased emphasis by industrial countries on capital account convertibility (and, consequently, the integration of capital markets).

Hedge funds are important institutional investors, but it is difficult to obtain comprehensive data on the majority of these private funds; their activities are therefore not included in the figures reported in Table II.6. There is no universally accepted definition of a "hedge fund," but two important features are that they are unregulated and are often highly

---

[63]See "America's Top 300 Money Managers" (1994).
[64]These countries are Canada, Germany, Japan, the United Kingdom, and the United States.
[65]International Finance Corporation (1994) and International Monetary Fund (1994).

Table II.6. Assets of Institutional Investors

(In billions of U.S. dollars)

	1980	1988	1990	1991	1992	1993
Pension funds						
Canada	43.3	131.3	171.8	188.4	191.7	...
Germany	17.2	41.6	55.2	58.6	62.6	53.5
Japan	24.3	134.1	158.8	182.3	191.9	...
United Kingdom	151.3	483.9	583.6	642.9	670.5	695.7
United States	667.7	1,919.2	2,257.3	3,070.9	3,334.3	3,571.4
Life insurance companies						
Canada	36.8	85.5	106.1	118.1	131.8	132.7
Germany	88.4	213.5	299.5	325.7	341.4	354.3
Japan	124.6	734.6	946.9	1,113.7	1,214.8	1,476.5
United Kingdom	145.7	358.9	447.9	516.7	574.7	619.3
United States	464.2	1,132.7	1,367.4	1,505.3	1,624.5	1,784.9
Non-life insurance companies						
Canada	9.2	22.7	26.8	23.3	...	...
Germany	36.7	87.6	126.3	127.4	187.9	198.8
Japan	34.6	156.1	190.3	215.5	218.5	167.9
United Kingdom	31.3	72.2	85.2	89.6	95.6	97.1
United States	182.1	453.9	529.2	591.6	628.7	640.8
Mutual funds[1]						
Canada	3.9	17.5	21.5	43.2	52.9	86.7
Germany[2]	22.4	99.9	145.5	166.2	171.6	205.2
Japan[3]	60.8	433.9	353.5	323.9	346.9	448.7
United Kingdom	16.8	76.7	91.5	104.4	91.2	141.3
United States	292.9	810.3	1,066.9	1,348.2	1,595.4	2,011.3
Total						
Canada	93.2	257.0	326.2	373.0	376.4	...
Germany	164.7	442.6	626.5	677.9	763.5	811.8
Japan	244.3	1,458.7	1,649.5	1,835.4	1,972.1	...
United Kingdom	345.1	991.7	1,208.2	1,353.6	1,432.0	1,553.4
United States	1,606.9	4,316.1	5,220.8	6,516.0	7,182.9	8,008.4
Total *(in percent of GDP)*						
Canada	35.2	52.2	56.8	63.3	66.1	...
Germany	20.3	37.1	41.7	42.7	42.7	47.4
Japan	23.1	50.3	56.3	54.8	53.8	...
United Kingdom	64.1	118.3	123.5	133.8	137.1	165.3
United States	59.3	88.1	94.5	113.9	119.0	125.6

Sources: Bank of Canada, *Bank of Canada Review*, various issues; Bank of Japan, *Economic Statistics Monthly*, various issues; Chuhan (1994); International Monetary Fund, *International Financial Statistics*; Investment Company Institute; United Kingdom, Central Statistical Office, *Financial Statistics*, various issues; United States, Board of Governors of the Federal Reserve System, *Flow of Funds Accounts*, various issues; and IMF staff estimates.

[1]The numbers in the first column are for 1983, except for Canada.
[2]Public and special funds.
[3]Investment trusts.

leveraged. Most hedge funds appear to be located in the United States.[66] The reason that they are unregulated is because either they have fewer than 100 investors, and thus do not have to comply with SEC disclosure and registration requirements (as stipulated by the Investment Company Act of 1940), or they are domiciled offshore. Onshore funds are structured as investment partnerships and the minimum investment is typically in the range of $350,000–10,000,000. The number of investors is generally much greater

and the minimum investment much smaller for offshore funds, which are often structured simply as open-end mutual funds, albeit with higher minimum investment than most retail mutual funds.

Hedge funds have been in existence since the 1940s, but first became prominent in the 1960s. The number of onshore hedge funds is not known, but most estimates are in the neighborhood of one thousand, up from around one hundred in 1987; assets under management have doubled since 1991.[67] The vast majority of hedge funds have capital below $100 million, and only about a dozen have assets currently

---

[66]The number of hedge funds located in Europe is not known, in large part because they are deliberately secretive.

[67]LaWare (1994) and Bennett and Shirreff (1994).

exceeding $1 billion. The largest hedge funds had assets between $6 billion and $10 billion in 1994. Although total assets of all hedge funds are estimated to be around $75–100 billion, the possible positions taken by hedge funds can be much larger. This is because these investors are not constrained by leverage restrictions on investment enterprises that fall under the purview of the Investment Company Act of 1940. In fact, some hedge funds committed to a particular investment opportunity may be leveraged between 5 and 20 times their capital. Factoring leverage into the net capital of hedge funds leads to the conclusion that they are a potentially important player in global capital markets.

Although there are hundreds of hedge funds, they differ markedly by investment objective. The lesser known "traditional" hedge funds are often interested in cross-security arbitrage within an equity market. The recently more visible hedge funds—commonly referred to as "macro," "opportunistic," or "directional" hedge funds—are chiefly interested in the currency and bond markets, typically taking highly speculative, and highly leveraged positions through liberal use of bank loans, options, futures, and other derivatives. Although it is estimated that there are only 15 or so of these macro hedge funds, they appear to control a very significant portion of the industry's assets.[68]

There are several regulatory considerations associated with the rise in the importance of institutional investors. As households increasingly delegate their investment management decisions to professional fund managers, the effective investor base is changing from a very large number of small investors toward a relatively small number of large investors. With greater concentration of wealth in the hands of professional fund managers, financial markets must cope with the effects of the attendant increase in the market power of market participants. Chief among these effects is the increased likelihood of market manipulation, and even less efficient markets.[69] Furthermore, as the investor base becomes more highly concentrated, the likelihood of coordination failures may increase and this can produce abrupt changes in market liquidity.[70] Market manipulation can be especially important in smaller markets, notably the emerging markets.

Hedge funds raise some unique regulatory considerations because of the unusually high degree of leverage. Hedge funds use banks for a variety of services, but the services that raise regulatory considerations are those that create credit risk to the banking

system—foreign exchange trading lines, repo lines, and loans. Foreign exchange trading lines and repurchase lines seem to be key services provided to hedge funds by banks in the United States.[71] But this is not surprising as banks are the principal providers of these services to all types of institutional investors. In fact, hedge funds appear to account for a relatively small portion of the total services provided by U.S. banks to institutional investors; however, care should be taken in drawing inferences about the exposure of any one bank when studying average exposures of all banks. An important consideration, therefore, is that individual banks have effective risk-management systems for all customers.

Are Institutional Investors Internationally Diversified?

In light of the substantial growth of assets under institutional management, an important question for international finance is the degree to which institutional investors have diversified their portfolios internationally. The evidence points to the accumulation of a substantial amount of foreign assets by institutional investors. The share of portfolio assets that are foreign securities also has increased for some institutional investors (Table II.7). Specifically, the foreign asset shares of pension funds have been on a gradual upward path at least since 1980, and in 1993 ranged from a low of 4.5 percent for German pension funds to a high of almost 20 percent for U.K. pension funds.

While there seems to be a clear but gradual trend toward internationally diversified portfolios of pension funds, the behavior of insurance companies is less clear. Insurance companies have in general not increased their international diversification over the same period, and in several countries even show some decrease in the 1990s. Insurance companies also are not as internationally diversified as pension funds, with the possible exception of Japan. Developments in Canada illustrate the more general trends in the period 1980–93: foreign asset shares of insurance companies are only about one sixth the size of pension funds, and, while pension funds have more than doubled their foreign asset share, insurance companies have cut their share by almost half.

The aggregate portfolio of mutual funds has several interesting features. First, mutual funds in Canada, Germany, and the United Kingdom are far more internationally diversified than U.S. or Japanese mutual funds. Second, U.S. mutual funds stand alone as displaying a clear trend toward increased international diversification. In fact, mutual funds in the other countries appear to have either leveled off in terms of foreign portfolio shares or to

---

[68]Four well-known macro funds—Quantum Fund, Tiger Management, Steinhardt Partners, and Ardsley Partners—had net assets of almost $25 billion mid-1994 ("Fall Guys?" (1994)).

[69]These possibilities are established formally by Kyle (1989).

[70]These ideas are formalized by Pagano (1989a) and (1989b).

[71]LaWare (1994).

Table II.7. Institutional Investors' Holdings of Foreign Securities

(In percent of total assets)

	1980	1988	1990	1991	1992	1993
Pension funds						
Canada	4.1	5.3	5.8	8.5	10.2	10.3
Germany	...	3.8	4.5	4.5	4.3	4.5
Japan	0.5	6.3	7.2	8.4	8.4	9.0
United Kingdom	10.1	16.5	18.0	20.8	22.0	19.7
United States	0.7	2.7	4.2	4.1	4.6	5.7
Life insurance companies						
Canada	3.3	1.9	1.6	1.9	2.3	1.8
Germany	0.6	0.6	1.0	1.0	...	...
Japan	2.7	14.2	13.5	12.5	11.4	9.0
United Kingdom	5.5	9.5	10.8	12.4	12.7	11.6
United States	4.1	3.6	3.6	3.6	3.7	...
Mutual funds						
Canada	19.9	19.5	17.5	16.2	16.7	17.1
Germany	...	...	56.3	53.5	47.6	45.2
Japan[1]	...	9.1	7.9	13.0	9.9	...
United Kingdom	...	...	37.1	39.2	37.9	36.0
United States	...	...	...	6.6	...	10.1

Sources: Bank of Canada, *Bank of Canada Review*, various issues; Bank of Japan, *Economic Statistics Monthly*, various issues; Bisignano (1994); Chuhan (1994); European Federation of Investment Funds and Companies; International Monetary Fund, *International Financial Statistics*; InterSec Research Corporation; United Kingdom, Central Statistical Office, *Financial Statistics*, various issues; United States, Board of Governors of the Federal Reserve System, *Flow of Funds Accounts*, various issues; and IMF staff estimates.

[1] Investment trusts.

have decreased their share of foreign assets.[72] Third, mutual funds in most countries (with the exception of Japan) are significantly more internationally diversified than other institutional investors. Even in the United States, where mutual funds are among the least internationally diversified of all countries, their foreign asset holdings are roughly double those of insurance companies and pension funds, as a share of total assets.

Despite the general trend toward international diversification, especially by mutual funds and pension funds, it is also clear that this trend in international diversification of portfolios is overshadowed by the small share of foreign securities in institutional portfolios, especially for insurance companies and pension funds. A well-known rule of thumb from modern portfolio theory is that an optimally diversified portfolio for an individual investor should have country weights corresponding to the ratio of

a country's market capitalization to the world market capitalization.[73] Using the market capitalization measures of the International Finance Corporation, this "world market portfolio" in 1993 would have had 37 percent of its investments in the United States, 21 percent in Japan, 8 percent in the United Kingdom, 22 percent in other industrial countries, and just under 12 percent in the emerging markets. Although, the degree of international diversification by aggregated mutual funds is greater than some other institutional investors, all types of institutional investors are much less internationally diversified than this world market portfolio.[74]

Although the share of foreign assets in the portfolios of some institutional investors is quite low relative to standard benchmarks, the level of cross-border securities holdings is substantial. For example, in 1993, a 5.7 percent foreign asset share in U.S. pension funds translated into foreign security holdings by U.S. pension funds of $203.6 billion. With U.S. mutual funds and insurance companies together holding roughly equivalent amounts, these three types of institutional investors in the United States alone control about $400 billion in foreign securities. Even though cross-border holdings seem to be far from an optimally diversified portfolio, these holdings could be an important source of funds.

One explanation for the low share of foreign securities in institutional portfolios is that the seeds of international portfolio diversification have only recently been planted and institutional investors are poised to make important advances in international diversification by the end of the century. For instance, estimates put U.S. private pension funds' foreign holdings at 9.5 percent of assets by year-end 1995, representing a more than 100 percent increase in three years.[75] These estimates are underscored by a recent poll of U.S. pension funds, which found that during 1995, 51.3 percent of them plan to increase their foreign equity holdings, 21.3 percent plan to increase their foreign fixed income holdings, and only about 2.0 percent plan to reduce either one.[76]

A second reason for the heavy bias of institutional investors' portfolios toward domestic assets is that it reflects the well-known tendency of individual investors in all industrial countries to display a very

---

[72] It is reported (e.g., Ito (1992)) that trust accounts of Japanese banks are much like mutual funds, and these data are not included in Tables II.6–II.7. The size of trust accounts for Japanese banks in 1993 was $1.89 trillion, up from $1.56 trillion in 1992. The share of total assets in trust accounts that are foreign securities is similar to the numbers reported in Table II.7 for mutual funds—8.9 percent in 1993, down slightly from 9.3 percent in 1992.

[73] In theory, these country weights should be based on all assets (stocks, bonds, real estate, and so on). A common simplification is, however, simply to use stock market capitalization.

[74] Justification for this might be that the world market portfolio is a good rule of thumb for individual investors and that institutional portfolios should mirror underlying investors' preferences. Some reasons are discussed below why institutional portfolios may be biased to domestic assets.

[75] See, for example, Money Market Directories (1995). This prediction matches closely that of the International Finance Corporation (1994).

[76] Richardson (1995).

marked "home-asset preference."[77] Many reasons have been put forward to explain this preference, including transactions costs, foreign exchange risk, uncertainties about expected returns, and unfamiliarity with foreign markets and tax laws. Institutional investors report that this aversion is an important consideration. Specifically, when asked why foreign asset holdings are such a small fraction of total assets, some fund managers report that the underlying investors or trustees of the funds they manage are "very conservative." This aversion to foreign markets seems to be largely a reflection of a lack of familiarity with foreign economies and financial markets.

A third possible reason for the limited degree of international diversification by institutional investors in industrial countries is that fund managers face binding, externally imposed, explicit quantitative constraints on foreign asset holdings. These types of constraints can arise from two sources. First, internal committees that set broad investment criteria for fund managers may restrict or even prohibit the fund from investing in foreign assets. In this case, the explanation for the observed low share of foreign asset holdings requires looking beyond the preferences of a fund's manager. The second reason is that government regulations of foreign asset holdings of institutional investors appear to be restrictive for at least some institutions in some countries (Table II.8). For example, a recent poll of Canadian pension fund managers found that 88 percent of them would increase foreign asset holdings in their portfolios above the 20 percent government-imposed ceiling if they could, with most favoring a 25–35 percent foreign asset allocation; only 18 percent would raise foreign holdings above 35 percent.[78] However, it is also reported that government-imposed restrictions on foreign asset holdings are not binding for many institutional investors in industrial countries.[79] This suggests that regulatory constraints on foreign asset holdings may explain some of the difference between institutional portfolios and the predictions of standard portfolio theory, but they do not fully account for investors' preference for home assets.

If government-imposed constraints on many institutional investors' foreign asset holdings are not important or binding, then there would appear to be a preference for home assets by all institutional investors, and a much more marked preference for home assets by pension funds and insurance companies than by mutual funds. The fact that these

differences exist may point to the influence of more considerations in portfolio management decisions than elementary portfolio theory suggests. Whereas the share of foreign assets in mutual funds probably reflects fairly accurately the preferences of the underlying investors in the long run, this may not be a valid conclusion about pension funds and insurance companies.

One reason that pension funds and insurance companies may display a preference for domestic assets is that pension fund trustees or investment management companies may display low-risk tolerance. Also important is the fact that most of the underlying investors are typically quite far removed from portfolio management decisions. A key reason why trustees or investment management companies might display lower risk tolerance than underlying claimants on the pension fund or insurance premium fund is shortfall risk. If the investment manager, or company, bears more downside risk than the underlying investors and, in addition, does not capture fully the upside potential, then the manager will optimally specialize the portfolio in safe, domestic assets.[80] In effect, contracts to manage asset pools for pensions or insurance companies typically generate a high degree of risk aversion on the part of fund managers because they do not share risk optimally.[81] These same contract-induced biases toward home assets may not be present in mutual funds because, given the mandate of a particular mutual fund (e.g., emerging markets), managers are typically compensated as a proportion of net asset value; this type of contract tends to share risk more efficiently between the fund manager or investment company, or both, and the underlying investors. Another key difference between mutual and defined benefit pension funds is that mutual funds are by definition fully funded: unlike a pension fund, there is no risk of a mismatch in its assets and liabilities. Further, in the case of mutual funds, it is easier for underlying investors to signal their investment preferences simply through fund selection.[82]

Institutional Investment in Emerging Markets

In 1993, the capitalized value of equity securities in emerging markets represented slightly less

---

[77]For instance, domestic ownership on the five largest stock exchanges is very high: 92 percent in the United States, 96 percent in Japan, 92 percent in the United Kingdom, 79 percent in Germany, and 89 percent in France (see French and Poterba (1991)).

[78]The Fraser Institute (1994).

[79]For instance, see Davis (1991), Chuhan (1994), and Gooptu (1993).

[80]See Bodie (1991).

[81]The reason that these sorts of contracts are entered into could be explained as a response to other incentives and prudential problems. For instance, a defined benefit pension plan typically requires that the fund return some specific rate of return over some planning horizon.

[82]Davis (1991) argues that it may be optimal for life insurance companies to concentrate their portfolios in domestic assets because matching currencies of assets and liabilities may be effective in limiting insolvency risk. This argument is essentially that shortfall risk may induce a home-asset preference.

Table II.8. Regulatory Constraints on Outward Portfolio Investment of Institutional Investors in Selected Industrial Countries[1]

Country/Region	Pension Funds	Insurance Companies	Mutual Funds
Canada	A December 1991 law progressively raised the ceiling on foreign investment from 10 percent to 20 percent in 1994.	A June 1992 regulation removed ceilings on foreign investments, but limits may be imposed based on prudential considerations.	Limit of 20 percent on foreign assets in the Registered Retirement Savings Plans (RRSP)-eligible funds.
France	At least 50 percent of assets must be invested in securities guaranteed by the state.	Investments are subject to the matching assets rule; the location rule; and the allocation of assets rule.	Subject to disclosure and asset diversification rules. A fund may not hold more than 10 percent of any one category of securities of one issuer.
Germany	Five percent of the assets of the technical provision fund and 20 percent of the other restricted assets in respect of business written in European Economic Area (EEA) States may be localized outside the EEA States. No restriction for free assets. Matching rules apply.	Five percent of the assets of the technical provision fund and 20 percent of the other restricted assets in respect of business written in European Economic Area (EEA) States may be localized outside the EEA States. No restriction for free assets. Matching rules apply.	None.
Japan	Private funds are subject to 30 percent foreign asset limit. Fifty percent of assets must be in guaranteed fixed return, domestic yen vehicles.	Holding of securities issued by nonresidents is limited to 30 percent of total assets; the same ratio applies to purchases of foreign currency denominated assets.	
United Kingdom	None.	Subject to matching and localization rules, which require them roughly to balance liabilities expressed in a particular currency with assets in the currency. A company must ensure that its liabilities are covered by assets of appropriate safety, yield, and marketability, having regard to the classes of business carried on, and that its investments are appropriately diversified and adequately spread and that excessive reliance is not placed on investments of any particular category or description.	Collective investment schemes (unit trusts) are required to invest at least 90 percent of their assets in transferable securities in markets, selected by the fund manager in consultation with the trustees, which are regulated, recognized, operate regularly, and are open to the public.
United States	Regulated by a special federal law—Employee Retirement Income Security Act (ERISA). Permissible investments subject to the "prudent expert" rule, which includes a requirement to give consideration to diversification and liquidity factors. Otherwise no explicit restrictions on holding foreign securities, including foreign equities and foreign currency denominated bonds.	U.S. state insurance regulations attempt "to prevent or correct undue concentration of investment by type and issue and unreasonable mismatching of maturities of assets and liabilities." These laws usually allow an unrestricted "basket" of investments for certain amount of assets, which can be allocated to foreign securities in the range 0–10 percent of total assets.	Primarily regulated by the U.S. Securities and Exchange Commission (SEC) under federal laws. An open-ended fund may not hold more than 15 percent of its net assets in illiquid assets. Otherwise no explicit restrictions are imposed on investment in foreign securities.
European Union		The EC life and non-life insurance directives intend to remove all legal barriers for the creation of a common market in insurance. They also set out provisions to harmonize rules on admissible investment.	None.

Sources: Chuhan (1994); International Monetary Fund (1993); Organization for Economic Cooperation and Development (OECD); and national authorities.

[1]For the securities houses of these countries, there are no explicit regulatory restrictions on foreign exchange positions and other cross-border investments.

Table II.9. Industrialized Country Securities Investment Flows in Emerging Markets

(In percent of foreign securities investment flows)

	1987	1988	1989	1990	1991	1992	1993
Africa	−0.6	−0.1	−0.1	−0.2	—	1.1	−0.1
Asia	1.6	0.2	0.8	0.6	1.5	2.3	2.7
Europe	0.2	0.6	0.6	0.4	0.3	1.0	1.7
Middle East	0.3	2.2	0.4	0.4	0.3	0.2	0.5
Western Hemisphere	−1.0	0.2	−0.4	10.7	8.1	10.2	11.4
Mexico	−0.8	0.5	0.1	2.0	4.2	5.6	5.7
All emerging markets	0.4	3.0	1.2	11.9	10.2	14.8	16.3
Memorandum items							
Outflows from industrialized countries *(in billions of U.S. dollars)*	123.4	207.5	276.4	170.1	306.8	320.3	495.3
Emerging markets capitalization as a share of world capitalization *(in percent)*	4.1	5.0	6.3	6.5	7.5	8.8	11.6
Mexican markets capitalization as a share of world capitalization *(in percent)*	0.1	0.1	0.2	0.3	0.9	1.3	1.4

Sources: International Finance Corporation, *Emerging Stock Markets Factbook*, various issues; and International Monetary Fund, *Balance of Payments Statistics Yearbook 1994*, Part 2; and IMF staff estimates.

than 12 percent of the capitalized value of all equity markets.[83] Even though it is not possible to provide a country breakdown of foreign asset holdings of institutional investors, on average they hold substantially less than 12 percent of their total assets in emerging markets securities.

An indirect measure of the degree to which institutional investors have increased their holdings of emerging markets securities is provided by data on portfolio flows from industrial countries to emerging markets. These data represent a reasonably good measure because, although gross portfolio outflows from industrial countries include some retail cross-border transactions (i.e., by individuals), most of the portfolio inflows to emerging markets are flows from institutional investors.[84] This suggests that the ratio of total portfolio inflows to emerging markets to outflows from all industrial countries provides a measure of the fraction of institutional flows to foreign markets that are targeted to emerging markets.

According to these ratios, the share of institutional investment in emerging markets appears to have increased at a rapid pace (Table II.9). Interpreted at face value, these figures suggest that, in 1993, more

than $16 out of each new $100 foreign investment went to emerging markets in 1993, up from about $0.50 in 1987. In addition, securities originating in the Western Hemisphere accounted for a large share of total inflows; Mexico alone accounted for half of these flows.[85]

It is conventional wisdom that the source of portfolio flows to emerging markets in the Western Hemisphere is primarily U.S. institutional investors, especially mutual funds. In contrast, the investor base for Asian emerging markets is more diverse, including institutional investors from Europe, the United States, and Japan. As a share of total funds invested, the amount of foreign securities held by institutional investors in the United States is smaller than the amount held by institutional investors in other countries. However, the sheer size of U.S. institutions means that the dollar value of U.S. institutional investments in emerging markets, and especially to countries in the Western Hemisphere, is quite substantial.

It is estimated that in 1993, U.S. institutional investors owned about 30 percent of the $425 billion in debt outstanding issued in emerging markets, including $80 billion in Brady bonds, $254 billion in bank debt, and $91 billion in Eurobonds, global bonds, and yankee bonds.[86] This proportion is in line with an IFC estimate that between 20 and 50 percent of all net inflows to emerging markets originated in the

---

[83]It should be noted that the definition of the category "emerging markets" differs slightly across institutions. For instance, Singapore is not included in the IFC's category, but it is included in the IMF's balance of payments statistics. Emerging markets share of world GDP in 1993 was 20 percent. World market capitalization was $14.1 trillion in 1993; $12.5 trillion was accounted for by developed countries, of which $5.2 trillion was the U.S.; Mexico accounted for 1.4 percent of world market capitalization in 1993 (International Finance Corporation (1994)).

[84]For instance, this view is held by Baring Securities. Howell (1993) holds that around 90 percent of flows to emerging markets are attributable to pension, insurance, and mutual funds.

[85]The one-year surge in portfolio flows to Middle Eastern countries in 1988 is attributable to international bond issues by Bahrain ($80.6 million) and Israel ($20.0 million) (Organization for Economic Cooperation and Development, *Financial Statistics Monthly*, various issues).

[86]"Emerging Markets Debt Comes of Age" (1994).

United States. This interest in emerging markets by U.S. institutional investors has been spearheaded by mutual funds. It is estimated that, in 1993, U.S. mutual funds invested the net amount of $20 billion in emerging markets, bringing their emerging market holdings to $100 billion at the end of 1993.[87] This translates into an emerging markets position in the neighborhood of 5 percent of total assets, and almost half of total foreign assets. Thus, U.S. mutual funds have significantly diversified their portfolios into emerging markets.

Closed end investment companies have also made significant investments in the emerging markets. The structure of closed end investment companies makes them an especially good vehicle for investing in less liquid markets. As a result, closed end funds are a relatively more important source of investment in emerging markets than in industrial countries.[88] It is estimated that, in September 1994, emerging markets assets held by U.S. and overseas closed end funds totaled $45 billion.[89]

The structure of closed end funds facilitates longer-term investments and therefore may be relatively more attractive to developing countries than some other portfolio flows. Specifically, portfolio weights in closed end funds are, on average, not nearly as sensitive to market volatility changes as open-end funds. One reason is that closed end fund managers are shielded from actual and expected redemptions because the claims on the pool of assets are traded on a stock exchange. In contrast, open-end funds are required to redeem claims on demand, which can have an important effect on portfolio decisions.[90] "Redemption risk" is probably one of the most important reasons for the much higher turnover ratios of open-end funds (on average) than closed end funds.[91] The consequence is that open-end funds tend to concentrate on an emerging market's larger firms because they often have the most liquid securities. Closed end funds, on the other hand, not only do not face redemption risk,

but they are able to select lesser known, less liquid, securities. Because the securities of the largest firms in emerging markets are often directly available to individual investors through ADRs and GDRs or direct transactions in that country, this puts open-end funds at a disadvantage.[92]

In 1994 and early 1995, U.S. open-end and closed end funds gave rise to substantial net inflows to emerging markets. Although it is well known that net contributions to U.S. mutual funds have slowed since 1993, contributions to international mutual funds that have investment mandates for emerging markets were strong for most of 1994 (Table II.10). Moreover, net contributions to emerging markets in the Western Hemisphere equity funds actually rebounded in early 1995 from the last few months of 1994, despite the Mexican crisis. Contributions in January 1995, however, were only a small fraction of those one year earlier. In addition, redemptions from bond funds continued to advance rapidly in early 1995.

In contrast to the appetite of U.S. mutual funds for emerging markets securities, U.S. pension funds appear to show limited interest in emerging markets. Emerging markets mandates for many pension funds in the past couple of years have been well below 1 percent of total assets, and average emerging markets holdings in 1993 are estimated at about 0.5 percent of total assets. This estimate places pension fund holdings of emerging markets securities at about $18 billion in 1993, less than one fifth of the holdings of U.S. mutual funds with emerging markets mandates in 1993 (Table II.6).[93]

There has been an important shift in recent years toward diversification into emerging markets by some institutional investors. However, as a percent of total assets, institutional investors are a long way from an emerging markets portfolio share representative of emerging markets capitalization relative to world market capitalization. Most estimates place the average share of emerging markets securities in institutional investors' portfolios around 1 percent. This low weight of emerging markets is consistent with the strong bias of pension funds and insurance companies away from foreign markets in general, and emerging markets specifically. There seems to be an

---

[87]International Finance Corporation (1994). For further analyses of the importance of U.S. and foreign mutual funds see the background paper "Capital Flows to Developing Countries," pp. 33–52.

[88]The Investment Company Act of 1940 stipulates that not more than 15 percent of the fund's assets can be invested in illiquid assets—those not salable within seven days without a substantial discount. For further details, see "Fund Management" (1994).

[89]Lipper Analytical Services.

[90]The Investment Company Act of 1940 requires that redemptions be met on seven days' notice.

[91]Turnover ratios for open-end funds vary widely. Index funds, for instance, typically have low turnover ratios, whereas actively managed funds often have turnover ratios above 100 percent, and many "aggressive" funds have turnover ratios of several hundred percent. The average open-end fund has a turnover ratio of about 100 percent. Closed end funds typically have turnover ratios below 50 percent, and often in the neighborhood of 20 percent.

[92]Gooptu (1993).

[93]This estimate is higher than existing direct measures of emerging markets holdings of pension funds. For U.S. corporate pension funds, which account for just over 25 percent of the pension assets recorded in Table II.6, Money Market Directories (1995) puts emerging markets bond holdings in 1995 at 0.09 percent ($992 million) and emerging markets equities at 0.15 percent ($1,590 million). Interestingly, these measures are not much greater than Chuhan's (1994) estimate for pensions funds' holdings of emerging markets securities in 1992: she puts them at only 3.4 percent of total foreign asset holdings in 1992 (or $5.2 billion), which translates into an emerging markets position of less than 0.2 percent.

Table II.10. International Mutual Funds Based in the United States[1]

(Net fund inflows monthly in millions of U.S. dollars)

	Jan. 1994	Feb. 1994	Mar. 1994	Apr. 1994	May 1994	June 1994	July 1994	Aug. 1994	Sept. 1994	Oct. 1994	Nov. 1994	Dec. 1994	Jan. 1995
International funds[2]													
(Equity)													
Growth	3,626	2,452	2,353	1,610	1,506	927	1,706	2,251	1,126	1,362	299	359	539
Emerging market equity	1,398	830	−150	455	346	157	224	688	411	341	−51	−58	89
Total return	495	352	208	125	173	−22	89	164	176	88	98	−94	24
Latin American equity	858	649	−256	−6	135	54	65	305	111	110	−24	−80	21
Single country equity	6	490	803	−2	30	−2	20	9	134	67	−6	−2	−14
Small cap	299	397	8	62	76	22	105	66	65	41	17	−23	−20
Chinese equity	75	85	57		—	15	23	12	10	−4	13	−20	−26
Canadian equity	47	18	19	−7	−1	88	67	20	19	−2	−13	−2	−35
Japanese equity	182	52	163	97	163	295	59	−127	−107	1	−47	−32	−55
European equity	435	372	25	119	257	−123	103	152	−182	−44	−128	−108	−109
Pacific equity with Japan	402	284	24	170	212	187	171	277	26	160	−39	−27	−74
Pacific equity without Japan	124	137	95	221	129	32	117	227	352	156	−116	−49	−83
Global funds													
Growth	1,468	1,338	704	789	771	459	702	987	679	703	252	373	259
Small company	285	193	128	104	105	80	93	210	87	76	60	28	78
Total return	320	263	198	121	102	76	78	122	78	62	53	26	27
Equity sector	336	241	102	49	49	249	27	170	45	126	39	−27	−9
Asset allocation	859	574	479	208	431	305	213	323	156	40	56	−114	−30
Total	11,214	8,727	4,959	4,114	4,483	2,798	3,864	5,857	3,185	3,282	664	151	583
(Taxable Bond)													
International funds													
Single country bond	−1	−1	—	−1	−1	—	−1	—	—	−1	−1	−1	—
Emerging market bond	142	74	−21	107	270	−20	11	57	14	−33	−146	−47	−40
Global funds													
Government bond	79	367	−12	−43	−30	−69	−32	−81	−103	−92	32	−88	−101
North American bond	554	313	−286	−335	−117	−77	−130	−87	−180	−156	−77	−442	−237
Short bonds	−218	−388	−509	−217	−340	−448	−305	−381	−370	−295	−314	−311	−329
Bond (general)	420	136	−39	−18	123	−119	−213	−179	−289	−196	−325	−233	−374
Total	976	502	−866	−507	−94	−733	−668	−671	−928	−773	−830	−1,123	−1,081
Grand total (equity plus taxable bond)	12,191	9,229	4,093	3,607	4,389	2,066	3,195	5,186	2,257	2,509	−166	−971	−498

Source: Strategic Insight Simfund.
[1] Open- and closed end funds.
[2] International funds invest in non-U.S. securities only; global funds invest in foreign and U.S. securities.

even stronger aversion of the more "conservative" types of institutional investors to emerging markets than to foreign markets. For example, a recent poll of U.S. pension funds indicated that 7 percent of them would allocate no additional contributions to emerging markets in 1995, 27 percent would allocate between 1 and 5 percent of new contributions, and only 2 percent would allocate more than 4 percent of new contributions to emerging markets.[94]

Despite these relatively small emerging markets portfolio weights of institutional investors, two facts are noteworthy. First, with an estimated 1 percent of assets invested in emerging markets, the share of emerging markets holdings in total foreign holdings is therefore above 10 percent (from Table II.7) for many institutional investors. This might indicate that investors' aversion is focused on foreign investments in general, not necessarily emerging market investments. Second, since 1990, the share of new foreign portfolio investment that has been targeted to emerging markets appears to have exceeded the market capitalization share. It is noteworthy that these general trends seem to be much more marked for Mexico, suggesting possibly an overweighting of Mexican securities.

---

[94]Richardson(1995).

Instead of interpreting the emerging markets portfolio weights of institutional investors in light of modern portfolio theory, one might instead question the benchmark that is used to gauge how far institutional investors have moved toward "optimal" international diversification. Portfolio managers from a variety of institutions report that the relevant benchmark for them is not a market-capitalization weighted portfolio, but instead a much narrower benchmark, such as a domestic stock index for mutual funds or an average of other institutional investors' portfolios for pensions, endowments, and trusts. Furthermore, the market-capitalization benchmark can be criticized for ignoring cross-country differences in liquidity, information, accounting practices, the market capitalization of traded firms as a percentage of market capitalization of all domestic firms, transactions costs, and custody and settlement systems. This seems especially relevant in light of the fact that institutional investors report that these factors—especially liquidity—are a fundamental reason why they hold such a small fraction of emerging markets securities. Even pension-fund and trust-portfolio managers, which, on the surface, might not appear to have the same concerns about liquidity as mutual funds (e.g., redemptions), state that annual turnover of their portfolios is often quite high—for example, 75 percent—and therefore liquidity figures prominently in portfolio allocation decisions.

VI

Bubbles, Noise, and the Trading Process in Speculative Markets

Remarkably little is understood about the short-run behavior of prices and trading volumes in highly liquid asset markets such as stock and foreign exchange markets. These markets, at times, experience very sharp price movements while at the same time other variables that are presumed to be economic fundamentals change very little, if at all. The surprisingly large value of trading in some markets also is difficult to explain based on the ideas in the economics literature about the fundamental reasons for trading. Although the reasons for short-term movements in asset prices remain enigmatic, the macroeconomic fundamentals suggested by many traditional models explain asset prices reasonably well over longer periods of time. One possible reason for this contrast in model performance is the presence of unmodeled short-run market influences that tend to abate over longer periods. While the long-run success of models is somewhat comforting, it is of little help to policymakers or short-term investors, who are under considerable pressure to understand short-term market movements.

As a first step toward understanding short-term developments in asset markets, researchers have introduced various pathologies into economic models. These pathologies, such as rational asset-price bubbles, are persuasive rationalizations only to the extent that they place restrictions on data. In other words, introducing pathologies as an explanation of asset-market behavior is useful only if the proposed pathologies are inconsistent with some types of behavior. An explanation that is consistent with everything is no explanation at all. In this section we introduce some of the pathologies, develop some of the restrictions they impose on the data, and review some relevant empirical work.

Problems Explaining Short-Run Price Movements

A simple and appealing model of rational stock pricing implies that the value of a share is related to the expected stream of dividends paid by that share in the future (the discounted dividend model).[95] One

influential extension of this model found that while prices deviate from the predictions of the basic model in the short run,[96] they have a tendency to move back toward the model's predictions in the long run; that is, the model works much better over a long adjustment period than it does over a short one.[97] The property of "mean reversion" is strongly supported by rigorous testing procedures. A similar study of the foreign exchange market found that while macroeconomic models explained exchange rates reasonably well in the long run, the forecasts of these models were substantially worse in the short run than the naive prediction that the exchange rate would stay constant.[98]

As an illustration of this tendency toward long-term mean reversion, consider the simple relative purchasing power parity (PPP) model of exchange rates. This model postulates that the percent change in the exchange rate between the currencies of two countries is equal to the inflation differential between those countries. Chart II.1 plots pairs of annual percent changes in dollar exchange rates for the industrial countries against each country's annual inflation rate relative to that of the United States.[99] If the PPP hypothesis is correct, then these pairs should coincide with the 45-degree diagonal line. On a year-to-year basis, the inflation differential is not closely related to exchange rate changes (see Panel 1 of Chart II.1). For countries with low-inflation differentials—10 percent or less in absolute value—the inflation differential is uninformative about the rate of depreciation of the exchange rate. The remaining panels in the chart plot the data averaged over 5, 10, and 20 years. Over long periods of time, inflation differentials are quite helpful in understanding average exchange rate changes (see Panels 2 through 4 of Chart II.1), and there does

---

[95]Shiller (1981) used simple statistics and graphs to suggest that annual stock prices are more variable than is warranted by

dividends. His methods were rigorously scrutinized by the profession, but his basic results have withstood many attacks. A survey of the work is given by Shiller (1991), see especially Chapter 4.

[96]Short-run price movements mean a short period between successive price observations (fewer than 90 days, for example). The long-run refers to a longer sampling period (more than one year, for example).

[97]See Fama and French (1988).

[98]See Meese and Rogoff (1983).

[99]The data are from *International Financial Statistics* for IFS 100-level countries.

Chart II.1. Relative PPP in *IFS* Industrial Countries, 1972–94[1]
(In U.S. dollar terms)

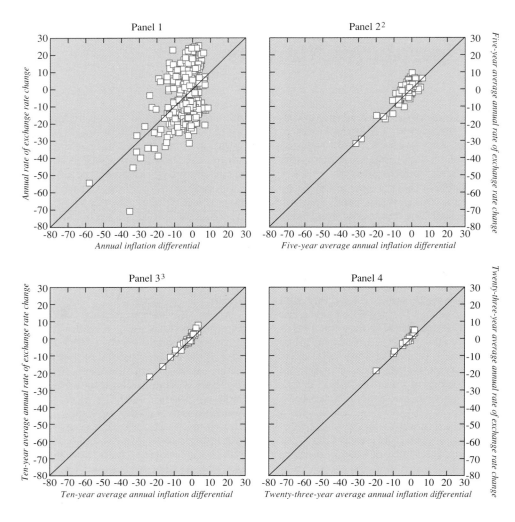

Source: International Monetary Fund, *International Financial Statistics (IFS)*.
[1]Excluding San Marino from the countries listed as industrial countries in the *IFS*.
[2]Five-year averages are for 1972–76, 1977–81, 1982–86, and 1987–94.
[3]Ten-year averages are for 1972–81 and 1982–94.

appear to be a strong tendency for exchange rate changes and inflation differentials to coincide.[100]

The failure of economic models to explain short-run movements in asset prices has generated interest in both academic and policymaking settings. Indeed, to many observers, the most glaring weakness of economic models is their inability to predict and to explain—after the fact—periods of turbulence in financial markets. There are several recent examples of sharp price and volume movements that

models could neither predict ex ante nor describe ex post. During the October 19, 1987 stock market "break," the Dow Jones Industrial Average (DJIA) fell 22.6 percent in one day, and totaled a 31 percent drop over four trading days starting on October 13, 1987.[101] During the subsequent October 13, 1989 mini-break the DJIA declined almost 7 percent. Other examples include the attack on currency parities in the European Economic and Monetary Union (EMU) in 1992–93, the rise and fall of the

---

[100]Balassa (1964) discusses deviations from the theory caused by structural growth differences.

[101]By contrast, the crash of October 29, 1929 caused a 24.5 percent reduction in the DJIA.

"bubble economy" in Japan in the early 1990s, the fall of the Mexican peso during and after December 1994 and the coincident stock market declines in many developing countries. Examples such as these seem particularly relevant to newly established stock markets all over the world and help place in context experiences such as the MMM stock scheme in Russia during 1994.

In each of these examples and in many other cases, price movements appear to be independent of movements in traditional market fundamentals. Researchers have only recently documented and accepted these short-run problems with popular models. Formal mathematical treatment of these problems is more recent still. The next section is very much a "report from the front" on the models that researchers are attempting to construct and test in order to account for short-run asset price movements.

A New Generation of Asset-Market Models

A new generation of financial models has been developed to try to overcome some of the weaknesses of the traditional models and to help explain some of the more dramatic market events. To explain short-term movements in prices, the new work differentiates between classes of investors, whereas traditional models assumed that all investors were alike. These new models add microeconomic detail in such a way that investor diversity is intrinsic and essential. Models that differentiate between economic agents generally yield the same long-term qualitative predictions as models with homogeneous agents, however.

Asset-Market Bubbles

Although a precise definition of a bubble requires a model of a particular market, when an asset price rises solely because agents expect it to rise, the asset is said to be "on a bubble." Two types of bubbles are studied in the literature: rational bubbles and other bubbles. Models of rational bubbles are interesting because the assumption of rationality produces simple statistical tests for the existence of bubbles. However, the assumption of rationality may be so restrictive that, in some cases, models do not explain the relevant data very well; that is, in some cases the model is rejected.

The rational bubble, which sounds like an oxymoron, is the mathematical formalization of the well-known greater fool theory. This theory postulates that an asset price is reasonable as long as a greater fool will later pay a sufficiently higher price for the asset. The value of a bubble-infected asset is driven, in part, by the expectation that the price of the asset will continue to increase. Once a rational bubble

has started, investors do not, on average, expect to get rich from buying into the bubble. Some investors might reap high returns before the bubble bursts, but others, of (mathematical) necessity, will hold on to the asset too long and suffer a considerable loss during the inevitable crash.

A Model of a Stock Market Bubble

It is useful to illustrate precisely what is meant by a rational bubble in the context of a stock market model.[102] Recent theoretical work indicates that bubbles may appear in models where generations of asset holders retire and are replaced by a new and sufficiently more wealthy generation of investors (the greater fools). This new generation is replaced by another one after a time, and so on. The appearance of successively more wealthy new generations of investors allows price bubbles to persist.[103]

Rational bubbles can occur in models in which the current price depends on the anticipated future price. One well-known, stock market model that generates bubbles is

$$P_t = \rho(P_{t+1} + \bar{D}). \tag{1}$$

P_t is the price of a share of stock now, $\bar{D}$ is the constant dividend paid to holders of the stock, and P_{t+1} is the prospective sale price of the stock next period. ρ is the discount rate (normally about .95 for inflation-adjusted annual data). This model adopts the fiction that all future dividends are constant and known currently and future prices are known also. Even with such simplifications, equation (1) is still a single equation in two unknowns, P_t and P_{t+1}. One equation in two unknowns determines a line relating P_t to P_{t+1}, not a point determining P_t. This simple notion is the basis of all work on rational bubbles.

Because P_t and P_{t+1} occur at different points in time the model's solution, multiplicity has an intertemporal dimension. According to equation (1), any price set this period will set next period's price also; and setting next period's price will determine price two periods into the future, and so on. This process is illustrated in Chart II.2, where equation (1) appears as the dashed line AA. Any point on AA is a solution to equation (1). The diagonal line shows points where price is constant over time ($P_t = P_{t+1}$). The solution of equation (1) with constant price occurs at the intersection of the two lines,

---

[102]Readers can ignore technical aspects of this subsection without losing the logical flow of the arguments. The important fact to be kept in mind is that the basis of all analytical work involving bubbles is that the model in question lacks a unique equilibrium price.

[103]This logic is developed by Tirole (1985).

Chart II.2. Stock-Market Bubbles

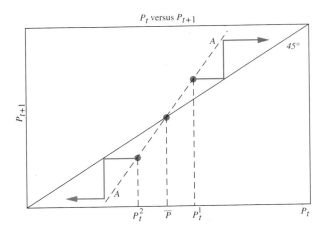

P_t versus P_{t+1}

$P_t = \bar{P} = (\rho/(1-\rho)) \cdot \bar{D}$. This is the fundamental solution of the model for P_t.[104]

If price is different from $\bar{P}$, equation (1) sets in motion some price dynamics. The arrows show the direction of price movement. If P_t is above $\bar{P}$, P_{t+1} must be even higher than P_t; if P_t is below, $\bar{P}_{t+1}$ must be even lower than P_t.[105] Prices like P_t^1 and P_t^2, which are away from the fundamental price $\bar{P}$, involve self-fulfilling expectations of future capital gains or losses. These departures from fundamentals are known as rational price bubbles.

Economists know very little about bubbles in practice, but quite a lot in theory. As an example, consider the price P_t^1 in the Chart II.2. Read P_t^1 off the horizontal axis and P_{t+1}^1 off the vertical axis. Evidently, since line AA is steeper than the diagonal (where P_{t+1} equals P_t), P_{t+1}^1 is above P_t^1. Of course, next period the higher P_{t+1}^1 will require an even higher capital gains, and so on. Current capital gains end up being justified by even larger future capital gains. For prices above the fundamental solution the market would take off on a self-fulfilling positive bubble as indicated by the arrow going northeast in Chart II.2.

Now suppose market price is below the fundamentals price (e.g., $P_t^2 < \bar{P}$). This may appear to result in a negative bubble, but a bit of introspection reveals that negative bubbles cannot exist. Following the negative bubble's path to the southwest, it is clear that the price must eventually fall below zero.[106] This makes no sense for assets like stocks,

which have limited liability—shareholders can lose no more than their initial investment. Any limited liability shareholder would gladly renounce ownership rather than hold an "asset" with negative value. A negative bubble, therefore, cannot be sustained by a rational forward-looking market.

Positive rational bubbles, on the other hand, make sense in some models. Their existence and description, therefore, becomes an empirical question. To study actual data, the simplifications of constant dividends and perfect anticipation of future prices and dividends must be removed. These simplifications are normally replaced by the condition that investors forecast future prices, dividends, and any other relevant variables as efficiently as possible, using all available information appropriately. This assumption, known as "rational expectations," preserves the mathematical structure so far developed, but allows investors to be wrong—perhaps disastrously so.[107]

Testing for Rational Bubbles

Models with rational bubbles have been popular in the literature because they embody the idea that bubbles drive prices away from their fundamental values. These models are also popular because they produce sharply defined predictions and hypotheses about prices and thus are amenable to empirical testing. The prospective bubbles cannot, however, be effectively separated from the models that generate them. Every test for bubbles is in the context of a model and is part of a joint hypothesis that the model is correct, that expectations are formed rationally, and that bubbles are absent. If the investigator is willing to maintain that the model is correct and that expectations are formed rationally and the hypothesis is statistically rejected, it may be concluded that bubbles may not be absent.

Models like that described in equation (1) generate testable hypotheses about market prices. The bubbles tests involve the difference between actual prices and a counterfactual price series—the one generated by the model and based on actual model-suggested fundamentals. The tests then use statistical theory to judge whether the difference is larger than would be given by chance and has the properties suggested by the relevant bubble.[108] For example, in the model portrayed in equation (1) the market fundamentals price is the constant $P_t = (\rho/(1-\rho)) \cdot \bar{D}$. In a bubbles test based on equation (1), if actual prices were significantly different from this constant and were growing on average at the rate $(1/\rho)$ then the investigator

---

[104]In general the fundamental price is the currently expected present value of future dividends, and $P_t = (\rho/1-\rho) \cdot \bar{D}$ is a special case of that result, which is appropriate for discounting of constant dividends at the rate ρ.

[105]In mathematical terms, this is because the line AA, whose slope is $1/\rho = 1/.95$, is steeper than the 45-degree line.

[106]This argument does not apply to models that are linear in the logarithm of price; a negative logarithm of price just means a price below unity.

[107]The ideas worked out here for bubbles and fundamentals in a simple model of a stock market have counterparts in other models and markets.

[108]See Flood and Hodrick (1990).

would not reject the presence of a rational bubble in this market.

Existing research constructs the counterfactual series in two ways. First, mathematical models are used, as above, to construct price series that would have been based appropriately on fundamentals.[109] The second approach compares prices in markets that are thought not to contain bubbles with prices in similar markets where bubbles are suspected.[110] Tests for bubbles always involve these counterfactual comparisons; in the first case, against the implications of a mathematical model and in the second case, against a similar market where bubbles are thought to be absent.

The tests are only as good as their counterfactuals, however. If one has great confidence in a model and the actual price series is different from the model-generated counterfactual in ways predicted by the presence of bubbles, then one might conclude that the data are consistent with bubbles.[111] If confidence in the model is low, however, then an apparent bubbles finding might be attributed to misspecification of the model-generated counterfactual series. For example, adopting equation (1) as the stock market counterfactual, one would generate a constant "fundamental" price in a market in which dividends actually grow on average but in an unpredictable way. Maintaining the model to be correct would lead to an apparent finding of a stock market bubble. In the example, bubbles might indeed be present, but because the model is so clearly wrong, a conclusion that bubbles are present would be ill founded because the counterfactual model is so weak.

Historical Bubble Reports: Tulipmania

Two kinds of empirical work have investigated bubbles: studies of purported historical bubbles, such as the Dutch Tulipmania of the 1630s, and more modern studies of prices and fundamentals in, for example, stock markets, foreign exchange markets, and land markets. Descriptions of events in the Dutch market for tulips in the period 1634–37 are often included in historical accounts of speculative market excesses.[112] During 1634–37, the Semper Augustus tulip bulb sold for 5500 guilders, a gold-price equivalent to $50,000 at $450 per ounce.[113] Historical descriptions of these events indicate that a speculative frenzy overtook the bulb market in early 1637 and drove prices to extreme heights, which was followed by a crash. After the crash, bulbs could not fetch prices that were as high as 10 percent of peak prices.

A more recent study using data from this period found that speculative run-ups and crashes were typical patterns in the historical flower bulb market.[114] Indeed, the pattern still persists in some ways; a 1987 prototype lily bulb sold for $480,000. The study compares the path of tulip bulb prices over 1634–37, for which bubbles are suspected, to bulb price paths in other markets that are thought not to contain bubbles. As the difference was found to be not significant, the so-called Dutch Tulip bubble probably was not a rational bubble.

Once the study's testing methodology is accepted, the explanation that Tulipmania is driven by the same fundamentals that drives other flower prices is convincing for some of the data. Not all of the events of 1637 can be rationalized, however. During the winter of that year, futures markets in bulbs flourished in taverns. In this market, the prices for common bulbs rose and exploded in a pattern otherwise unique to the rarest species.

Bubbles have also been studied using formal econometric models.[115] The first such test examined whether the tremendous acceleration of inflation during 1922–23 in post–World War I Germany was partly due to a price level bubble. The hypothesis that no bubbles were present was not rejected. Possible price level bubbles in one economy, of course, have exchange rate implications. Other related work testing for foreign exchange market bubbles was unsupportive of the existence of such bubbles.[116]

Tests for bubbles also were applied to stock prices.[117] Studies have found evidence for bubbles in the stock market using state-of-the-art methods. The tests, however, suffer from the problem that a bubble can be identified only relative to a particular model of price fundamentals. A fully credible model has remained elusive in the stock market. Rejecting the hypothesis that bubbles are absent could just as well indicate that the model generating the counterfactuals is wrong.

The Japanese Bubble Economy

Among the best-known modern asset-market disturbances is the "bubble economy" in Japan in the late 1980s. Stock prices and land prices in Japan

---

[109]See Flood and Garber (1980) and Blanchard and Watson (1982).

[110]See Garber (1989).

[111]Actually, it can only be concluded that the data might be inconsistent with the absence of bubbles.

[112]The Mississippi Bubble, 1718–20, connected to John Law's French government finance schemes and the temporally related South Sea Bubble, connected to the British government, are reviewed by Garber (1990).

[113]See McKay (1852).

[114]See Garber (1989).

[115]Such work began with Flood and Garber (1980).

[116]See Flood and Hodrick (1990).

[117]Two notable investigations were by West (1988) and by Froot and Obstfeld (1991).

increased at a very rapid pace.[118] The Nikkei 225 index of stock prices went from 9,500 in December 1983 to 18,700 in December 1986, and then to 38,000 in 1989, more than doubling every three years. Average land prices in Tokyo doubled between the end of 1986 and the end of 1988. Although the timing of price increases differed across different types of assets, the capital gains from owning stocks and real estate greatly exceeded the interest rates. High returns on property attracted many investors, driving prices up further, which is characteristic of a bubble process.

Stock prices peaked at the end of 1989, and land prices peaked around 1990–91. Once a turning point was reached, asset prices plummeted. In the process, stock and land prices lost most of their gains from the rise during the bubble period. Asset owners suffered capital losses; many real estate companies and developers, who had borrowed to acquire assets, became insolvent. Although there is some work testing whether the price movements in Japan can be explained by microeconomic or macroeconomic fundamentals, the evidence appears to be mixed.[119]

Other Bubbles

Some researchers feel that the assumption of rationality is too restrictive. Although the possibility that asset prices in models could be driven by expectations rather than by fundamentals has been in the literature for some time, the older literature was unsatisfactory in that not only were destabilizing expectations not self-fulfilling, they were increasingly self-deluding.[120]

Recent work in this tradition does not require rationality and need not be self-deluding in the long run. This work examines a foreign exchange market populated by three types of traders: fundamentalists, chartists, and portfolio managers.[121] Fundamentalists assume that the exchange rate will take on its fundamental value; chartists forecast the future exchange rate by extrapolating from past exchange rates; and portfolio managers forecast an exchange rate that is

a weighted average of those expected by the chartists and fundamentalists. The type of adaptive learning used by the model's portfolio managers generates nonlinear dynamics. For some specifications of this model, price moves away from the path that would prevail if all expectations were formed by the fundamentalists, due to nonrationality. For different parameter configurations, the model is able to mimic the speculative run-ups and crashes that characterize foreign exchange markets.

Another notion of a bubble has been investigated in experiments with a computerized stock market, allowing subjects to "trade" in the market.[122] In the experiments, both researchers and experimental subjects (college students and businessmen) knew the price that should be determined by fundamentals, the random final-period cashflow. One would expect that in such a controlled setting, the stock price would quickly attain the expected value of the final payout, but it did not. In 14 of 22 experiments, the authors found a boom-bust pattern typical of a bubble. This kind of bubble is different from those discussed previously because the subjects knew all possible terminal prices, but prices still fluctuated wildly. The authors interpreted this as the result of traders' learning about the market and possible strategic behavior by market participants.

Noise Trading

Much empirical work suggests that trading volume is related to price changes. This leads some to suspect that something in the trading process is generating what appears to be excess price volatility. Several new approaches have emerged to address this possibility.

Trading based only on rationally processed differences in information is impossible. If traders agree on what information is important, and how to interpret that information, differences in information will generate no trading. Suppose there are two traders: one who knows the value of the dividend to be paid out next period, and one who does not. Suppose also that the information is favorable; the stock is a bargain at current prices, given knowledge of the future dividend. The informed trader will want to profit from his information, and buy the uninformed traders' shares. When the informed trader offers to pay more for the shares of the second than the going price, he signals to the uninformed trader that the prospective buyer has superior information, and that his information indicates that the market price is too low. The uninformed trader will rationally refuse the offer, now knowing that the market price is too low.

---

[118]See Ito (1992) for a general introduction to the asset price inflation in Japan. See also Schinasi and Hargraves (1993) for a description and an analysis of the asset price cycle in Japan and other industrial countries.

[119]See Ito (1992) and (1993) and Ito and Iwaisako (forthcoming). Hoffmaister and Schinasi (1995) explain a significant part of land price movements in Japan in the late 1980s on the basis of macroeconomic fundamentals.

[120]Much of this work involves adaptive expectations, which is a simplified error-learning mechanism that was popularized in Cagan (1956). In Cagan's model, and those based on his work, if expectations adapt sufficiently quickly then price will be driven away from the long-run fundamental value instead of being driven toward it.

[121]See Frankel and Froot (1990) and Smith, Suchanek, and Williams (1988).

[122]This market lasted a fixed number of "trading periods" (15–30), also known to the experimental subjects. The real time market exists for only one to two hours, so that discounting of future payouts is not important.

In fact, he will refuse any price that the informed trader finds acceptable (up to the actual value of the stock given dividend information). Hence, no trading will take place. This simple but powerful result is known as a no-trade theorem and prompted several responses.[123]

In one type of response non-information-based reasons are introduced for trade. Some people sell stocks to finance purchases, adjust portfolios, generate retirement income, and so on. In these new models, some traders are (realistically) allowed to have fundamentally changing life circumstances—death, retirement, changes in tastes, or changes in labor income, all of which would prompt rational trade. Likewise, some people no doubt trade because they do not understand the market, because they receive bad investment advice, because they think they can outguess other traders, or simply because they like to trade. Hence, in another type of response, the full rationality requirement is relaxed so that some traders do not have a complete understanding of the information-processing abilities of other traders or, more simply, about how to process information themselves.

These latter traders, who do not act rationally, are known as noise traders. The idea that traders act in a fully rational manner, whose expectations are consistent with the reality of the model, is a modern innovation.[124] Consideration of viable noise traders in addition to rational traders is modern also and is different from the idea of rational bubbles. Roughly speaking, noise trading involves short-run deviations from a fundamentals equilibrium, while bubbles involve deviations that are expected to last a long time.[125]

Noise trading is not necessarily all bad. A well-known contribution in this area[126] pointed out that in the absence of frequent trading, markets are illiquid—death, retirement, and other circumstances simply cannot generate much trading. Illiquid markets do a poor job of impounding relevant information into prices; the liquidity generated by noise traders makes markets more efficient in revealing this information.

While the early work on noise was quite general, later work became more specific by concentrating on the price effects of noise.[127] In this work, there are two types of traders. The first kind is a typical utility-maximizing "information trader" who knows about fundamentals and takes informed positions. The second kind is a "noise trader," who takes positions that are not in accordance with standard economic principles. Either the noise trader is behaving irrationally for unspecified reasons, escapes the norms of economists' models, or simply likes to trade.

At one time, most mainstream economists discounted the notion of noise traders because traders that are systematically wrong would quickly lose all their money to fundamentals traders, and be driven out of the market.[128] However, this new model of noise traders shows that this need not happen. Noise traders' activity creates price fluctuations in risky assets they hold; this makes fundamentalists, who dislike risk more than noise traders do, less apt to hold these assets. The noise traders thus create a space for themselves in the market, which is insulated from the information traders by the very risk the noise traders create.

Herd Behavior

In most of the work discussed so far, it has been assumed that investors make their decisions ignorant of the decisions of others. A different kind of assumption is explored in models of herd behavior.[129] In this work, not all information is publicly available, and agents make decisions in turn. The sequencing of decisions is crucial since decision-makers toward the end of the queue can learn from the decisions made by those before them. Hence, individual decisions can have externalities, and the cumulative effect of these externalities may lead to inefficient investment allocations. With this kind of information, an investor's decision is predicated both on his private information about market fundamentals and by his observations of others' decisions. The decision of other investors yields information, as it might reveal what other investors know.

As an example, suppose that all investors have access to public information about an investment project, such as balance sheets and accountants reports. Suppose also that each investor has a private information source that may or may not be reliable. Suppose there are two investors, A and B, considering one project, and investor A is first in line. Suppose investor A has a "tip" that the project is good, while B has a tip that it is bad. A, going first, follows his tip and invests. B observes A's decision, and weighing his own information decides to follow A and invest, inferring that A must know something he doesn't. Now suppose that, in reality, A's private information was wrong. Although B may have correct private information, that private signal was swamped by knowledge of A's actions. The asset market would misprice the project because of the

---

[123]The "no-trade" theorems are developed by Grossman and Stiglitz (1980) and by Milgrom and Stokey (1982).

[124]See Muth (1961).

[125]The presence of noise traders can, however, influence the fundamental equilibrium by injecting additional risk.

[126]See Black (1986).

[127]See De Long and others (1989).

[128]See, for example, Friedman (1953).

[129]See, for example, Bikchandani, Hirschleifer, and Welch (1992).

externality imposed by sequential decision making with private information.[130] Models based on similar ideas have been used to explain diverse phenomena, such as political bandwagons; medical fads known as treatment-caused epidemics (iatroepidemics), such as tonsillectomies; and financial-market behavior, such as bank runs in which depositors' observations of other depositors actions can trigger a cascade of further withdrawals.

Conclusion

At one time it was widely asserted that pathologies such as bubbles and noise were inconsistent with well-functioning rational markets. Careful theoretical work, however, has established conditions such that these alleged pathologies could logically endure in models. This, no small achievement, has altered the way many researchers approach markets.

Establishing the pathologies in theory is quite different from confirming that they are relevant to actual markets. The biggest obstacle is, again, that the tests are only as good as the counterfactuals. This applies to tests for bubbles, noise, or any other source of concern about market outcomes. All of the tests require a comparison of actual market outcomes against a model of the outcomes the market would have generated had the alleged pathologies been absent.

The current generation of models of asset pricing based on fundamentals, the counterfactuals, is simply not very convincing. According to these models virtually all asset markets are too volatile and always have been so. While that is a consistent position, it is not persuasive or informative as to the urgency of concerns about asset-market volatility.

When researchers see prices change in ways that are inconsistent with their models, they have two polar responses. One response is that the model is wrong, and the market, right. The solution is to change the model. The other response is that the model is wrong because certain pathologies inhabit the market; the model is right, and the market, wrong. Although respectable researchers inhabit both poles, most are somewhere in the middle, concerned about large and unmotivated price changes but unimpressed by theories that have not held up to empirical testing.

---

[130]This becomes much more complicated when investor A tries to account for the effects of his actions on the decisions of investor B, who, in turn understands A's motives.

Bibliography

"America's Top 300 Money Managers," *Institutional Investor* (July 1994), pp. 113–48.

Balassa, Bela, "The Purchasing Power Parity Doctrine: A Reappraisal," *Journal of Political Economy*, Vol. 72, No. 6 (December 1964), pp. 584–96.

Bank for International Settlements, "Public Disclosure of Market and Credit Risks by Financial Intermediaries" (Basle: Bank for International Settlements, September 1994).

———, "Issues of Measurement Related to Market Size and Macroprudential Risks in Derivatives Markets" (Basle: Bank for International Settlements, February 1995).

Basle Committee on Banking Supervision, "International Convergence of Capital Measurement and Capital Standards" (Basle: Basle Committee on Banking Supervision, July 1988).

——— (1993a), "The Prudential Supervision of Netting, Market Risks and Interest Rate Risk" (Basle: Basle Committee on Banking Supervision, April 1993).

——— (1993b), "The Supervisory Recognition of Netting for Capital Adequacy Purposes" (Basle: Basle Committee on Banking Supervision, April 1993).

——— (1993c), "The Supervisory Treatment of Market Risks" (Basle: Basle Committee on Banking Supervision, April 1993).

——— (1993d), "Measurement of Banks' Exposure to Interest Rate Risk" (Basle: Basle Committee on Banking Supervision, April 1993).

——— (1994a), "Basle Capital Accord: The Treatment of the Credit Risk Associated with Certain Off-Balance-Sheet Items" (Basle: Basle Committee on Banking Supervision, July 1994).

——— (1994b), "Risk Management Guidelines for Derivatives" (Basle: Basle Committee on Banking Supervision, July 1994).

——— (1994c), "Report of International Developments in Banking Supervision," Report No. 9 (Basle: Basle Committee on Banking Supervision, September 1994).

——— (1995a), "Proposal to Issue a Supplement to the Basle Capital Accord to Cover Market Risks" (Basle: Basle Committee on Banking Supervision, March 1995).

——— (1995b), "An Internal Model-Based Approach to Market Risk Capital Requirements" (Basle: Basle Committee on Banking Supervision, March 1995).

——— (1995c), "Planned Supplement to the Capital Accord to Incorporate Market Risks" (Basle: Basle Committee on Banking Supervision, March 1995).

Bennett, Rosemary, and David Shirreff, "Let's Bash the Hedge Funds," *Euromoney* (April 1994), pp. 26–33.

Bikchandani, Sushil, David Hirschleifer, and Ivo Welch, "A Theory of Fads, Fashion, Custom and Cultural Change as Informational Cascades," *Journal of Political Economy*, Vol. 100 (October 1992), pp. 992–1025.

Bisignano, Joseph, "The Internationalization of Financial Markets: Measurement, Benefits, and Unexpected Interdependence," Cahiers économiques et monétaires, no. 43, Banque de France (November 1994), pp. 9–71.

Black, Fischer, "Noise," *Journal of Finance*, Vol. 41 (July 1986), pp. 529–43.

Blanchard, Oliver, and Mark Watson, "Bubbles, Rational Expectations and Financial Markets," in *Crises in the Economic and Financial Structure*, ed. by P. Wachtel (Lexington: Lexington Books, 1982).

Bodie, Zvi, "Shortfall Risk and Pension Fund Management," *Financial Analysts Journal* (May–June 1991), pp. 57–61.

"Books of Revelations?" *Risk*, Vol. 7 (September 1994), pp. 91–102.

Borchardt, Klaus-Dieter, "The ABC of Community Law" (Luxembourg: Office of Official Publications of the European Communities, 1993).

Cagan, Phillip, "The Monetary Dynamics of Hyperinflation," in *Studies in the Quantity Theory of Money*, ed. by Milton Friedman (Chicago: University of Chicago Press, 1956), pp. 25–117.

Chuhan, Punam, "Are Institutional Investors an Important Source of Portfolio Investment in Emerging Markets?" World Bank Policy Research Working Paper, No. 1243 (Washington: The World Bank, 1994).

Claessens, Stijn, and Sudarshan Gooptu, eds., *Portfolio Investment in Developing Countries*, World Bank Discussion Papers 228 (Washington: The World Bank, 1993).

Davis, E.P., "International Diversification of Institutional Investors," *Bank of England Discussion Paper, No. 44* (September 1991), pp. 1–53.

De Long, J. Bradford, and others, "The Size and Incidence of the Losses from Noise Trading," *The Journal of Finance*, Vol. 44 (July 1989), pp. 681–95.

"Emerging Markets Debt Comes of Age" *Institutional Investor* (April 1994), pp. 63–68.

European Community, Council Directive 93/6/EEC, "On the Capital Adequacy of Investments Firms and Credit Institutions," *Official Journal of the European Communities* (Luxembourg, March 1993).

"Fall Guys?" *Business Week*, April 25, 1994, pp. 116–21.

Fama, Eugene, and Kenneth French, "Permanent and Temporary Components of Stock Prices," *Journal of Political Economy*, Vol. 96 (April 1988), pp. 246–73.

Federal Reserve Bank of New York, "Wholesale Transaction Code of Conduct" (New York: Federal Reserve Bank of New York, January 1995).

Financial Accounting Standards Board, "Statement of Financial Accounting Standards No. 119: Disclosure About Derivative Financial Instruments and Fair Value of Financial Instruments" (Norwalk, Connecticut: Financial Accounting Standards Board, October 1994).

Flood, Robert, and Peter Garber, "Market Fundamentals Versus Price Level Bubbles," *Journal of Political Economy*, Vol. 88 (August 1980), pp. 745–70.

Flood, Robert, and Robert Hodrick, "On Testing for Speculative Bubbles," *Journal of Economic Perspectives*, Vol. 4 (Spring 1990), pp. 85–101.

Frankel, Jeffrey A., and Kenneth A. Froot, "Chartists, Fundamentalists, and Trading in the Foreign Exchange Market," *American Economic Review, Papers and Proceedings*, Vol. 80 (May 1990), pp. 181–85.

Fraser Institute, *Survey of Senior Investment Managers: Results for Winter, 1994/95* (Vancouver: December 19, 1994).

French, Kenneth R., and James M. Poterba, "Investor Diversification and International Equity Markets," *American Economic Review, Papers and Proceedings*, Vol. 81 (May 1991), pp. 222–26.

Friedman, Milton, "The Case for Flexible Exchange Rates," in *Essays in Positive Economics*, ed. by Milton Friedman (Chicago: University of Chicago Press, 1953).

Froot, Kenneth, and Maurice Obstfeld, "Intrinsic Bubbles: The Case of Stock Prices," *American Economic Review*, Vol. 81 (December 1991), pp. 1189–1214.

"Fund Management," Special Supplement *International Financial Law Review* (February 1994).

Garber, Peter, "Tulipmania," *Journal of Political Economy*, Vol. 97 (June 1989), pp. 535–60.

———, "Famous First Bubbles," *Journal of Economic Perspectives*, Vol. 4 (Spring 1990), pp. 35–54.

Gooptu, Sudarshan, "Portfolio Investment Flows to Emerging Markets," in *Portfolio Investment in Developing Countries*, ed. by Stijn Claessens and Sudarshan Gooptu, World Bank Discussion Papers 228 (Washington: The World Bank, 1993), pp. 45–77.

Grossman, Sanford, and Joseph Stiglitz, "On the Impossibility of Informationally Efficient Markets," *American Economic Review*, Vol. 70 (June 1980), pp. 393–408.

Group of Thirty, *Derivatives: Practices and Principles* (Washington: Group of Thirty, July 1993).

——— (1994a), *1994 Annual Report* (Washington: Group of Thirty, 1994).

——— (1994b), "Derivatives: Practices and Principles—Follow-Up Surveys of Industry Practice" (Washington: Group of Thirty, December 1994).

Hayworth, P.C., "Basle Committee on Bank Supervision," in *The New Palgrave Dictionary of Money and Finance*, Vol. 1, ed. by Peter Newman, Murray Milgate, and John Eatwell (New York: Stockton Press, 1992), pp. 185–87.

Hoffmaister, Alexander W., and Garry J. Schinasi, "Asset Prices, Financial Liberalization, and Inflation in Japan," in *Saving Behavior and the Asset Price "Bubble" in Japan: Analytical Issues*, ed. by Ulrich Baumgartner and Guy Meredith, IMF Occasional Paper, No. 124 (Washington: International Monetary Fund, April 1995).

Howell, Michael J., "Institutional Investors and Emerging Stock Markets," in *Portfolio Investment in Developing Countries*, ed. by Stijn Claessens and Sudarshan Gooptu, World Bank Discussion Papers 228 (Washington: The World Bank, 1993), pp. 78–87.

Institute of International Finance, Inc., "A Preliminary Framework for Public Disclosure of Derivatives Activities and Related Credit Exposures" (Washington: Institute of International Finance, Inc., August 1994).

International Finance Corporation, *Emerging Stock Markets Fact Book 1994* (Washington: International Finance Corporation, 1994).

International Monetary Fund, *International Capital Markets: Part I. Exchange Rate Management and International Capital Flows*, World Economic and Financial Surveys (Washington: International Monetary Fund, April 1993).

———, *International Financial Statistics* (Washington: International Monetary Fund, August 1993).

———, *International Capital Markets: Part II. Developments, Prospects, and Policy Issues*, World Economic and Financial Surveys (Washington: International Monetary Fund, September 1994).

International Organization of Securities Commissions, *1994 Annual Report* (Montreal: International Organization of Securities Commissions, 1994).

Ito, Takatoshi, *The Japanese Economy* (Cambridge, Massachusetts: MIT Press, 1992).

———, "The Land/Housing Problem in Japan," *The Journal of the Japanese and International Economies*, Vol. 7 (March 1993), pp. 1–31.

———, and Tokuo Iwaisako, "Explaining Asset Bubbles in Japan," *Bank of Japan, Monetary and Economic Studies* (forthcoming).

———, and Keiko Hirono Nosse, "Efficiency of the Tokyo Housing Market," *Bank of Japan, Monetary and Economic Studies*, Vol. 11 (July 1993), pp. 1–32.

J.P. Morgan & Co Incorporated (1994a), "Introduction to RiskMetrics" (New York: Morgan Guaranty Trust Company, October 1994).

——— (1994b), "RiskMetrics Technical Document" (New York: Morgan Guaranty Trust Company, October 1994).

Kupiec, Paul, and James O'Brien, "A Pre-Commitment Approach to Capital Requirements for Market Risk" (mimeograph, Washington: Board of Governors of the Federal Reserve System, March 1995).

Kyle, Albert S., "Informed Speculation with Imperfect Competition," *Review of Economic Studies*, Vol. 56 (July 1989), pp. 317–56.

LaWare, John P., Testimony on Hedge Funds Before the Committee on Banking, Finance, and Urban Affairs of the U.S. House of Representatives (Washington: April 13, 1994).

McKay, Charles, *Memoirs of Popular Delusions and the Extraordinary Madness of Crowds* (London: Office Nar. Illustrated Library, 2nd ed., 1852).

Meese, Richard, and Kenneth Rogoff, "Out-of-Sample Failure of Empirical Exchange Rate Models: Sampling Error of Misspecification?" in *Exchange Rates and International Macroeconomics*, ed. by Jacob A. Frenkel (Chicago: University of Chicago Press, 1983).

Milgrom, Paul, and Nancy Stokey, "Information, Trade and Common Knowledge," *Journal of Economic Theory*, Vol. 26 (January 1982), pp. 17–27.

Moody's Investors Service, "Asset Quality Looms as Major Problem for Mexican Banks," January 1995.

Money Market Directories, *Directory of Pension Funds and their Investment Managers 1995* (McGraw-Hill, 25th ed., 1995).

Muth, John, "Rational Expectations and the Theory of Price Movements," *Econometrica*, Vol. 29 (July 1961), pp. 315–35.

Noel, Emile, "Working Together—The Institutions of the European Community" (Luxembourg: Office of Official Publications of the European Communities, 1993).

Organization for Economic Cooperation and Development, *Financial Statistics Monthly*, various issues.

Pagano, Marco (1989a), "Trading Volume and Asset Liquidity," *Quarterly Journal of Economics*, Vol. 104 (May 1989), pp. 255–74.

——— (1989b), "Endogenous Market Thinness and Stock Price Volatility," *Review of Economic Studies*, Vol. 56 (April 1989), pp. 269–87.

Richardson, Portia, "Outlook 95: The Rugged Singles Scene," *Institutional Investor* (January 1995), pp. 115–25.

Schinasi, Garry J., and Monica Hargraves, " 'Boom and Bust' in Asset Markets in the 1980s: Causes and Consequences," in *Staff Studies for the World Economic Outlook*, World Economic and Financial Surveys (Washington: International Monetary Fund, 1993), pp. 1–27.

Shiller, Robert, "Do Stock Prices Move Too Much to Be Justified by Subsequent Changes in Dividends?" *American Economic Review*, Vol. 71 (June 1981), pp. 421–35.

———, *Market Volatility* (Boston: MIT Press, 1991).

Smith, Vernon L., Gerry Suchanek, and Arlington W. Williams, "Bubbles, Crashes and Endogenous Expectations in Experimental Spot Asset Markets," *Econometrica*, Vol. 56 (September 1988), pp. 1119–51.

Technical Committee of the International Organization of Securities Commissions, "Operational and Financial Risk Management Control Mechanisms for Over-the-Counter Derivatives Activities of Regulated Securities Firms" (Montreal: International Organization of Securities Commissions, July 1994).

Tirole, Jean, "Asset Bubbles and Overlapping Generations," *Econometrica*, Vol. 53 (September 1985), pp. 1071–100.

Ueda, Kazuo, "Are Japanese Stock Prices Too High?" *Journal of the Japanese and International Economies*, Vol. 4 (December 1990), pp. 351–70.

United States, General Accounting Office, "Financial Derivatives: Actions Needed to Protect the Financial System" (Washington: U.S. General Accounting Office, May 1994).

West, Kenneth, "Bubbles, Fads and Stock Price Volatility Tests: A Partial Evaluation," *Journal of Finance*, Vol. 43 (July 1988), pp. 639–56.

Statistical Appendix

Appendix Table 1. Sources of International Capital Markets Financing

	1987	1988	1989	1990	1991	1992	1993	1994
	(Gross issues in billions of U.S. dollars)							
Syndicated loans	91.7	125.5	121.1	124.5	116.0	117.9	136.7	202.8
Euronotes	102.2	93.2	81.6	73.2	87.9	134.6	160.2	279.8
Euro-commercial paper	55.8	57.1	54.1	48.3	35.9	28.9	38.4	31.8
Euro-medium-term notes	8.0	12.6	15.5	16.0	43.2	97.9	113.2	243.0
Bonds	180.8	227.1	255.7	229.9	308.7	333.7	481.0	426.9
Straight bonds	121.3	160.2	154.6	158.9	242.7	265.4	369.1	288.8
Floating rate bonds	13.0	22.3	17.8	37.1	18.3	43.6	69.8	96.3
Convertible bonds	18.2	11.3	14.1	10.6	10.1	5.2	18.1	21.7
Bonds with warrants attached	24.8	29.7	66.2	21.2	31.6	15.7	20.6	9.9
Other bonds	3.5	3.6	3.0	2.1	6.0	3.8	3.4	10.3
International equity offerings	20.4	9.1	14.0	14.2	23.8	25.3	36.6	58.1
Depository receipts								
(ADRs/GDRs/Rule 144A)	4.6	1.3	2.6	1.7	4.6	5.3	9.5	11.0
Total	395.1	454.9	472.4	441.8	536.4	611.5	814.5	967.6
Memorandum items								
Global bonds	—	—	1.5	9.7	15.4	25.1	34.4	49.0
Cross-border equity trading[1]								
Gross equity flows	1,377.8	1,166.7	1,562.6	1,390.9	1,322.5	1,404.9	2,266.1	2,550.0
Cross-exchange trading	508.6	342.6	582.9	873.9	779.1	968.7	1,547.5	2,000.0
Net equity flows	16.4	32.9	86.6	3.2	100.6	53.7	196.3	119.6
Cross-border mergers and								
acquisitions	70.9	109.6	117.5	128.4	83.7	91.0	95.1	156.2
	(In percent of total)							
Syndicated loans	23.21	27.59	25.64	28.18	21.63	19.28	16.78	20.96
Euronotes	25.87	20.49	17.27	16.57	16.39	22.01	19.67	28.92
Euro-commercial paper	14.12	12.55	11.45	10.93	6.69	4.73	4.71	3.29
Euro-medium-term notes	2.02	2.77	3.28	3.62	8.05	16.01	13.90	25.11
Bonds	45.76	49.92	54.13	52.04	57.55	54.57	59.05	44.12
Straight bonds	30.70	35.22	32.73	35.97	45.25	43.40	45.32	29.85
Floating rate bonds	3.29	4.90	3.77	8.40	3.41	7.13	8.57	9.95
Convertible bonds	4.61	2.48	2.98	2.40	1.88	0.85	2.22	2.24
Bonds with warrants attached	6.28	6.53	14.01	4.80	5.89	2.57	2.53	1.02
Other bonds	0.89	0.79	0.64	0.48	1.12	0.62	0.42	1.06
International equity offerings	5.16	2.00	2.96	3.21	4.44	4.14	4.49	6.00
Depository receipts								
(ADRs/GDRs/Rule 144A)	1.16	0.28	0.55	0.39	0.86	0.86	1.17	1.14
Total	100.00	100.00	100.00	100.00	100.00	100.00	100.00	100.00

Sources: Bank of New York; Baring Securities; and Organization for Economic Cooperation and Development, *Financial Market Trends*, various issues.

[1]The data for 1994 are estimates.

Appendix Table 2. Net Crossborder Equity Flows[1]
(In billions of U.S. dollars)

	1986	1987	1988	1989	1990	1991	1992	1993	1994
Investor from									
North America	3.7	−2.2	4.0	21.0	12.0	48.3	46.7	89.1	55.0
United States	2.6	−2.7	2.0	19.0	10.3	43.3	42.3	84.8	49.0
Canada	1.1	0.5	2.1	2.0	1.8	4.9	4.4	4.3	6.0
Japan	8.2	16.9	3.0	17.9	6.3	3.6	−3.0	15.3	13.5
Europe	21.4	9.5	14.4	38.3	4.6	40.0	8.0	61.0	46.3
United Kingdom	8.9	3.8	9.7	24.2	−0.9	25.6	−3.1	19.4	14.2
Rest of the world	8.8	−7.7	11.4	9.4	−19.7	8.7	2.0	30.9	4.8
Equity from									
North America	19.8	20.3	−3.7	13.8	−15.9	9.6	−3.9	32.3	6.3
United States	19.1	16.5	−1.4	11.4	−14.5	11.0	−4.1	24.3	1.8
Canada	0.7	3.8	−2.3	2.4	−1.3	−1.4	0.3	7.9	4.5
Japan	−15.8	−42.8	6.8	7.0	−13.3	46.8	8.9	20.4	45.5
Europe	33.6	29.7	23.0	47.7	15.9	24.2	25.5	68.5	29.1
United Kingdom	7.8	19.5	9.7	11.2	5.4	5.8	10.1	19.6	11.1
Emerging markets	3.3	5.9	3.5	10.1	13.2	15.8	21.2	62.4	39.9
Hong Kong, China, and Singapore	2.7	4.8	1.9	1.9	2.4	3.9	5.9	17.1	9.0
Other Pacific Rim countries	0.7	1.3	0.6	1.4	1.5	0.9	5.0	23.0	7.0
Latin America	0.2	0.4	0.7	7.0	9.9	11.2	9.6	20.0	14.9
Other[2]	−0.3	−0.6	0.3	−0.3	−0.6	−0.1	0.7	2.2	9.0
Rest of the world	1.0	3.4	3.2	8.1	3.3	4.2	2.0	12.3	1.8
Total	42.0	16.4	32.9	86.6	3.2	100.6	53.7	196.3	119.6

Source: Baring Securities.
[1]The data for 1994 are estimates.
[2]Africa, Middle East, and Eastern Europe.

Appendix Table 3. Developments in International Bond Markets

	1987	1988	1989	1990	1991	1992	1993	1994
	(In billions of U.S. dollars)							
Total gross international bonds	**180.8**	**227.1**	**255.8**	**229.9**	**308.7**	**333.7**	**481.0**	**426.9**
Amortization	76.0	82.9	89.2	107.9	149.3	222.5	305.2	223.5
Net issues[1]	104.8	144.2	166.6	122.0	159.4	111.2	175.8	203.4
By residence of borrower								
Industrial countries	156.3	198.3	224.4	190.2	255.9	265.0	368.5	339.9
Developing countries[2]	3.2	5.2	3.6	4.9	10.2	17.5	43.3	41.3
Offshore centers[3]	0.2	0.3	0.2	0.2	0.1	—	6.2	4.9
Countries in transition	0.6	1.4	2.2	1.7	1.5	1.3	5.8	2.4
Other, including international organizations	20.6	22.0	25.3	32.9	40.9	49.9	57.3	38.2
By category of borrower								
Governments	23.8	24.7	20.2	24.5	44.4	63.6	104.3	83.9
Public enterprises	21.3	32.1	32.1	41.0	48.3	52.8	66.1	57.7
Banks	38.8	61.8	62.1	56.0	55.9	67.3	109.9	136.0
Private corporations	78.0	88.8	119.8	79.0	123.7	108.7	152.8	120.5
International organizations	18.8	19.7	21.6	29.4	36.4	41.3	47.9	28.8
By currency of denomination	*(In percent)*							
U.S. dollar	36.2	37.2	49.6	34.8	31.1	37.9	38.1	38.1
Japanese yen	14.7	10.0	9.3	13.4	13.4	12.3	12.4	18.4
Deutsche mark	8.3	10.4	6.4	8.0	6.6	10.1	11.4	7.4
Swiss franc	13.4	11.6	7.3	10.1	6.5	5.4	5.6	4.7
Pound sterling	8.3	10.5	7.7	9.2	8.4	7.0	8.9	7.1
ECU[4]	4.1	4.9	4.9	7.8	10.6	6.4	1.5	1.8
Other	14.9	15.3	14.8	16.9	23.4	20.9	22.2	22.5
Interest rates	*(In percent a year)*							
Eurodollar deposits[5]	7.9	9.4	8.4	7.8	4.5	3.6	3.3	6.3
Dollar Eurobonds[6]	10.2	9.7	8.7	9.1	7.9	7.3	6.2	8.4
Deutsche mark international bonds[6]	6.5	6.2	7.9	9.6	8.6	7.8	6.4	7.7
Memorandum items	*(In billions of U.S. dollars)*							
Net issues of medium-term or Euronotes	23.3	19.9	8.0	33.0	34.9	40.4	72.1	140.2
Bonds purchased or issued by banks	53.0	67.0	57.9	79.0	34.8	69.4	127.5	69.1

Sources: Bank for International Settlements, *International Banking and Financial Market Developments*; Organization for Economic Cooperation and Development, *Financial Market Trends* and *Financial Statistics Monthly;* and IMF staff estimates.

[1]Gross issues less scheduled repayments and early redemption.
[2]All developing countries except the seven offshore centers (listed in footnote 3).
[3]The Bahamas, Bahrain, the Cayman Islands, Hong Kong, the Netherlands Antilles, Panama, and Singapore.
[4]European currency unit.
[5]Three-month deposits, at end of period.
[6]Bonds with remaining maturity of 7–15 years, at end of period.

Appendix Table 4. Financial Futures and Options: Exchanges, Contracts, and Volume of Contracts Traded

Exchange/Type	Face Value of Contract[1]	Volume of Contracts Traded					
		1989	1990	1991	1992	1993	1994
		(In thousands of contracts)					
United States							
Chicago Board of Trade (CBOT)							
Interest rate							
Futures							
Thirty-day federal funds	$5,000,000	68	81	116	234	182	416
U.S. Treasury notes[2]	$100,000[3]	7,891	8,698	10,013	18,105	25,257	37,480
U.S. Treasury bonds (15-year)	$100,000	70,303	75,499	67,887	70,005	79,428	99,960
Municipal bond index	$1,000 × index	1,068	697	549	776	1,121	1,601
Mortgage-backed securities	$100,000	25	17	6	—	—	—
Interest rate swap (three- and five-year)	$25,000,000	n.t.	n.t.	7	2	—	—
Canadian Government bonds (ten-year)	Can$100,000	n.t.	n.t.	n.t.	n.t.	n.t.	27
Options							
Options on U.S. Treasury note futures[4]	$100,000	1,168	1,024	1,020	3,236	6,829	9,125
Flexible options on U.S. Treasury note futures (two-, five-, and ten-year)	$100,000[5]	n.t.	n.t.	n.t.	n.t.	n.t.	66
Options on U.S. Treasury bond futures	$100,000	20,784	27,315	21,926	20,259	23,435	28,143
Flexible options on U.S. Treasury bond futures	$100,000[5]	n.t.	n.t.	n.t.	n.t.	n.t.	174
Options on municipal bond index futures	$1,000 × index	89	86	53	38	69	25
Options on mortgage-backed securities futures	$100,000	14	19	10	—	—	—
Options on interest rate swap futures (three- and five-year)	$25,000,000	n.t.	n.t.	6	—	—	—
Options on Canadian Government bond futures (ten-year)	Can$100,000	n.t.	n.t.	n.t.	n.t.	n.t.	1
Stock index							
Futures							
Major market index (MMI)	$500 × index	1,087	951	703	361	155	n.t.
Wilshire Small Cap index	$500 × index	n.t.	n.t.	n.t.	n.t.	2	n.t.
Options							
Options on MMI futures	$500 × index	n.t.	n.t.	3	2	1	n.t.
Wilshire Small Cap index options	$500 × index	n.t.	n.t.	n.t.	n.t.	—	n.t.
Chicago Board Options Exchange (CBOE)							
Interest rate							
Options							
U.S. Treasury bonds and notes	$100,000	144	7	—	n.t.	n.t.	n.t.
Stock index							
Options							
Standard & Poor's (S&P) 100 options	$100 × index	58,371	68,847	63,936	62,427	64,032	81,825
S&P 500 options	$100 × index	6,274	12,089	11,925	13,420	16,454	28,017
Russell 2000 index options	$100 × index	n.t.	n.t.	n.t.	40	495	651
Financial Times stock index (FT-SE) options	$100 × ¹⁄₁₀ of index	n.t.	n.t.	n.t.	16	22	7
Chicago Mercantile Exchange (CME)							
Interest rate							
Futures							
London interbank offered rate— LIBOR (one-month)	$3,000,000	n.t.	84	450	919	1,128	1,911
Eurodollar (three-month)[6]	$1,000,000	40,818	34,696	37,244	60,531	64,411	104,823
Euro-deutsche mark (three-month)	DM 1,000,000	n.t.	n.t.	n.t.	n.t.	26	1
U.S. Treasury bills (90-day)	$1,000,000	1,502	1,870	2,012	1,337	1,017	1,020
U.S. Treasury bills (one-year)	$500,000	n.t.	n.t.	n.t.	n.t.	n.t.	1
Options							
Options on LIBOR futures (one-month)	$3,000,000	n.t.	n.t.	75	99	91	79
Options on Eurodollar futures (three-month)	$1,000,000	6,002	6,860	7,875	13,763	17,009	28,146
Options on Euro-deutsche mark futures	DM 1,000,000	n.t.	n.t.	n.t.	n.t.	9	—
Options on U.S. Treasury bill futures	$1,000,000	17	32	49	30	14	5
Currency							
Futures							
Japanese yen[6]	¥ 12,500,000	7,824	7,437	6,017	4,520	6,023	6,613
Deutsche mark[6]	DM 125,000	8,186	9,169	10,929	11,593	12,866	10,956

Appendix Table 4 (*continued*)

Exchange/Type	Face Value of Contract[1]	Volume of Contracts Traded					
		1989	1990	1991	1992	1993	1994
		(In thousands of contracts)					
Deutsche mark rolling spot	$250,000	n.t.	n.t.	n.t.	n.t.	29	127
Deutsche mark forward	$250,000	n.t.	n.t.	n.t.	n.t.	n.t.	47
French franc	F 500,000	n.t.	n.t.	n.t.	n.t.	19	49
Pound sterling[6]	£62,500	2,518	3,410	3,746	3,053	3,701	3,563
Pound sterling rolling spot	$250,000	n.t.	n.t.	n.t.	n.t.	2	—
Canadian dollar	Can$100,000	1,264	1,409	1,139	1,172	1,411	1,740
Australian dollar	$A 100,000	114	105	76	90	199	355
Swiss franc	Sw F 125,000	6,094	6,525	5,835	5,135	5,605	5,217
Cross-rate deutsche mark/ Japanese yen	DM 125,000 × DM/¥ cross rate	n.t.	n.t.	9	11	—	—
Options							
Options on Japanese yen futures	¥ 12,500,000	3,127	3,116	2,397	1,518	2,262	2,946
Options on deutsche mark futures	DM 125,000	3,795	3,430	5,643	6,354	5,916	4,794
Options on deutsche mark rolling spot futures	$250,000	n.t.	n.t.	n.t.	n.t.	—	—
Options on French franc futures	F 500,000	n.t.	n.t.	n.t.	n.t.	6	1
Options on pound sterling futures	£62,500	406	501	650	597	528	920
Options on pound sterling rolling spot futures	£250,000	n.t.	n.t.	n.t.	n.t.	—	—
Options on Canadian dollar futures	Can$100,000	274	284	337	307	177	186
Options on Australian dollar futures	$A 100,000	23	27	38	13	3	8
Options on Swiss franc futures	Sw F 125,000	1,489	1,130	998	1,027	628	768
Options on cross-rate deutsche mark/ Japanese yen futures	DM 125,000 × DM/¥ cross rate	n.t.	n.t.	3	29	—	—
Stock index							
Futures							
S&P 500 index	$500 × index	10,560	12,139	12,340	12,414	13,204	18,709
Nikkei stock index average	$5 × index	n.t.	52	247	384	357	548
S&P MidCap 400 index	$500 × index	n.t.	n.t.	n.t.	103	219	286
Goldman Sachs commodity index	$250 × index	n.t.	n.t.	n.t.	36	122	155
Major market index (MMI)	$500 × index	n.t.	n.t.	n.t.	n.t.	49	150
Russell 2000 stock price index	$500 × index	n.t.	n.t.	n.t.	n.t.	19	36
Options							
Options on S&P 500 index futures	$500 × index	1,162	1,638	1,813	2,210	2,916	3,821
Options on Nikkei stock index average futures	$5 × index	n.t.	9	12	14	10	8
Options on S&P MidCap 400 index futures	$500 × index	n.t.	n.t.	n.t.	3	5	4
Options on Goldman Sachs commodity index futures	$250 × index	n.t.	n.t.	n.t.	8	38	34
Options on MMI futures	$500 × index	n.t.	n.t.	n.t.	n.t.	—	1
Options on Russell 2000 stock price index futures	$500 × index	n.t.	n.t.	n.t.	n.t.	1	3
New York Mercantile Exchange, COMEX Division							
Stock index							
Futures							
Eurotop 100 index	$100 × index	n.t.	n.t.	n.t.	26	56	62
Options							
Options on Eurotop 100 index futures	$100 × index	n.t.	n.t.	n.t.	n.t.	1	—
Philadelphia Board of Trade							
Currency							
Futures							
Foreign currencies[7]		· · ·	1	1	83	25	42
Philadelphia Stock Exchange (PHLX)							
Currency							
Options							
Japanese yen	¥ 6,250,000	3,328	2,990	1,783	1,305	1,302	999
Deutsche mark	DM 62,500	5,277	4,892	7,472	7,966	6,218	3,445
French franc	F 250,000	60	40	146	1,261	3,979	4,508
Pound sterling	£31,250	482	646	587	789	529	411
Canadian dollar	Can$50,000	362	475	204	189	221	158
Australian dollar	$A 50,000	417	309	186	143	160	70

Appendix Table 4 (*continued*)

Exchange/Type	Face Value of Contract[1]	Volume of Contracts Traded					
		1989	1990	1991	1992	1993	1994
		(In thousands of contracts)					
Swiss franc	Sw F 62,500	1,114	773	460	434	450	428
European currency unit (ECU)	ECU 62,500	3	10	6	4	8	20
Cross-rate pound sterling/deutsche mark	£31,250	n.t.	n.t.	n.t.	18	153	28
Cross-rate deutsche mark/Japanese yen	DM 62,500	n.t.	n.t.	1	49	82	33
Cash-settled deutsche mark	DM 62,500	n.t.	n.t.	n.t.	n.t.	n.t.	43
Customized currency[8]		n.t.	n.t.	n.t.	n.t.	n.t.	7
Stock index							
Options							
PHLX index options[9]	$100 × index	137	185	391	288	847	1,933
New York Cotton Exchange, FINEX Division							
Interest rate							
Futures							
U.S. Treasury notes[10]	$250,000[11]	599	292	81	81	51	73
Currency							
Futures							
U.S. dollar index	$1,000 × index	743	565	716	678	599	558
ECU	ECU 100,000	16	12	2	1	—	n.t.
U.S. dollar/deutsche mark	DM 125,000	n.t.	n.t.	n.t.	n.t.	n.t.	30
Cross-rate deutsche mark/Japanese yen	DM 125,000	n.t.	n.t.	n.t.	n.t.	n.t.	31
Cross-rate deutsche mark/Paris	DM 500,000	n.t.	n.t.	n.t.	n.t.	n.t.	10
Cross-rate deutsche mark/Italian lira	DM 250,000	n.t.	n.t.	n.t.	n.t.	n.t.	4
Cross-rate pound sterling/deutsche mark	£125,000	n.t.	n.t.	n.t.	n.t.	n.t.	12
Options							
U.S. dollar index	$1,000 × index	5	100	1,418	470	68	42
Options on ECU futures	ECU 100,000	n.t.	n.t.	n.t.	5	—	n.t.
New York Futures Exchange (NYFE)							
Stock index							
Futures							
New York Stock Exchange (NYSE) composite stock index	$500 × index	1,580	1,575	1,486	1,315	849	729
Commodity Research Bureau (CRB) index	$500 × index	125	70	61	56	92	110
Options							
Options on NYSE composite stock index futures	$500 × index	39	26	35	43	30	27
Options on CRB index futures	$500 × index	4	4	4	4	7	7
American Stock Exchange (AMEX)							
Stock index							
Options							
AMEX index options[12]	$100 × index	8,265	6,690	5,976	6,247	4,495	3,668
Mid-America Commodity Exchange (Midam)							
Interest rate							
Futures							
Eurodollar (three-month)	$500,000	n.t.	n.t.	n.t.	3	7	9
U.S. Treasury bills (90-day)	$500,000	9	4	1	2	1	1
U.S. Treasury notes (five- and ten-year)	$50,000	n.t.	n.t.	n.t.	n.t.	12	35
U.S. Treasury bonds (15-year)	$50,000	1,307	1,461	1,397	1,342	1,126	1,386
Options							
Options on U.S. Treasury bond futures (15-year)	$50,000	n.t.	n.t.	2	4	2	3
Currency							
Futures							
Japanese yen	¥ 6,250,000	59	54	41	39	63	68
Deutsche mark	DM 62,500	54	83	94	106	124	113
Pound sterling	£12,500	24	26	30	44	67	66
Canadian dollar	Can$50,000	7	9	4	5	9	10
Swiss franc	Sw F 62,500	61	76	74	63	74	65
Kansas City Board of Trade							
Stock index							
Futures							
Value Line index	$500 × index	41	36	58	46	46	50
Mini Value Line	$100 × index	8	14	27	34	41	52

Appendix Table 4 (*continued*)

Exchange/Type	Face Value of Contract[1]	Volume of Contracts Traded					
		1989	1990	1991	1992	1993	1994
		(In thousands of contracts)					
Options							
Options on Mini Value Line futures	$100 × index	n.t.	n.t.	n.t.	1	2	3
Pacific Stock Exchange (PSE)							
Stock index							
Options							
Financial News composite index options	$100 × index	226	130	72	70	3	n.t.
Wilshire Small Cap index options	$100 × value of index	n.t.	n.t.	n.t.	n.t.	153	73
New York Stock Exchange (NYSE)							
Stock index and equity							
Options							
NYSE index options[13]	$100 × index	577	262	153	131	42	31
Equity options		3,606	2,480	1,864	1,982	1,990	2,226
Japan							
Osaka Securities Exchange							
Stock index							
Futures							
Nikkei 225	¥ 1,000 × index	5,443	13,589	21,643	11,927	8,461	6,209
Nikkei 300	¥ 10,000 × index	n.t.	n.t.	n.t.	n.t.	n.t.	4,184
Options							
Nikkei 225 options	¥ 1,000 × index	6,610	9,188	11,836	9,257	6,090	4,274
Nikkei 300 options	¥ 10,000 × index	n.t.	n.t.	n.t.	n.t.	n.t.	269
Tokyo International Financial Futures Exchange (TIFFE)							
Interest rate							
Futures							
Eurodollar (three-month)	$1,000,000	103	8	3	—	—	—
Euro-yen (three-month and one-year)	¥ 100,000,000	4,495	14,414	14,666	14,969	23,391	37,451
Options							
Options on Euro-yen futures (three-month)	¥ 100,000,000	n.t.	n.t.	332	486	687	570
Currency							
Futures							
U.S. dollar/Japanese yen	$50,000	n.t.	n.t.	149	86	48	14
Tokyo Stock Exchange							
Interest rate							
Futures							
U.S. Treasury bonds (20-year)	$100,000	141	518	125	118	113	116
Japanese Government bonds (JGB) (10- and 20-year)	¥ 100,000,000	18,971	16,319	12,829	11,872	15,165	13,003
Options							
Options on ten-year JGB futures	¥ 100,000,000	n.t.	2,288	1,850	1,141	1,507	1,692
Stock index							
Futures							
Tokyo Stock Price Index (TOPIX)	¥ 10,000 × index	3,728	3,091	1,677	1,358	2,157	2,623
Options							
TOPIX options	¥ 10,000 × index	4,806	463	120	49	38	20
Germany							
Deutsche Terminbörse (DTB)							
Interest rate							
Futures							
Frankfurt interbank offered rate— FIBOR (three-month)	DM 1,000,000	n.t.	n.t.	n.t.	n.t.	n.t.	429
Medium-term notional bond (Bobl)	DM 250,000	n.t.	n.t.	236	1,668	4,534	5,648
Notional German Government bond (Bund)	DM 250,000	n.t.	60	2,283	5,328	7,625	14,160
Notional German Government long-term debt securities (Buxl)	DM 250,000	n.t.	n.t.	n.t.	n.t.	n.t.	89
Options							
Options on Bobl futures	DM 250,000	n.t.	n.t.	n.t.	n.t.	54	46
Options on Bund futures	DM 250,000	n.t.	n.t.	163	498	252	261
Stock index and equity							
Futures							
German Stock Index (DAX)	DM 100 per DAX index point	n.t.	51	1,251	3,271	3,977	5,141

Appendix Table 4 (*continued*)

Exchange/Type	Face Value of Contract[1]	Volume of Contracts Traded					
		1989	1990	1991	1992	1993	1994
		(In thousands of contracts)					
Options							
Options on DAX futures	One DAX futures contract	n.t.	n.t.	n.t.	136	63	50
DAX options	DM 10 per DAX index point	n.t.	n.t.	2,046	13,945	21,420	23,500
DTB stock options	50 shares of underlying stocks	n.t.	6,688	9,390	9,996	12,253	9,885
France							
Marché à Terme International de France (MATIF)							
Interest rate							
Futures							
Paris interbank offered rate—PIBOR (three-month)	F 5,000,000	2,296	1,901	3,000	6,437	11,864	13,176
Medium-term French Treasury bond	F 500,000	n.t.	n.t.	n.t.	n.t.	99	—
ECU bond	ECU 100,000	n.t.	56	546	1,354	873	619
Long-term French Treasury bond	F 500,000	n.t.	n.t.	n.t.	n.t.	29	—
Notional bonds[14]	F 500,000	15,005	15,996	21,088	31,063	36,805	50,153
Options							
Options on three-month PIBOR futures	F 5,000,000	n.t.	710	1,374	2,660	4,830	3,361
Options on ECU bond futures	ECU 100,000	n.t.	n.t.	21	83	8	1
Options on notional bond futures	F 500,000	7,150	7,410	8,412	10,047	11,573	18,025
Currency							
Options							
Options on U.S. dollar/French franc	$100,000	n.t.	n.t.	n.t.	n.t.	n.t.	75
Options on U.S. dollar/deutsche mark	$100,000	n.t.	n.t.	n.t.	n.t.	n.t.	225
Stock index							
Futures							
CAC 40 stock index	F 200 × index	581	1,641	2,311	3,601	5,909	7,464
Marché des Options Negociables de Paris (MONEP)							
Stock index							
Options							
CAC 40 stock index options (short-term)	F 200 × index	816	2,470	3,718	3,171	2,452	2,755
CAC 40 stock index options (long-term)	F 50 × index	n.t.	n.t.	87	547	1,761	2,996
Italy							
Mercato Italiano Futures							
Interest rate							
Futures							
BTP (five-year)	Lit 250,000,000	n.t.	n.t.	n.t.	49	1,637	667
BTP (ten-year)	Lit 250,000,000	n.t.	n.t.	n.t.	521	2,777	3,703
Options							
Options on BTP futures (ten-year)	Lit 250,000,000	n.t.	n.t.	n.t.	n.t.	n.t.	71
United Kingdom							
London International Financial Futures Exchange (LIFFE)							
Interest rate							
Futures							
Eurodollar (three-month)	$1,000,000	2,061	1,249	994	709	245	92
Euro-deutsche mark (three-month)	DM 1,000,000	952	2,660	4,784	12,173	21,319	29,312
Euro-lira (three-month)	Lit 1,000,000,000	n.t.	n.t.	n.t.	376	1,479	3,456
Short sterling (three-month)	£500,000	7,114	8,355	8,064	11,296	12,136	16,603
Euro-Swiss (three-month)	Sw F 1,000,000	n.t.	n.t.	548	1,970	1,846	1,699
ECU (three-month)	ECU 1,000,000	16	64	115	317	721	622
Medium-term German Government bond (Bobl)	DM 250,000	n.t.	n.t.	n.t.	n.t.	1,050	73
U.S. Treasury bonds	$100,000	967	756	463	272	5	n.t.
Japanese Government bond (JGB)[15]	¥ 100,000,000	117	46	106	221	421	611
German Government bond (Bund)	DM 250,000	5,330	9,582	10,112	13,605	20,440	37,335
Italian Government bond (BTP)	Lit 200,000,000	n.t.	n.t.	483	3,773	6,344	11,824
Long gilt (government bond)[16]	£50,000	4,063	5,643	5,639	8,805	11,809	19,048
Spanish Government bond	Pta 20,000,000	n.t.	n.t.	n.t.	n.t.	28	n.t.
ECU bond	ECU 200,000	n.t.	n.t.	54	7	n.t.	n.t.
Options							
Options on Eurodollar futures (three-month)	$1,000,000	82	65	31	73	20	12

Appendix Table 4 (*continued*)

Exchange/Type	Face Value of Contract[1]	Volume of Contracts Traded					
		1989	1990	1991	1992	1993	1994
		(In thousands of contracts)					
Options on Euro-deutsche mark futures (three-month)	DM 1,000,000	n.t.	248	514	1,964	2,906	2,944
Options on short sterling futures (three-month)	£500,000	824	1,377	1,594	2,648	2,667	4,058
Options on Euro-Swiss futures (three-month)	Sw F 1,000,000	n.t.	n.t.	n.t.	17	32	19
Options on U.S. Treasury bond futures	$100,000	76	87	40	68	3	n.t.
Options on Bund futures	DM 250,000	469	1,804	2,453	2,750	4,416	8,574
Options on BTP futures	Lit 200,000,000	n.t.	n.t.	16	395	602	1,031
Options on long gilt futures	£50,000	727	790	844	1,813	2,059	2,357
Stock index							
Futures							
Financial Times stock index (FT-SE 100)	£25 × index	1,028	1,444	1,727	2,619	3,120	4,227
FT-SE Mid 250 index	£10 × index	n.t.	n.t.	n.t.	n.t.	n.t.	41
Options							
FT-SE 100 options	£10 × index	n.t.	n.t.	n.t.	3,063	3,439	4,787
Canada							
Montreal Exchange							
Interest rate							
Futures							
Canadian Bankers' Acceptances[17]	Can$1,000,000	28	88	194	443	749	1,931
Canadian Government bonds (ten-year)	Can$100,000	87	454	421	516	895	1,497
Options							
Canadian Government bond options	Can$25,000	323	139	47	51	61	51
Options on Canadian Government bond futures	Can$100,000	n.t.	n.t.	15	5	9	6
Options on Canadian Bankers' Acceptances futures (three-month)	Can$1,000,000	n.t.	n.t.	n.t.	n.t.	n.t.	29
Toronto Futures Exchange							
Stock index							
Futures							
Toronto Stock Exchange (TSE) 35 index	Can$500 × index	35	53	61	59	69	104
TSE 100 index	Can$500 × index	n.t.	n.t.	n.t.	n.t.	n.t.	11
Options							
TSE 35 index options	Can$100 × index	487	698	465	302	221	247
TSE 100 index options	Can$100 × index	n.t.	n.t.	n.t.	n.t.	n.t.	13
Toronto Stock Exchange							
Equity							
Options							
Canadian equity options	100 shares	2,435	1,411	1,015	889	1,155	1,207
Spain							
Meff Renta Fija							
Interest rate							
Futures							
Madrid interbank offered rate—MIBOR[18]	Pta 10,000,000	n.t.	17	456	747	2,363	4,176
Notional bond (three-, five-, and ten-year)	Pta 10,000,000	n.t.	171	535	1,015	4,553	13,204
Options							
Options on MIBOR futures (90-day)	Pta 10,000,000	n.t.	n.t.	n.t.	8	140	307
Notional bond (three- and ten-year)	Pta 10,000,000	n.t.	n.t.	n.t.	382	1,088	2,048
Currency							
Futures							
Spanish peseta/U.S. dollar	$100,000	n.t.	n.t.	4	12	—	n.t.
Spanish peseta/deutsche mark	DM 125,000	n.t.	n.t.	11	55	3	n.t.
Meff Renta Variable							
Stock index							
Futures							
IBEX 35 index	Pta 100 × index	n.t.	n.t.	n.t.	2,864	10,856	27,647
Options							
IBEX 35 index options	Pta 100 × index	n.t.	n.t.	n.t.	2,447	3,563	7,566

Appendix Table 4 (*continued*)

Exchange/Type	Face Value of Contract[1]	Volume of Contracts Traded					
		1989	1990	1991	1992	1993	1994
		(In thousands of contracts)					
The Netherlands							
European Options Exchange (EOE)							
Interest rate							
Options							
Dutch Government bond options	f. 10,000	486	260	232	270	436	447
Flexible Dutch Government bond options	f. 10,000	n.t.	n.t.	n.t.	n.t.	n.t.	181
Options on Dutch Government bond futures	f. 250,000	n.t.	1	8	1	1	—
Currency							
Options							
U.S. dollar/guilder and	$10,000						
pound sterling/guilder options	£10,000	469	200	373	538	673	483
Stock index and equity							
Options							
EOE stock index and	f. 100 × index and						
MMI U.S. stock index options[19]	$100 × index	1,995	2,003	2,384	2,471	2,701	2,853
Dutch Top 5 index options	100 × value of index	n.t.	174	330	493	412	394
Eurotop 100 index options	50 × value of index	n.t.	n.t.	10	10	3	1
Dutch stock options	100 shares	9,998	7,525	7,013	6,809	8,035	7,943
Financial Futures Market							
Interest rate							
Futures							
Notional guilder bond	f. 250,000	62	54	29	25	70	14
Currency							
Futures							
U.S. dollar/guilder	$25,000	n.t.	n.t.	2	11	22	13
Stock index							
Futures							
EOE stock index	f. 200 × index	238	437	485	492	812	1,031
Dutch Top 5 index	f. 200 × index	n.t.	43	47	52	58	62
Eurotop 100 index	ECU 50 × index	n.t.	n.t.	1	2	1	—
Australia							
Sydney Futures Exchange							
Interest rate							
Futures							
Bank bills (90-day)	$A 500,000	5,911	5,081	4,652	5,698	6,415	9,369
Treasury bonds (three-year)	$A 100,000	967	1,608	2,112	5,435	6,940	9,710
Commonwealth Treasury bonds (ten-year)	$A 100,000	3,222	3,174	3,602	4,253	4,782	6,815
Options							
Options on bank bill futures (90-day)	$A 500,000	515	606	719	610	663	944
Options on Treasury bond futures (three-year)	$A 100,000	25	75	107	317	515	507
Options on Commonwealth Treasury bond futures (ten-year)	$A 100,000	709	512	670	746	713	800
Overnight options on Commonwealth Treasury bond futures (three-year)	$A 100,000	n.t.	n.t.	n.t.	n.t.	—	2
Overnight options on Commonwealth Treasury bond futures (ten-year)	$A 100,000	n.t.	n.t.	n.t.	n.t.	2	19
Stock index							
Futures							
All-ordinaries share price index	$A 25 × index	326	314	388	342	981	2,553
Options							
Options on All-ordinaries share price index futures	$A 25 × index	140	186	248	154	467	834
Switzerland							
Swiss Options and Financial Futures Exchange (SOFFEX)							
Interest rate							
Futures							
Euro-Swiss franc (three-month)	Sw F 1,000,000	n.t.	n.t.	122	184	—	n.t.
Swiss franc (five-year)	Sw F 100,000	n.t.	n.t.	59	200	29	n.t.
Swiss Government bond	Sw F 100,000	n.t.	n.t.	n.t.	234	271	950
Options							
Options on Swiss Government bond futures	Sw F 100,000	n.t.	n.t.	n.t.	n.t.	n.t.	50

Appendix Table 4 (*continued*)

Exchange/Type	Face Value of Contract[1]	Volume of Contracts Traded					
		1989	1990	1991	1992	1993	1994
		(In thousands of contracts)					
Stock index							
Futures							
Swiss market index	Sw F 50 × index	n.t.	31	591	847	914	1,694
Options							
Swiss market index options	Sw F 5 × index	2,115	4,683	6,175	7,794	5,595	6,679
Belgium							
Belgian Futures and Options Exchange (BELFOX)							
Interest rate							
Futures							
Brussels interbank offered rate—							
BIBOR (three-month)	BF 25,000,000	n.t.	n.t.	n.t.	52	191	150
Belgian Government bonds	BF 2,500,000	n.t.	n.t.	13	264	585	688
Options							
Options on Belgian Government bond futures	BF 2,500,000	n.t.	n.t.	n.t.	n.t.	n.t.	52
Currency							
Options							
U.S. dollar/Belgian franc	$10,000	n.t.	n.t.	n.t.	n.t.	n.t.	30
Stock index and equity							
Futures							
Bel 20 index	BF 1,000 × index	n.t.	n.t.	n.t.	n.t.	12	155
Options							
Bel 20 index options	BF 100 × index	n.t.	n.t.	n.t.	n.t.	346	561
Stock options	20 shares of underlying stocks	n.t.	n.t.	n.t.	104	275	280
Sweden							
Stockholm Options Market							
Interest rate							
Futures							
Interest rate	SKr 1,000,000	n.t.	n.t.	4,134	7,420	11,272	14,124
Swedish Treasury bills	SKr 1,000,000	n.t.	206	1,980	3,930	3,990	3,696
Swedish Government bonds (two-, five-, and ten-year)	SKr 1,000,000	n.t.	116	1,646	2,342	3,814	4,582
Options							
Interest rate options	SKr 1,000,000	2	19	94	20	—	86
Stock index and equity							
Futures							
Stock futures	SKr 100 × index	—	3	5	21	119	208
OMX index	SKr 100 × index	—	4	117	450	628	1,707
Options							
Stock options	SKr 100 × index	3,195	2,849	4,074	3,543	7,068	10,055
OMX index options	SKr 100 × index	5,016	5,169	4,826	5,605	4,073	5,812
Austria							
Austrian Futures and Options Exchange (ÖTOB)							
Interest rate							
Futures							
Austrian Government bonds	S 1,000,000	n.t.	n.t.	n.t.	n.t.	43	124
Stock index and equity							
Futures							
Austrian Traded index (ATX)	S 100 × index	n.t.	n.t.	n.t.	67	174	348
Options							
ATX options	S 100 × index	n.t.	n.t.	n.t.	176	673	1,253
ATX long-term equity options	S 100 × index	n.t.	n.t.	n.t.	n.t.	n.t.	9
Denmark							
Guarantee Fund for Danish Options and Futures (FUTOP)							
Interest rate							
Futures							
Danish Government bonds	DKr 1,000,000	11	22	283	548	580	520
Mortgage credit bonds	DKr 1,000,000	229	329	100	34	30	172
Copenhagen interbank offered rate—							
CIBOR (three-month)	DKr 5,000,000	n.t.	n.t.	n.t.	n.t.	35	33

Appendix Table 4 (*continued*)

Exchange/Type	Face Value of Contract[1]	Volume of Contracts Traded					
		1989	1990	1991	1992	1993	1994
		(In thousands of contracts)					
Options							
Options on Danish Government bond futures	DKr 1,000,000	n.t.	n.t.	53	153	86	101
Options on mortgage credit bonds	DKr 1,000,000	41	87	35	—	n.t.	n.t.
Stock index and equity							
Futures							
KFX stock index	DKr 1,000 × index	7	243	336	407	339	429
Options							
Options on KFX stock index futures	DKr 1,000 × index	n.t.	55	135	194	87	80
Options on Danish equities	100 underlying shares	n.t.	3	143	187	164	110
Norway							
Oslo Stock Exchange							
Interest rate							
Futures							
Norwegian Government bonds (ten-year)	NKr 1,000,000	n.t.	n.t.	n.t.	n.t.	28	165
Norwegian Government bonds (five-year)	NKr 1,000,000	n.t.	n.t.	n.t.	n.t.	n.t.	44
Stock index							
Futures							
OBX index	NKr 100 × index	n.t.	n.t.	n.t.	15	17	4
Options							
OBX index options	NKr 100 × index	n.t.	39	224	445	386	422
Long OBX options	NKr 100 × index	n.t.	n.t.	n.t.	n.t.	1	1
Finland							
Finnish Options Market Exchange and Clearing House							
Stock index							
Futures							
FOX index	Fmk 100 × index	70	43	35	37	54	70
Options							
FOX index options	Fmk 100 × index	931	747	636	398	378	415
Ireland							
Irish Futures and Options Exchange							
Interest rate							
Futures							
Dublin interbank offered rate—							
DIBOR (three-month)	£Ir 500,000	15	7	5	6	4	3
Short gilt	£Ir 100,000	n.t.	1	3	2	—	1
Long gilt	£Ir 50,000	4	8	10	4	10	12
New Zealand							
New Zealand Futures and Options Exchange							
Interest rate							
Futures							
Bank bills (90-day)	$NZ 500,000	118	281	408	392	463	608
Government stock (three-, five-, and ten-year)	$NZ 100,000	349	308	267	208	146	144
Options							
Options on bank bill futures	$NZ 500,000	2	3	30	39	8	7
Options on Government stock futures (three-, five-, and ten-year)	$NZ 100,000	27	9	22	29	3	4
Stock index							
Futures							
Forty index	$NZ 20 × index	n.t.	n.t.	3	5	4	7
Options							
Forty index options	$NZ 20 × index	n.t.	n.t.	—	1	1	2
Hong Kong							
Hong Kong Futures Exchange (HKFX)							
Interest rate							
Futures							
Hong Kong interbank offered rate—							
HIBOR (three-month)	HK$1,000,000	n.t.	55	1	—	—	—

Appendix Table 4 (*continued*)

Exchange/Type	Face Value of Contract[1]	1989	1990	1991	1992	1993	1994
		*(In thousands of contracts)*					
Stock index							
Futures							
Hang Seng index	HK$50 × index	236	236	536	1,087	2,416	4,193
Options							
Hang Seng index options	HK$50 × index	n.t.	n.t.	n.t.	n.t.	282	607
Singapore							
Singapore International Monetary Exchange (SIMEX)							
Interest rate							
Futures							
Eurodollar (three-month)	$1,000,000	3,862	3,469	3,433	5,618	5,536	8,688
Euro-yen (three-month)	¥ 100,000,000	169	816	1,492	2,473	3,533	6,821
Euro-deutsche mark (three-month)	DM 1,000,000	n.t.	57	33	5	23	231
Japanese Government bond (ten-year)	¥ 50,000,000	n.t.	n.t.	n.t.	n.t.	29	444
Options							
Options on Eurodollar futures (three-month)	$1,000,000	10	13	5	12	7	14
Options on Euro-yen futures (three-month)	¥ 100,000,000	n.t.	62	81	81	57	126
Options on Japanese Government bond futures (ten-year)	¥ 50,000,000	n.t.	n.t.	n.t.	n.t.	n.t.	40
Currency							
Futures							
Japanese yen	¥ 12,500,000	287	116	47	20	21	17
Deutsche mark	DM 125,000	84	64	60	45	16	9
Pound sterling	£62,500	3	3	4	4	4	2
Deferred spot U.S. dollar/Japanese yen	$100,000	n.t.	n.t.	n.t.	n.t.	13	69
Deferred spot U.S. dollar/deutsche mark	$100,000	n.t.	n.t.	n.t.	n.t.	26	131
Options							
Options on Japanese yen futures	¥ 12,500,000	2	—	—	—	—	n.t.
Stock index							
Futures							
Nikkei stock average	¥ 500 × index	859	881	722	3,349	5,162	5,801
Options							
Options on Nikkei stock average futures	¥ 500 × index	n.t.	n.t.	n.t.	269	898	1,497

Sources: American Stock Exchange; Austrian Futures and Options Exchange; Nick Battley, ed., *The World's Futures & Options Markets* (Chicago: Probus Publishing Company, 1993); Belgian Futures and Options Exchange; Chicago Board of Trade; Chicago Board Options Exchange; Chicago Mercantile Exchange; Deutsche Terminbörse; European Options Exchange; Financial Futures Market; Finnish Options Market Exchange and Clearing House; Futures Industry Association; Futures Industry Institute, *Fact Book*, various issues; Guarantee Fund for Danish Options and Futures; Hong Kong Futures Exchange; Irish Futures and Options Exchange; London International Financial Futures Exchange; Marché à Terme International de France (MATIF); Meff Renta Fija; Meff Renta Variable; Mercato Italiano Futures; Mid-America Commodity Exchange; Montreal Exchange; New York Cotton Exchange; New York Mercantile Exchange; New York Stock Exchange; Oslo Stock Exchange; Pacific Stock Exchange; Philadelphia Stock Exchange; Singapore International Monetary Exchange; Stockholm Options Market; Swiss Options and Financial Futures Exchange; Tokyo International Financial Futures Exchange; Tokyo Stock Exchange; Toronto Futures Exchange; and Toronto Stock Exchange.

Note: n.t. = not traded; — = either zero or fewer than 500 contracts; $A = Australian dollar; S = Austrian schilling; BF = Belgian franc; Can$ = Canadian dollar; DKr = Danish krone; DM = deutsche mark; ECU = European currency unit; Fmk = Finnish markka; F = French franc; HK$ = Hong Kong dollar; £Ir = Irish pound; Lit = Italian lira; ¥ = Japanese yen; f. = Netherlands guilder; $NZ = New Zealand dollar; NKr = Norwegian krone; £ = pound sterling; Pta = Spanish peseta; SKr = Swedish krona; Sw F = Swiss franc; and $ = U.S. dollar; Options volume is puts and calls combined.

[1]Blanks in this column indicate that information is not available.
[2]Data on 6½–10-year and 5-year notes for 1988 and 1989; from 1990 onward it also includes 2-year notes.
[3]Face value of contract is $100,000 for 6½–10-year and 5-year notes, and $200,000 for 2-year notes.
[4]Data on 10-year notes for 1988–89; 10- and 5-year notes for 1990–91; and 10-, 5-, and 2-year notes from 1992 onward. Face value of contract is $100,000 for 5- and 10-year notes; and $200,000 for 2-year notes.
[5]Minimum size to initiate a request for quote and/or to trade is 100 contracts, each having a face value at maturity of $100,000.
[6]CME deutsche mark, Eurodollar, Japanese yen, and pound sterling contracts are listed on a mutual offset link with the Singapore International Monetary Exchange.
[7]Covers Australian dollar, Canadian dollar, deutsche mark, ECU, French franc, Japanese yen, pound sterling, and Swiss franc. Contract units are $A 100,000; Can$100,000; DM 125,000; ECU 125,000; F 500,000; ¥ 12,500,000; £62,500; and Sw F 125,000, respectively.
[8]Determined by the underlying currency as follows: $A 50,000; Can$50,000; DM 62,500; ECU 62,500; F 250,000; ¥ 6,250,000; £31,250; Sw F 62,500; and $50,000.

Appendix Table 4 (*concluded*)

⁹Include value line index, national OTC index, and utility index. Bank stock index has also been included since 1992. For 1994, semiconductor sector index, phone sector index, and Big Cap sector index have also been added.

¹⁰Five-year notes for 1988; and 2- and 5-year notes from 1989 onward.

¹¹Commodity size is $250,000 for 5-year notes and $500,000 for 2-year notes.

¹²Amex/Oscar Gruss Israel index, biotechnology index, biotechnology LEAPS index, computer technology index, Eurotop 100 index, Hong Kong option index, Hong Kong option LEAPS index, institutional index, institutional index LEAPS, institutional index capped options (a.m. settled index capped options; delisted September 21, 1992), international market index (delisted June 21, 1991), Japan index, Japan index LEAPS, major market index, major market index LEAPS, major market index capped options (delisted June 22, 1992), Mexico index, Mexico LEAPS index, Morgan Stanley consumer index, Morgan Stanley cyclical index, natural gas index, oil index, North American telecommunications index, pharmaceutical index, pharmaceutical LEAPS index, Securities broker/dealer index, S&P MidCap 400 index, and S&P MidCap 400 index LEAPS.

¹³Includes NYSE composite index, NYSE beta index (discontinued trading in 1988), and NYSE utility index (since 1993).

¹⁴A contract identical to the MATIF treasury bond future is also traded on an over-the-counter basis outside exchange hours and is cleared by the clearinghouse.

¹⁵Trading began on July 13, 1987, for the old JGB. A new JGB was launched on April 3, 1991, with modified specifications.

¹⁶The 1988 data also contain 54,108 contracts traded on medium gilts (£50,000).

¹⁷Includes one- and three-month futures. Face value of contract for the one-month futures is Can$3 million and for the three-month futures, Can$1 million.

¹⁸Includes 90-day MIBOR. Beginning from 1993, it also has data for 360-day MIBOR.

¹⁹The MMI option is also listed on the American Stock Exchange.

World Economic and Financial Surveys

This series (ISSN 0258-7440) contains biannual, annual, and periodic studies covering monetary and financial issues of importance to the global economy. The core elements of the series are the *World Economic Outlook* report, usually published in May and October, and the annual report on *International Capital Markets*. Other studies assess international trade policy, private market and official financing for developing countries, exchange and payments systems, export credit policies, and issues raised in the *World Economic Outlook*.

World Economic Outlook: A Survey by the Staff of the International Monetary Fund

The *World Economic Outlook,* published twice a year in English, French, Spanish, and Arabic, presents IMF staff economists' analyses of global economic developments during the near and medium term. Chapters give an overview of the world economy; consider issues affecting industrial countries, developing countries, and economies in transition to the market; and address topics of pressing current interest.

ISSN 0256-6877.
$34.00 (academic rate: $23.00; paper).
1995 (May). ISBN 1-55775-468-3. **Stock #WEO-195.**
1994 (May). ISBN 1-55775-381-4. **Stock #WEO-194.**
1994 (Oct.). ISBN 1-55775-385-7. **Stock #WEO-294.**

International Capital Markets: Developments, Prospects, and Policy Issues

This annual report reviews developments in international capital markets, including recent bond market turbulence and the role of hedge funds, supervision of banks and nonbanks and the regulation of derivatives, structural changes in government securities markets, and recent developments in private market financing for developing countries

$20.00 (academic rate: $12.00; paper).
1995 ISBN 1-55775-516-7. **Stock #WEO-695.**
1994. ISBN 1-55775-426-8. **Stock #WEO-694.**

Staff Studies for the World Economic Outlook
by the IMF's Research Department

These studies, supporting analyses and scenarios of the *World Economic Outlook*, provide a detailed examination of theory and evidence on major issues currently affecting the global economy.

$20.00 (academic rate: $12.00; paper).
1995. ISBN 1-55775-499-3. **Stock #WEO-395.**
1993. ISBN 1-55775-337-7. **Stock #WEO-393.**

Issues in International Exchange and Payments Systems
by a Staff Team from the IMF's Monetary and Exchange Affairs Department

The global trend toward liberalization in countries' international exchange and payments systems has been widespread in both industrial and developing countries and most dramatic in Central and Eastern Europe. Countries in general have brought their exchange systems more in line with market principles and moved toward more flexible exchange rate arrangements in recent years.

$20.00 (academic rate: $12.00; paper).
1995. ISBN 1-55775-480-2. **Stock #WEO-895.**

Private Market Financing for Developing Countries
by a Staff Team from the IMF's Policy Development and Review Department

This study surveys recent trends in private market financing for developing countries, including flows to developing countries through banking and securities markets; the restoration of access to voluntary market financing for some developing countries; and the status of commercial bank debt in low-income countries.

$20.00 (academic rate: $12.00; paper).
1995. ISBN 1-55775-456-X. **Stock #WEO-994.**
1993. ISBN 1-55775-361-X. **Stock #WEO-993.**

International Trade Policies
by a Staff Team led by Naheed Kirmani

The study reviews major issues and developments in trade and their implications for the work of the IMF. Volume I, *The Uruguay Round and Beyond: Principal Issues*, gives and overview of the principal issues and developments in the world trading system. Volume II, *The Uruguay Round and Beyond: Background Papers*, presents detailed background papers on selected trade and trade-related issues. This study updates previous studies published under the title *Issues and Developments in International Trade Policy*.

$20.00 (academic rate: $12.00; paper).
1994. *Volume I. The Uruguay Round and Beyond: Principal Issues*
ISBN 1-55775-469-1. **Stock #WEO-1094.**
1994. *Volume II. The Uruguay Round and Beyond: Background Papers*
ISBN 1-55775-457-8. **Stock #WEO-1494.**
1992. ISBN 1-55775-311-1. **Stock #WEO-1092.**

Official Financing for Developing Countries
by a Staff Team from the IMF's Policy Development and Review Department led by Michael Kuhn

This study provides information on official financing for developing countries, with the focus on low- and lower-middle-income countries. It updates and replaces *Multilateral Official Debt Rescheduling: Recent Experience* and reviews developments in direct financing by official and multilateral sources.

$20.00 (academic rate: $12.00; paper)
1994. ISBN 1-55775-378-4. **Stock #WEO-1394.**

Officially Supported Export Credits: Recent Developments and Prospects
by Michael G. Kuhn, Balazs Horvath, Christopher J. Jarvis

This study examines export credit and cover policies in major industrial countries.

$20.00 (academic rate: $12.00; paper).
1995. ISBN 1-55775-448-9. **Stock #WEO-595.**

Available by series subscription or single title (including back issues); academic rate available only to full-time university faculty and students.

Please send orders and inquiries to:
International Monetary Fund, Publication Services, 700 19th Street, N.W.
Washington, D.C. 20431, U.S.A.
Tel.: (202) 623-7430   Telefax: (202) 623-7201
Internet: publications@imf.org